HITLER'S PIANO PLAYER

HITLER'S
PIANO
PLAYER

The Rise and Fall of Ernst Hanfstaengl, Confidant of Hitler, Ally of FDR

Peter Conradi

Carroll & Graf Publishers
New York

To my family

HITLER'S PIANO PLAYER
The Rise and Fall of Ernst Hanfstaengl, Confidant of Hitler, Ally of FDR

Carroll & Graf Publishers
An Imprint of Avalon Publishing Group Inc.
245 West 17th Street
11th Floor
New York, NY 10011

AVALON
publishing group incorporated

First Carroll & Graf edition 2004

Library of Congress Cataloging-in-Publication Data is available.

ISBN: 0-7867-1283-X

Printed in the United States of America
Distributed by Publishers Group West

CONTENTS

CONTENTS

IT is not a name that rolls easily off the tongue, but the first time I came across Ernst Hanfstaengl in an article in the *Boston Globe* in April, 2001, I was immediately intrigued. The article, by Mark Fritz, was prompted by the CIA's release of a number of files containing a mass of fascinating personal material about Adolf Hitler and other leading Nazis. One of the oddest items, Fritz wrote, was a profile of the Führer that had been written by a "former Hitler crony" named Hanfstaengl. Running to sixty-eight pages, the profile provided a "surreal, secret agent's view" of everything from Hitler's eating habits and fondness for American football marches to his phobia about people seeing him naked. Little was revealed in Fritz's article about Hanfstaengl himself, however, except that he was a Harvard graduate who had been part of Hitler's circle in the early 1920s, but had later apparently gone over to the Allied side.

I set out to learn more about this curious and little-known link between Nazi Germany and Franklin D. Roosevelt's America. Hanfstaengl's own autobiography, written in the 1950s, provided his own version of his relationship with Hitler, but revealed little about his secret role in the Allied war effort in the United States during World War II. An unpublished 1988 PhD thesis by David Marwell provided a wealth of other detail. Many contemporary accounts and histories of 1930s Germany each contained a tantalizing few pages about him, whilst documents and letters preserved in libraries in Munich, Germany, and Hyde Park, New York, and in the Public Records Office in London helped fill in the picture.

As I dug deeper, an intriguing portrait emerged of a larger-than-life character who helped create the monster that was Adolf Hitler and then spent the rest of his life rueing what he done. It also brought forth a long and eclectic list of famous names who crossed his path; not just Hitler and his henchmen, but others such as Theodore Roosevelt Jr., Winston Churchill, Randolph Hearst, Djuna Barnes, and Diana and

Unity Mitford, all of whom were Hanfstaengl's friends.

Sadly, Putzi had already been dead for more than a quarter of a century when I embarked upon this book. I nevertheless had the pleasure of meeting his son, Egon, in December, 2002, in his home in Munich, a city in which I had studied twenty years ago. I should like to thank him for sharing with me his memories both of his father and of his godfather, Adolf Hitler. Egon's son, Erik, read my manuscript and compared the man I had written about with the grandfather whom he had known as a boy. My agent, Andrew Nurnberg, was his usual upbeat self, whilst Philip Turner and Keith Wallman at Carroll & Graf were excellent editors. Ginny Buechele trawled through the hundreds of pages of material on Hanfstaengl at the Franklin D. Roosevelt Library. Alison Graham at the *Sunday Times* in London provided expert guidance on the choice of pictures.

Like it or not, my family was drawn into the project. My children, Elisabetta, Alexander, and Matthew found it difficult to grasp the fascination that this figure from a far-away age could hold for their father. As they grow older, I am sure they will begin to understand. Elisabetta used her technical skills to good effect to scan in the photographs. Roberta, my wife, was not only obliged to share her husband with a long-dead Nazi for almost three years, but also read the manuscript and provided invaluable advice on how to improve it.

This book is dedicated to them all—and to Gaston, my father, who served in the Royal Air Force, and to Marjorie, my mother, who as a teenager in wartime London lived through the hell which Hitler unleashed and who, sadly, did not live to see this work completed.

ALL dialogue between the historical characters in this book has been culled from Ernst Hanfstaengl's own memoirs, legal submissions and other writings, from accounts in contemporary newspaper and magazine articles, and from letters and books by the parties themselves.

HITLER'S PIANO PLAYER

FROM MUNICH TO FIFTH AVENUE

1

THE posters had been out on the streets of Munich for days; in blood-red type they promised salvation to a people who knew only desperation. The crowds had been gathering for several hours and the mood inside the Kindlkeller was tense with anticipation. The L-shaped beer cellar on the Rosenheimer Strasse was packed.

A distinctive patrician figure walked in. In his mid-thirties, he was six feet four inches tall, with a prominent lantern jaw and a flick of hair that hung across his forehead. Ernst Sedgwick Hanfstaengl paused for a moment. This was not the Germany he had left behind a decade ago to run the family art business in New York.

The meeting was about to start. Looking through the haze of tobacco smoke, he studied the careworn faces of the petty bourgeois crowded around him, many of whom had brought their wives along. Here and there were more refined characters, *Beamtentypen* (civil servants), or former military officers. The majority, though, were young men, some of them in the traditional costume of lederhosen and long woolen socks. What could have brought such a disparate collection of people to one place? The atmosphere reminded Hanfstaengl of a ball he had attended during his military service in the Bavarian Life Guards.

He pushed his way through to the stage. There near the podium was a table for the press. Hanfstaengl sat down and turned to an elderly, bespectacled journalist sitting to this left.

"Which of the men over there at the head table is actually Herr Hitler?" he asked, speaking in his native German.

The journalist peered at him over the edge of his steel-rimmed glasses. "You can't be from here, colleague, if you don't know him of all people," he said in a thick Bavarian accent. "Where are you from, then? "From out of town," Hanfstaengl replied. "I've been abroad a lot and I'm now a correspondent for German-language newspapers overseas." "That explains it, then," the man concluded. And he began to point out those present: the small man over on the left, with one arm, was Max Amann, the party's manager. He had been Hitler's sergeant in the army during the war. And there in the middle, with the glasses, was Anton Drexler, the real founder of the party, even though he did not have much to say these days. Then there was the man who ran the show, the one with the little mustache—Hitler.

"A real *Teufelskerl* (a devil of a fellow), I can tell you. I have never heard a speaker like him," the man said. Whether they would actually hear Hitler's normal rhetoric that night, the journalist did not like to predict. Hitler had only just been released after spending a couple of months in jail for breach of the peace and so would have to watch his words carefully. Anything too inflammatory and he would be locked up again.

While his neighbor was speaking, Hanfstaengl studied Hitler carefully. He could not seem to see anything remarkable in this *Teufelskerl*. On the contrary. Everything about him looked very normal and ordinary: average kind of build, with a comic little Charlie Chaplin mustache over a soft collar; a dark cheap-looking suit with a leather jacket and a pair of clumsy old army boots that he was stamping around in. He looked like a waiter in a station buffet, perhaps, or a barber's assistant, even though both would have been better dressed.

As Drexler introduced Hitler to the crowd, a storm of applause broke out in the hall. Bolt upright, with quick, rigid steps, he strode to the podium, instantly recognizable as a soldier in civilian clothes. He was barely nine feet or so away from Hanfstaengl, who could see every nuance of his gestures and the play of his features. Most striking were his piercing, deep blue eyes. Hitler waited for the applause to die down and began to speak.

"Pay attention now; it's going to start," the journalist whispered to Hanfstaengl, pushing his glasses higher on his nose in anticipation.

EARLIER that week the telephone had rung in the tiny apartment in Schwabing, the bohemian quarter of Munich, that Hanfstaengl shared with his tall American wife, Helene, and their one-year-old son, Egon. It had been a long continuous ring, which meant an official call. Hanfstaengl was surprised; it was barely a year since homesickness had driven him to swap his family's comfortable life in New York for the turmoil of postwar Germany. Few people even had their telephone number. "Remain on the line and keep repeating your name," said an anonymous woman's voice. "You are being called from Berlin. We will shortly be connecting you to an official call on a special line."

"Berlin, an official call on a special line," Hanfstaengl whispered to his wife, and began to repeat his name with the piety of a Tibetan monk.

It was November 18, 1922, a gray and cloudy day. The mood in Germany was grim. The country was tearing itself apart under the weight of the punitive reparations imposed by the victorious wartime allies. It seemed only a matter of time before civil war would break out between Prussia and Bavaria, the two most powerful states in the recently declared Weimar Republic. The economy was deteriorating sharply: industrial production, already badly dislocated by war, was further hit by labor strikes. Food and winter fuel were beyond the reach of many. The only thing thriving was the black market.

Hanfstaengl's thoughts were interrupted by a voice that crackled out of the ether; it was Warren Robbins, a former classmate from Harvard. The two men knew each other from one of the university's riotous Hasty Pudding shows in which they had both performed. Hanfstaengl, all six feet four inches of him, had incongruously yodeled his way in drag through the starring role of Gretchen Spootspfeifer in their 1908 show, *The Fate Fakirs*. Robbins had played one of Gretchen's admirers.

Robbins, newly installed as second-in-command at the American embassy in Berlin, was looking for a favor. The embassy wanted to see for itself what was going on in Bavaria and was sending down Capt. Truman Smith, the assistant military attaché, to have a look around and talk to as many people as possible.

"Admittedly, he's a Yale man, but in spite of that he is a nice, bright chap," Robbins said. "He'll come and see you in the next few days. Please look after him and get him a few introductions, will you, please?"

"Of course, old fellow, no problem," Hanfstaengl replied. Before he could ask anything more the line had gone dead.

Truman Smith arrived a couple of days later. In his thirties, he was friendly and open-minded. He struck Hanfstaengl as someone who knew what he wanted but who also realized there were two sides to most things in life. Like Hanfstaengl, he was a music lover and was especially keen on Wagner. After a brief welcoming meal, the American turned the conversation to the aim of his mission and presented his host with a long wish list of politicians he wanted to meet. Hanfstaengl felt embarrassed. "The best I can offer you are a few society connections," he said. "And I don't even know whether they have much political weight or not." He proposed instead introducing his guest to Paul Nikolaus Cossmann, publisher and editor in chief of the *Münchener Neueste Nachrichten*, one of the city's most important newspapers. Truman Smith went to see him in his office in the Sendlinger Strasse.

Four days later, Truman Smith came back for lunch. He had been very busy: to Hanfstaengl's surprise, he had already spoken to almost all the big names in Bavarian politics, from Crown Prince Rupprecht to Gen. Erich Ludendorff, the war hero. Truman Smith had found them all interesting, but there was something blandly similar about them all too—they replied with the same answers to his questions and had no new original solutions to Germany's mounting political and economic problems. There was another politician he had met that morning who was really different, though; he seemed like a real fighter. He was due to make a speech in Munich that evening and had given Truman Smith a pass for the press table. The American officer was convinced he was someone to watch. Unfortunately, he had to catch his train back to Berlin and wondered whether Hanfstaengl could go to the meeting on his behalf and report back.

Intrigued, Hanfstaengl asked the politician's name.

"Adolf Hitler," Truman Smith replied.

Hanfstaengl was certain he had confused the name with that of another nationalist politician whom he had already come across and of whom he had a rather low opinion.

"Your apparent discovery is actually called Hilpert and—if you allow someone who generally abstains from politics but happens to know him to express his modest opinion—he is a political no-hoper."

Truman Smith retorted there was no doubt the man was called Adolf Hitler—something Hanfstaengl would have realized himself if he had taken the trouble to look at all the posters around Munich that bore Hitler's name.

"I'm telling you, he's got such a way with words and says exactly what the hungry Germans want to hear today," Smith continued. "Nationalistic but with a socialist side—and anti-Jew. He'll probably tone things down over time, as others before him have done, but this guy has a concept and a talent for speaking that takes people along with him. So, are you going along or not?"

Hanfstaengl could not refuse. He agreed to accompany Truman Smith to the railroad station and then go on to the meeting.

When they arrived that evening at the platform from which the Berlin train was due to leave, a dubious-looking man of indeterminate ethnic origin was waiting for them. Hanfstaengl took an instant dislike to him. His face was pale and almost without expression and he looked unkempt. He had the air of a police spy about him.

"That's Herr Rosenberg, Herr Hitler's press chief," Truman Smith said as they approached. After making the introductions, he explained to Rosenberg that he would be sending Hanfstaengl to represent him that evening.

Hanfstaengl stared at both men and wondered if he had heard right. Could someone who was supposed to be a skilled politician really have such a desperate-looking character as his press spokesman and adviser? All sorts of questions went through his head. Chief among them was, What *was* this Hitler doing with such an unsavory fellow?

The comedy continued: Rosenberg suddenly bowed in front of Truman Smith and, with a heavy Baltic German accent, proceeded to deliver in English a farewell address that he had obviously carefully memorized.

"Captain," he declared with a raised voice. "I have the honor to convey to you on your departure the soldierly greetings of Herr Hitler and at the same time to express to you his thanks for your interest in our movement. Herr Hitler wishes you a good journey."

Hanfstaengl could not help but laugh to himself at the absurdity of the tableau unfolding in front of him. If the Hitler show had a few more novelties like this, then the evening would be amusing, at least. In fact, the last few minutes until the train left passed in a relatively pleasant way: even Rosenberg's rather hostile features were lightened by a forced smile when Hanfstaengl, in somewhat exaggerated form, translated into German the positive things Truman Smith had told him about Hitler. Soon afterward, the whistle blew and the train steamed slowly out of the station, bound for Berlin.

Alone with Rosenberg, Hanfstaengl felt awkward as he clutched the press pass Truman Smith had given him. What was he, as a German, doing representing the American embassy at a political rally held by such a nonentity? Should he treat the whole thing as a joke, perhaps, or else give up his job as Truman Smith's envoy and just slip off home? But he was intrigued. Half an hour later, he and Rosenberg arrived at the Kindlkeller.

WHEN Hitler began to address the meeting, Hanfstaengl was immediately struck both by the broadness of his register and the scope of his rhetoric. He had listened to a number of great orators in his time. President Theodore Roosevelt, whom he had met personally while studying at Harvard with his son, was one. Thomas Pryor Gore, the blind senator from Oklahoma, was another. But none of them had such an incredible range of effects as Hitler, who spoke freely and rhapsodically and was completely without the professorial manner of other German politicians. He would absorb all the irrational feelings and wishful thinking of his audience and then express it back to them in such a way that he could turn it to his own purpose—in the process turning them into a kind of sounding board. Making use of the same talent for mimicry that he would often display when with friends, Hitler displayed an empathy with his listeners that allowed him to translate his intentions and goals into their terms and language. In this way he mastered with equal success the vocabulary of the troubled housewife at the empty Viktualienmarkt, Munich's food market, the jargon of the disaffected common soldier or high military officer, and the intellectual world of the property owner dispossessed by inflation.

Hitler was also tremendously compelling because of his total belief in his own words. He had the kind of faith that moved mountains. Engaging with a mass audience, he was later to tell Hanfstaengl, was like talking to a woman who had heard a lot of negative things about you. You had to try to talk her around and gradually she would become your most ferocious supporter. Not that, as Hanfstaengl wryly noted, Hitler had had that much experience with women.

Hitler spent the first ten minutes of his speech on a brief summary of what had happened to Germany since November 1918: the breakup of the monarchy, the proclamation of the republic, the consequences of the Versailles Treaty—with the enforced acceptance by Germans of guilt for the war—and the deception behind the words of the pacifists and the Marxists. When Hitler saw he was getting his point across, he relaxed his left leg—like a soldier standing at ease—and began to illustrate his words with a variety of gestures, of which he had many. His tone became more aggressive, but there was also a mocking humor. Hanfstaengl noticed the sparkling wit of the Vienna coffeehouse in the sly malice of some of his intimations and the elegance of his sentences. Hitler denounced the kaiser and his advisers for their weakness at the decisive moment of German surrender and sneered at the left-wing politicians for having conceded to the victors everything that could have alleviated their own people's suffering. Nor did he have any more sympathy for the Bavarian separatists and confessional Catholics; he contrasted their attitude with that of the noble soldier on the front who would come to the aid of his wounded colleague regardless of whether he was Bavarian or Prussian, Catholic or Protestant.

"That is the spirit that we Germans need more than any other at this time of emergency," Hitler declared. "This is the spirit that accomplishes miracles and leads those who have been conquered and deceived into a new future." His audience had only to look at the example of Benito Mussolini, the Italian fascist leader, who just weeks earlier had led his Blackshirts on their triumphant march on Rome, he said. Tumultuous applause followed.

The more Hitler warmed to his theme, and the louder the applause, the more he stepped up the speed and volume of his speech. He gesticulated. If anyone tried to heckle, he would lift up his hands as if he were catching a ball and defuse their protest with a sly smile. Two or three sentences full of humor and he had the crowd on his side again. His agile performance reminded Hanfstaengl of a master violinist, who rarely needs to use the full length of his bow.

Waking from his revery, Hanfstaengl looked around the room. There was little left of the dull, seething mass of flat triviality through which he had pushed his way an hour earlier. They had been replaced by a community of people, all deeply moved. The beer had grown tepid in their half-empty mugs; the audience was too busy drinking in every one of Hitler's words. Not far away, Hanfstaengl saw a young woman who had raised her arms as if in the presence of the Messiah.

Years later, after Hitler had translated the vision he had outlined that evening into a terrible reality, Hanfstaengl would often wonder how he had allowed himself to be so impressed by what he had heard in the Kindlkeller. How could he ever have been taken in by such a man? It may have been because Hitler had moderated his words for fear of being arrested and imprisoned again. Or maybe it was because Mussolini's recent seizure of power in Italy had made his arguments seem especially pertinent. Either way, when Hitler finished after two hours, Hanfstaengl found himself applauding in just as enthusiastic and unrestrained a way as everyone else in the beer cellar. Giving the journalist next to him a friendly farewell tap on the shoulder, he stood up and went over to the speakers' platform, where Hitler, bathed in sweat, was being congratulated by his supporters.

Hitler acknowledged Hanfstaengl's greetings with a self-confident smile, but without any arrogance, and listened carefully when the well-wisher introduced himself as Truman Smith's emissary. Hitler paused in the middle of wiping the sweat from his brow with a handerchief and looked at Hanfstaengl.

"So, you are a friend of the big captain who called this morning," Hitler said. "He mentioned you were coming. So, what are you going to report to him?"

"One thing," Hanfstaengl replied. "I will tell him that I personally agree with ninety-five percent of what you have said and that I have expressed the wish to discuss the remaining five percent with you at an appropriate moment."

Hitler laughed. "I will happily fulfill your wish," he replied. "For I'm sure, Herr Hanfstaengl, that we will also agree on the remaining five percent."

They bade each other farewell and Hanfstaengl went home. He found it difficult to sleep that night. He sat at his desk trying to compose the report he would send Truman Smith; first one draft of his text and then the other were tossed into the wastepaper basket. He could not get Hitler's rhetoric out of his mind, the dynamism of his speech and the striking formulation of his program. On the other hand, he was struck by the portion of the Kindlkeller speech he had found absurd and paradoxical.

Hanfstaengl found himself gradually coming to agree with Truman Smith. However ordinary Hitler seemed at first glance, here was someone who played like a virtuoso on the keyboard of the human soul and seemed destined one day to play a decisive role in some form or other. He had the air of the unusual about him. As Hanfstaengl sat there, he also reflected on the enthusiasm and spontaneity with which he had gone over to Hitler and told him he agreed with ninety-five percent of his speech.

One thing was clear: after what he had heard that night, Hanfstaengl could not just shrug his shoulders and continue with his life as if nothing had happened. He shared the same sadness and anger at the fate of his beloved Germany as the rest of the audience in the Kindlkeller.

Unlike other politicians, Hitler actually articulated these sentiments and appeared to offer solutions.

Hanfstaengl had to admit, though, that some of Hitler's ideas seemed downright absurd and the paucity of his knowledge of the world called out for urgent correction. Hanfstaengl thought, in particular, of Hitler's dismissal of the significance of America—the country in which Hanfstaengl had spent almost all the previous seventeen years; of his demand for an end to the payment of all reparations to France, and to resist the military occupation, which was almost certain to lead to a guerrilla war; and finally, of his wild anti-Semitism, a mixture of mythical theories of race and the kind of clichéd anti-Jewish tirades common among the petty bourgeois of Vienna.

Hanfstaengl could not help but think back to a conversation with Rudolf Kommer, a brilliant Austrian Jewish journalist from the Czernowitz ghetto, whom he had gotten to know when they were both working in New York. "In a lunatic asylum, where there is also a shortage of food, everyone is mad in his or her own way," Kommer had told him. "But once the situation in Germany is normal again, then things will calm down and all this madness will just fade away."

It was a reassuring thought, and it was something to which Hanfstaengl would repeatedly turn for comfort in the following years as he became closer and closer to Hitler. It was also wrong.

2

ERNST Hanfstaengl's parentage ensured that his loyalties would always be divided—a factor that would color his life from earliest childhood and prove both his salvation and his undoing. He was born on February 11, 1887, into one of the most prominent and well-connected families in Bavaria. His grandfather, Franz, was a pioneer in the art reproduction business who had made his reputation throughout Europe when he was commissioned by the state of Saxony in 1835 to reproduce the entire collection of the Dresden Gallery. Franz, who had already achieved his fame as a lithograph portraitist, was swift to grasp the opportunities presented by the development of photography and in 1853 opened his own photographic atelier. Kaiser Wilhelm, Queen Victoria, and Franz Liszt were among his more prominent subjects.

Franz's son, Edgar, followed in his father's footsteps, turning the family firm into one of the most respected names in its field and opening branches in New York and London. The success of the business brought the Hanfstaengls considerable wealth. Along with the money came social status: Edgar, like his father and grandfather before him, was a privy councillor to the duke of Saxe-Coburg-Gotha.

Ernst, however, was no purebred Bavarian. His mother, Katherine Sedgwick Hanfstaengl, née Heine, was an American whose pedigree was no less impressive than her husband's. Katherine's father, William Heine, who fled to the United States from Germany after the failure of the liberal revolution of 1848, was an architect and celebrated illustrator who had worked on the Paris Opéra. He became a Civil War general and was one of the pallbearers at the funeral of Abraham Lincoln. Katherine's mother, Catherine, was a member of the Sedgwick family, one of the leading New England clans. General John Sedgwick, the Civil War hero whose statue stands at West Point, was her uncle.

Edgar and Katherine, or Kitty, as everyone called her, lived in grand style in a large house at Liebigstrasse 30, close to the River Isar, in one of the most prestigious parts of Munich. Villa Hanfstaengl, as it was known, was built for them in 1889 by the prominent Berlin architects Heinrich Kayser and Karl von Grossheim. Its windows afforded an impressive view of the river, the Isar bridge, and the Maximilianeum, now the seat of the Bavarian Landtag (parliament). Situated on extensive grounds, the house measured almost ninety feet across; the ground floor alone had more than fifteen rooms. Pride of place went to the music room, which was modeled on the antechamber of the Bishop rooms in the Munich Residenz and measured more than four hundred and eighty square feet. The work of a number of talented artists and skilled craftsmen, it was decorated with various woods and marble, as well as glass, leather, and silk. The wood-paneled dining room had space for twenty to thirty people; there were also numerous bedrooms and servants' rooms, a large kitchen complex, stables for six horses, a winter garden, two terraces, and four bathrooms—a considerable luxury for the time. Kitty had decorated some of the rooms green, apparently because this was the favorite color of Queen Victoria. A signed portrait of the monarch, dedicated to Edgar, was on display in a heavy silver frame.

Kitty had met Edgar in 1872 when she was just thirteen. Returning after the American Civil War to a newly united Germany, her father had sought out Edgar in Munich to discuss having some of his illustrations published, and he took his daughter with him. Edgar, who was thirty, made a strong impression on the teenage girl. Just back in Germany after seven years in China, he was fascinating and handsome and had been cited as the cause of the breaking of the engagement between Sophie Charlotte, duchess of Bavaria, and King Ludwig II of Bavaria.

Edgar and Kitty finally married a decade later, in November 1882. Their first son, Edgar II, was born the following July; another boy, Egon, arrived in July 1884 and their only daughter, Erna, in 1885. The last child, Erwin, was born in 1888, the year after Ernst. It was according to a tradition established by Edgar's father, Franz, that they were all given names beginning with *E*. Franz and his wife, Franziska, had lost several children in infancy, and they had heeded a prophesy by the wife of a forester, who worked for Duke Ernst of Saxony-Coburg-Gotha, that names beginning with an *E*—like that of the duke himself—would ensure that their bearers reached adulthood.

Despite his name, Ernst almost did not live to see his second birthday. A few weeks earlier he had come down with an especially bad case of diphtheria; his throat was so badly swollen, he was unable to eat for several days. It was the third day of his fast and the doctors, beginning to despair, told his father there was little they could do for him. Desperate to get away from the misery, Edgar went fishing. When he came back, he hesitated for a moment before going into the house, fearing his son might be dead.

He hadn't accounted for Kati, an elderly peasant woman who worked for the family. She was determined to save the boy and fed him patiently with a spoon, repeating all the while, "Putzi, eat this now, Putzi." And to everyone's amazement, the little boy who had refused to respond when addressed as Ernst was suddenly eating. Edgar could not believe what he saw when he walked in.

In the Bavarian dialect of the time, Putzi—pronounced to rhyme with *tootsie*—meant "little fellow," and the name stuck. From then on, it was the only name to which the little boy would answer. However hard his parents tried to drop it, he refused to respond to Ernst. And so the nickname continued to be used, even when the child had grown into a strapping young lad. Indeed, for the rest of his life Ernst was referred to as Putzi—however much he tried as an adult to shake it off.

The Hanfstaengls chose British women to care for their children, adding a third culture to the mix of American and German. The young Putzi's first nursery maid was Bessie Clapp, a small girl with thick steel-rimmed glasses. After a year or so she was replaced by Bella Farmer, a pretty young woman from Hartlepool in northern England. Putzi particularly took to her, but alas, after a few years she left to marry and start a family. She was replaced in 1895 by Caroline Jones, a staunch Methodist from Swansea, in South Wales. Putzi, writing later, would recall Jones's innocence and conviction that life was little more than a test set by God. Her talk, he recalled, was "Redolent of god-fearing copybook maxims and earnest endeavor viz. 'everyone should develop his god-given talents.'" She also used to tell him of the might of the British Empire and recounted tales from friends who had gone to Africa as missionaries.

Jones tried to drum into Putzi's head the basics of good manners, which, as she never hesitated to tell him, "maketh the man": stand up straight and keep your shoulders back; don't scratch yourself or fidget; don't grumble or gobble your food; and don't discuss things that are "below the tablecloth." She despaired at times of her young charge's uncontrolled tempers and used to scold him when he turned around in the street to watch pretty girls walk by. "It is not nice," she would tell him. "It is not done." The young Putzi was not impressed. Of his governess he later wrote: "Beneath the façade of Victoria Puritanism, lay a stifled soul—yearning for love and finding expression in Beethoven's 'Pathetique' and Chopin's nocturnes."

Edgar was also conscious of the need "to put a bit of stuffing into a quartet of sons in danger of getting spoiled by too many artistically minded adults." And so, every Sunday afternoon, Sgt. Maj. Franz Streit, from the Bavarian Royal Guard, would come to teach the boys military drill, marching them up and down the lawn. A soldier on guard, Putzi was taught, should shout three times *"Halt! Wer da?"*—Halt! Who goes there?—and then shoot. To her horror, Putzi's sister, Erna, was also obliged to take part.

Besides bawling commands at them, Streit would also entertain the children with tales of military heroics—which, as Putzi later remarked, was strange, since he could not recall the Bavarian army ever having won a victory on the battlefield. Streit, who sported an impressive mustache, nevertheless made a great impression on the boy. The sergeant major, he wrote, was "my first encounter with Militarism à la Bavarois, and in a certain sense an unforgettable element within my weltanschauung." Without military training, the young Putzi was told, a young man is only a "half person."

Music was an even greater influence on the boy. From an early age, Putzi's bedroom wall was decorated with pictures of Brahms, Hans von Bülow, Wagner, Liszt, Tchaikovsky, and others, which he had torn out of a musical calendar—early inspiration for his dream of a musical career. The famed Hertha Hauptmann Emmerich taught him the piano; Heinrich Bihrle, the violin; and Josef Horbelt, a musician from the Bavarian court who also taught at Munich's Akademie der Tonkunst, took care of music theory and singing. Although seemingly clumsy and badly coordinated, Putzi proved from an early age to be a talented pianist, to the delight of his father, who often invited friends around to hear his son play. Putzi's mother hoped he might one day become a conductor.

Befitting their status, Putzi's parents liked to entertain the cream of Munich society. Mark Twain, Buffalo Bill Cody, John Philip Sousa, and Richard Strauss were among the illustrious names who graced their guest book. On Sunday afternoons Edgar often had guests, and they would gather in his study, discussing politics. Putzi would sometimes sit in and listen; he subsequently dated the beginning of his political consciousness to the late 1890s.

There were two contrary political trends in Bavaria at the dawn of the twentieth century: on one side were the democratic federalists, who believed strongly in the rights of the individual and of the states, such as Bavaria, that made up the German federation. As such, they were closely identified with Kaiser Wilhelm I and with Bismarck, the former chancellor, who had been dismissed in March 1890. Ranged against them were the adherents of the *"junge Kaiser,"* Wilhelm II, believers in a strong, centralized, and militaristic Germany. A demonstration of this credo—and of the "Wilhelmscult"—came that May when the emperor appeared at the Wiesbaden opera house. He was greeted with a standing ovation by the audience, which chanted *"Ein Kaiser, Ein Reich, Ein Glaube"* (One Emperor, One Empire, One Faith). Edgar and other liberal Munich intellectuals like him were firmly in the federal camp. To them, sentiments of the sort expressed at Wiesbaden sounded like a declaration of war by the authoritarian, Protestant Prussia on their Catholic Bavaria.

As he grew up, Putzi also became aware of another strand of thought that was to play a decisive role in his life: he must have been about thirteen when he first heard talk of a National-Social Association, founded by Friedrich Naumann, a liberal German pastor. Naumann's aim was to improve the situation of the country's working classes by developing a new kind of Christian-based national socialism that, he hoped, would wean them away from Marxist-inspired ideas of class struggle and integrate them into the newly unified German nation-state. *Die Hilfe*, the weekly newspaper founded by Naumann in 1896, was for many years to be found among the various publications on Edgar's desk. By chance, the central distribution point for the newspaper was close to the family home.

In September 1897, Putzi was admitted to the Royal Bavarian Wilhelmsgymnasium in Munich, an imposing building of red and yellow sandstone on the Thierschstrasse next to the Maxmonument, where his two elder brothers were already studying. Founded by Jesuits in 1559, it was the oldest Gymnasium (high school) in the Bavarian capital and one of the most prestigious. Putzi, whose education had hitherto been entrusted to governesses, was delighted at last to be taught by men.

His first-form teacher was Gebhard Himmler, whose son, Heinrich, was later to become one of the leading Nazis. The senior Himmler had once been a tutor to Prince Heinrich of Bavaria; Putzi considered him a terrible snob who favored those pupils who had titles and was tough on the "commoners"—even those who came from wealthy, prominent families like the Hanfstaengls. Heinrich was several years younger than Putzi, so their paths did not cross at school. Putzi occasionally saw him, though, when he went to deliver work to the Himmlers' home on the Sternstrasse. He remembered him as a "pallid, moon-faced brat" who had a reputation as a sneak, running to his father to tell tales on other boys.

Such snobbery was commonplace in a school proud to be attended by the royal pages of the court of Wittelsbach, the Bavarian royal family. Five decades after graduating, one of Putzi's fellow classmates still vividly remembered the haughty behavior of the members of the "vain, yet petty little Bavarian nobility" who were keen to distance themselves from the "poor white trash known as the *Bürgerliche*. When these noble boys met, during the morning intermission, in a huddle in the courtyard of the Gymnasium, woe unto the petit bourgeois, who innocently and unawares of the established exclusive iron curtain attempted a friendly approach to one or the other of these scions of the supposed elite."

Despite his undoubted talents, Putzi lacked dedication to his studies. He was, he subsequently admitted, "the world champion in staying back," and had to repeat both the second class—after failing Latin and geography—and the fourth, after problems with Latin again. Greek, "painfully arrived at and darkly understood," proved another challenge. "Greek has three qualities," he noted. "It requires lots of time to learn, it is quickly forgotten, and it makes one educated." Putzi's failings were undoubtedly due in part to the considerable time he was devoting to music; his teachers, Bernhard Stavenhagen and August Schmidt-Lindner, had studied under Liszt and were extremely demanding.

Unlike his elder brothers, Putzi wanted to continue his education not in Germany but in America. This was not just because it was the land of his mother's birth. It was also planned that he should take over the branch of the family business set up by Edgar in the 1880s on Fifth Avenue in New York. This meant getting to know the country in which he was to start his career. Kitty was enthusiastic, and an American friend of hers helped Putzi secure conditional admission to Harvard University's freshman class. He finished at the Gymnasium in July 1905 and spent the summer with his family on Lake Starnberg, southwest of Munich. Before leaving Germany he met a recent Harvard graduate, William Chase, at the Hotel Vierjahreszeiten in Munich. Chase gave Putzi some valuable advice on how to behave at his future school: "Keep away from the Yard, from so-called grinds, from cheap clubs; get to know the 'right people'; go out for rowing, the Deutsche Verein (the German Union), the Musical Clubs; beware Dean Hurlbut; get on the good side of the headwaiter at the Hotel Tourraine in Boston."

On September 12, Putzi bade farewell to his family and set off by train for Hamburg, where, two days later, he would board the steamer S.S. *Hamburg*, bound for America. He arrived ten days later. During the crossing he was asked by some elderly ladies about his future plans and the job he intended to get in America. "I am a *Kunstmensch* [man of art] and come from a fine arts publishing family and therefore intend to become only that which my father and grandfather were before me," he replied rather pompously.

The period from the beginning of the twentieth century until the outbreak of the First World War has been described as the last years of innocence for the United States. It was a time during which the union of forty-eight contiguous states was completed, and its citizens largely concentrated their attention on domestic issues. The outside world was of no real concern to the American people, and the United States was of no real concern to the outside world.

Harvard was at the heart of the American establishment: it was here that the country's future political, intellectual, and business elites were formed and networked with one another. For Putzi, the university's preeminence was summed up by John Collins Bossidy's "On the Aristocracy of Harvard," which mocked the prominence of old families like the Lowells and the Cabots, both of whom had crossed the Atlantic from Bristol in the seventeenth century.

And this is good old Boston,
The home of the bean and the cod
Where the Lowells talk only to Cabots,
And the Cabots talk only to God.

Despite his mother's impressive pedigree, Putzi—or Hanfy, as he was to be known during his Harvard years—was something of an outsider who was teased about his foreign roots. Among his papers is a list of American preconceptions about Germans, apparently compiled at the time. "Germans are too sentimental, German humor is too heavy, and German women are too fat," his American classmates told him. The German language was impossible; Germany's Gothic churches were not really Gothic at all; and its artillery and submarines were inferior to their French counterparts. As for German sausages, they just made one fat, while Munich beer was not as good as American. Putzi was also mocked by some of his classmates for the traditions of German student life, especially their obsession with dueling. Putzi's parents had had little time for sword fighting and so he had never learned. But he was enough of a German patriot to be annoyed by such criticism, even though he couldn't quite bring himself to take up fencing just to prove to his classmates what they were missing.

Putzi was able to rise above such stereotypes; his larger-than-life character and the determination with which he threw himself into extracurricular activities soon made him one of Harvard's most popular and best-known students. His size and bulk won him a position on the Harvard crew; his voice made him cheerleader for the football team; and his general exuberance gained him many friends during the four years he was there. He was remembered by his contemporaries, according to *The New York Times*, "chiefly for his thundering renditions of Wagnerian music and the apprehension felt by his hearers for any piano which he attacked at the university and later at the Harvard Club in New York City."

Putzi also achieved hero status soon after he arrived. In early 1906, a canoeist nearly drowned after he capsized in the freezing water of the Charles River. Putzi, who happened to be walking past, plunged in and fished him out. The story quickly got around Harvard and Putzi was praised in a *Boston Herald* headline: "Hanfstaengl Harvard's Hero."

Proud of his German roots, Putzi also became president of the Deutsche Verein. Its constitution, accepted on May 7, 1909, proclaimed the "object of the club shall be to unite Harvard men who are interested in the promotion of the Knowledge of German Language and Culture." Its activities consisted of lectures, an annual play, and a series of sessions in the Kneipe—a German-style bar. In his second year, Putzi took to presiding over meetings of the Deutsche Verein with a sword that had been presented to him by the captain of the German cruiser *Bremen* when it visited Boston.

While he tended to his studies, Putzi also played hard—as he demonstrated one warm spring evening in 1909 when he climbed the stairs of one of Harvard's most prestigious clubs, called the Sphinx. A score or so men were sitting at small tables, smoking, talking quietly, and downing beer and stingers; one of them caught sight of Putzi and called him over. He ordered beer and joined the conversation until one of them suddenly urged: "Play us something, Hanfy." Putzi did not need much convincing: he walked over to the upright piano against the wall and let his massive hands range across the keys. The music, which began light, soon became heavier and more martial. "Soldiers' Field," came the cry, and Putzi crashed out the stirring music from one of Harvard's football songs. "'O'er the stands in flaming crimson Harvard's banners fly,'" someone sang, and more and more people joined in.

Word soon spread that Putzi was playing, and increasing numbers of men from other clubs wandered into the Sphinx. As the room filled, Putzi began to play opera. Then, fueled by more beer, he turned his hand to Wagner. And so he continued through the small hours, with short pauses only for rest and more beer. As dawn drew near, the crowd became more boisterous. "Let's get a truck and have Hanfy play through the streets of Cambridge," one of the students yelled.

Pandemonium broke out. Some people managed to get hold of a truck and backed it up to the door of the club. It took eight of the revelers to manhandle the piano down the stairs and load it onto the truck. A piano stool followed. Putzi was literally mobbed by the crowd and hustled down the stairs. He climbed onto the truck and immediately began pounding out more football marches. He played like a demon, the crowd around him laughing, yelling, singing, and running to keep up. The whole wild throng then flowed down the street and around the corner. Heads began to appear at windows, their anger at having been awoken giving way to fascination at the strange goings-on in the street below. Just as they were setting off, Putzi had spotted four nuns going to the early mass in the church opposite. When he raised his hand, the crowd fell momentarily silent: the nuns scurried into the church, horrified at the mob scene they had just witnessed. Then he struck up the music again.

Just as he was gaining the affection of his classmates, Putzi was making inroads into the American establishment, becoming a frequent guest at the home of Charles William Eliot, the president of Harvard. He became a friend, too, of the eldest son of Theodore Roosevelt, who in September 1901 had become America's youngest president at the age of forty-two. Indeed, Putzi became so close to Theodore junior that he was invited to the White House in 1908 for the Christmas festivities. Putzi was flattered at how the president spoke to him as an equal and invited him to play the White House's magnificent Steinway grand piano. Thereafter he was a frequent guest at other functions in Washington, D.C. During one official ball, Putzi and several other young guests slipped away and staged their own private party in one of the underground rooms. Putzi played another, more modest, piano they found there so enthusiastically that he broke seven of its bass strings.

During this time, he also met the other branch of the Roosevelt family, from which the future president Franklin Delano Roosevelt was to come. Among the luminaries with whom he made friends were Hamilton Fish, later to be a leading force in the isolationist camp in the House of Representatives, T.S. Eliot, Walter Lippman, Hendrik von Loon, Hans von Kaltenborn, Robert Benchley, and John Reed.

Inevitably, given the energy that he put into his social life, Putzi's academic performance was far from glittering. He had initially been admitted to Harvard only as a special student "on trial," and although he earned regular status within a few weeks, his subsequent work was disappointing. In November of 1906 he was put on probation for the first time. In a letter to his father, the dean, Byron Satterlee Hurlbut, put the blame on his extracurricular activities.

"The boy frankly admits that his failure is due to his too great devotion to matters outside of the regular business of college," Hurlbut wrote. "I think that he has spent too much time on his music." Suitably chastened, Putzi put in enough work to ensure that the probation was lifted the following April; but then he started to slack off again and three months later had been dropped a class-year and was back on probation.

As Putzi left to spend the summer holidays in Germany, Hurlbut wrote him a warning letter in which he advised him "not to return unless you are prepared to put college ahead of your fun." A similar warning was sent to his father, who had been ailing since suffering a serious heart attack a month or so after Putzi had left for Harvard. And so it continued for the rest of his academic career.

By spring 1909, Putzi was close to graduating. The news from home was not good: his father's condition had taken a turn for the worse. Putzi's studies were still not going especially well and he was in danger of narrowly missing his degree; he had become so carried away with his thesis on Goethe's Italian journey that he missed the Friday deadline and delivered it to his professor's home first thing on Monday instead. In what seemed to Putzi an appalling example of small-mindedness, it was rejected and he was faced with the alarming prospect of returning to Germany without the much-coveted diploma. Not for the first or last time in his life, music became his salvation. Putzi was accepted into a summer school on harmony by Professor Marshall, a former pupil of Joseph Reinberger's, a prominent name in sacred music in Bavaria. The generous final mark gave Putzi the missing point in lieu of a passing thesis that he needed for his degree.

Equipped with his liberal arts degree in art, literature, history, and philosophy, Putzi returned to Munich later in 1909 to perform one year of voluntary military service in the infantry Life Guards. After four years in America, it was like stepping back into the eighteenth century: the young recruit shouldered arms, trooped the color, and stood guard outside the royal palace and other important buildings. Putzi joked that his only taste of action happened when some Harvard friends, led by Hamilton Fish, came across him on guard duty during a visit and threatened to knock off his spiked helmet and play football with it. They ran off when he threatened to call some of his comrades.

Despite such larks, the months after his graduation were a time of sadness. On May 29, 1910, after a long deterioration in his condition, Putzi's father died. Putzi, along with the rest of the family, was at his deathbed. In his last words to his son, Edgar urged him to do his duty. After his military service was complete Putzi went to Vienna to study lithography, before working for six months at the family firm in Munich to learn the workings of the art publishing business. The time had come for a new challenge.

3

IN the fall of 1911, Putzi returned to America. Although just twenty-four, he was put in charge of Galerie Hanfstaengl, the New York branch of Kunstverlag Franz Hanfstaengl. He was helped by Friedrich Denks, the son of a Lutheran minister who had been working for the family in Munich and had just arrived in America. Putzi may have been a new-comer to the art business, but his lack of experience was more than out-weighed by his outgoing personality and the wealth of society contacts he had garnered at Harvard. He threw his all into the job, working most days from 7 AM until 8 PM. The gallery thrived and the annual dividend sent back via Amsterdam to the family firm in Munich rose steadily.

By early 1913, business was doing so well that Putzi moved its prem-ises to one of the busiest—and most expensive—corners of Fifth Avenue. The gallery, at number 545, on the corner of Forty-fifth Street, was a "delightful combination of business and pleasure," he recalled later. "The famous names who visited me were legion: Pierpont Morgan, Toscanini, Henry Ford, Caruso, Santos-Dumont, Charlie Chaplin, Paderewski and the daughter of President Wilson." Carl Muck, the famous conductor of the Wagner Festival in Bayreuth and director of the Boston Symphony Orchestra, used to drop in to chat about art and music when he was in New York. Other German musicians on tour in America would visit too. Indeed, Putzi consciously tried to turn the gallery into a meeting place for music and art lovers, not just for his own entertainment but also because it was good for business. During his subway ride home, Putzi would take out his diary and memorize the names of all the people he had met in order to be able to greet them by name at their next encounter.

Putzi carefully cultivated his contacts with the Roosevelts and was an occasional guest at their retreat at Sagamore Hill in Oyster Bay, on Long Island. One weekend in 1912, Theodore Roosevelt took Putzi aside and questioned him about his military service. To Putzi's surprise, he then launched into praise of the German army "as an excellent school. . . . As long as the German *Volk* has an army in which they must perform military service, then it can and will not degenerate," he told him. Roosevelt also gave him an insight into politics that was to stay with him throughout his life. It was not a choice between the better of two options, but rather which of the two would have fewer bad and unpleasant consequences, he said. Bismarck may have spoken of politics as an art, but "If I said what I understand as politics, it is the choice of the lesser evil," Roosevelt told Putzi.

He also had the chance to renew the acquaintance of Franklin D. Roosevelt, who was then a lawyer and a state senator in New York. With little time or inclination to cook for himself, Putzi used to take most of his meals in the New York Harvard Club, which was conveniently nearby on West Forty-fourth street. FDR would take breakfast in the club's large dining room when he came to New York City from Albany. Putzi was often already there, seated at the Steinway grand piano in the corner, playing his familiar repertoire of Bach, Beethoven, Schubert, Liszt, Brahms, and Wagner.

FDR, then in his early thirties, was still an energetic man with a lively spring in his step. He would give Putzi a friendly nod as he came in and sat down at his favorite table near the fireplace, reading his newspaper and listening to the music. Putzi was impressed by the parade of well-known names who would often join him there: Walter Lippmann, who was then only just starting his journalistic career; Jack London, the author; John Reed, who was to become world famous for his eyewitness account of the Russian revolution; and Harold Laski, one of the great thinkers of the British labor movement. Their politics were all somewhat too liberal for Putzi's taste, but this did not prevent him from developing a close friendship with the future president.

In business as well as in his private life, Putzi was already beginning to show signs of the eccentricities that were to mark his career. On one occasion, he noticed a man with a violin case looking wistfully at a portrait of Paganini in the window of his gallery. The man finally summoned the courage to come in and ask the price, but he looked crestfallen when he learned how expensive it was. Putzi suggested payment in kind. The violinist was delighted and within a few weeks a string ensemble was playing there every afternoon.

▬

ONE day in 1914, while Putzi was working in the gallery, a beautiful young woman walked in carrying a portfolio of drawings under her arm. In her early twenties, she was five feet eight inches tall, with a curvaceous figure, gray eyes, auburn hair, and a mole near her left eye. Her name was Djuna Barnes and she was destined to become one of the most prominent writers of her generation. At this time, though, she was just starting out as a journalist and freelance illustrator. When she caught sight of Putzi, selling her drawings suddenly did not seem so important anymore. The two of them "sort of looked at each other and fell in love," she recalled later.

They quickly became lovers; Putzi appears to have been undeterred to learn early in their relationship that Barnes was bisexual and, if anything, preferred women to men. There was a rather strong physical attraction. On one occasion Putzi reportedly suffered an extremely painful burst blood vessel in his penis while dancing with her. But Putzi's love ran deeper. One day, Barnes mentioned to him that her editor had assigned her to take a flight on a homemade plane. Putzi thought it extremely foolhardy and offered her the twenty-five dollars she would have earned if she promised not to go. It was a fortuitous call. The plane crashed, killing everyone on board. Putzi also became a frequent visitor at the Barnes's family home in Morris Park, New York (on Long Island), striking up a friendship with her teenage brother, Saxon, to whom he gave a stamp album. The boy found Putzi likable, and he was genuinely struck by his soldierly air and impressed by how convincingly he could go through a military drill with a rifle.

Putzi's feelings for Barnes were reciprocated—as was shown in a section deleted from the final version of *Nightwood*, her celebrated and largely autobiographical novel, published in 1936. The section, preserved in Barnes's papers, describes the heroine falling for a German who seemed "so tall and melancholy and humorous, with a head with the curse of madness in it." When they kissed as they walked together across the Brooklyn Bridge, it was "the first time I had been kissed or cared [for] in six years, and I loved him with all my heart," she wrote. "And it went on three years and I said, 'I will be married.'"

A real marriage was not to be, however, in part because of events in faraway Sarajevo. The assassination on June 28, 1914, of Archduke Franz Ferdinand, the heir to the Austro-Hungarian throne, set off a chain of events that was to lead within weeks to the outbreak of the First World War. The immediate impact on life in the United States, though, was negligible. Woodrow Wilson, who had succeeded Theodore Roosevelt as president the previous year, declared that his country would stay out of the conflict. Despite America's traditional ties with Britain, Wilson had no desire to give up its long-standing policy of isolationism in favor of participation in a European war. He also had to take into account the potential reaction of the large number of Germans and Austrians who lived in the United States.

By virtue of his service in the Life Guards, Putzi was a reservist and had military obligations in Germany, but he was thousands of miles from his unit. He claimed subsequently that he had been keen to return home and had presented himself to Franz von Papen, the German military attaché in New York. Von Papen gave him an address to which to report, to arrange his journey, but the information was delivered in such an open and careless fashion that Putzi was convinced the place would be infested with British spies. Given that American ships were often searched by the Royal Navy as soon as they left their own waters, and all German men of military age on board were detained, Putzi decided not to risk it. A number of other men his age nevertheless made the journey successfully.

Putzi's failure to take part in the conflict and enjoy the camaraderie of the trenches was to weigh heavily on him during the years that followed. While his unit was fighting on the Western Front and in Italy, Serbia, and Romania, he was safe in New York. "Somehow I never managed to rid myself of the oppressive feeling that I was not at the front during those difficult years that claimed the lives of so many of my childhood friends and regimental comrades," he wrote.

Life for a German in New York, meanwhile, was not as comfortable as it had been. Even before the outbreak of war, the American newspapers had become increasingly critical of the kaiser's militarism and, by extension, of Germans as a whole. As tension grew in the Balkans and the European powers began to rearm, it seemed to Putzi that his countrymen were being blamed for everything that went wrong in the world.

This increasingly hostile mood was typified for Putzi by an incident in 1912 during a memorial concert at the Metropolitan Opera for those who died during the sinking of the the *Titanic*. Putzi had been invited there by Mrs. Fairfield-Osborn, the wife of the director of the Museum of Natural History, but as he went to leave her box at the end of the performance, she turned on him and said the disaster was all Germany's fault, for building faster and faster ships. The only way the *Titanic* had been able to compete, she told him, was by taking the fateful northern route across the Atlantic, which led to disaster.

On another such occasion shortly afterward, a society hostess declared to Putzi: "I could kill all Germans."

"Please, madam, then you had better start with me," he replied.

Despite President Wilson's policy of neutrality, such anti-German outbursts gave way to concerted, open hostility once the war began. German governesses were dismissed, Wagner operas were removed from artistic programs, and the paintings of German masters were taken from the walls of art galleries and confined to cellars. The windows of Galerie Hanfstaengl were often smashed.

Even Putzi's beloved Harvard Club was not immune to anti-German sentiment. In his memoirs, he describes an incident in which Donald Rogers, the red-haired playboy son of a rich Newport family, came to the bar, demanded a "Bullfighters Dream" and, seeing Putzi, added: "The kaiser is a son of a bitch." Putzi was faced with a dilemma: either throw his glass of German beer at Rogers and risk being thrown out of the club or sit there and lose face. He was reaching for his glass when Jimmy, the Irish barman, saved the day. Smiling, he handed Rogers the drink with the words: "You are right, sir, his mother was British."

Matters only got worse after the sinking of the *Lusitania*, a 32,000-ton British ocean liner, by a German submarine, on its way from New York to Liverpool, in the Irish sea near Queenstown on May 7, 1915. Of the 1,959 passengers and crew on board, 1,198 died—among them 128 U.S. citizens. The loss of so many American lives provoked a wave of indignation that nearly persuaded the U.S. government to give up its policy of neutrality. But it was still not quite ready to join in on the Allied side.

According to one account, when news came through of the sinking of the ship, Putzi stood at the bar of the Harvard Club and toasted those responsible, prompting something of a fracas. Until his last days he would deny the incident ever happened, dismissing it as baseless libel. "I have tried to run down the source but have always come up against a stone wall of silence," he wrote almost two decades later. "My classmates at Harvard have done their best to dispel that horrible libel—but to no avail."

Such a reaction was all the more unlikely because Putzi had a number of friends on the ship. He was also still in mourning for his beloved elder brother, Egon, a lieutenant in the reserve of the Bavarian Field Artillery Regiment, who had fallen at Peronne four days earlier. It was a particularly heavy blow. Putzi was suddenly afflicted with a "stabbing, convulsive homesickness" as he thought of those "now doing their duty in Germany or else at forward positions." It was the second personal tragedy of the conflict he had suffered: the previous August, his younger brother, Erwin, died of typhoid fever in Paris, at age twenty-six.

Whatever the truth of the Harvard Club incident, there is little doubt that Putzi was increasingly uncomfortable in the pro-Allied atmosphere of the club, and he spoke out against some of the anti-German sentiments increasingly heard there. He finally resigned his membership in May 1916.

Thanks to his mother's citizenship and his Harvard education, Putzi could have played up his American side and tried to pose as a model citizen of his adoptive homeland, but both his surname and temperament mitigated against it. If anything, the outbreak of war in Europe had made him feel more German and more determined to speak out on behalf of the country of his birth.

His relationship with Barnes was one of the first casualties. Now almost thirty, Putzi felt it was time to settle down and have children. He was equally convinced that the woman he married should be a German. One day in 1916 he announced he was leaving Djuna.

Asked about Putzi toward the end of her life, Barnes tried to make light of their relationship. "I was engaged to Putzi for about twelve hours," she said, before adding, laughingly, "and that was long enough! What would I have done with all those German children?"

The deleted section of *Nightwood*—which may, admittedly, present an embellished version of what really happened—tells a different story. In it Barnes describes how the German of the story came to the heroine one Sunday morning, wearing his top hat, and said simply, "I can't marry you, because you must be German for that now." The two of them then went together to her garret room on Washington Square and cried until it was night. When he left and stood under the trees below, she leaned out of the window. She came close to throwing herself out to her death on the street below, before being dissuaded by a neighbor. Two days later, she could stand it no longer and rushed around to the German's home. "I love you anyway, and you can do as you like," she declared. He was not to be swayed, however, and accused her of trying to trap him into marriage by having his child. After a dramatic and violent quarrel, they parted again—this time for good. His future wife, he insisted, "will be German."

Barnes's nationality may not have been the real reason for the breakup, especially considering that Putzi took up almost immediately afterward with Mimsey Benson, a stunning blonde who was no more German than she was. He was to claim later that the real reason was Barnes's continuing interest in women. Indeed, her next affair appears to have been with a woman: Mary Pyne, a beautiful redheaded journalist who, like her, was writing for *New York Press*. When Barnes arrived in Paris in the early 1920s, she was to tell her friend, the poet Mina Loy, that she had already had nineteen lovers; the women, she told her, were better in bed than the men.

Barnes was not Putzi's only entrée into New York's bohemian society. During the war years he also struck up friendships with two other literary enfants terribles who had turned up in the city: Hanns Heinz Ewers, the German author and epicurean; and Frank Harris, the Irish dramatist and Shakespeare expert, and friend of Oscar Wilde and George Bernard Shaw. Through Harris, Putzi was introduced to Aleister Crowley, the occultist writer, who was also spending the war in the United States. Putzi appears to have been attracted, above all, to their disdain for the hypocrisy of conventional Anglo-Saxon morality and their admiration for German freethinking. It also helped that they were fervently anti-British.

Ewers, who had shocked the literary world back home with his stories of atavism and bloodlust, cut a colorful figure in New York with his monocle and sabre scars. Although he was to marry twice, he appears to have been attracted to men and moved in homosexual circles. He and Putzi met late in 1914, apparently in the gallery, and although Ewers was sixteen years Putzi's senior, the two men were to remain close for many years.

Ewers had been traveling in South America at the outbreak of the war and made his way up to New York. Like Putzi, he was trapped on the wrong side of the Atlantic and could not return home. Unable to serve his nation on the battlefield, he turned his hand to pro-German propaganda, writing for an English-language magazine, *The Fatherland*, "devoted to Fair Play for Germany and Austria." Ewers was more than just a political propagandist: he was also determined to savor for himself everything that New York had to offer. His experiences there during the war served as the basis for his novel, *Vampir*, which appeared in Germany in 1920. The book, which tells of a bizarre illness suffered by a German, Frank Braun, that can be cured only by drinking the blood of a Jewess, shocked many with its depiction of sex and mescal-taking. It was variously described by critics as an amoral "maze of paths through a sexually pathological swamp" and a "divine comedy and satyr play combined." Ewers was described by one critic as a German Marquis de Sade.

Putzi did not reveal the extent to which he, too, participated in libertine activities with Ewers. He admitted, however, in the German version of his own autobiography, that *Vampir* was "a reproduction, in sharply alienated form, of his [Ewers's] and our experiences in New York—a mixture of sex and homesickness for Germany." Tellingly, Putzi was also to try in later life to downplay the extent of his relationship with Ewers, claiming in a German magazine article published in 1951—eight years after the writer's death—that they had met only in 1917. He was obliged to come clean, however, after an angry exchange of letters with Ewers's widow, Josephine. "I know as well as you do about the long-standing friendship that existed between yourself and HHE [Ewers]," she wrote. Putzi's bending of the truth may have been attributable in part to his keenness to disassociate himself from a man who had remained closely identified with the Nazis. It is difficult to avoid the impression, however, that he was also reluctant to reveal the real extent to which they had ventured into the seamier side of New York life together.

THE sinking of the *Lusitania* was not the only cause of growing anti-German feeling in America. Anger was also being fueled by a series of mysterious explosions at factories producing munitions and other much needed supplies for the Allied war effort. The most dramatic was on the night of July 29, 1916. The Black Tom pier in New Jersey, opposite the Statue of Liberty and packed with a thousand tons of munitions, caught fire and exploded. The resulting blast shattered windows in Times Square, rocked the Brooklyn Bridge, and awoke sleepers as far away as Maryland. The munitions on the pier had been destined for Britain, France, and Russia for use in their war against Germany. It did not take authorities long to realize the blast was the work of German saboteurs waging a campaign to prevent supplies from neutral America reaching their country's enemies.

Wilson had won reelection on the slogan "He kept us out of war," but the United States was, in any case, drifting toward joining the conflict. On February 3, 1917, two days after Germany stepped up the activities of its submarines, relations were severed between Washington and Berlin. Then, on March 9, Wilson ordered the arming of American merchant ships to allow them to defend themselves against U-boat attacks. A month later, after the appropriate resolutions were passed by both the Senate and the House of Representatives, the president declared war. Putzi's mother, who unlike her son had managed to cross the Atlantic, was visiting New York at the time. She returned home on May 5 on the "embassy ship."

America's entry into the war had immediate and disastrous consequences for the family business. Putzi operated the gallery under a power of attorney that had been granted him by his mother in March 1912. As such it was treated as a foreign business under the Trading with the Enemy Act and needed a license to continue operating. Although Putzi was at first refused, his lawyers finally managed to get him a temporary license that allowed him to conduct business under the supervision of the Alien Property Custodian.

While Putzi struggled to keep the business going, he was, like other prominent Germans, being closely watched by U.S. authorities. A report for the Department of Justice's Bureau of Investigation in February 1917 expressed misgivings about his potential loyalties. Putzi, it said, was a "German reservist, a very high-class educated gentleman." Its author recalled how before the war Putzi had explained to several fellow members of the Harvard Club, using a map of Europe, how the German army would pass through Belgium, seize Paris, and then dictate Berlin's own terms to Russia. Such a conflict, he assured them, would be over in six weeks—Britain would not have enough time to land an army to do much harm. "In as much as the majority of the members of the Harvard Club are pro-Ally, he resented it and resigned from the Club," the document continued. "He is not a man of criminal instinct, but if war was declared between Germany and America it probably would be best that he be interned because he has the ability of an officer to lead men either here or in Mexico."

Similar concerns were voiced in another letter sent to authorities that May by a member of the Roosevelt clan. "I have known Mr. Hanfstaengl for many years and while I have not seen him since May of last year, I know him to be violently anti-American; to have been in close touch with the German embassy before it left; to be highly intelligent and capable and an almost fanatical supporter of his fatherland," wrote Nicholas Roosevelt. His conclusion was harsh: "In consequence, I consider him a most dangerous man to have about, and in fact believe he would be best off on Ellis Island."

But Putzi had a good lawyer in Elihu Root, a former senator who had been Theodore Roosevelt's secretary of state. And so, in return for a promise not to indulge in anti-American activities, Putzi was allowed to retain his liberty. His business affairs took a dramatic turn for the worse, however, in the closing months of the war. Despite the granting of his temporary license, the Alien Property Custodian took over the gallery's assets and finally sold them at forced auction in July 1919. They fetched just eight thousand two hundred dollars—a fraction of the half a million dollars Putzi considered they were worth.

After the Armistice, Putzi was allowed to set up a small business of his own again at 153 West Fifty-seventh Street, just opposite Carnegie Hall. He named it the Academy Art Shop. But the war had shaken up the old economic order. "People who had got rich quickly had no interest in fine art," Putzi wrote. "People who had interest in such art were penniless."

4

ON December 13, 1919, a young woman walked into the Academy Art Shop. Like Putzi, Helene Elise Adelheid Niemeyer was of mixed German-American origins. She was also tall, blonde, and extremely attractive.

Putzi was delighted to see her again. They had met several weeks earlier at a charity ball in the Waldorf-Astoria Hotel. Helene had been accompanied by Otto Julius Merkel, a friend of Putzi's who was later to become head of Lufthansa, the German airline. The new acquaintances were immediately attracted to each other, but loyalty to Merkel prevented Putzi from making a move. Hence he was delighted, if not a little surprised, when she suddenly appeared in his shop. The reason for her visit, she claimed, was a postcard from Germany that she had just received from their mutual friend Ewers, who had returned home after the war. The writer had asked her to pass on his best wishes to Putzi. It was only the flimsiest of pretexts and they both knew it. Helene had been intrigued by Putzi and was eager to meet him again. The speed with which events unfolded surprised both of them, however. They were engaged that evening; their wedding date was set for two months later.

On the morning of February 11, 1920, Putzi's thirty-third birthday, the couple married on Long Island in a civil ceremony lasting just twelve minutes. Afterward, Putzi went back to the shop and Helene to the office where she was working as a secretary. The newlyweds had dinner that evening at Helene's parents' house in Elmhurst, Queens. There were plenty of tears a few hours later when Putzi left with his bride and they made their way with their suitcases through the heavy snow to the railroad station. They were bound for the Judson Hotel on Washington Square in New York, where they were to begin their married life.

For years, Putzi had been alone, disoriented, and as if "wasted away by the long, solitary, delayed life." Helene had walked into his life at precisely the right moment. "In the psychological moment when I, so to speak, found myself before the abyss, Helene Niemeyer appeared—or rather, Schnappel, as I call her," he wrote to his mother that May. Despite the apparent impetuousness of his actions, he was prepared to declare their union a success: although wary of making prophecies, the intervening three months had shown "the steps I had undertaken to be correct," he said.

Even before the wedding, Putzi had begun to question whether his future lay in America or back in Germany. The gallery provided a steady income, but it was not great and scarcely enough to support both him and Friedrich Denks, who had become his partner in the new venture. Putzi's marriage made the financial question more acute. Relations between the two men were deteriorating, and it seemed sensible that one should go back to Germany. Putzi was certainly keen to see his homeland again, but he was apprehensive about returning and uncertain of what role he could play in the family firm. The main problem was his elder brother, Edgar, who had taken over the business after their father's death and was openly dismissive of Putzi's talents. A letter Edgar sent him a month after his wedding, effectively ruling out a job back in Munich, particularly rankled.

"He apparently seems to think that I am a total idiot who always needs a wet nurse nearby in order to live," Putzi wrote somewhat despairingly to his mother that May. "What kind of activity can he promise me within the Munich firm if he considers me to be so incapable?" The idea of becoming a "parasite" back home in Bavaria was not appealing. Edgar's criticism seemed all the more unfair to Putzi because of the progress he was making with the New York gallery. After a successful, if extremely tiring, few months, it was doing well and had paid back its debts to the parent company in Munich. All in all, Putzi seemed proud of his business and was reluctant to give it up. "The best thing is if I stay with the business here, which is now maintaining me completely, and continue to run it until it is turned into a proper Munich Franz Hanfstaengl subsidiary or another advantageous solution is found," he concluded. It looked as if it would be Denks who would be returning home.

Circumstances soon changed: Helene became pregnant with their first child. Egon was born on February 3 the following year in Lenox Hill

Hospital in Manhattan. Although Egon therefore automatically qualified for U.S. citizenship, Putzi preferred that his son grow up in Germany. Nostalgic for his native land, and despite the roots he had established during his time in America, he still felt a German at heart: as German as his father and as his two brothers who had fallen during the war; so German that he had returned home after Harvard to do his military service. If he had appeared to desert his homeland after the outbreak of the war, he told himself, this was merely because any attempt to return home would have led to a "ninety-nine percent chance" of capture by the British.

Helene felt much the same way. Although she had been brought up in America, it had been in a distinctly German environment. Her father, Johann, a watchmaker, had emigrated in the 1880s from Bremen to America, where he had married Elina Magnus, a seamstress, who was herself a recent immigrant. German rather than English continued to be spoken in their New Jersey home. Helene, too, was keen to return to the land of her parents' birth.

Putzi began negotiations with Denks about how his partner could continue running the store and eventually take it over as his own. Before crossing the Atlantic, Putzi had one more administrative hurdle to overcome, though: as a German, he needed permission from the State Department to leave America. By the summer of 1921 he had finally obtained it, and on July 5, he, Helene, and Egon left Hoboken on board the liner *Amerika* bound for the northern German port of Bremen. Putzi was traveling with documents issued by the Swiss consulate in New York, which was handling German interests in the immediate postwar period.

It had been a decade since he had last set foot on his homeland and he and Helene had high hopes of what they would find there: they expected to be able to "mend the broken fragments of . . . [their] lives, hoping to find in Germany a chance of regaining economic independence." Matters did not prove quite that simple. The crossing gave him plenty of time, however, to ponder the motives and expectations of those Germans who, like him, had decided to return home. "The clock had stopped on the day when their steamer left the shores of the Fatherland," he wrote later. "The last impression taken away having formed a cherished wish-picture—a vision of an idealized, unchanging Germany."

They stayed for a few days in Bremen with Helene's uncle and aunt before taking the train south to Bavaria. The journey was meant to take twelve hours; it lasted an interminable twenty. Germany's train services still had some way to go before they attained their prewar regularity and efficiency. The couple was met at Munich's main railroad station by Putzi's family, which with the loss of his father and two brothers had been reduced to his mother, eldest brother, Edgar, and sister, Erna. They then took a rickety old bus to the Hotel Vierjahreszeiten, where they were to start their new life. As they made their way through the city, Putzi was struck by the shabby, unpainted appearance of the houses and the peeling façade of the Great Court Theatre.

The hotel was one of the finest in Munich, but apparently without food service. The most immediate problem was finding some milk for Egon, who was howling with hunger. Milk was strictly rationed and the only solution was to order copious amounts of coffee, each of them accompanied by a tiny jug of cream. Helene soon learned that staples she had taken for granted in America, such as milk, butter, and eggs, were scarcely available in the misery of postwar Germany. Fortunately, Putzi's mother had in the meantime bought a small farm on the Staffelsee at the foot of the Alps; Egon soon had a reliable source of milk.

The couple rented a small apartment at Gentzstrasse 1, in Schwabing, a part of town north of the university, which Putzi liked to call the Montparnasse of Munich. It belonged to the stepdaughter of the painter Franz von Stuck. It was fairly miserable: just three rooms plus a balcony on which they kept the coal and dried the laundry. Their new home was yet another shock for Helene: the high-ceilinged rooms could be bitterly cold in winter.

Putzi's first challenge was to clarify his own position vis-à-vis the family firm. His fears that Edgar would try to exclude him proved correct. In October 1917, while Putzi was away in America, a new contract had been drawn up under which Edgar represented the interests of his absent brother and Putzi's own status was reduced to that of a sleeping partner. Putzi was livid, especially since no attempt had been made to contact him before the document was signed, and a bitter battle between the two brothers ensued.

A truce, of sorts, was finally declared in April 1923, when the contract was replaced by a new one. Under its terms, Edgar and Putzi were each given RM (reichsmark) 2,100,000 worth of shares, with RM 900,000 worth to Kitty and Erna. Edgar, however, was the only general partner, while the three others had the status of limited partners. If Putzi wanted to enjoy equal status with his brother, he would first have to work for the company for a year and then could only be elevated to the status of general partner by unanimous vote. Putzi never forgave Edgar for the way he was treated; like so many family feuds, things were only to get worse as the years passed.

Putzi was forced to come up with another plan for making a living. Now in his early thirties, he decided to devote himself again to academic studies, despite his less than glittering performance at Harvard. His aim was eventually to get a job teaching at a university. He chose history, concentrating on two very different figures—a reflection of the two different directions in which he as a German American felt himself pulled. His first subject was "mad" King Ludwig II—the eccentric Swan King of Bavaria, best known for building the fairy-tale castle of Neuschwanstein—who drowned in Lake Starnberg, south of Munich, in 1886. The king, who had been an admirer and patron of Richard Wagner, was an attractive subject to Putzi and the born-again student plunged enthusiastically into the task at hand, talking to opera singers and servants who had known him and retracing Ludwig's movements.

The second of Putzi's subjects was Benjamin Thompson, later elevated to Count Rumford, the American patriot and social reformer who reorganized the administration and public life of Bavaria in the 1780s on behalf of the archbishop-elector of Mainz, Karl Theodor. If Ludwig appealed to Putzi's romantic side, then Rumford appeared to offer the model of someone, coming from America, who was able to make a significant contribution to life in Germany—something Putzi, himself, yearned to do. Appointed in 1784, Rumford had set about dealing with the considerable social problems of the era: soup kitchens were set up where the so-called Rumford Soup was distributed; beggars were taken off the streets and put into the army or highly regimented work battalions, where they carried out public works and helped a state-subsidized manufacturing industry grow.

Putzi, seeing parallels between the problems of Count Rumford's time and his own age, set out to write a book about him; Rudolf Kommer, an Austrian writer whom he had met in New York, was so intrigued by the subject that he suggested it might even make a film. The pair worked on a script at a villa in Garmisch-Partenkirchen, but, according to Putzi, ended up with "something that had the dimensions of Tolstoy's *War and Peace*." Not surprisingly, the film was never made. Putzi enjoyed himself, however; through Kommer he met Fritzi Massary, Berlin's famous opera diva, and her eccentric husband, Max Pallenberg. Even if Putzi and Kommer often had differences about their work, they could both agree on Pallenberg's motto—*cogito, ergo bibamus*—I think, therefore let's have a drink.

—

AS Putzi had feared when crossing the Atlantic, the Germany to which he returned was very different from the country he had last seen before the war; he felt a stranger in an even stranger land. Writing a decade later, after the Nazis had seized power, he painted a grim picture. "Germany was a tame bear, sick, bewildered, being led about by scheming tricksters," he wrote; the overwhelming characteristic of his countrymen was apathy, coupled with a lack of self-respect. "Germany was like a horse which ran up against a stone wall, not because it was blind but because it just didn't give a damn."

The enforced resignation of the kaiser in November 1918 and proclamation in August the following year of a new German constitution in Weimar had heralded the birth of a new country. But the Weimar Republic, as it became known, was unloved by its citizenry from the start. It was also hopelessly divided into a bewildering number of political parties: at one end of the spectrum were the Communists, buoyed with confidence after the Bolshevik revolution of 1917 and convinced that Germany was poised to follow suit. At the other were the *völkisch* nationalists. In between the two extremes was a plethora of other parties.

The nation's troubles were further complicated by the rivalry between the federal authorities in Berlin and the state government of Bavaria. This only intensified after the appointment in March 1920 of Gustav Ritter von Kahr, an old fashioned right-wing monarchist, as the Bavarian prime minister. Von Kahr was determined to turn his state into a "cell of order" committed to true nationalist values, even if this put him on a collision course with the Social Democrats who dominated in Berlin. Under von Kahr, Bavaria swiftly became a haven for the *völkisch* groups, who were united by their extreme nationalism, anti-Semitism, and a desire to hark back to a glorious if largely mythical Teutonic past. The various local militias and private armies, which already counted more than three hundred thousand soldiers, were swollen by the influx of right-wingers and nationalists from elsewhere in Germany determined to use Bavaria as a base for their struggle against what they dismissed as the "Jews' Republic." It was against this background that Adolf Hitler, the Austrian-born former house painter recently discharged from service as a volunteer in the Bavarian army, was making his first tentative forays into Munich politics.

Putzi, by temperament and background, was naturally drawn to many of the ideals of the nationalists, not least because he too felt nostalgia for the certainties of the prewar era. He was also conscious that many of the groups were little more than relics of a lost age. After almost a decade living in America, he might have been expected to have sympathy for the democratic parties that sprung up within the Weimar Republic. Yet they seemed to him little more than a "pitiful caricature" of the real thing that he had seen during his time in Boston and New York.

Like many German intellectuals, Putzi was saddened by what was happening to his country, yet he did not believe the groups on either the left or the right had a solution to its problems. Besides, he had never involved himself in politics and did not intend to do so now. With books to write on both King Ludwig and Benjamin Thompson—as well as a new wife and young son—he had more than enough to occupy himself. All that was to change, though, when at Truman Smith's bidding he went for the first time to hear Hitler speak.

CIVILIZING HITLER

5

NOT long after Putzi first saw Hitler in the Kindlkeller, he had a second chance to hear him speak. The impression this time was far less powerful: Hitler's voice seemed to have lost much of its magnetic appeal and strength. It may have been because Putzi was late arriving and, unwilling to make too noisy an entrance, had watched the distant speaker from the door. Even from afar, the text was not to his taste. The French government was threatening to reoccupy the Ruhr and Hitler was calling for resistance using guerrilla warfare if they did so. To Putzi, this was the language of a desperado, not a rational politician: a densely populated country like Germany did not easily lend itself to a military campaign by "irregular bands of francs-tireurs." Such a call to arms was also symptomatic of the alarming views that Hitler expressed whenever he strayed into foreign policy—a product, as Putzi saw it, of his ignorance of the world beyond Germany and Austria.

Yet there was undoubtedly something about Hitler that attracted and intrigued Putzi: "a certain cosmopolitan ingredient, the flair of the Danube—that richer German political horizon which I had encountered when a student in polyglot Vienna." He was eager to meet him again, ideally alone, to find out what was "at the back of this curious man's brain." As for Hitler's views on foreign policy, Putzi was beginning to entertain an idea—later to become almost an obsession—that he could teach him to take a more reasonable and rational approach.

Putzi went to Max Amann's publishing office, which served as a base for the fledgling national socialist movement. Amann, himself, was there; so too were Hermann Esser, a journalist and gifted orator who had previously been a socialist, and Christian Weber, a rough-hewn former horse trader, almost broader than he was tall, with an enormous kaiser mustache. They were amused by this lanky newcomer, with his huge forehead, strongly protruding chin, and eccentric mannerisms. Putzi, who was accustomed to moving in more exalted social circles in Germany, as he had been in America, was not impressed at the sight of them either. When the question of joining the party came up, he asked to be put on a secret membership list. He was worried that an overt avowal of his enthusiasm for the movement would expose him to the mockery of smart Munich society.

Another man present, Kurt Lüdecke, was nevertheless quick to realize the benefits that someone of Putzi's social standing would bring the Nazis. "Hitler's pot-pie needed a bit of upper crust," he recalled later. "We could probably find special work for such a man to do." And so he whipped out a gold pencil and, thrusting a membership form in front of Putzi, tried to persuade him to sign up for the princely sum of one dollar a month—which, with the German currency already beginning to depreciate rapidly as hyper-inflation took hold, was worth about six thousand marks. Putzi felt he was being pushed by Lüdecke and stalled him until Amann came out from his inner office.

It was no coincidence that Lüdecke took the lead in signing up the new recruit. Like Putzi, he was something of an outsider who brought a cosmopolitan flavor to what was initially a largely Bavarian phenomenon. Three years Putzi's junior, he had been born in Berlin but after performing his military service left for London and then France. He claimed to have become a successful gambler—so successful, in fact, that he could live comfortably off the proceeds; in reality, he appears to have been a blackmailer who specialized in having homosexual encounters with wealthy friends and then extorting money from them afterward to buy their silence. The war put a temporary end to his activities and he joined the German army. He was discharged after only two years, however, and by 1921 had settled in Munich, where he devoted himself to various business projects and appeared to have a substantial number of dollars to his name. Like Putzi, he had also joined the movement after hearing Hitler speak.

Putzi took an immediate dislike to this "flashy figure," who he considered a "pathological case of megalomania, or an impostor, a crook or even a spy." Later, when he had ingratiated himself sufficiently with the party, Putzi asked the others about Lüdecke and was reassured that

Amann shared his suspicions. "He tries to give the impression of a grand seigneur with access to money abroad," Amann told him. "We get all sorts in here and he may be useful, but we are keeping an eye on him."

———

SOON after his secret initiation, Putzi had a chance for the more intimate meeting with Hitler that he craved. He and Helene went with a few friends to hear him speak at the Zirkus Krone. After the speech, Putzi approached Hitler and introduced him to his wife. Hitler was immediately taken with this enchanting German American and readily accepted an invitation to visit their home. Hitler was soon dropping by almost daily at the little apartment on the Gentzstrasse for lunch or for coffee—which he would drink with a lump of chocolate dissolved in it. He nicknamed their home Café Gentz and sometimes brought along Hermann Göring, an early member of the movement to whom Putzi took an immediate liking, and Göring's aristocratic Swedish wife, Karin.

Their conversations were wide-ranging: much of the time, inevitably, their talk would turn to the political situation and how best to exploit it. Putzi would share with Hitler his knowledge of the world beyond Germany, and especially America. Putzi claimed later that the chant of *Sieg Heil*—and the accompanying arm movement—that became a feature of Nazi rallies was a direct copy of the technique used by American football cheerleaders, which he had taught Hitler. It was also on Putzi's initiative that the Nazis began to use American-college-style music at political rallies to excite the crowds, heightening the contrast with the dry political lectures offered by most of the other parties.

Putzi would also urge Hitler to read the Lutheran bible, which he felt "contains a perfect arsenal of forceful passages, highly useful in the fight against the atheistic Bolsheviks, and doubly suited for Bavaria, the home of the Oberammergau Passion Plays." Afterward he was to recognize increasing numbers of biblical phrases creeping into Hitler's speeches: Hitler's description of himself as the "drummer" marching ahead of a great movement of liberation, for example, seemed to reflect a tendency to identify himself with John the Baptist. More often than not, though, the conversations in Putzi's apartment would turn to Hitler's wartime experiences and he would describe in detail the battles of the Somme or Aisne, using his skill as a mimic to imitate the different sounds of the British, French, and German small arms, bombs, and artillery.

Putzi was not afraid to speak his mind during such conversations, even on personal matters. He disliked Hitler's little mustache—nicknamed a Rotzbremse, or snot brake, in the Bavarian dialect—and during one visit urged him to let it grow so it extended right across his mouth.

"Look at the portraits by Holbein and Van Dyck; the old masters would never have dreamt of such an ugly fashion," Putzi told him.

"Don't worry about my mustache," Hitler retorted. "If it is not the fashion now, it will be later because I wear it."

Hitler also swiftly established a rapport with young Egon and became his godfather. On one of his first visits, he arrived as the boy was crying after knocking his knee against a chair. Putzi slapped the chair, which had armrests carved in the form of lions' heads, as if to punish it, and Hitler quickly joined in. After that, whenever Hitler came there, he would make a habit of striking the lion and asking Egon if it was behaving itself. The boy took to the man he soon came to know as Uncle Dolf. Years later, Egon recalled how Hitler would go down on his hands and knees and play trains with him, doing convincing impressions of everything from the puffing of steam locomotives to the shriek of signalmen's whistles. "He was an extremely good entertainer," he said. "He had a very marked histrionic talent."

Hitler enjoyed such tastes of family life, since he was without close family of his own. His father, an aggressive and violent man who regularly beat his children, had died when he was fourteen and he lost his mother just before he was twenty—which was, he told Putzi during one of their talks in the first few months after they met, the "greatest loss I ever had." The Hanfstaengls were fast becoming a sort of surrogate family for the future Führer.

As their companionship grew, Putzi and Hitler would go out together, one day that spring taking in a film about the life of Frederick the Great. Hitler especially enjoyed the scene in which the Prussian king ordered his son to be executed for high treason after he absconded to England.

"It is imposing to think that old king would have beheaded his own son to enforce discipline," Hitler told Putzi. "That is how all German youth will have to be brought up someday."

"Not all German mothers will agree to that," Putzi answered, as Hitler made a contemptuous gesture.

That same night, Hitler spoke again at the Zirkus Krone. Inspired by the example of Frederick, as his speech came to a close he shouted: "German youth, victory depends on you! You must be hard. You must accept stern discipline to become supreme." The crowd cheered him in a frenzy, reinforcing the Prussian king's place as his hero.

Putzi returned Hitler's visits by calling on him in his modest apartment on the Thierschstrasse. Often Hitler would be sitting at his desk, working on a speech, dressed in a simple black jersey and thick-soled gray slippers. It could take him as long as six hours to compose one, sketching out a plan on a dozen or so large sheets of paper. Invariably he would work alone. But in the last hour or so before he was due to appear, as he began walking up and down rehearsing in his mind the various phases of his argument, telephone calls would come pouring in from his closest aides describing the moods on the streets and how quickly the hall was filling up.

A couple of years later, Hitler was to write in a letter to Alfred Rosenberg how he had come to know "a man whose fanaticism is divided into love of the movement and hatred for its enemies." Putzi, he said, "had become a friend to me personally." But how is it possible to explain fully the attraction between them?

For Putzi, the chief appeal was undoubtedly his conviction, even at this early stage in Hitler's political career, that this man's "brilliant gifts would take him to the top." With his plain manner of speech and ability to put his finger on the needs of the people, Hitler could have been another Theodore Roosevelt, Putzi thought. If Hitler was going to rise, then Putzi wanted to rise with him. But he also wanted to play a part in shaping the movement. For this reason, he would spend hours hunting through history books looking for the best analogies with past leaders in order to steer Hitler on what he considered a more reasonable path. "At that time my only thought, day in, day out, was: where can I find material, models, suggestions and ideas for Hitler—ideas that would help him widen his emotional appeal," Putzi wrote.

The attraction, for Putzi, was not promoted only by his own ambition. Although alarmed by much of what Hitler said, he saw in some of his policies a clear remedy for his country's ills. There may also have been a more subtle psychological reason for allying himself with Hitler: Putzi found it difficult to shake off the guilt he felt for sitting out the war while in New York, and so could not fail to be impressed by a man of action who had not only served his country but also had been decorated for it. In some respects, perhaps, Hitler may even have reminded Putzi of Egon, his fallen elder brother.

They nevertheless made an odd couple, the former Austrian corporal in his tight blue serge suit and the patrician Bavarian American. Hitler was respectful toward Putzi and, in conversation, always employed a form of address Putzi claimed was "still de rigeur in Germany between people of lower rank when speaking to those of better education, title or academic attainment."

In his memoirs, written after the Second World War, Putzi dismissed suggestions that he "civilized" Hitler or taught him table manners. He nevertheless admits to having been constantly taken aback by his strange tastes, especially his sweet tooth, which manifested itself in his love of Austrian cakes piled high with whipped cream. On one occasion, he watched in horror as Hitler, thinking himself alone, dropped a heaped tablespoon of sugar into the glass of wine Putzi had just poured him—Prince Metternich's best Gewürztraminer.

If Hitler seemed a rough diamond, then the other members of his entourage in the early days were even lesser gems. One of the most powerful figures was Alfred Rosenberg, whom Putzi had met as he was seeing Truman Smith onto his train. The son of a cobbler, he was born in 1893 in the Estonian city of Tallinn, which was then part of the Russian empire. Fancying himself as something of a party theoretician, he had become anti-Semitic and anti-Bolshevik as a result of the Russian revolution, which he experienced firsthand while studying architecture in Moscow. In 1919 he had settled in Munich.

Putzi took an instant dislike to him. Part of it was personal: Putzi was appalled by Rosenberg's liking for garish clothes, claiming he had "the taste of a costermonger's donkey." Rosenberg, he claimed, "had some theory about it being a waste of money to wash shirts and used to throw them away when they became unbearable even by his standards." There was also something dubious about his sex life, "a reflection, perhaps, of the Tatar in him." Although only recently married, there were "innumerable stories about his unsavory love life, which usually involved multiple intercourse with half a dozen men and women companions at a time in some grubby back-street flat."

Putzi was equally appalled by what he saw as the pernicious influence that Rosenberg had on shaping Hitler's unsophisticated view of the world. Indeed, until the arrival on the scene several years later of the even more powerful Joseph Goebbels, the future propaganda chief, Putzi considered Rosenberg "the principal antagonist in my attempts to make Hitler see reason." The main problem, as Putzi saw it, was that Hitler's ideas and military strategy were rooted in the past, in the ideas of Clausewitz and his obsession with the balance of power on the continent of Europe. To Putzi's dismay, Hitler had little appreciation of the importance of the United States and the need to pursue friendship with it. The main lesson of the First World War had been that any future conflict would necessarily be won by whichever side America joined, but if Hitler showed any interest in the United States at all, it was only in its technological achievements rather than its geopolitical significance. The only American figure for whom he had any time at all was Henry Ford, and then only because his reputation as an anti-Semite made Hitler see him as a possible source of funding. Putzi was also dismayed to see that Hitler had a fascination for the Ku Klux Klan, mistakenly seeing it as a powerful political movement with which he could make an alliance.

Although Rosenberg was to remain Putzi's nemesis, the others gathered around Hitler during those early years were hardly any more impressive: Anton Drexler, a blacksmith and the original founder of the party, who had since been reduced to little more than honorary president; Weber, the burly horse dealer who "enjoyed knocking Communists about"; and mysterious Lieutenant Klintzsch, a storm trooper leader who had been involved in the abortive Kapp putsch in Berlin in 1920. One of the few intellectuals, and thus impressive figures, in Putzi's eyes was Dietrich Eckart, a poet and author of the standard German translation of *Peer Gynt*. Thanks to the royalties from his books, Eckart made a substantial contribution to party funds; it was also Eckart who had first taken Hitler under his tutorial wing, but, as Putzi noted, he was beginning to regret it.

If it was difficult to see why Putzi should be drawn to Hitler, it was clear what the former Austrian corporal saw in him. Hitler may have suffered from an acute inferiority complex, but he was also aware of the advantages of gaining access to high society. As Lüdecke put it, "Putzi's comfortable and cultivated house was unquestionably the first of the kind to open its doors to Hitler." Putzi soon became Hitler's "admirer in chief . . . made himself a sort of social secretary to Hitler, zealous in introducing him to hostesses."

Putzi hoped that by bringing Hitler into contact with illustrious figures, some of their learning, culture, and civilized ways would rub off. And so, largely thanks to his introductions, Hitler began to mix with Hugo Bruckmann, a prominent anti-Semitic Munich publisher, and his wife, Elsa, and with the Bechsteins, the piano makers. They, in turn, invited him to their country residence near Berchtesgaden and introduced him to the Wagners at Bayreuth. Hitler was in rapture at his first visit that October to Haus Wahnfried, the shrine of his hero, Richard Wagner.

Wagner's son, Siegfried, thought Hitler a fraud; Winifred, his Welsh-born wife, thought he was "destined to be the savior of Germany."

Hitler's entrance into Munich bourgeois society was uncomfortable: he cut a curious figure in the salons of the rich when he turned up wearing his gangster hat and trench coat and carrying a heavy dog-whip. Putzi was just as amused as his bourgeois hosts by Hitler's reaction when he encountered the trappings of wealth. On one occasion, Putzi and Helene listened with scarcely concealed amusement after Hitler returned from dinner with the Bechsteins at their private suite in a luxury Munich hotel and started enthusing about the hot water in their bathroom. On another night, at the Bruckmanns', Hitler was confronted for the first time with an artichoke.

"But, madam," he said in a quiet voice to his imposing hostess. "You must tell me how to eat this thing. I never saw one before."

Yet far from counting against him, Hitler's shyness and naïveté delighted his society hosts, especially elder women like Frau Bechstein and Frau Bruckmann, who treated him almost as an adoptive son. Bechstein was clearly thinking of pairing Hitler with her daughter, Lotte. Apparently with that in mind, she started working on his wardrobe, persuading him to wear formal evening clothes and shined boots in place of his usual cheap blue suit on social occasions. She even lent the party her jewelry for use as collateral for a loan of 60,000 Swiss francs from a Berlin coffee merchant.

And then there was Putzi's piano playing. Putzi dropped in at Hitler's home around noon one day, and catching sight of a rickety old instrument in the hallway outside Hitler's flat, he sat down and began idly to work his way through a Bach prelude. Hitler listened without appearing to pay much attention, then asked if he knew any Wagner.

Putzi immediately gave him the crashing chords of *Die Meistersinger von Nürnberg*. Hitler swung up and down the room in a state of high excitement, keeping time with his hands. When Putzi finished, Hitler stood transfixed, staring blankly into space. "You must play for me often," he said. "There is nothing like that to get me into tune before I have to face the public."

And with that, Putzi's role was established as Hitler's mood maker. He would play for him almost every time he visited, often for as long as two hours at a stretch. Hitler would literally yell with delight as Putzi played "with Lisztian fioritura and fine romantic verge." His repertoire was broad, encompassing American football marches and college songs as well as the classics. But his greatest success was with Wagner, especially the *Meistersinger* prelude or the "Liebestod" from *Tristan und Isolde*. Putzi played Wagner beautifully, and Hitler, who loved music, placed Wagner among the demigods. "That was it! I must have played from it [*Tristan und Isolde*] hundreds of times, and he couldn't have enough of it," Putzi recalled. "It did him good physically. . . . He chuckled with pleasure." The music brought Hitler the "relaxation" that he sought, and he was hooked—so much so that he soon took to calling Putzi and demanding he come over and play. Putzi felt himself inconvenienced by the "imperious claims" Hitler put on his time, but dutifully set off for the Thierschstrasse regardless.

Keen to reinforce his role as Hitler's court musician, Putzi published a "Hitler song book" in 1924. Despite his better judgment, the lyrics of the songs, which had titles like "Hitler-Lied" ("Hitler Song"), "Deutsche Voran" ("Germans First"), and "Die Hitler-Medizin" ("Hitler Medicine"), were the purist kind of *völkisch* propaganda, warning of a Jewish conspiracy and urging the "resurrection" of the German Reich under the Nazis' swastika symbol. But Putzi knew how to compose a catchy tune and the songs always went down well at party rallies.

Another appealing side of Putzi for Hitler was undoubtedly the two women in his life—his sister, Erna, and his wife, Helene. In spring 1923, the *Münchener Neuste Nachrichten*, the most widely read newspaper in Munich, wrote a story claiming that Hitler was rumored to be getting engaged to Erna. It was complete invention, but Hitler was clearly flattered. When Putzi asked him what he should say to other journalists who tried to follow up on the story, he replied: "I authorize you hereby to tell the press that I shall never engage myself to a woman nor marry a woman. The only true bride for me is and always will be the German people." The parallel with the description in Christian literature of the church as Christ's true bride was all too clear: this, according to Putzi, was confirmation of what was later to become Hitler's "messiah complex."

Hitler, nevertheless, continued to be fascinated by Helene, who possessed the twin virtues in his eyes of being both glamorous and from a good family. Nor did he seem to make any attempt to hide this attraction—much to the annoyance of many in the party. In what was clearly a reference to Helene, Gottfried Feder, an important figure in the movement, wrote a circular complaining that Hitler "put the company of beautiful women above his duty as party leader." Almost two decades later, during the Second World War, Hitler reminisced to aides about a party he had attended at the Bayerische Hof Hotel during those early days: there had been plenty of women there, but then "one entered [who was] so beautiful that next to her everyone disappeared . . . it was Frau Hanfstaengl," he said. Putzi does not appear to have been jealous—he realized it was little more than infatuation on Hitler's part; the attraction was never physical, expressing itself instead in "flowers and hand-kissings and an adoring look in his eyes."

Helene, by contrast, did not initially think much of Hitler; indeed, her first impression of him was of "a slim shy young man with a far-away look in his very blue eyes." As for his appearance, it was "really quite pathetic." Yet her fascination appears to have grown over the years: decades later, she recalled the "expressive, vibrant quality" of Hitler's voice; its "immense power," she said, had also appealed to her husband, who was profoundly moved by its "unique sound effects." She appears to have had no illusions about any kind of sexual relationship, however. When Putzi discussed rumors with her that Hitler was having an affair with Jenny Haugg, the sister of his driver, Helene was dismissive. "Putzi," she replied. "I tell you he is a neuter."

———

AS significant for the future of the Nazi movement as Putzi's relationship with Hitler was his financial contribution; his most important funding regarded *Völkischer Beobachter*, the party's modest four-page weekly newspaper. Hitler knew he had to improve the paper if he was going to build on the name he was making for himself as a speaker, but he lacked the money to do so. By a stroke of fortune, Putzi had just received fifteen hundred dollars, one of the installments for giving up his share in the Academy Art Shop in New York to Friedrich Denks. One thousand of those dollars, converted into rapidly depreciating marks, would be enough to buy two American rotary presses that could be used to turn the *Beobachter* into a full-size daily, like the newspapers Putzi was familiar with from the United States. He had originally earmarked the money to put toward buying a house in Munich, but in March 1923 agreed to give it to the party as an interest-free loan, to be repaid in full two months later. Helene, who wanted desperately to get out of their cramped apartment, was opposed, warning her husband that he might never see his money again. Such was Putzi's enthusiasm for the movement that he could not be dissuaded, and Helene let him have his way.

Putzi eagerly helped shape the newspaper, hiring a cartoonist from *Simplicissimus*, a left-wing satirical magazine, to design the masthead.

He also devised its slogan: *Arbeit und Brot*, work and bread. Underlying his involvement was the hope that the extra space available would help transform the *Beobachter* from a shrill pamphlet to a more balanced newspaper, but he was to be disappointed.

The first large-format edition was published on August 29, 1923—giving Hitler's movement an important propaganda boost. As *The Times* of London put it: "At a time when many newspapers in Germany have been forced to cease publication, and others, owing to the enormous cost of production, are only able to continue with difficulty, Herr Hitler's paper, the *Völkischer Beobachter*, has been doubled in size, and with one exception is the largest daily paper published in Bavaria."

Dietrich Eckart, who was in increasingly poor health, was forced to step down as editor. To Putzi's horror, Alfred Rosenberg was appointed in his place, dashing his hopes that the newspaper would pursue a more moderate and reasoned editorial line. The financial aspects of Putzi's involvement were no more satisfying: when the debt fell due for repayment in May 1923, Max Amann said he could not afford to repay it and demanded an extension to the following January. But it soon became clear that what Putzi had intended as a loan was seen by the party as a gift; when he insisted on getting his money back, he was rudely rebuffed. It was all the more annoying because Putzi and his wife had in the meantime found the ideal house. Located at Pienzenauerstrasse 52, in the affluent Herzogpark district on the outskirts of Munich, it was being sold by Duchess Ruth Vallombrosa, who had formerly been married to Walter Goldbeck, an American artist from St. Louis who had built the house with American dollars during the great inflation. In the end, Putzi sold on the debt to Weber at a twenty-five percent discount and they bought the house. They named it Villa Tiefland.

Their new home was a great improvement on the apartment on the Gentzstrasse. Putzi at last had the feeling that he was living somewhere appropriate to his status. Large and with a beautiful garden, it was filled with fine old furniture, great paintings and drawings, and thousands of books. A sliding door with big glass panes separated the dining room from the breakfast room, which was modeled after the rooms of the Bavarian peasants of the High Alps—although without the wood paneling. The door itself had been painted by Goldbeck with figures of the Madonna and with saints and angels.

Most of the treasures in the house were in the library, a huge room that had been Goldbeck's studio. Here was the family's most prized antique: a squat cupboard known as an *Ulmer Schrank*, made of oak and walnut, inlaid with other fine woods, dating back to Martin Luther's time. Beside it, on a table, stood a delicate Chinese cabinet brought back from Canton by Putzi's father, Edgar, in 1865; beside that was a faded photograph of him surrounded by a dozen Chinese workers, which had been taken during the seven years he spent there working for an English tea company. There was also an enormous Steinway grand piano and on it a terra-cotta bust of Benjamin Franklin by Jean-Antoine Houdon, the French sculptor. The room was dominated by the bookshelves: there was a whole shelf for music literature, a complete collection of Punch cartoons, large numbers of historic works, and an entire section about Putzi's favorite king, Ludwig II. The Hanfstaengls' background in art publishing meant there were also a large number of etchings, woodcuts, and other pictures. The room was rounded off by a French Empire clock on the mantelpiece above the open fireplace.

Egon later recalled how the curious mixture of bits from China, Italy, America, France, and England had been thrown together to form a harmonious whole. "The fact that balance reigned, that everything lived and breathed, that you were never pained by the lack of something here, or the super-abundance of something there—that was almost entirely due to Father," he wrote. "He had fashioned this little world, and he saw to it that it kept moving; as aesthetic needs changed, so did the house. . . . It was never quite the same for long."

———

THE troubles Putzi faced in having his debt repaid may have dented his enthusiasm for the movement but did not kill it completely. Gradually, he became accepted into Hitler's official inner circle. Soon he was attending the Monday evening *Stammtisch* at the Café Neumaier, a coffeehouse by Munich's Viktualienmarkt on the corner of Petersplatz, where Hitler would hold court for his closest supporters. The patrician Putzi stood out among the predominantly middle-aged couples who would listen as Hitler tried out his ideas on them while they ate their frugal suppers.

The movement, meanwhile, was permanently in need of money—and runaway inflation ensured that they quickly spent their way through anything they were given. Hitler was forever on the lookout for wealthy benefactors and often would take Putzi along for fund-raising. As he recalled, "Hitler seemed to think that I would give an air of respectability to his begging expeditions and we went on several trips around Munich and its environs visiting prominent citizens."

One of the most eventful of such trips was in April 1923, when they set off for Berlin in Hitler's old Selve with his driver, Emil Maurice, at the wheel. As they rounded a corner in Delitzsch, in northwestern Saxony, a Communist stronghold, they ran into a roadblock manned by armed members of the Communist police—sworn enemies of Hitler and his party. According to Putzi, it was only his own swift action that saved the day: climbing out, he produced the Swiss passport he had used to travel back from the United States.

"Hanfstaengl. . . . So, *Deutsch Amerikaner*," the policeman said as he examined the document.

"*Ja*, my friend," Putzi replied, and, affecting his most atrocious German American accent, he introduced himself as a paper manufacturer from Milwaukee on the way to the Leipzig trade fair.

"And this," Putzi added, jerking his thumb at Hitler, "is my man, Johann. I hired him and the chauffeur in Hamburg."

Putzi held his breath as the policeman glanced at Hitler. But although his description had been widely circulated, the policeman did not immediately recognize him. To bring matters to a conclusion, Putzi offered the policeman a cigar and he waved them on. Hitler was grateful to his friend and mentioned the incident several years later; Putzi nevertheless believed he never forgave him for calling him "my man."

The Berlin visit itself was not very productive—but it was rich in comic value. Putzi was worried about being spotted in Hitler's company and was reluctant to spend the night in the same place as him. So while Hitler, Maurice, and Fritz Lauböck, an eighteen-year-old supporter who joined them, stayed at accommodations arranged by a local admirer, Putzi set off for the night to an evangelical hospice behind the state theater in Unter den Linden, one of Berlin's main avenues.

Hitler was just as secretive as Putzi, and when they set off on their calls the next day, it was inside a closed van. Putzi, with his tall frame curled up like a grasshopper in the back, never really knew why Hitler wanted him there—but assumed it was probably just to keep his spirits up. The canvassing went badly, which left them plenty of spare time, part of which they spent at the National Gallery. Putzi was appalled both by Hitler's ignorance of art and by his insistence on judging artworks through an ideological prism. Another insight into Hitler's character came the same afternoon, when Putzi suggested killing a couple, of hours with a visit to a funfair. Hitler was fascinated by the groups of scantily clad women boxers who were putting on a show, and he insisted on staying right until the end.

One evening, Hitler took Putzi along to dinner at the Bechsteins, who also had a large house in Berlin. Inevitably they talked about politics and the National Socialist Party and its future, but whenever the question of money came up, their hosts tried to change the subject. Seeing the huge diamonds on Frau Bechstein's fingers, Putzi temporarily forgot his manners and suggested that she could keep the party going for months if she were to raise money on them. It was only later that he found out she had done precisely that with other jewelry. In the meantime, though, all she gave them was an expensive grayish-yellow fedora, for Hitler to replace the broad-brimmed black gangster hat he had been wearing.

Putzi's growing influence on Hitler was not going unnoticed. "In 1923, it was an open secret that Hitler listened to no one more readily than to E. Hanfstaengl, Hitler's in-house foreign minister at that time," the *Münchener Post* claimed in an article in 1930, in which it gave him credit for "developing American methods in propaganda and the press." It was Putzi, the newspaper said, who "gave the impetus for ten mass meetings in a day" and came up with the idea of mass leafleting.

Yet certain members of the party were hostile toward Putzi's closeness to Hitler; some considered his patrician ways inappropriate in a party that was pitching for working-class support; others felt his enthusiasm for all things American sat uncomfortably with the Nazis' fierce nationalism.

Count von Treuberg, an early aristocratic supporter, took particular exception to Putzi's foreign mannerisms and flamboyant behavior, urging Hitler to break with him completely. "To put it briefly, Hanfstaengl is . . . a complete *Hanswurst* [a clown]," he wrote to Hitler that July. "How shall one otherwise describe a man who, born German, is absolutely incapable of conducting a conversation—even a serious one—without spoiling his words with English fragments in American slang?" The count was also annoyed by how Putzi was the only one to turn up at political meetings wearing a tuxedo, "in complete lack of regard for good German simplicity." Even worse, when there was music, he would mount the stage like an impresario or a "crazy cabaret comic" and lead the singing. Friedrich Plümer, another early party member, was unhappy, too, with the way Putzi used his influence "to Americanize the entire operation completely unnecessarily"—even down to the format of the *Beobachter*. Hitler did not pay any attention to such rumblings, however. Putzi was still extremely useful to him.

6

NOVEMBER 8, 1923, was destined to go down as one of the most significant days in Nazi history, but Putzi did not let the prospect of the dramatic events ahead spoil his appetite. He had arranged to have lunch with Larry Rue, an American journalist who wrote for the *Chicago Tribune*. The first course had barely arrived when Rue began to rib Putzi about Hitler's boast that he would soon stage a coup d'état with the help of the Sturmabteilung (SA). Established in 1921, and otherwise known as the Brownshirts, the SA was a squad of some eight hundred youths, who, as Rue mockingly noted, "wore brown shirts, marched in military formation and were armed with broomsticks."

"That's right," Putzi replied (about Hitler's boast) as they tucked into a meal of caviar, pheasant, raspberries and cream, brandy, and coffee, for which Rue—or more likely his newspaper—was picking up the tab.

"When?" Rue asked him.

"That's a secret," Putzi replied. "But you are wise to stick around. You won't be disappointed."

Rue said he was going that evening to the Bürgerbräu Keller, a beer hall on the outskirts of Munich, to hear a speech by Gustav Ritter von Kahr, the Bavarian leader. He invited Putzi to accompany him.

"I can't go with you, but I may be there" was his cryptic reply.

Putzi had been given an inkling of what was to come a few hours earlier when he visited Rosenberg's little whitewashed office to discuss the next edition of the *Beobachter*. These were turbulent times; the economic situation in the country had deteriorated even further in the two years since Putzi had returned from America. Germany was bankrupt and in the grip of hyperinflation: by September 1923 the cost of a loaf of bread had passed one million marks; a month later it reached fifty-eight million. The German currency, noted *The Times* of London, had "outstripped the rouble in the race to worthlessness," wiping out a lifetime of one's savings in a few hours. The middle classes were especially badly hit. *The Observer* (London) told of the increasing number of suicides and the "unprecedented number of women taken to lunatic asylums, either raving or desperate or sunk in apathy, covering sheets of paper with endless noughts."

Revolution was in the air. Mass discontent led to strikes and radicalization of politics that benefited both the extreme left and extreme right. The previous month, communists in Hamburg staged an uprising but were crushed. In the west, there were calls for the proclamation of a Rhineland republic. Other risings elsewhere were also suppressed. Munich, too, had been bubbling for weeks with rumors of plots and counterplots. *The Times* warned on September 11 that an armed attempt by Bavaria to secede could not be ruled out. It noted three possible leaders of such a revolt: Dr. von Kahr, Dr. Heinrich Held, leader of the Catholic Bavarian People's Party (BVP), and Herr Adolf Hitler. Von Kahr, it suggested, was the most likely.

Von Kahr, who had briefly headed the right-wing government in Bavaria in 1920, did not need to stoop to such action. On September 26, he was named state commissioner with dictatorial powers. An ardent monarchist and close friend of Rupprecht, the former Bavarian crown prince, von Kahr was a divisive figure. He was hated not just by the Communists but also by the Socialists and the Republican Democrats. He soon added Hitler to their ranks: one of his first acts the next day was to ban all Nazi Party meetings, including fourteen gatherings scheduled for that evening. Hitler did not attempt to challenge the ban but was furious at von Kahr's actions and under pressure from his storm troopers to act. "My organization and I shall continue along our way," Hitler declared a few days later in one of his first interviews with a foreign newspaper. "Dr. von Kahr knows where to find us."

As Putzi and Alfred Rosenberg sat talking that morning in the office of the *Beobachter*, Hitler burst in, his trench coat tightly belted and his riding whip in his hand. From his air of urgency, it was clear that he had decided it was time to seize the initiative.

"Swear you will not mention this to a living soul," he told them. "The hour has come. Tonight we act. You, Comrade Rosenberg, and you,

Herr Hanfstaengl, will be part of my immediate escort. Rendezvous outside the Bürgerbräu Keller at seven o'clock. Bring your pistols."

Although several others had also been told, Anton Drexler, the party's founder and still its honorary chairman, had been left in the dark. It was a measure of Putzi's closeness to Hitler that he was one of those who had been let in on the secret—and proof of the extent to which he had fallen under the Nazi leader's spell that he was ready to go along with such a harebrained and dangerous scheme.

Putzi's first thought was for Helene, who had just become pregnant for a second time, and for Egon, now two and a half. Without giving his wife any more details, he told her to pack their things and go that afternoon to a house the family owned in Uffing, south of Munich, one and a half hours away by train. Besides Rue, he also encouraged H. R. Knickerbocker, another prominent American journalist, to come to the meeting at the Bürgerbräu Keller, but did not say why.

Putzi arrived as instructed at the beer hall at 7 PM, only to find the building surrounded by police. They refused to admit either him or the small group of foreign journalists trailing in his wake. And there they stood for at least half an hour or so, until a red Mercedes-Benz drew up, disgorging Hitler, Amann, Rosenberg, and Ulrich Graf, Hitler's bodyguard. A few words from Hitler and they all swept into the hall.

The beer hall was packed with nearly three thousand people. Von Kahr, a short fat man, was well into his speech, which was timed to coincide with the fifth anniversary of the November revolution of 1918, which drove the kaiser from power—or, as von Kahr put it, "the night on which the Red International conquered Germany." It was, according to one contemporary account, "a very long, emotional apotheosis of the middle-class virtues and a manifesto against the spirit of international socialism." Hitler and a few associates stood by a pillar about twenty-five yards from the platform and tried to make themselves inconspicuous. Bored by von Kahr's words, Putzi went to the serving door and bought three liter jugs of beer. Both he and Hitler took deep drinks.

Then, at around 9 PM, there was a sudden commotion at the entrance: Göring burst in at the head of twenty-five heavily armed Brownshirts. The meeting descended into chaos. As people clambered onto their seats to get a better view, Hitler emerged from beside the pillar and pushed his way toward the stage, accompanied by two armed bodyguards. Chairs were overturned and beer glasses went flying. Trying and failing to make himself heard above the din, Hitler took his pistol and fired a single shot into the ceiling.

"The national revolution has begun," he cried out to the stunned audience. "The hall is surrounded by six hundred armed men. No one may leave the premises. Unless quiet is restored immediately, I have a machine gun placed in the gallery. The Bavarian government and the national government have been overthrown, and a provisional national government is being formed. The barracks of the Reichswehr and the state police have been occupied; the Reichswehr and the state police are already appearing under the swastika flag."

With that, Hitler ordered von Kahr, Otto von Lossow, and Hans Ritter von Seisser to accompany him into the next room. Hitler had everything worked out: in the new revolutionary government that he was to form, he would be chancellor, von Kahr the head of Bavaria, Lossow the Reichswehr minister, and Seisser the minister of police. The three men were taken aback by Hitler's proposal and reluctant to go along with him. Von Kahr was especially cool. When Hitler threatened to kill them all—and then commit suicide—if they refused, von Kahr replied calmly, "Herr Hitler, you can have me shot; you can shoot me yourself. But whether or not I die is of no consequence to me."

But Hitler would not give up that easily. While the captive members of his putative future government waited in a side room, he went back into the hall and made an impassioned appeal to the crowd to back him in his bold attempt to find "a solution to the German question."

"Tomorrow morning will either find Germany with a German nationalist government—or us dead," he proclaimed. The crowd was swayed by the power of his oratory. It also undoubtedly helped that he gave the strong impression that von Kahr and the others had agreed to back him.

The unhappy trio had in the meantime been joined by Ludendorff, the World War I hero. He had not been in on the plot, but a car had been sent for him and he duly appeared at the Bürgerbräu Keller, resplendent in his Imperial army uniform. He was cheered noisily as he entered but his features were rigidly set; his head never turned on his bull-like neck. Hitler had put him down to be in charge of the national army. Ludendorff was offended at not having been offered a more important role but went along with Hitler anyway, immediately launching into an impromptu speech in which he urged the others to follow suit. When Hitler assured them that the crowd was behind them, even von Kahr, reluctantly, had to give in.

In the main hall, Putzi, meanwhile, had climbed on a chair and was holding an impromptu press conference for Rue, Knickerbocker, and the handful of other foreign journalists who had come. As they gathered around him, he announced that a new government had been formed that would restore order and discipline in Germany.

Among the reporters was Rue, who undoubtedly appreciated the irony of being taken prisoner by the same youths he had mocked when he had seen them drilling with their broomsticks a few days earlier. This time, though, they had machine guns. Rue was close to deadline, so Putzi managed to find a telephone at the back of the hall for him to call his story in to his colleague, John Clayton, who was waiting in the Berlin office of the *Chicago Tribune*. In his story, which was billed by his newspaper as the "first eye-witness account of the Hitler-Ludendorff *opera-bouffe* revolt in Bavaria," Rue described the hysterical shouts and confusion of the meeting. Hitler, he wrote, "looked ready to shoot any man opposing him."

After about half an hour Hitler and his still-reluctant coconspirators returned to the hall. Putzi was amused to see that he had taken off his trench coat to reveal a black tailcoat and waistcoat. Hitler could not have looked less like a professional revolutionary: he instead reminded Putzi of "a collector of taxes in his Sunday best." Hitler was determined not to waste any more time and so made only a short announcement that a new national government had been formed. The five then swore a solemn oath and led the crowd in the most impressive rendition of "Deutschland über Alles" that Putzi had ever heard.

The meeting broke up at about 10:30 PM and both the plotters and their hostages went their separate ways. "Better times are coming," Hitler told Ernst Röhm, the Brownshirt leader, as he embraced him. "We shall all work day and night on the great task of rescuing Germany from shame and suffering." He then issued a proclamation to the German people and two decrees establishing a special tribunal to try political crimes.

The revolution had begun—but it was already starting to fall apart. Hitler had made the mistake of letting von Kahr and the others leave unattended. It was, as Putzi pointed out, an error that proved Hitler was an amateur when it came to plotting revolution. Even the most cursory reading of the history books suggested that if you are trying to over-throw a government you should control the movements of those you have ousted. Putzi had suggested commandeering a hotel and keeping them there overnight to keep an eye on them, but Hitler did not think it necessary.

Once von Kahr was out of Hitler's clutches, he issued a proclamation rescinding the statement he had made in the Bürgerbräu Keller on the grounds that it had been extracted from him at gunpoint. After an acrimonious meeting with his officers, Lossow followed suit. Neither told Hitler of their change of mind, but when midnight came and he had still not heard from either of them, he realized something was going wrong. Calls to the Bavarian government office, where the Nazis wrongly thought von Kahr had sought refuge, revealed nothing. Hitler's supporters, meanwhile, were busy settling old scores: an armored car and machine gun detachment were dispatched to the offices of the *Münchener Post*, the socialist newspaper, where they smashed windows, overturned tables and chairs, and stole all the typewriters. Gangs roamed the streets and invaded the more expensive restaurants in search of Jews or profiteers. Hitler, who spent the night in the beer hall, was becoming increasingly despondent and was on the verge of giving up, but Julius Streicher, one of the most rabid and anti-Semitic of his followers, persuaded him to stand firm. It was decided to order a demonstration the following morning. Putzi was sent out to gauge the mood on the streets, but quickly became bored and quietly returned home to bed.

The following morning a correspondent from *The Times* of London drove through the streets of Munich with one of Hitler's staff in a requisitioned car and found the streets filled with his men, posting proclamations. The bridges were all heavily guarded and the town appeared to be at the mercy of his forces. Some of the posters announced the formation of military tribunals to deal with looting and other crimes. Those found guilty faced summary execution.

The atmosphere back in the beer hall reminded the reporter of the early days of the First World War: uniforms, rations, and equipment were being issued; small squads were drilling in the various courtyards; and rows of trucks, packed with troops, munitions, and supplies, moved off from time to time. Everywhere the utmost enthusiasm and optimism prevailed. Hitler, himself, was closeted in a small, barely furnished room upstairs with Ludendorff and half a dozen officers. A little man in an old waterproof coat, with a revolver at his hip, the would-be ruler of Bavaria was unshaven, his hair disordered, and he was so hoarse he could hardly speak.

Ludendorff, anxious and preoccupied, had had enough of waiting. "We shall march," he declared, and toward noon, several thousand men lined up behind the Nazi standard-bearers. Both he and Hitler joined them. They set off through Munich. The balance of power had already shifted dramatically against them, however; after their brief moment of weakness the evening before, von Kahr and Lossow were back in control. Almost simultaneously, Reichswehr reinforcements arrived from various outlying depots while a strong detachment with an armored car and machine guns took up a position in the Odeonsplatz.

Hitler's supporters, many of them oblivious to what was happening, marched past the National Opera House and into the narrow streets leading to the square, where they received the command to halt. They obeyed, but then a shot rang out—it is not clear from where. It was followed by an exchange of fire that lasted just a minute. Max Erwin von Scheubner-Richter, an engineer and early convert to the cause, dropped to the ground, fatally wounded. As he fell, he pulled Hitler down with him, pulling his shoulder out of joint.

By the end, another thirteen marchers and three policemen lay dead or dying. Many others, including Göring, were wounded. Ludendorff, who according to one eyewitness had thrown himself flat on the paving stones, stood waiting to be arrested by the commanding officer. Drexler, Wilhelm Brückner, and several others followed suit. Röhm, who with his men had seized army headquarters during the night, capitulated after a firefight.

Hitler took advantage of the confusion to flee the chaos and make his way out of Munich. But his shoulder was injured and the pain was becoming intolerable; his car was also running out of gas. Unsure where to seek refuge, he suddenly remembered that Putzi had a country house in Uffing and made for it.

That evening, Helene, who had arrived in Uffing the previous day with Egon and the maid, was surprised by a knocking at the door. Outside stood Hitler, Dr. Walter Schultze, a doctor from one of the SA battalions, and two or three others.

Hitler was suffering badly from his shoulder injury. Helene, oblivious to the dramatic events of the previous twenty-four hours, let him in and gave him a little room in the attic where her husband kept his books. The doctor thought the shoulder was merely dislocated and tried in vain to reset it, prompting a yelp of pain from Hitler. More thorough medical examinations were later to reveal that he was suffering from a broken collarbone. Hitler was almost incoherent, but Helene finally managed to piece together his story. He assured her that a car would come and pick him up in a few hours.

Putzi himself was not with him. He had arrived back at the Bürgerbräu Keller at eight that morning to find a band of several hundred SA men still hanging around; most had not eaten since the evening before, and despite the bitter cold and occasional snow flurries many were wearing only thin shirts. Putzi spent the morning shuttling between the beer hall and the center of Munich, so he could report back to Hitler what was going on in the city. He also tried to brief the foreign journalists who were camped out at the *Beobachter* offices, hungry for information. While he was in the Briennerstrasse, which leads off from the Odeonsplatz, near where the battle had taken place, he saw a crowd streaming toward him. With some exaggeration, they told him what had happened. As Putzi hurried back to his apartment, he saw Hermann Esser, Max Amann, Dietrich Eckart, and Heinrich Hoffmann, Hitler's friend and official photographer, driving past in an open car. They all went to Hoffman's nearby home to discuss what to do next. It was decided that they should all flee over the Austrian border and regroup there.

Putzi had a problem. In yet a further sign of how badly the putsch had been organized, he did not even have a passport. Fortunately, Admiral von Hintze, one of the coconspirators, had a couple of spares and was ready to help out. By that evening, Putzi had reached Rosenheim, on the German side of the border. He crossed the frontier and the following evening arrived in the Austrian town of Kufstein, where he found a small group of pro-Nazi railwaymen. The family of one of them had a flower shop. While Hitler was sleeping in Putzi's attic room in Uffing, Putzi spent his first night in exile on a tiled floor underneath a bank of chrysanthemums.

7

IT was pouring rain on the evening of November 11, 1923. Soaked through and in a bad mood, police Sgt. Georg Schmiedel ended his evening rounds in Uffing. All was quiet at 9 PM when he went back to his small house in the village and sat down to drink the tea his wife had prepared for him. Suddenly there was a ferocious ringing at the door. His immediate superior, Kommissar Mehringer, was waiting on the doorstep.

"Schmiedel," Mehringer demanded, "do you know an Adolf Hitler? Could he be here?"

Schmiedel, forty-six, six feet tall, with a short military haircut and a mustache, paused for a moment before replying slowly.

"He was often here, at the Hanfstaengls', Herr Kommissar," he replied. "We could try there. But why do you ask?" Wearily, he picked up the gun and saber he had just put down for the night. Mehringer told him to hurry.

"Didn't you hear anything about the putsch in Munich?" he asked. Schmiedel shook his head; he had heard Hitler speak a couple of times and had seen him going in and out of the Hanfstaengls', but the putsch was news to him.

As they stepped back out into the torrential rainfall, Schmiedel felt he had walked onto the set of a film. There were two trucks outside, each with thirty Munich police in them. Another two officers were sitting in a private car. Schmiedel and Mehringer got in. They drove first to a farmhouse belonging to Putzi's mother. They spent an hour or so searching through the hay in the barn with bayonets, and even picked up a man they found lurking there; but when they shone the flashlight on him they discovered he was just the farm manager. So they went back to Putzi's own house in the village. While the thirty men surrounded the building, Schmiedel, the two officers, and the kommissar rang the doorbell. The maid answered and Schmiedel asked if he could speak to Hitler.

As Helene walked toward Hitler's room, she saw him coming toward her with a gun in his hand. They met in the living room. He was feverish and still in considerable pain and looked ready to turn the gun on himself.

"It's the end," he cried. "Let myself be arrested by these swine, never! I would be better off dead."

The formidable Helene was having none of it: she calmly walked up to Hitler and took the gun away. He did not resist or even say a word.

"What do you think you are doing?" she demanded. "You have gotten all these people interested in your ideas about saving the country and now you are just going to take your life and leave them behind. They are rooting for you to carry on."

Then, as the police waited outside, she produced a notebook. "Now, look," she continued. "You've got all your workers depending on you. They have to know what to do. You are going to be incarcerated for a while, there is no doubt about that. Tell me what you want each one of them to do and I will write it down."

Hitler calmed down and began to dictate. He ran through the names of his small band of supporters one by one, telling Helene which tasks he wanted assigned to each. When he finished, she hid the notebook in a drawer and promised to take it to his lawyer in Munich.

Whether Hitler would actually have pulled the trigger is not clear. Asked about the incident several years later, he denied Helene had saved him from suicide but added: "Naturally my spirits were very low—the mere presence of a woman may have kept me from the thought of ending my life."

Whatever the truth of Hitler's mind-set then, Helene sent the maid a few minutes later to open the door.

"Herr Hitler is here and asks that you don't make a scene," she told the kommissar. "He is completely at your disposal." With that, the four policemen went in. Hitler was standing in the living room on the ground floor, his injured arm still in a sling. He was dressed in a pair of Putzi's pajamas and a blue terry-cloth bathrobe.

Schmiedel walked to Hitler's right side. One of the officers went to his left and told him he was under arrest. For a moment Hitler went pale, and then he said, "*Bitte, meine Herren*," and walked to the door. He climbed into the car and was taken to Munich.

In a report two days later, *The New York Times* noted the curious fact that Hitler, "leader of the Fascisti in Bavaria," had been arrested in the villa of a former New York art dealer. Putzi, the newspaper reported, was "credited in Berlin as being one of Hitler's financial backers." Francis Rogers, secretary of the Harvard Club, described in the piece how Putzi had openly denounced the Allies and resigned his membership in March 1916 in protest over anti-German feeling there. Friedrich Denks claimed not to have heard from him during the previous year.

Putzi himself was still in Austria. But he slipped back across the border to visit Hitler in Munich, while he awaited trial, in the cells under the court on the Blutenburgstrasse. To Hitler's delight, Putzi even brought along three-year-old Egon. The boy later recalled a bright, well-furnished, almost cheery room; the bars on the windows were the only thing that suggested a jail. He claimed to have been struck by the deep, sonorous quality of Hitler's voice. Another pleasant memory was the offer of cookies that Hitler produced from a tin box in his wardrobe. A prison psychologist who visited Hitler soon after he began his detention found him deeply depressed. Putzi, in contrast, did not detect any sign of the earlier despair that may have driven him close to suicide. In fact, Hitler seemed to be looking forward with relish to the chance of embarrassing the Bavarian authorities in court by revealing the extent of their links with the radical right.

"What on earth can they do to me?" Hitler demanded. "All I have to do is to tell some of the things I know about von Lossow and the whole thing will collapse. Those in the know are well aware of this."

The trial of Hitler and the other putsch leaders began on February 26, 1924, and continued for just over a month. Hitler turned the proceedings into a political rally, speaking on one occasion for as long as four hours, and interrogating the prosecution witnesses at great length. He was helped in this by the court's president, Judge Georg Neithardt, who made no secret of his sympathy for the Nazi plotters. Ludendorff was acquitted. The others were all found guilty, although Hitler was given just five years in prison, with the prospect of parole after six months. It was an extraordinarily light sentence considering that the putschists had been plotting to overthrow the state and had killed four policemen in the process. The court also waived a provision in the law under which Hitler should have been deported to his native Austria. He was sent to serve his time in the jail in Landsberg, thirty-five miles west of Munich.

Hitler's imprisonment was subsequently depicted by the Nazis as a form of martyrdom. In reality his stay there was almost completely devoid of hardship. "Landsberg," noted *The Times* of London, "is by no means an unpleasant place of confinement. The prisoners are mostly political offenders and are allowed a considerable amount of personal liberty, books to read, special food and opportunities for exercise and sport, practically the only restriction being that they may not leave the grounds of the fortress." Numerous sympathizers among the prison staff ensured that Hitler had an even more comfortable time than most.

He was allocated cell number 7, a large and well-furnished room hitherto occupied by Count Arco-Valley, a right-wing nobleman who in February 1919 murdered Kurt Eisner, a former theater critic who led a short-lived left-wing government in Bavaria. The cell afforded an impressive view of the Bavarian countryside. Hitler the prisoner enjoyed many other privileges: when he ate in the large common room, he did so at the head of a special table with his followers, under a swastika banner. Fellow inmates were ordered to clean and tidy his room. He was also excused both work and prison athletics, while the rules on visiting hours were bent to allow people to come see him for up to six hours a day.

One of the most valuable of those privileges was the right to receive food parcels. They poured in from across the country, including from wealthy admirers such as Frau Bruckmann and from the Wagners, who had restarted the Bayreuth Festival in 1924, where they held a collection for the "political prisoners" of Landsberg. The quantity of food was far more than Hitler could consume himself and he made a point of spreading it liberally among the guards and fellow prisoners, which further enhanced his standing. Putzi was impressed during one of his visits by the piles of flowers and fruit and bottles of wine, which made the place look more like a delicatessen than a jail. It put him in mind of a "fantastically well equipped expedition to the South Pole." He was also struck by the way the jailers would announce their arrival with a cheery cry of "Heil Hitler."

On one such visit, Putzi took with him a copy of the April 1 edition of the liberal satirical magazine *Simplicissimus*, which had a fantastical picture of Hitler riding on horseback through the Brandenburg Gate, accompanied by banner-waving supporters. It was, of course, intended as a biting April Fools' Day satire of the failed putsch. For Putzi, though, it was instead a vision of what one day could become reality. The caricature became a "secret inner impulse for all of us to bring about what then, in April 1924, seemed impossible."

That July, Hitler started work on the first volume of *Mein Kampf.* Entitled *Die Abrechnung (The Reckoning),* it set out his poisonous creed. He completed it in just three and a half months. Many of those who have plowed their way through the book have sneered at its style, which has been variously described as turgid, repetitive, and meandering. Its first edition was also full of grammatical and stylistic errors—a reflection of Hitler's poor education. It nevertheless displayed his demagogic style to great effect in the way it managed to appeal to the various dissatisfied elements in Germany; there was something there for the anti-Semites, ultranationalists, anti-Marxists, and all the other groups that made up Hitler's potential supporters. It also contained a political philosophy that, in retrospect, proved an all-too-accurate description of what he would do if he came to power—from the identification of Aryans as the "genius" race and condemnation of the Jew as "the parasite" to the declaration of the need for the Germans to seek *Lebensraum* in the east at the expense of both the Slavs and the hated Bolsheviks.

That summer, Putzi received a request from the secretary of his Harvard class asking for a note to put in the annual class book. "I still have a faith in Hitler and the future of his platform," Putzi wrote. "I believe that he and his platform will save Germany." He could not fail to be impressed by his own powers of prophecy when he went back to Harvard for his twenty-fifth reunion almost a decade later, at a time when Hitler was nearing the height of his powers, and saw again what he had written.

Hitler's time in what he called his "university at state expense" was drawing rapidly to a close. A report made up at the request of the state prosecutor by the prison warden in September 1924 praised him as a man of order and discipline, making parole almost a certainty. And so, despite a somewhat half-hearted attempt by the Munich police commissioner's office to have him deported, Hitler was released on December 20. Only a small group of friends was waiting with a car at the prison gate to meet him. One of his first actions was to contact Putzi, who invited him to spend Heilige Abend—Christmas Eve—at his new house, which Hitler had not yet seen. The evening of Christmas Eve is the high point of the German celebration, and Putzi's asking Hitler to share it with him and his family illustrated the closeness of their relationship.

———

THE snow was falling and little Egon was delighted at the prospect of a white Christmas. He was also excited at the thought of seeing his uncle Dolf again. Hitler arrived at Putzi's house at five o'clock and, after kicking the snow from his boots, went to the room where the others were waiting. When he saw Egon he walked immediately toward him, picked him up, and congratulated him on how big he had grown. Catching sight of the armchair with the lions' heads carved into the armrests, he laughed to Egon about how naughty it had been in the past. The boy had, of course, forgotten their joke and Hitler reminded him of the scene in the Gentzstrasse apartment when he punished the chair after Egon knocked his knee against its leg. He also showed the boy how to march up and down with his toy sword.

Later, as Hitler, Helene, Egon, the cook, and the maid listened, Putzi sat down at the Steinway to play *"Stille Nacht! Heilige Nacht!"* Although the others sang along, Hitler did not join in. Putzi then followed with a number of other pieces, including some of his own patriotic marches, one of which was in honor of Albert Leo Schlageter, a German executed for sabotage by the French forces of occupation in the Ruhr.

Despite the festive atmosphere that evening, Hitler's mood was somber and he looked tired and gaunt. Conditions in Landsberg may not have been hard, but his imprisonment had left him confused and disoriented. To Putzi, he seemed genuinely at a loss as to what to do next.

"What now, Hanfstaengl?" Hitler asked him.

"You will go on. Your party still lives," Putzi replied. At that point, he handed Hitler as a talisman an autograph of Frederick the Great, whom he knew to be one of his great heroes.

"He once sat beside a broken drum. He was once in the depths of despair after his defeat on the field of battle," Putzi told Hitler. "But today Germans worship his memory and glory in his achievements."

Then Hitler asked Putzi to play the piano for him. He wanted to hear the last part of the third act of *Tristan und Isolde*. Putzi obliged. He played, he recalled later, "as I never played before." Hitler thanked him and bade them all good night.

THE Nazi party had withered during Hitler's time in jail. Rosenberg had been put in charge, but he was not a charismatic leader and it began to degenerate into rival factions. Hitler did not seem worried; indeed, he was probably pleased by the confusion. The worse the party's state while he was away, the more his case to lead it on his release would be strengthened. When the second Reichstag elections of the year were held on December 7, 1924, the entire *völkisch* movement together picked up just three percent of the votes—a far worse result than the previous poll that May. The various radical-right parties—and the Nazi among them—seemed be in terminal decline. Indeed, this was one of the reasons that the authorities had been prepared to release Hitler.

The debacle of the putsch was not solely to blame. The situation in the country had become far less conducive to Hitler's inflammatory propaganda. The hyperinflation that had ruined many in the middle class in 1923 had been eliminated, thanks in part to a currency reform. Unemployment, the cause of more misery, was receding. American capital was beginning to flow in. The Dawes Plan of 1924 provided a framework for the repayment of the massive reparations imposed on Germany as "punishment" for the First World War; the French also indicated a willingness to evacuate the Ruhr, which they had occupied in January 1923 ostensibly because Germany was behind on its coal deliveries. A much-needed air of normality and stability was returning to Germany. The Weimar Republic, widely despised at birth, was finally acquiring a degree of respectability.

Putzi remained in contact with Hitler in the months following his release, continuing to receive him in his new home. On one occasion, Hitler turned up with a handful of galley proofs from *Mein Kampf*, which he wanted help correcting. Putzi obliged but was appalled by what he read, although as much by the stylistic errors as by its political premises. Whatever the book's shortcomings, Putzi was nevertheless convinced it would be a commercial success and tried to persuade his brother, Edgar, that the family publishing company should buy the rights. Edgar, a convinced Social Democrat and highly conservative in business, demurred. Although the firm had published several political works, Edgar considered Hitler a dangerous charlatan and, like many other Germans, wanted nothing to do with him.

Hitler, meanwhile, continued to have a crush on Helene—as he demonstrated one evening when he found her sitting alone on a sofa in the giant artist's studio in Villa Tiefland. Putzi had left the room to call a taxi, and taking advantage of his absence, Hitler suddenly sank to his knees and thrust his head into Helene's lap, proclaiming himself her slave.

"If only I had someone like you to look after me," he declared.

Helene scolded him, asking him why he did not simply look for a wife.

"I can never marry because my life is dedicated to my country," Hitler replied.

Convinced it was all little more than a show, Helene told him to pull himself together. "Look, this won't do, Herr Hitler," she told him sternly. Suitably chastened, he got up and was back on his feet before Putzi came back into the room.

After Hitler had left, an embarrassed Helene described to Putzi what had happened. "Don't take it too seriously," he told her; it was not the first time Hitler had behaved like that with a woman.

Reflecting on the incident more than four decades later, Helene doubted Hitler had been making a serious pass at her. His attitude, it seemed to her, had been almost childlike. Either that, or the whole thing had been play-acting. Yet there was little doubt that Hitler was smitten by the statuesque blonde, who at five feet nine inches was an inch or so taller than he was. "As far as he was able to be in love with anyone, I suppose I was one of the ones perhaps he was in love with," Helene admitted. It was not reciprocated: many women were mesmerised by his penetrating blue eyes or attracted by his characteristically Austrian gallantry, but he was not Helene's type.

Undaunted by such embarrassing displays, Helene and Putzi continued their futile attempts at "civilizing" Hitler. Determined to widen his horizons, Putzi tried in vain to persuade him to travel—to America, ideally, or just around Europe. One evening, he also urged him to learn English so he could better understand the United States or Britain.

"Quite unnecessary," Hitler retorted tartly. "I know the British, Americans, French, and Russians. I saw them all as prisoners. I understand them perfectly." And with that he launched into a bloodcurdling monologue about how the future of the world would be decided on the battlefields of France. Putzi rather regretted having started the conversation.

Even more bizarre was an attempt Putzi and Helene made to encourage Hitler to take lessons in dancing and social deportment. Although the Charleston was all the rage, Putzi thought the waltz would have a much-needed calming effect on his character. Needless to say, Hitler rejected the idea out of hand as unworthy of a budding statesman. Putzi argued in vain that Napoleon, George Washington, and Frederick the Great had not been averse to a quick whirl around the ballroom.

"No, I won't do it," Hitler retorted. "It is a stupid waste of time and these Viennese waltzes are too effeminate for a man to dance. This craze is by no means the least factor in the decline of their empire. This is what I hate about Vienna."

Putzi was beginning to distance himself from Hitler, though, and it was because of more than just his reluctance to take to the dance floor. To his dismay, Hitler was reverting to his old ways and surrounding himself with his former cronies. Rosenberg, previously sacked for incompetence from his job as editor of the *Beobachter*, was reinstated when the newspaper started appearing again as a daily on April 1.

Putzi also began to resent the pernicious influence of Rudolf Hess, who had become very close to Hitler during their time together in Landsberg. Hess, notably, was one of the few to address Hitler with the familiar "*du*" form. It was during this period of enforced isolation and sexual privation that the affinity between the two men turned into what, in Putzi's mind, "might have possibly bordered on the sexual." This impression was to be strengthened a decade later when Putzi learned that Hess's nickname among homosexual members of the party was Fräulein Anna and that he was notorious for attending balls dressed in women's clothes. Putzi was also struck by how upset Hitler had been to leave Hess behind when he was released just before Christmas 1924. "If only I could get him out of Landsberg," he used to tell Putzi, referring to him by the affectionate diminutive "Hesserl." "I can't forget the way his eyes filled with tears when I left the fortress. The poor fellow."

After he was finally released in 1926, Hess began to build up a cult of personality around Hitler, whom he increasingly referred to as *der Chef* or *der Führer*—which was apparently inspired by the *Il Duce* used by Mussolini's supporters. Putzi noted later that it was also at about this time that the "Heil Hitler" greeting began to be used among his small band of supporters. Putzi refused to go along with what he saw as nonsense.

In the years that followed, Hitler was trying both to rebuild the party, which in 1925 was still smaller than it had been at the time of the putsch, and to assert his leadership of the entire *völkisch* movement. He became an increasingly aloof figure, however, spending more and more time in the mountains above Berchtesgaden near the Austrian border, where he rented and then bought a house, Haus Wachenfeld, which was later to be become massively extended and turned into the complex known as the Berghof. It was a difficult period for the Nazis. The economy continued to improve, cutting away at the discontent on which the party fed. Both industrial production and real wages passed prewar levels; the first signs of a modern consumer society emerged, with ownership of radios, telephones, and automobiles growing. Music, art, and architecture flourished. Hitler also continued to be subject to a speaking ban imposed in Bavaria, Prussia, and other German states.

In the 1925 presidential election, prompted by the death of Friedrich Ebert, the Weimar Republic's first head of state, Hitler threw his weight behind Ludendorff. He polled just 1.1 percent. Field Marshal Hindenburg, another war hero, eventually won the runoff. It was not the blow that it might have seemed, however. Ludendorff's humiliation effectively finished him off as a rival to Hitler for the leadership of the *völkisch* movement. Hindenburg, although initially suspicious of Hitler, was eventually to have no alternative but to accept him.

The far right, nevertheless, continued to enjoy only marginal support—as was demonstrated to dramatic effect by the Reichstag elections of May 20, 1928, which were entered into by no fewer than thirty-two parties. The main winners were the two leftist parties, the Social Democrats and the Communists. Hitler's Nationalsozialistische Deutsche Arbeiterpartei (NSDAP), campaigning for the first time under its own name, polled just 2.6 percent, giving them just twelve seats out of 491. Hitler—who had renounced his Austrian citizenship but had not yet been allowed to become a German—was not among those elected. Despite the fighting talk of Goebbels and the others elected to parliament, the movement seemed little more than an irrelevance.

Meanwhile, Putzi was drifting away from not just Hitler but from politics altogether. Despite his brother's hostility, he was still involved with the family business. In 1928, in a demonstration of his skills as a negotiator, he obtained permission from the French government to reproduce all the pictures in the Louvre and the Musée du Luxembourg. His heart lay with writing and the academic world, however. Every morning, he would set off from home through Munich's English Garden on his way to the library on the Ludwigstrasse on a huge old British-made Swift bicycle, acquired by his father during the Boer War. The bike's giant frame allowed him to ride it without knocking his chin on his knees. He nevertheless cut an eccentric figure as he pedaled through town. Years later, when he had moved to Berlin, he would continue to use the bicycle—at a time when other leading Nazis were driving around in their large flashy Mercedes-Benzes. Putzi prided himself on never owning a car; he preferred to spend his money on pianos, books, and sailing boats.

Music also remained a dominating passion: a full four hours a day were devoted to piano practice, probably more than at any other time in his life. Starting soberly with Bach, to get properly warmed up, he would move on to tackle some of the more difficult études and preludes by Chopin, his favorite. He had eclectic taste: Gabriel Fauré, Richard

Strauss, and Rossini were often mixed in with a Harvard football song or the "Londonderry Air." Putzi was also a frequent concertgoer, often taking Egon along with him.

In February 1928, Putzi obtained a doctorate from Munich University with his thesis on Bavaria and the Austrian Netherlands in the eighteenth century. He was now entitled to be addressed as Herr Doktor, no small matter in title-conscious Germany. He also decided to turn the work into a book. It was published in September 1930 by Sudost-Verlag Adolf Dresler in Munich with the title *Amerika und Europa von Marlborough bis Mirabeau (America and Europe from Marlborough to Mirabeau)*. Running to 491 pages, including dozens of pages of detailed footnotes, it was a serious academic work. Putzi sent a proof to Oswald Spengler, the historian, whom he had met recently in Munich. Spengler wrote back full of praise, describing it as "the first example of original historical thought in two decades." Putzi was delighted: it seemed possible he might really be able to make his name as a historian.

There was tragedy, too: his academic achievements were overshadowed by the continuing sickness of his second child, Hertha, who was born in 1924. She suffered from Hirschsprung's disease, a chronic colon disorder, and soon entered a long and pitiful decline. It was in July 1929, when Putzi was returning home from a business trip to Paris, that he learned she had died. Although five years old, she weighed just twenty-one pounds. It was only superstition, but Putzi could not help but regret that he had not followed the family tradition begun by his grandparents and given her a name beginning with *E*. He composed a funeral anthem in her memory.

Putzi continued to see Hitler, who continued to visit Villa Tiefland occasionally, although far less often than before. Other visitors included Hermann Esser, whom Putzi would help with his speeches, and Göring, who struck up a particular rapport with Egon and sometimes stayed at the house. Göring's wife, Karin, also became fast friends with Helene.

Joseph Goebbels, who was rising up the Nazi ranks, began to drop in too. One evening that November, he and Göring went back to Putzi's house after the three of them had gone together to see a comedy at the theater. While Göring lay snoring on the sofa, Goebbels and Putzi sat by the fireplace talking about politics. Goebbels found Putzi clever and witty but was taken aback by the way he criticized both Hitler and Rosenberg. "But apart from that, a well-read man with whom it is worth being acquainted," he recorded in his diary.

Sometimes Putzi's vast library would be used to host meetings of the senior party leadership; besides Hitler himself, Hess, Goebbels, Röhm, and occasionally Heinrich Himmler would be present. They would sit in the splendid surroundings, arguing for hours on end about election strategy. Egon, who was allowed to watch from a chair in the corner, was struck by how supposedly sacrosanct principles like anti-Semitism and anti-Communism were discussed coolly with a view to their political effectiveness rather than their ideological sanctity. Indeed, the whole discussion seemed to be inspired by a rivalry between those present to impress Hitler, who would listen to all the arguments before announcing his decision on a particular matter. Putzi was one of the few who would openly disagree with Hitler—often provoking him to loud bursts of fury.

On occasion, Hitler would stay on in the house after the others had left, giving Putzi the opportunity to speak on his favorite subject—the dangers posed by Rosenberg. Putzi would try to tell Hitler how little the Balt understood Russia and how his misguided policies would necessarily plunge the country into war. Hitler listened to what he had to say, but never acted on it.

—

THE Nazis' fortunes were transformed by events on Wall Street. The share price collapse of October 24, 1929—Black Friday—and the depression that followed in its wake had a disastrous impact on Germany. The foreign loans—many of them short term—that had helped the country's economic recovery since the mid-1920s were swiftly withdrawn; exports fell and world market prices for agricultural products dropped sharply. German stock prices followed their American counterparts downward and companies began to lay off workers. Unemployment began to rise and by September 1930 had reached three million.

The crisis in Germany was more than purely economic. Unlike in the United States or Britain, it swiftly took on a political character that threatened the very existence of the Weimar Republic, the legitimacy of which many still refused to recognize. The grand coalition under Chancellor Hermann Müller, a Social Democrat, was already under strain. In March 1930 it fell apart in a relatively minor dispute over plans to increase employers' contributions to unemployment insurance. Müller was replaced by Heinrich Brüning, of the Zentrum Party, who spurned compromise in favor of dissolving the Reichstag. New elections were set for

September. The Nazis could scarcely have hoped for a more propitious set of circumstances.

Despite Hitler's aloofness, the party organization had continued to grow throughout the mid-1920s, drawing support from those who failed to benefit from Weimar's Golden Years. Although they enjoyed only limited success in wooing workers away from the Communists and Social Democrats, the Nazis began increasingly to target small shopkeepers and farmworkers. The number of hard-core activists was also growing sharply. By October 1928, despite the party's disastrous performance at the polls, its membership had reached 100,000—double the amount there were on the eve of the putsch five years earlier. In early 1927, first Saxony and then Bavaria lifted the speaking ban on Hitler; Prussia, the largest state, finally followed suit in fall 1928. The party was also forging a young and dynamic image for itself: Baldur von Schirach, who was to take over leadership of the Hitler Youth in 1931, built up membership among students and other young people. Far more cohesive than before, the party was a burgeoning cult of personality centered on Hitler, who was now, more than ever before, its undisputed leader. Some of its smaller rivals on the right had either faded away or been absorbed into its ranks.

In 1929 the Nazis enjoyed a substantial boost from an alliance with Alfred Hugenberg, a wealthy industrialist and newspaper baron. The catalyst was the coming together of different groups on the radical right in opposition to the Young Plan, a series of arrangements to deal with the reparations issue, drawn up by a committee headed by an American banker, Owen D. Young. Although the plan would have meant an improvement for Germany over the existing terms, opposition to it became an article of faith on the nationalist right, and Hugenberg and his allies launched a campaign to force a popular plebiscite against it. In the process, Hitler was able to make use of Hugenberg's newspapers to reach a nationwide audience, targeting the lower middle classes and the newly unemployed with his promise to make Germany great again. The Hugenberg connection also opened the door for Putzi to collect from other industrialists keen to fund his party as a bulwark against communism. Many naïvely thought they were manipulating Hitler for their own purposes.

The campaign against the Young Plan ended in a humiliating defeat: the plebiscite, held on December 22, won just fourteen percent of the vote. Hitler broke with Hugenberg and his conservative allies, blaming them for the defeat. The campaign nevertheless had the desired effect; for Hitler any publicity was good publicity.

This new money pouring in to the party helped to bring electoral success in various local and state elections during 1929, with the Nazis regularly winning four or five percent; although small, this was almost double the party's tally in the May 1928 general election. In October, even before Black Friday was to swell the ranks of the disaffected, the Nazis won seven percent in state elections in Baden; in Lübeck city elections two weeks later, they passed eight percent. Then in December in Thuringia, they won 11.3 percent and Wilhelm Frick was appointed interior minister, becoming the first Nazi to serve in a provincial government.

The general election of 1930 was to be the first real test for Goebbels, recently appointed as Reich propaganda chief. The two to three thousand graduates of the Nazi party's schools were dispatched throughout the country to agitate. In the last two days of the campaign, the Nazis held two dozen demonstrations in Berlin alone. Their energy and enthusiasm was in dramatic contrast to the established parties', many of which seemed merely to go through the motions of electioneering. Hitler began his own campaign with a mass meeting in Weimar before setting off around the country. The Nazis had nothing much in the way of a program and were unable to offer any concrete solution to the depression. But Hitler knew who was to blame for Germany's woes: the Marxists, the Jews, the Allies, and the corrupt and incompetent politicians of the Weimar Republic. He also had a talent for presenting his arguments in the form of powerful political slogans. In a letter to a supporter on February 2 that year, he predicted "with almost clairvoyant certainty" that his movement would be victorious "at the most in two and a half to three years."

8

THE results of the election of September 14, 1930, proved a political sensation. The Nazis won 6.5 million votes and 107 (of 577) seats in the Reichstag; two years earlier they had polled just 800,000 and won a mere 12 mandates. Putzi was staggered; he had expected the party to end up with forty seats at most. He was also annoyed with himself for missing a golden opportunity. During the preceding months, he had drifted away from Hitler and his inner circle as he devoted more time to his academic work. In the run-up to the election, Göring had urged him to come back into the fold and had held out the prospect of a prominent place on the Nazi Party list, which would have ensured Putzi a seat in the Reichstag. Putzi had not listened, however, and now it was too late.

A day or so later, the telephone rang at his home on the Pienzenauerstrasse. It was Rudolf Hess.

"Herr Hanfstaengl, the Führer is very anxious to talk to you," Hess said. "When would it be convenient for us to call on you?"

Putzi was surprised, but he was also struck by Hess's polite and courteous tone. *What do I have to lose?* he asked himself.

"Yes, certainly, come along whenever you like," he replied.

Half an hour later, the pair of them appeared in Putzi's library. Hitler did most of the talking, while Hess provided silent support. Putzi immediately launched into congratulations for their triumph, but Hitler cut him short.

"Now we're on our way!" he exclaimed, striding up and down the room. "Hanfstaengl, I want you to take over the foreign press department. You know England and America. Watch what they say about us. Also, make sure that they hear what we're doing; perhaps they'll wake up to the importance of what we are trying to accomplish."

Putzi was flattered that Hitler still looked to him as the only member of his entourage with the experience, sophistication, and language skills needed to look after his image in the world's eyes. But he was not without his misgivings. His archenemy, Rosenberg, had been swept into the Reichstag on Hitler's coattails, which could only help him to spread his misguided and dangerous ideas. Hitler proved persuasive, though, and tried to assuage Putzi's concerns by promising that Rosenberg and the *Beobachter* would have far less influence once the Nazis came to power. Putzi eventually agreed, but made it clear that he was taking the job only on a trial basis and without pay and would continue to pursue his other interests.

Hitler was profuse in his thanks. "Hanfstaengl, you will be part of my closest entourage," he told him.

Putzi could not help but recall the definition Theodore Roosevelt had given him all those years before, of politics being the choice of the lesser evil. It was partly as a result of this advice that he had originally chosen to support Hitler. As he had then, he now hoped to use his proximity to Hitler to influence him and his policies. But Hitler, as Putzi was to find, was not someone to be steered toward regular, systematic work.

A reminder of the challenge facing Putzi came the day after the victory, when Nazi mobs smashed windows on Unter den Linden, one of the main streets in Berlin.

"This will not do," he told Hitler. "The world now expects you to take charge of this empire. We are the second biggest party in the Reichstag and now we have window-breaking parties. All that looks very bad in the world press." To Putzi's dismay, though, Hitler just shook his head and denied it ever happened.

The practical arrangements for Putzi's work were vague and chaotic. No mention was made of where he would have his office or who would work with him. Matters improved in January 1931 when the party opened its new headquarters in the Palais Barlow on the Brienner Strasse in Munich. The building, which had been owned by a wealthy British-German widow, was turned into a showcase of pseudoclassical pomposity and decorated with Nazi flags, brown eagles, and other such heraldry. It was renamed the Braun Haus (the Brown House). Putzi was given a small room on the third floor. Next door was Heinrich Himmler, who had been entrusted with setting up a special bodyguard to protect Hitler, which was later to become the SS.

Putzi took to his job with gusto, and quickly turned it to his personal advantage. His role as Hitler's gatekeeper put him in a powerful—and potentially lucrative—position vis-à-vis the growing number of people who were eager to ingratiate themselves with the Nazi leader. But it was deeply frustrating too. Hitler thought nothing of working twenty or more hours a day for weeks on end, but was chaotic and ill-disciplined and a notoriously bad timekeeper. After staying up late into the night, he would often not turn up at the Braun Haus until 11 AM or midday, regularly breaking appointments with journalists that Putzi had set up for him. Lunch was meant to be at one o'clock, but Hitler was invariably one and a half or two hours late, driving his fat, witty chef, Artur Kannenberg, to despair. If Putzi really needed to see Hitler, he would often have to chase him across Munich, tracking him down at the Café Heck, where he used to hold court at a *Stammtisch* of his regulars every day at 4 PM.

Putzi's personal relationship with Hitler recovered some of its previous closeness as a result of the death of the Nazi leader's beloved niece, Geli Raubal, which drove him to seek out the company of his old friends again. Geli, a tall, attractive blonde in her early twenties, had gone with her mother, Angela—Hitler's half sister—to live with Hitler in a luxurious nine-room apartment on Munich's Prinzregentenplatz. Hitler had been able to move there in 1929 thanks to money poured into the party by Hugenberg and his fellow industrialists. The object of a lengthy infatuation of Hitler's, Geli began appearing with him in public wearing expensive gowns and furs—prompting angry comments from the party rank and file, who had been told the ideal Nazi woman should dress plainly. It was clear to Putzi that the pair had some kind of relationship, but it seemed a one-sided affair. While Hitler had a "moon-calf look in his eyes," Geli demonstrated no affection toward him. When Putzi and Helene had dinner with them once, he glimpsed the girl's unease as Hitler emphasized a point by cracking the dog whip he invariably carried with him.

Helene, who had previously gone to the same singing teacher as Geli, noticed the same unease on the occasions the two women walked together across the English Garden. Geli told her she felt oppressed and complained that Hitler prevented her from living the life she wanted. "I always had the feeling he [Hitler] was trying to run her life and tyrannizing her," Helene recalled. "She did not have the people around her whom she would have liked."

On the evening of September 18, 1931, while Hitler was away from Munich, Geli locked herself in her bedroom and shot herself in the chest with his revolver. Her body was found the next morning. Although it was clear that she had suffered an emotional crisis of some sort, the reason for her suicide was not clear. It was only some six years later that Putzi was to learn an intriguing possible explanation from Bridget Hitler, an Irishwoman who had married Hitler's half brother, Alois. She claimed Geli had killed herself after becoming pregnant by a young Jewish art teacher she had met in the Austrian town of Linz.

The Nazis tried to hush up the affair, but Putzi was convinced the death of the one woman whom Hitler really loved had a dramatic effect on his character. "The relationship, whatever form it took in their intimacy, had provided him for the first and only time in his life with a release to his nervous energy, which only too soon was to find its final expression in ruthlessness and savagery," he claimed. Hitler's later relationship with Eva Braun was to prove a poor substitute. With Geli's death, "the way was clear for Hitler's final development into a demon," Putzi believed. It also had the effect of reviving Hitler's infatuation with Helene.

Putzi, meanwhile, was spending more and more time at the Braun Haus, and at the end of 1931 he began to carry out his duties there on a full-time paid basis. The explanation lay in the parlous state of his finances. He had the upkeep of a large house and all the other trappings of bourgeois life to finance, but the depression had sharply reduced his income from the family firm. He would have preferred to work there full-time as a director, but when he proposed it to Edgar, his brother dismissed the suggestion out of hand. "As far as I am concerned, you and your family can go and jump in the lake," he said during one especially acrimonious meeting that left Putzi bewildered and outraged.

The next day, Putzi sought out Hitler in a Munich hotel and persuaded him that he needed a full-time foreign press chief. It was, Putzi told his son, far from pleasant to have to ask for such a favor: "If Ettl [nickname for Edgar] had made it possible for me to work in the firm, I would never have had the idea of offering my services to the party in this way."

It was at about this time, too, that Putzi finally joined the Nazi Party. Although it was almost a decade since he had first met Hitler and begun providing money and advice, he had so far refrained from formally becoming a member. On November 1, he rectified the omission and was granted membership number 668 027. Also joining at that time was Hanns Heinz Ewers, Putzi's epicurean writer friend from his New York days, with whom he had remained in contact after his return to Germany.

Like Putzi, Ewers had been drawn to the movement after hearing Hitler speak. It was not immediately clear whether he would be allowed to join, though; the scandalous nature of his books led more conservative-minded Nazis to question whether he was the kind of person with whom the movement should be associated. Putzi put in a good word for him with Hitler, however. The writer's case was further helped by his plans to write a book about Horst Wessel, a young SA agitator who had been turned into a Nazi martyr after he was killed in January of the previous year. Hitler presided over the ceremony at which Putzi and Ewers were admitted; Rudolph Hess and Ernst Röhm were also in attendance.

At this time, Hitler, too, was pondering an important symbolic step. Despite his political success, he was still an Austrian citizen and so disqualified from holding office in Germany. One way around this, it was suggested, was for him to be made a professor of politics at Brunswick Technical University, which would have carried with it citizenship. Putzi found this deeply amusing. Hitler had always despised education, having dropped out of school so early himself, and was so scathing of what he called "the professor type" that Putzi could not help teasing him.

"Well, now you are about to become a professor after all," he joked.

It was all too much for Hitler to stomach. There was a danger, too, that his appointment could prompt a protest by students. In the end he chose instead to obtain his citizenship in February 1932 by being made an Oberregierungsrat—a member of the local government—in Brunswick.

———

INTEREST in Hitler's political rise was growing dramatically abroad. The question most foreigners wanted answered was simple: did Hitler mean war? Some days Putzi was receiving more than a hundred telephone calls from journalists who wanted him to interpret and explain the Nazi leader's speeches. Other times, if Hitler was not too tired, Putzi would arrange interviews, especially with the Americans and the Britons.

The American correspondents who covered Germany were an impressive group, and they set themselves the task of educating their isolationist homeland about the outside world. Articulate and intelligent, most spoke good German, knew the country well, and had sources at least as good as those of the diplomats with whom they mixed. Many had been in Berlin for several years and so were in a strong position to describe the Nazi takeover, and with it the personalities and events that were to push Europe and the world inexorably toward war. The 1930s, wrote John Gunther, who reported for the *Chicago Daily News* from a number of European countries, "were the bubbling, blazing days of American foreign correspondence in Europe. . . . Most of us traveled steadily, met constantly, exchanged information, caroused, took in each other's washing and, even when most fiercely competitive, were devoted friends."

Despite—or perhaps because of—his eccentric manner, Putzi made a good impression on the English-speaking correspondents. At times, his fluent English and experience of American life made him seem almost one of them. They, in turn, liked him not just because he was an affable companion but also because he gave them advance information about the Nazis' plans. Edgar Mowrer, a Berlin correspondent for the *Chicago Daily News*, was not alone in finding Putzi an enigma—and wondering what he was doing with the Nazis at all. "Big, dark, blessed with a cultured New England mother, subjected to American society at an early age, he should have been Nazi-proof," he wrote. He was not. Although apparently setting little store by Nazi ideology, Putzi nevertheless "did a good job in playing down the repulsive aspects of Nazism for visiting correspondents."

Putzi's media contacts were indeed impressive. Especially useful was a friendship with William Randolph Hearst, the newspaper baron. Hearst, the model for Orson Welles's *Citizen Kane*, had known Putzi's mother and done business with his father. Hearst had established a practice of encouraging foreign leaders to write for his publications. Their pieces were mostly published on Sundays in the "March of Events" section of his many newspapers. Mussolini—and Margherita Sarfatti, his mistress and ghostwriter—signed an exclusive deal in April 1930 to provide twelve articles at fifteen hundred dollars each. Argentina's President, General José Félix Uriburu, and Emilio Portes Gil, the Mexican leader, also wrote for him.

The dramatic surge in support of the Nazis in the 1930 election convinced Hearst that Hitler was the coming man, and so he signed him up too. Hitler's first article appeared on September 28, two weeks after the poll. Previewed in Hearst's newspapers throughout the preceding week, it was entitled: "Adolf Hitler's Own Story: He Tells What Is the Matter with Germany and How He Proposes to Remedy It." Alongside it was a photograph of Hitler in a full-length leather jacket. Putzi had arranged everything and was gratified when Hitler gave him thirty percent of his fee. Hitler continued to write for Hearst over the following few months, but he proved an unreliable contributor. Although the Nazi leader's inflammatory ideas made excellent copy, he was terrible at meeting deadlines and often failed to deliver promised exclusives—frequently announcing policies openly rather than through the columns of Hearst's newspapers. Thanks to Putzi, though, the newspaper baron was able to keep channels to him open.

Among those eager to interview Hitler was Putzi's former lover, Djuna Barnes. By now a prominent journalist and writer, she visited Munich in October 1931 with her latest partner, Charles Henri Ford. She and Putzi had remained in touch, despite the bitterness of their breakup in New York fifteen years earlier. During her stay, Barnes visited Putzi's home on several occasions, one time taking tea there with the historian Oswald Spengler. Putzi introduced his guests to the Wittelsbachs, the Bavarian royal family, and took them to see King Ludwig II's castle. Naturally, he played the piano for them too. Barnes, meanwhile, was pushing for the interview with Hitler and proposed it to *Hearst's International-Cosmopolitan*. The magazine cabled back around Christmas expressing interest, but then Putzi told her that Hitler wanted two dollars for each word printed—a preposterous sum, although it was not clear how much of it Putzi himself would be taking. She was forced to decline.

Plenty of other newspapers were ready to pay Hitler, though, often as much as two to three thousand dollars an article, thereby providing him with an important source of income and effectively funding his political campaign. Hitler badly needed the money. When he traveled to the Kaiserhof Hotel he would bring with him so many aides that he often needed to take the entire floor. With the cost of meals added, the bill for a week's stay could be as much as ten thousand reichsmarks.

Even though Hitler came to depend on such income, such monetary negotiations often proved a matter of contention between Hitler and Putzi. Hitler later complained that his foreign press chief was so obsessed with earning commissions for himself that he treated the Nazi leader's writing as a purely moneymaking venture rather than as a forum for political ideas. On one occasion, when Hitler asked him to place a time-sensitive article in the world's press as quickly as possible,

Putzi lost precious time trying to extract a higher fee. Eventually, he managed to sell it to one foreign correspondent for a thousand pounds, but Hitler was livid at the delay and refused to agree.

"Hanfstaengl, stop being so greedy," he told him. "If it is a matter of the article being read all over the world, then financial considerations don't play even the smallest role."

Putzi was left wondering how he was going to get by without the thousand pounds he had already counted on receiving.

▬

IT was an invitation no journalist could resist. In December 1931, Louis P. Lochner, the short, bald-headed Berlin bureau chief of the Associated Press, received a call to meet Hitler at the Kaiserhof Hotel. It was worded in such a way that he expected to be alone with the Nazi leader, hence his surprise when he arrived to find the room full of twenty-five to thirty correspondents from at least a dozen countries. Putzi was showing that he already had an understanding of the spin doctor's craft: no journalist can pass up the offer of an exclusive.

Once the press conference started, it was quite clear to Lochner that Putzi had carefully coached Hitler on the burning questions of foreign policy. Before anyone was allowed to ask a question, Putzi had supplied a question of his own. "A few hours later," Lochner recalled, "the world press was full of snappy, pithy, direct quotations from the man who had hitherto been regarded as a crack-brain and political amok-runner."

Thanks to Putzi's adroit handling of the meeting, Hitler was now able to command the attention of both foreign governments and newspaper readers. Among those itching to meet him face-to-face was Dorothy Thompson, the journalist wife of the writer Sinclair Lewis and one of the best-known American reporters of the day. Thompson had tried to interview Hitler in 1923 after the putsch while he was staying at Putzi's house in Uffing, but she had arrived just after he had been taken away by the police. Stunned by Hitler's electoral success and back in Europe with a commission from *Hearst's International-Cosmopolitan*, she decided to try again. Putzi was happy to oblige.

It was clear to both sides that the interview was an important affair. Thompson was on her way to becoming a highly influential figure in America and, as she noted, the Nazis were suddenly interested in making a good impression abroad. Hitler was "going very high hat and frock coat," she wrote. "He associates with industrialists. He goes to tea with princesses . . . is in control of propaganda and organization funds estimated at $8,000 per day." Thompson was nevertheless surprised by the fussiness of the preparations for their meeting, which was "not, somehow, what one would expect from a man to whom The Deed is everything." She was also scathing about what she saw as the homo-erotic side of the movement—or the "wavy-haired bugger-boys," as she later called them, the "pink-cheeked mediocrities" who made a fetish of the virtues of brotherhood and "talking about woman's function in bearing *sons* for the state."

Despite Putzi's role in arranging the interview, Thompson had no kinder words for him, dismissing him as "an immense, high-strung, incoherent clown. . . . Fussy. Amusing. The oddest imaginable press chief for a dictator." Her harshest words were reserved for Hitler, however. Her first impression, as she saw him shooting past through the hotel lobby, accompanied by a bodyguard who looked rather like Al Capone, was of "a man who owns an army. A man who terrorizes the street." Indeed, she was so nervous that she considered taking smelling salts.

The interview was something of a disappointment. Thompson found Hitler shy, almost embarrassed, and incapable of normal conversation; he behaved instead as if he were addressing a mass meeting, leaving his desperate interlocutor struggling to put forward her questions.

"In every question he seeks a theme that will set him off," she complained. "Then his eyes focus in some far corner of the room; a hysterical note creeps into his voice which rises sometimes to a scream. He gives the impression of a man in a trance. He bangs the table."

The interview, published in the April 1932 edition of *Hearst's International-Cosmopolitan*, was scathing:

When finally I walked into Adolf Hitler's salon in the Kaiserhof Hotel, I was convinced that I was meeting the future dictator of Germany. In something less than fifty seconds I was quite sure I was not. It took just about that time to measure the startling insignificance of this man who has set the world agog. He is formless, almost faceless, a man whose countenance is a caricature, a man whose framework seems cartilaginous, without bones. He is inconsequent and voluble, ill-poised, insecure. He is the very prototype of the Little Man. . . . Looking at Hitler, I saw a whole panorama of German faces; men whom this man thinks he will rule. And I thought: Mr. Hitler, you may get, in the next elections, the fifteen million votes which you expect. But fifteen million Germans CAN be wrong.

Thompson never quite lived down the dismissive few sentences of the interview, which was also to form the basis of a short book, *I Saw Hitler*, published later in 1932. Her fellow American reporters were particularly critical: for William L. Shirer, it "was a rather surprising judgment of so veteran and astute a Berlin correspondent." John Gunther of the *Chicago Daily News* was even harsher, calling it "her comico-terrible gaffe."

For Putzi, however, things had already moved on dramatically by the time Thompson's article appeared. This was to be Germany's year of elections. As well as the presidential election, caused by the expiry of Hindenburg's seven-year term, there were various state and regional polls in 1932. There were also two elections to the Reichstag—a sign of growing political instability that was soon to put an end to democracy in Germany. The rise of the Nazis, on the right, and the continued strong showing of the Communists, on the left, combined with the inability of the centrist parties to set aside their differences, was making it impossible for anyone to form an enduring democratic government. Matters only got worse as the year went on. Against the backdrop of the deepening economic crisis that sent the unemployment rate to almost thirty percent, the way was open for Hitler to deal the Weimar Republic the coup de grace.

The first election of 1932 was the presidential poll, which was set for March 13. Hitler began his campaign with his usual energy, embarking on an exhaustive tour of the country to get his message across. His team varied from trip to trip but usually included his adjutant, Wilhelm Brückner, a beefy ex-army captain; Julius Schaub, another ex-soldier with a wooden leg whom he used as his secretary-valet and general factotum; Sepp Dietrich, his bodyguard, who later became an SS general; and Heinrich Hoffmann, who was establishing a lucrative monopoly on Hitler photographs. Putzi was a permanent fixture, even though he found the touring process both dull and chaotic.

In the early stages, the group would travel in a great convoy of cars. They would be met on the outskirts of town by a pilot, who would take them through the backstreets to a meeting hall where Hitler would deliver an incendiary speech. It could be a danger-fraught experience; their convoy was often attacked by local communist sympathizers. A wrong turn could easily take them into a street covered in red flags, which Hitler and his supporters would literally have to fight their way through. In the Bavarian city of Nuremberg, for example, a bomb was thrown at a car in their convoy; in Bamberg a couple of windshields were shattered by bullets. Hitler liked to have a street map handy just in case a quick escape route was needed. On one occasion, in Brunswick, Emil Maurice failed to bring one and was soundly reprimanded by Hitler. Putzi was amused to see him stand his ground.

"Herr Hitler, what are you getting so excited about?" his long-time driver said to him. "Just remember Christopher Columbus."

"What do you mean?" Hitler retorted.

"Well, Columbus had no map, but that did not keep him from discovering America."

Communists and other opponents were not the only problem the entourage had to deal with on the early tours. Hitler spent considerable time locked behind closed doors trying to sort out quarrels within the local party organizations, which, in a reflection of the Nazis' origins, were an often uncomfortable mixture of nationalists and socialists. Hitler had little time for most of them. "I know why these Gauleiters are always harrying me to speak for them," he told Putzi. "They take the biggest hall in town, which they could never fill themselves. I cram it to the roof for them and they pocket the proceeds. They are all at their wits' end for money and I have to tear around Germany like a maniac to see that they don't go bankrupt."

The whole experience was akin to accompanying a musician on tour. Hitler would arrive in his town, give his performance, pack his bags, and move on to the next venue. Putzi became frustrated by the lack of opportunity for intellectual input. If the chance came, along the way, to meet someone important who could be of use to the movement, Hitler would do so alone. He was no longer a believer in sitting down with his aides and working out a campaign strategy; he preferred to talk to each of them in turn and then make his own decision.

All the while, as Putzi noted, Hitler's mind was increasingly set on his single goal: winning unilateral power. Unlike other politicians operating in the confused final days of the Weimar Republic, he wasted little time trying to work out tactical alliances or coalitions with other parties. He was already acutely aware of the force of his oratory and convinced that, provided he made enough speeches, he would eventually be swept into office by the masses.

Putzi, meanwhile, was finding himself swept into the familiar role of court minstrel. Often, toward midnight, tired after a day of speeches and meetings with local Gauleiters, Hitler would suddenly demand he play something on the piano. Putzi never had time to practice these days but would expertly busk for an hour or more, starting perhaps with some

Bach or Chopin or some of his own marches, but always finishing with *Tristan und Isolde* and the *Meistersinger*. Putzi tried to introduce Hitler to more modern works, such as Rachmaninoff's Second Piano Concerto, but it was too adventurous for the Nazi strongman. Hitler did, however, develop an unexpected passion for the work of Irving Berlin and made Putzi play his arrangement of a Russian lullaby over and over again. Putzi did not have the heart to tell him that Berlin was Jewish. While Putzi played, Hitler would sit in a half doze, literally gurgling with delight, and his entourage would not dare interrupt. Such interludes provided only a brief respite from the rigors of the campaign.

Despite Hitler's intense electioneering, the result of the March 13 presidential poll was a disappointment. When the votes were counted, he had just 30.1 percent to Hindenburg's 49.6 percent. Ernst Thälmann, the Communist candidate, was third with 13.2 percent. Although a distant second, Hitler had nevertheless narrowly prevented the elderly president from winning an absolute majority, triggering a second round of voting. The next election was set for April 10.

Determined to close the enormous gap that separated him from Hindenburg, Hitler decided on a change of tactics. So far, he had traveled by car and train, which meant he could address two meetings at most in the course of an evening. Although deeply wary of air travel, he now decided to campaign by plane instead. Hans Baur, who flew for Lufthansa, the German airline, was recommended to Hitler as a first-class pilot and was summoned to the Nazi leader's office in the Braun Haus. Baur was happy to take up the challenge: the first Deutschlandflug (Germany flight) was set for April 3, the day campaigning resumed after a truce declared for the Easter break. To Putzi's horror, he was required to fly with the entourage. He liked planes even less than cars.

That first day's itinerary set the pace for the hectic schedule they were to adopt throughout the week. They flew first from Munich to Dresden, where Hitler spoke for half an hour, then on to Leipzig, where he addressed a rally in the famous Exhibition Hall. Three-quarters of an hour later, they were in the air again, this time bound for Chemnitz. The final leg took them to Plauen, where Baur successfully carried out a landing in the darkness. At the end of the day, Hitler picked the largest of the many bunches of flowers he had been given during the day and handed it to the pilot. Hitler had suffered badly from airsickness in the past; at Baur's suggestion, this time he sat in the front and felt perfectly well.

"Baur, you've done your job well," he told him. "I'm enthusiastic about air travel from now on."

At Putzi's insistence, a seat on the plane was reserved for a journalist, often a foreign one, an idea taken from Franklin D. Roosevelt's campaigns. Ostensibly, it was all about publicizing the movement. Some of the reporters who were invited along suspected their presence was also about providing slightly more erudite company for Putzi. The first such passenger was Denis Sefton "Tom" Delmer, who wrote for the *Daily Express*, a leading British tabloid newspaper with a circulation of two million. Delmer, a fluent German speaker and one of the brightest young reporters of his generation, had assiduously courted Putzi, even renting a Bechstein grand piano for his flat, to encourage him to drop by. This flight was his reward.

Putzi and Delmer were the first to arrive at Tempelhof Airfield on April 5. It was a gray and drizzly morning as Hitler's election team gathered on the tarmac beside the chartered three-engined JU 52 Lufthansa D 2001. Heinrich Hoffmann, the hard-drinking official photographer, was there. Also on the tarmac was Prince August Wilhelm, who, as Delmer was amused to see, was "lounging around as chinless and knock-kneed as ever, joking and making himself affable to all." Then Goebbels drove up in a brand-new beige and brown Mercedes convertible, which he had just been delivered that morning. With him was his glamorous new wife, Magda, looking "most attractively unproletarian and very un-Nazi in her black Persian lamb coat with a little Persian lamb cap perched rakishly on her wheat-blond hair." A few minutes later, two black Mercedes Saloons drew up, disgorging Hitler and his SS bodyguards onto the tarmac.

Magda Goebbels rushed over to Hitler, seized him by the hand, and dragged him over to their new car.

"Mein Führer," she declared. "You simply must try it out. It is a dream." And so Hitler, the great connoisseur of automobiles, was taken by the Goebbelses' chauffeur for a couple of spins around the airfield. He returned, suitably impressed, proclaiming it a "most delightful car." And with that, smiling and saluting as he went, Hitler clambered up the steps and boarded the plane. Delmer, Putzi, and the others followed.

In the stern, nearest the door, sat Sepp Dietrich, who was the head of the bodyguard, together with four or five of his men. The men were undoubtedly tough, but some, to Delmer's eyes, looked too strangely delicate and effeminate to be bodyguards. He was even more startled when they took photographs out of their wallets and began passing them around with exclamations like "Isn't he sweet!" Delmer saw in their appointment the hand of Ernst Röhm, the flamboyant SA leader, whose homosexuality was a badly kept secret.

Besides Hitler and Goebbels, others on the plane included Brückner, Schaub, and Willi Krause, a reporter from Goebbels's newspaper, *Der Angriff*. At the far end of the cabin sat the prince, who had brought along a large box of chocolates, which he passed around. Despite his legendary sweet tooth, Hitler was the only passenger to refuse one. Opposite the prince was Goebbels's secretary, the bearded Karl Hanke. Putzi sat behind. Although obliged by his job to go along, he found the whole thing deeply uncomfortable as he squeezed his tall frame with difficulty into the cramped cabin. Like Hitler, he was prone to airsickness and would douse his hands and face with Yardley's lavender water to try to overcome the stink of aviation fuel and hot rubber. Every time Delmer looked over, he found Putzi rubbing his hands together and holding them to his nose.

It was all too much for Hitler. "That stuff of yours, Hanfstaengl, smells worse than a pimp parlor," he told him. "Put it away." Thereafter, Putzi had to make use of smelling salts instead—although his comrades were not above taking an occasional furtive sniff. It would, he wryly noted, have been "very un–National Socialistic" to be airsick.

Despite the conversational possibilities offered by the presence of a journalist such as Delmer, Putzi found it all rather depressing. He quickly tired of his fellow companions—a "stupid, inartistic, inarticulate bunch." It also annoyed him that they traveled to so many towns, but never took the time to visit the local museum or any other buildings of historical significance. Sometimes, as their interminable journey continued, he could be seen gazing for inspiration at a couple of picture postcards that he had plucked from his pocket of Goethe's workroom in Weimar.

Hitler, meanwhile, was sitting in what was to become his habitual position, in the mechanic's seat, up near the pilot. And there he would stay for the duration of the flight, dozing—or pretending to—or looking out the window or at his map. He would put wads of cotton wool in his ears. According to Delmer, everyone—with the exception of himself, Putzi, and the bodyguards—kept trying to attract Hitler's attention, showing him some newspaper article or making some comment that demonstrated their zeal for the National Socialist cause. Hitler was distinctly unimpressed: he would rarely talk and instead retreated behind a newspaper or some other document whenever another member of the party tried to engage him in conversation.

Delmer was surprised by how quiet and tired Hitler seemed and found it difficult to reconcile the man he encountered on the plane with the rabble-rousing character he had just seen on the tarmac. Hitler reminded him of a "tired and not very successful salesman flying with his samples to a client who had no great wish to see him and whom he himself had no wish to see." Was this the real Hitler, Delmer wondered, and the other, more familiar, one merely the product of "a terrific effort of will and imagination"?

The familiar Hitler was back on display when they landed at their first stop, Stolpe, in eastern Germany. The campaigning was a hectic affair; disembarking from the plane, the party drove to a disused factory, where crowds had already been waiting for several hours. At Putzi's insistence, Delmer jumped out of the car and ran after Hitler to ensure a good seat in the packed hall. They had to fight their way through a crowd of up-stretched arms and cheering and adoring fans. Like an American football player setting blocks, Putzi used his bulk to insert himself between the fans and Hitler. Then, when the speech was over, Hitler abruptly left and it was the same mad dash all over again for Putzi, Delmer, and the rest of the entourage, on their way back to the airfield to catch the plane before it took off again. And so it continued for the next few days as their flying circus crisscrossed Germany.

Hitler's new electioneering technique proved its worth in the second round of the presidential poll: although Hindenburg emerged victorious with fifty-three percent of the vote, Hitler had increased his share to thirty-seven percent—picking up thirteen million votes, two million more than in the first round. The Communist candidate, Thälmann, won just over ten percent.

From an obscure and unsavory small cult, by 1932 the Nazis had secured their position as a mass party that could count on the support of a third of the population. There was little time to pause for celebration, though: state elections were set for Prussia, Bavaria, and several other states on April 24, and again Hitler took to the air. After a few days, the Nazis chartered a second plane for Sepp, Dietrich, and one or two journalists. They would fly ahead, ready to report on the situation to Hitler as he arrived, before taking off for the next destination.

ONE day in April, when Hitler's plane landed home at Munich's Oberwiesenfeld Airport, Putzi found a telephone message waiting for him from Randolph Churchill, the son of future British prime minister Winston Churchill, who was out of government and a backbench member of Parliament. Putzi had struck up something of a rapport with Randolph, who was working as a journalist, and had invited him along a couple of times on Hitler's plane.

"My mother and father are here and it would be awfully nice if you and your boss would come this evening to a little supper at the Hotel Continental," Randolph Churchill told him.

"Of course, it would be lovely," Putzi told him. "I will try what I can do, but of course Hitler is very busy."

Hitler had already gone into town, so Putzi took a taxi and hurried to the Braun Haus. After throwing his bag into his tiny office, Putzi went to find Hitler; he found him sitting in his far-larger corner office, reading a stack of newspapers.

"Something very important's come up," Putzi told him. "Winston Churchill is here—you know, the father of the young man who has flown with us. He has heard so much from him." The whole thing was quite relaxed, Putzi assured Hitler: Winston Churchill had brought his family along as well, so they would not have to stick to political discussions; they could talk about Albrecht Dürer, Richard Wagner, or any of the other members of the German Valhalla. The elder Churchill was also a good singer; he could perform some Scottish songs and Putzi could accompany him on the piano.

Hitler insisted he was busy with the papers. "I've got too much to do," he said.

Putzi was not going to give up that easily. Winston Churchill was the coming man, he insisted, and this was the chance of the century, the first step toward a future Anglo-German alliance that Bismarck could only have dreamed of.

"I implore you," he continued. "Go home, shave, put a nice shirt on and come with me this evening. We'll have a great time. He's a real English gentleman. And his wife is charming. They're really looking forward to seeing you."

But Hitler continued to insist he was too busy. And who was Churchill, anyway? He was only a backbencher and without any real political power.

Desperate not to have Hitler squander the opportunity, Putzi suggested a compromise: maybe he could just drop by at the end of the meal while they were having coffee. Hitler could not be persuaded, though. Putzi put it down to his inferiority complex. The Nazi leader was in his element when manipulating a mass audience but could be extremely uncomfortable in one-to-one meetings, especially with as skilled a politician as Churchill.

Putzi went along to the Hotel Continental anyway, making his excuses for Hitler and saying he might join their party later. Apparently in view of their expected audience with Hitler, the Churchills had taken a private room. Besides Winston, his wife, and Randolph, there were a half dozen or so people sitting around the long table. The conversation quickly moved to politics. Putzi outlined the Nazis' views, making clear that they saw Bolshevik Russia as the main danger to Germany. Churchill gave Putzi a hearing, but pressed him about Hitler's anti-Semitism. Putzi tried to give what he considered as mild an account as he could, but it was still too much for Churchill.

"Tell your boss anti-Semitism is a good starter, but a bad sticker," he told Putzi.

The air nevertheless remained cordial as coffee and cognac were served with the cigars. Then, toward 2 AM, to Putzi's delight, Churchill pushed back his chair and, behind his cognac glass, asked him in an almost conspiratorial tone what Hitler thought of a possible alliance between Britain and Germany. Putzi was thrilled at the very thought of it; such an alliance would not only give Hitler prestige abroad, it would also, he hoped, hold him in check and save him from some of his own more outlandish and dangerous ideas.

"What about Italy?" Putzi asked.

"No, no, that would make the club far too large," Churchill retorted.

The dinner was easily living up to Putzi's expectations, but Hitler, of course, was not there to share it. Claiming he had to telephone his wife, Putzi slipped out to a phone booth in the hall and telephoned the Braun Haus. Hitler was not there. Nor, according to housekeeper Anny Winter, was he at home either. Frustrated, Putzi turned to go back to the party. No sooner had he stepped out of the phone booth than he saw Hitler on the staircase a few steps above him. Dressed in a green hat and a dirty white trench coat, he was saying good-bye to a Dutch friend of Göring's who had helped finance the Nazi Party.

"Herr Hitler, what are you doing here?" he demanded. "Don't you realize the Churchills are sitting in the restaurant? They may well have seen you come in and out. They will certainly learn from the hotel servants that you have been here. They are expecting you for coffee and will think this is a deliberate insult."

Hitler began to make excuses again, saying he hadn't shaved and would have to go home to do so. Putzi said he would pretend he had telephoned him at home and that Hitler had said he would be over in an hour or so. "I'll go on playing the piano and keep them here until breakfast if necessary," he told him.

Despite Hitler's reluctance, Putzi still had not completely given up hope and went back into the room. Sitting down at the piano, he began pounding out the "Londonderry Air" and a selection of Scottish songs as well as some of his own football marches. The cognac loosened Churchill's tongue and he was soon singing along; so, too, was Putzi, in his best Hasty Pudding falsetto.

To Churchill's disappointment and Putzi's fury, Hitler never turned up. When Putzi got home in the early hours of the morning, he found a note saying they had to leave at 7 AM for Nuremberg for an important meeting with Julius Streicher, editor of *Der Stürmer*, a fiercely anti-Semitic newspaper.

The car, with Maurice at the wheel, was outside on the dot of seven. Hitler was already in the front passenger seat, but Putzi was not going to let the matter of the missed meeting rest.

"You should have been there," he said, leaning forward. "Among other things, Churchill sketched out the idea of an alliance, with a request you should think about. He also wished you success in the elections."

If Hitler had any regrets, he did not show them. "In any case, what part does Churchill play?" he demanded. "He is in opposition and no one pays any attention to him."

"People say the same thing about you," Putzi retorted.

That was the end of the discussion, however. The Churchills stayed on in Munich for another couple of days, but Hitler made no attempt to contact them. Putzi liked to think that the meeting, if it had taken place, would have changed the course of history. At the very least, he thought, such a confrontation would have been the "delight of historians."

—

HITLER'S intense campaigning brought further success in the state elections of April 24, 1932. With 36.3 percent of the vote, the Nazis emerged easily as the biggest party in Prussia, the largest state, increasing their share of seats in its Landtag from just six in 1928 to an overwhelming 162. In Bavaria, they won 32.5 percent, putting them within 0.1 percent of the ruling BVP, and in Anhalt, to the east, they achieved 40.9 percent.

Then on July 31 came the first of the year's two national elections to the Reichstag—and another chance for the Nazis. Germany had been ruled at federal level since 1930 by a coalition headed by Chancellor Heinrich Brüning, a member of the Catholic Zentrum Party. Brüning had been unable to secure a stable parliamentary majority for the harsh austerity program he wanted to force through and, in a suspension of the normal democratic rules, had been allowed by President von Hindenburg to rule by decree. By late May 1932, however, the president was beginning to find Brüning insufficiently pliable and replaced him with the more conservative Franz von Papen, an urbane former diplomat. But Papen, too, enjoyed little support in the Reichstag and asked the president to make use of his power under the constitution to dissolve it. Hindenburg granted Papen's request.

Far from solving Germany's growing political problems, however, the July election made matters worse. The Nazis won 230 out of the 608 seats, making them by far the strongest party in the Reichstag. Even though Hitler had not achieved the absolute majority he had hoped for, he still could have expected to be named chancellor. But Hindenburg was deeply suspicious of his intentions and refused to call him. As the president told Papen, he was prepared to see "the Bohemian corporal" in the government, but could not countenance the idea of him becoming chancellor. Hitler, however, would settle for nothing less than the top job. The idea, as Goebbels put it, of the Führer becoming vice-chancellor within a cabinet dominated by the bourgeois parties was "too grotesque to be taken seriously."

The result was to plunge the political system into a fresh crisis. Although Papen remained chancellor, the Nazis and their archfoes the Communists together enjoyed a blocking majority in the Reichstag. It seemed to Papen and his advisers that the only solution was to dissolve the chamber again, postpone new elections indefinitely, and have the government granted special, wide-ranging powers. Again, Hindenburg readily agreed. The result would have been an authoritarian state, but at least one that was not dominated by the Nazis.

Yet Papen lost his nerve. When the Reichstag met on September 12, the Nazis and several other parties backed a no-confidence vote by the Communists. With Hermann Göring, newly elected president of the chamber, presiding, the government suffered a humiliating 512–42 vote before Papen could even serve the dissolution notice. When his cabinet met two days later, it was decided that now was not the time to start tampering with the constitution. And so new Reichstag elections were set for November 6.

Hitler embarked with enthusiasm on the fifth and last long campaign of the year, again taking to the air to relay his message to the nation. His most fiery oratory was directed against Papen and the small circle of "reactionaries" who had kept him in power—an outrage, in Hitler's eyes, since the September Reichstag vote had shown that the Papen government had only minimal popular support. The voters were weary after all these elections, and the Nazis' coffers were drained by the numerous other campaigns of the year, but Hitler pressed on with his punishing program of rallies and speeches. Putzi was again at his side.

In the closing days of the campaign, Putzi had another unexpected meeting. He was staying with Hitler and other members of the team in the Hotel Kaiserhof in Berlin when he received a message that an American named John Franklin Carter wanted to see him. The name did not mean anything to him, but he was intrigued and agreed to meet the man.

Carter, a personable young journalist in his early thirties, said he was bringing a greeting on behalf of Putzi's fellow Harvard alumnus, Franklin Delano Roosevelt, who was in the final stages of his battle with Herbert Hoover for the White House. Roosevelt had not forgotten Putzi and had fond memories of the early-morning piano concerts he used to give in the Harvard Club in New York, Carter said. There then followed a strange appeal: Carter said Roosevelt realized that Hitler was the coming man in German politics, but hoped that, as his adviser on foreign matters, Putzi would do his best to prevent any rashness or hotheadedness.

"Think of your piano playing and try and use the soft pedal if things get too loud," Carter told him. "If things start getting awkward, please get in touch with our ambassador at once."

For all of Roosevelt's concern, though, it was beginning to look as if the Nazis might already have peaked. In the days before the November 6 election, their support was falling away and even Hitler was beginning to have trouble attracting large enough crowds to fill halls. The leadership began privately to accept as much—even though the propaganda machine continued full tilt.

When the votes were counted after the November 6 election, the result provided confirmation that the Nazis' apparently inexorable rise had been broken. They received two million fewer votes than in July, pushing their share of the poll down from 37.4 percent to 33.1 percent and the number of Nazi seats in the Reichstag from 230 to 196. Many Germans, it seemed, had become weary of Hitler's strident propaganda and turned back to the traditional "bourgeois" parties. Others turned to the Communists, who won 100 seats, 11 more than in July.

The result had not helped Chancellor von Papen either. He tried to cling to office by reviving the idea of a broad nationalist coalition with Hitler as his junior partner, but the Nazi leader was having none of it. Papen was also being undermined by his defense minister, General Kurt von Schleicher, a powerful figure with a thoroughly deserved reputation as a master of intrigue, who had long been close to Hindenburg. Unable to gather enough support to form a stable administration, Papen stepped down—only to see Schleicher appointed in his place on December 3.

Introducing himself as a "social-minded general," Schleicher set about trying to build a coalition with the social democratic labor unions and began secret talks with Gregor Strasser, a popular and powerful figure on the left of the Nazi Party who was one of Hitler's only real rivals. Putzi, who had been watching all this plotting from the sidelines, was tipped off about Schleicher's intentions by Tom Delmer of the *Daily Express*, and he told Hitler, who was furious at what he saw as Strasser's betrayal.

Schleicher's strategy soon ran into problems. His concessions to labor failed to win over the Social Democrats and merely antagonized the employers, while the large landowners were angered by his proposed land resettlement program. Strasser, too, spurned the general's advances, but only after a furious showdown with Hitler, who never forgave him for his treachery. The general's well-known predilection for intrigue only added to the suspicion with which many regarded him.

Papen, meanwhile, was itching for revenge on Schleicher and was prepared to make use of Hitler to achieve it. At a series of meetings starting in mid-December, the two men ironed out their differences and agreed to jointly lead a coalition government. Buoyed by support from prominent industrialists such as Alfried Krupp and Fritz Thyssen, they approached President von Hindenburg's son, Oskar, to lobby on their behalf with his father.

Schleicher was belatedly beginning to realize the precariousness of his own situation, and on January 23 he called on the president. Admitting he had been unable to secure a majority for his government, he asked for powers to dissolve the Reichstag, declare a state of emergency, and ban both the Nazis and the Communists. This time Hindenburg refused. There was a public outcry when news of Schleicher's intentions was leaked to the press.

The days that followed saw more frantic plotting, as Papen lobbied others in the nationalist camp to support his proposed coalition,

Schleicher made one last attempt to reassert control, and the aging Hindenburg tried to avoid coming down on either side. By January 28 the president could delay no longer, and in what was to be one of the most fateful political decisions of the twentieth century, he warily gave his assent to the plan hatched by Papen and Hitler.

Two days later, Hitler was appointed chancellor, with Papen as his deputy and the premier of Prussia. Just a decade after Putzi had first spotted him as an unknown in a Munich beer cellar, Hitler had become the most powerful man in Germany—and Putzi was to be at his side.

HIS
MASTER'S
VOICE

9

THE strains of "Young Heroes," one of Putzi's own marches, rang out as the massed ranks of the SA and SS staged a torch-lit parade down the Wilhelm Strasse in the heart of Berlin. From 7 PM until midnight on January 30, 1933, twenty-five thousand of Hitler's uniformed followers marched through the Brandenburg Gate and past the chancellery. The streets were a mass of flags and flaming torches, and the mood was one of jubilation. From behind a closed window in his palace, President von Hindenburg, dressed in his traditional black coat, surveyed the scene below, his face a grim mask. Erect and immobile, he bowed only slightly to the marchers. Fifty yards farther on, in the chancellery, stood the subject of their adulation: Adolf Hitler. Lights played on him, "a halo of illumination for the man whom young Germany looks upon as its messiah," as one newspaper account put it. From time to time, Hitler would lean forward over the railing, his right hand raised in the Nazi salute.

The crowds had begun gathering earlier that afternoon. Göring had emerged first from the chancellery to announce the news of Hitler's appointment as chancellor. A few moments later, Hitler himself was applauded as his car drove out; the roof was down and he was standing up. Putzi had missed most of the celebrations because he was busy fielding telephone calls from foreign correspondents desperate for information. Dozens more forgotten acquaintances from the past had also called, claiming to have been with Putzi at school or to be a close friend of the family. But he still managed to slip away and join the spectators waiting expectantly on the first floor of the Kaiserhof when Hitler returned after his audience with the president.

"We've done it," Hitler declared, as he emerged from the elevator and was mobbed by supporters. Even the waiters and chambermaids pushed forward to shake his hand.

Putzi claimed to have been "singularly unmoved by the clamor and hysteria" of the day. He was amused nevertheless by the sight of Joachim von Ribbentrop, a liquor salesman who had just joined the Nazis, putting on his "Bismarckian airs" and Göring popping up every-where in his most resplendent uniform. Putzi even managed a mocking joke at Hitler's expense: "Well, Herr Reichskanzler [chancellor]," he told him. "At least I am not going to have to call you Herr Oberregierungsrat [a state councillor] anymore."

The torch-lit parade that evening, and the other Nazi pomp, vastly overstated the constitutional significance of what had happened. In the strictest sense, January 30 had merely seen the replacement of one apparently unstable governing coalition by another—an all-too-frequent occurrence in the Weimar Republic. Although Hitler had become chan-cellor, the Nazis had only two other posts in his cabinet: Wilhelm Frick was interior minister; while Göring, one of the most highly decorated flying aces of the First World War, was Reich commissioner for aviation, and deputy commissioner for the interior in Prussia.

Papen, by virtue of his special relationship with Hindenburg, was expected to continue to play a prominent role in the government. Indeed, he and his supporters congratulated themselves on having harnessed Hitler and turned him into the puppet of the industrialists and wealthy landowners. Experienced conservative ministers were also to remain in control of foreign policy, finance, economics, labor, and agriculture.

Much of the American and British press shared Papen's view—but in many cases they were prepared to give the new chancellor the benefit of the doubt. "Hitler did not seize power like Mussolini, he accepted it. There is a difference," said the *Daily Express* in an editorial headlined "Hitler's Hour." "What will he do now? . . . Mountebank or hero? There have been many who have called Hitler either name. Events will now decide which of them history will fix on him." For its part, *The Times* of London was reassured by the retention of Baron Konstantin von Neurath as foreign minister and Count Schwerin von Krosigk, who was in charge of finance.

The New York Times got it even more wrong: in an editorial the same day it predicted that any attempts by the new chancellor to "translate the wild and whirling words of his campaign speeches into political action" would founder on the resistance of his cabinet colleagues, of organized labor, and, above all, of President Hindenburg, who could "unmake Hitler as quickly as he made him." There was therefore "no warrant for immediate alarm," it continued. "It may be that we shall see the 'tamed Hitler' of whom some Germans are hopefully speaking." Wall Street, too, took everything in its stride: the mark fell five cents against the dollar, while German bonds ended the day only a fraction weaker.

Opinions from national capitals closer to Berlin were less sanguine. Edouard Daladier, struggling to form a new cabinet in France, expressed concern. The Poles, fearful of Hitler's demands for a revision of the Polish-German frontier, responded with a defiant show of military aircraft over Warsaw. The newspapers in Mussolini's Italy reacted with predictable joy.

Hitler moved swiftly to impose his will on Germany. To pass the kind of constitutional changes that would concentrate power in his hands, he needed the support of two-thirds of the Reichstag—something he did not currently enjoy, even with the support of Papen's nationalists. The only solution was to hold yet another election, but it was Hindenburg, rather than Hitler, who had the power to dissolve the Reichstag. When Schleicher made the same request a few days earlier, the president had refused, sealing the general's fate and paving the way for his replacement by Hitler. This time, however, Hindenburg granted Hitler's wish immediately. The new elections were set for March 5 and the Reichstag was dissolved before it could meet to proclaim its judgment on the new government.

For Putzi, the exhilaration of victory was mixed with concern at Hitler's intentions. Confirmation of his fears came quickly. The offices in the Reichskanzlei (chancellery) had still not been vacated by the outgoing ministers and Hitler continued to hold court in the Kaiserhof. It was in one of the rooms in the hotel that Putzi overheard a conversation between Hitler and Frick. Rosenberg, whom Putzi blamed for feeding Hitler some of his most dangerous ideas about foreign policy, was to be installed as state secretary in the foreign office. Putzi was appalled—not least because he felt he had been deceived. Hitler knew only too well how Putzi loathed Rosenberg and had assured him the Balt's influence would diminish once the party came to office. Yet here he was being propelled into an important post—indeed into one that Putzi would have liked for himself.

Putzi hurried to see von Neurath. Appointed as foreign minister the previous June, the conservative aristocrat had served under both Papen and Schleicher. He was alarmed at the prospect of having such a virulent Nazi as his deputy, fearing it would undermine his own position, and swiftly vetoed the appointment. Rosenberg had to make do instead with becoming head of the Nazi Party's foreign policy section, but he was at least able to console himself with a luxurious villa in the Tiergarten. Von Neurath was grateful for Putzi's tip-off. Although it was the first time the two men had met, they became firm allies and he took Putzi with him that summer to the World Economic Conference in London.

Putzi was given a set of offices in Hess's Verbindungsstab (Liaison Staff), diagonally opposite the chancellery. He moved later into a building on the corner of Wilhelm Strasse and Unter den Linden. He was allowed to appoint his own staff: his deputy, Harald Voigt, was a member of the Nazi party, but the others were not. As his secretary he chose Agnethe von Hausberger, a Quaker who had grown up in the United States. Putzi had little time for what he called the "superficial Nazi flummery." Those who worked in his office greeted each other with "good morning" or "good day" rather than the "Heil Hitler" or Nazi salute that were quickly becoming commonplace in Germany. The office was to become a civilian island in a sea of uniforms.

Although the volume of Putzi's work increased dramatically, he still received the same expense allowance as before. Once party dues, tax, and insurance had been deducted, this left him just 850 reichsmarks a month—not a great sum. His post, technically, was not a Nazi party position: he was answerable only to Hitler; he did not receive instructions from party officials and he did not have the power to give any, either. Nor did his position feature in the Nazis' Organizationsbuch (Organization Book). Putzi's salary was paid not by the party but instead out of one of Hitler's special accounts. Such distinctions were of more than mere academic interest. They were seized on by Putzi after the Second World War, when he and others had to justify their work for the regime; this was, he claimed, proof that he could not be judged as a Nazi. Putzi's part ownership of the family art firm provided another source of income, but it was never enough and he was forever involved in moneymaking schemes to try to make ends meet. He was all the more annoyed when he learned Rosenberg was being paid much more than he.

Putzi's duties were relatively circumscribed. His chief responsibility was to organize interviews for Hitler both with foreign journalists—mostly American and British—and with prominent personalities. In his capacity as foreign press chief he also had to fly the flag at the many diplomatic dinners and receptions held at the various embassies. Putzi needed little persuading. Naturally gregarious, he enjoyed party-going and relished contact with foreign correspondents and diplomats; he far preferred their sophisticated company to spending time with those he called the *chauffeureska*, the old, ill-educated party hacks still gathered around Hitler.

As part of his work cultivating the press, Putzi went often to Die Taverne, a restaurant on the corner of the Kurfürstenstrasse, which served as a rendezvous for foreign correspondents, leading young Nazis, and storm troopers. They were joined there by actors, dancers, singers, and other habitués of the old nightlife of Weimar Berlin, which was largely being closed down by the new regime in its first fervor of idealism.

Thick with smoke and the aroma of wine, beer, and coffee, Die Taverne was a place of low rooms, long tables, and wooden benches, where those who claimed to know the secrets of the new regime would exchange confidences well into the early hours of the morning. It was, in short, a clearinghouse for all the political gossip of Germany, and as such, it was infested with spies. Although indiscretions were partially shielded by the orchestra pumping out the latest American jazz, only the unwary newcomer would dare to speak in too loud a voice or without first looking around to check who was within earshot.

Die Taverne was more than just a center for gossip. Setting aside personal competition, the foreign correspondents who gathered there nobly pooled information; in those first awful days of Nazi rule, the common task of telling the world what was really happening in Germany seemed more important than who filed the better story. As one observer put it, "One man alone could see little: five, ten, twenty men experienced at their job, knowing the country, each in touch with half a dozen diplomats and quantities of Germans of every class and kind, could cover the situation pretty well." The Nazis raged and tried to find the "miserable informers," sending German newspapermen to try to find out what was going on, but to no avail.

Putzi's work proved frustrating. Hitler had been followed relentlessly by foreign journalists during the recent election campaigns and had become heartily sick of them. When Putzi passed on a suggestion from a French reporter that the Nazis should mark their victory by organizing a joint reconciliation celebration of French and German soldiers along the border, Hitler dismissed it out of hand. Putzi was deeply disappointed: this would have been a golden opportunity to improve the new regime's reputation with an important neighbor. Instead the French press stuck to their simple—if ultimately correct—slogan of *"Hitler C'est la Guerre"* (literally, "Hitler means war"). Nor could the Nazi leader grasp the fact that Putzi could not order foreign correspondents around in the same way Goebbels bullied the German press. As Putzi told him, there was no point in threatening critical writers with expulsion: most could make their living just as well in another country as in Germany.

Soon Putzi had the first of what was to be a series of clashes with Hitler and his entourage. He had heard reports that people were being tortured in Columbia House, a building near Berlin's Tempelhof Airfield used by the SA as a private prison and interrogation center. Count Schönborn, one of Putzi's acquaintances, confirmed the details to him. When Putzi confronted Göring, he became evasive and demanded the name of his informant. Naïvely, Putzi gave him Schönborn's name. The unfortunate aristocrat was then himself locked up in Columbia House until Putzi could get him out. Putzi was careful not to make the same mistake again.

When the cabinet met for the first time on February 2, Hitler devoted most of the time to preparations for the election. Every tactical move he took from then on was directed to March 5—named by Goebbels the Day of the Awakening Nation. Hitler launched his campaign with a major speech in the Berlin Sportpalast. In the weeks that followed he crisscrossed the country, often by air with Baur at the controls, to spread his message. Thanks to Goebbels, Hitler also exploited a powerful new propaganda tool: radio. As he visited city after city, the local radio station would broadcast each speech. He was helped, too, by Hindenburg, who approved several emergency decrees that gave Hitler the power to forbid meetings of rival parties and ban their newspapers and other publications. The Nazis were also making inroads into the administrative apparatus: Göring installed his own men in the police force and turned a minor department in police headquarters into the notorious Geheime Staatspolizei (secret state police)—known more simply as the Gestapo.

Putzi accompanied Hitler on many of his campaign trips; in the last days before the election the pace became frantic. On February 26, after a twelve-hour plane tour that took in three cities hundreds of miles apart, he returned to Berlin feeling tired and feverish and with swollen glands. Ever the socialite, he forced himself to keep a dinner appointment that evening with Prince Viktor zu Wied and his wife at their plush home on the Kurfürstenstrasse. When he left, the prince sent him away with a bottle of aquavit and instructions to drink himself into a fever.

Putzi was too tired to try it out that night, but the next afternoon he put on a couple of sweaters, covered his bed with blankets, and settled down in the room that Göring had temporarily allowed him to use on the first floor of the Reichspräsident's palace, opposite the Reichstag. The aquavit was to complete the cure.

Putzi had been due to go to Goebbels's house on what is now Theodor-Heuss-Platz that evening. But he had begged off because of his fever, even though Hitler was going to be there. Shortly after Putzi settled down in bed, the telephone rang. It was a member of Hitler's staff.

"The Führer insists that you come to the Goebbels's this evening," he told him. "You are to play something on the piano for him." Putzi insisted that he was not well enough.

Then, just as he was settled back into bed, the telephone rang again; this time it was Magda Goebbels. Putzi was ruining everyone's evening by not turning up, she told him. But Putzi stood his ground and went back to bed. This time he took the phone off the hook. At last he was going to get some rest.

As he lay drifting in and out of sleep, he suddenly became aware of a bright light. At first he thought he must have forgotten to turn off the desk lamp in the adjoining room, but it was too bright and was flickering unlike any electric bulb. At that moment, Frau Wanda, the housekeeper, burst in.

"Herr Doktor," she cried. "The Reichstag is on fire."

For a moment Putzi forgot about his fever. He jumped out of bed and ran to the window. He had always disliked the Reichstag building, which he likened to a giant gasworks. Now, as he looked across the square, he could see it was enveloped in flames.

He rushed to the telephone and called the Goebbels's home, where dinner was in full swing. Trout was on the menu for all but the vegetarian Hitler, who was eating eggs and vegetables. The host picked up the phone himself and Putzi demanded to speak to Hitler. Goebbels wanted to know what it was about, and Putzi in the end lost patience with him.

"Tell him the Reichstag is on fire," Putzi said angrily.

"Hanfstaengl, is this one of your jokes?" Goebbels retorted. It was not such a bizarre question. In order to amuse Hitler, Goebbels had played a telephone hoax on Putzi just four days earlier and he suspected Putzi was now trying to get him back.

"If you think that, come down here and see for yourself," said Putzi and hung up. He then called Tom Delmer of the *Daily Express*. Delmer was already on his way to the Reichstag, after being tipped off by one of his network of gas station attendants who served as occasional informants. Since he had already put his car away in the garage and there were no taxis around, he had to run the mile and a half from his office to the Reichstag. He nevertheless arrived just forty minutes after the first alarm had been given. Putzi also called Lochner of the Associated Press.

No sooner had Putzi put the receiver down than it rang once more. It was Goebbels again. He had been so convinced Putzi was trying to trick him that at first he had not told Hitler, who was in the next room with Magda and a blonde film starlet who'd been invited along for his delectation. But after making a few calls, he suspected the building might really be on fire.

"I have just talked to the Führer and he wants to know what is really happening," Goebbels said. "No more of your nonsense."

Putzi lost his temper; Goebbels still seemed to think he wanted revenge for the previous joke. "I tell you to come down here and see whether I am talking nonsense or not," he retorted. "The whole place is in flames and the fire brigades are already here."

He demanded Goebbels bring Hitler to the phone. Goebbels finally gave in, but Hitler initially did not believe Putzi's story either.

"What's happening, Hanfstaengl?" Hitler demanded. "Stop that now. Are you suffering from hallucinations or have you drunk too much whiskey? What? You can see flames from your window?"

Hitler was at last convinced, to Putzi's satisfaction. Putzi felt he had done enough; he was due to drive with Hitler to Breslau the next day and wanted to finish his cure. Although the Reichstag was only a few minutes' walk away, he returned to his bed.

Had he chosen to cross the road, the scene he would have encountered was one of considerable destruction and devastation. It was also of enormous historical significance. Göring, massive in a camel hair coat, was already there. When Hitler and Goebbels arrived shortly afterward in their black Mercedes-Benzes after a sixty-mile-an-hour dash down the Charlottenburger Chaussee, he promptly took them on a tour of the building, past pools of water, charred debris, and clouds of evil-smelling smoke.

"This is undoubtedly the work of Communists, Herr Chancellor," Göring declared, looking flushed and excited. "A number of Communist deputies were present here in the Reichstag twenty minutes before the fire broke out. We have succeeded in arresting one of the arsonists."

"Who is he?" demanded Goebbels.

"We do not know yet," replied Göring, with an ominously determined look around his thin, sensitive mouth. "But we shall squeeze it out of him, have no doubt."

The fire was still smoldering when they opened a varnished yellow door that led into the oak-paneled debating chamber. Göring picked up a piece of cloth soaked in gasoline near one of the charred curtains and showed it to Hitler. "Here, you can see for yourself, Herr Chancellor, how they started the fire," he told him.

Delmer, who had managed to join them after getting approval from Hitler, was struck by Göring's automatic assumption that more than one person was involved. Despite the apparent lack of any conspiratorial evidence, Hitler swiftly seized upon a theory. As the party walked farther along a corridor, he dropped back from the others and took the journalist to one side.

"God grant that this be the work of the Communists," Hitler told him. "You are now witnessing the beginning of a great new epoch in German history, Herr Delmer. This fire is the beginning." He then added: "You see this flaming building. If this communist spirit got hold of Europe for but two months it would be all aflame like this building."

Hitler repeated his thoughts to Papen when he appeared a few moments later. Arriving straight from the Herrenklub, where he had been entertaining Hindenburg for dinner, the vice-chancellor looked very much the aristocrat in his dress suit and beautifully cut gray tweed overcoat. "This is a God-given signal," Hitler told him. "If this fire, as I believe, is the work of the Communists, then we must crush this murderous plague with an iron fist." Papen looked uneasy.

Hitler invited Papen to join him and Göring to decide immediately on what measures to take. The vice-chancellor, who had a sense of what was to come, declined, saying he needed to report back to Hindenburg.

The only apparent perpetrator was quickly identified by police as Marinus van der Lubbe, a left-wing Dutch anarchist. Wearing only shoes and trousers in spite of the icy cold, he was dripping with sweat and crying "Protest! Protest!" It soon emerged that he was a renowned arsonist who had already tried to set fire to a number of buildings in both Germany and his native Holland. He confessed almost immediately to having added the Reichstag to his list. He was wrapped in blankets and taken for interrogation at the headquarters of the political police on the Alexanderplatz. Van der Lubbe insisted that he—and he alone—had set the Reichstag on fire; furthermore, he had done so on his own initiative and without any outside help. His aim, he said, was to incite the workers of Germany to "do something about Hitler" before it was too late. Prosecutors were reluctant to believe him; they were under considerable pressure to follow the official line that this was a Communist conspiracy. And so, Ernst Torgler, a Communist Reichstag member who had been the last person to leave the building before the fire, was arrested. So too were Blagoi Popoff, Wassil Taneff, and Georgi Dimitroff, three Bulgarian Comintern agents. All four men had alibis.

But would one man have been physically capable of causing so much damage to such a large building on his own? Or was the fire deliberately started by the Nazis in order to discredit the Communists, as was immediately claimed by Hitler's critics? It is a question that has continued to divide historians ever since: witness statements have been examined and reexamined, and claims by contemporary technical experts suggesting the fire could have been the work of one man have been challenged by more recent analysis.

Delmer was scornful of what he saw as clumsy attempts by the German Communist Party to blame the fire on the Nazis, especially since their case was based largely on forged documents. "I rather suspect there was really just one incendiary who lit that fire—the lunatic van der Lubbe," he claimed in an article in 1939. Writing again in 1961, he said he no longer suspected this was the case; he was *sure* of it.

Putzi himself was not able to shed much light either way on the matter. In his memoirs, written during the 1950s, he pointed to the existence of a tunnel—about one hundred and twenty yards long—that ran from the cellar of the palace where he had been sleeping, under the Friedrich-Ebert-Strasse, to the Reichstag. He wrote that he had noticed nothing, however, that would confirm one prevalent conspiracy theory, that SA leader Röhm had used the tunnel to lead a team of Nazi arsonists into the parliament building.

On the other hand, he had been in bed with a fever, the building was huge, and Röhm and his team could easily have slipped in without anyone, least of all him, noticing. Putzi was even more intrigued by the reaction of Goebbels. The man was, of course, a practiced liar. Yet the suspicious and angry way in which he reacted when Putzi telephoned him seemed genuine rather than mere dramatics. One possibility, he thought, was that Göring, with Hitler's knowledge, had cooked up the whole thing but had deliberately failed to tell Goebbels, whom he hated.

Whatever the role of Hitler and the other Nazi leaders in causing the blaze, there was no doubting their determination to make full use of it for their own purposes. Just after 11 PM, Hitler went to a meeting at the Prussian interior ministry to discuss the security implications for the state. He then went with Goebbels to the Berlin office of the *Beobachter*, where a new front page was made up to reflect the drama of the evening's events. Göring immediately gave the order to round up communists; within an hour and a half, hundreds of plainclothesmen, accompanied by policemen armed with automatics, began their arrests. The fire itself, which had broken out at around 9:45 PM, was finally brought under control by 12:30 AM. Two press rooms were still alight, but there was no danger of the blaze spreading, although the building's dome had burst and crashed to the ground.

The next morning, while the newspapers splashed banner headlines about the "Communist Plot," Hitler went to see Hindenburg and presented him with the text of two emergency decrees, ready to sign. Together the decrees suspended indefinitely certain rights, such as freedom of speech, association, and the press, as well as the privacy of postal and telephonic communications, which had been guaranteed under the Weimar constitution. The Reich government also gave itself the power to intervene throughout the country to restore order—eliminating the autonomy of the individual Länder (states).

Hitler spoke to the cabinet as well. The time had come, he told them, for a showdown with the Communist Party—the struggle against them should not be based on "juridical considerations." Within the next two weeks, in Prussia alone, an estimated ten thousand people were arrested.

——

HITLER continued to campaign for the last few days; much of the time Putzi was at his side. Their electioneering reached a climax on March 4 with a grandiose rally in Königsberg, the capital of East Prussia, which was to become the Russian city of Kaliningrad after the Second World War. Hitler ended the speech with an appeal to the German people: "Now hold your heads high and proud once again!" He declared, "Now you are no longer enslaved and unfree; now you are free again . . . by God's gracious aid." As he finished, the strains of a hymn rang out, mingling with the pealing of bells from the cathedral. All radio stations had been ordered to broadcast the rally live; SA columns marched through the country and so-called freedom fires were lit along the borders.

The result was dramatic: the Nazis increased their share of the vote to 43.9 percent, ensuring them 288 of the 647 seats in the Reichstag. Their success was not only due to the ferocious repression of the Communists and other left-wing parties, although this undoubtedly played an enormous part. The Nazis also had considerable popular support. Germany was a deeply polarized society and Hitler was able to play on a strong fear, especially among Catholics, of both the Socialists and the Marxists.

Goebbels spoke of a "glorious triumph" for the Nazis; it was not quite that, however. Despite the mass hysteria and intimidation, the Social Democrats still managed to win 18 percent and the Communists 12.3 percent. Although Hitler emerged from the poll with his position considerably strengthened, he still did not have an absolute majority—and he remained dependent on his nationalist coalition partners, who won a crucial eight percent.

Hitler did not allow this lack of a majority to constrain him unduly. At a cabinet session on March 7, he declared the election result a "revolution." In the next few days, he staged a virtual coup d'état in each of Germany's constituent states. Storm troopers marched through the streets and laid siege to official buildings, forcing local and state governments to resign and replacing them with "nationalist" cabinets. Five days later, he visited Munich, where Franz von Epp, the nationalist general, had effectively seized power and declared the "first part of the struggle," namely the Gleichschaltung, or "coordination," of the political will of the state with the will of the people, to have been completed.

The tone of the new regime was set on March 21 when the new Reichstag held its first session. The Nazis called it the Day of the National Rising. It was marked with a solemn state function in the Potsdam Garrison Church, above the tomb of Frederick the Great. The display of traditional German imperial values was carefully orchestrated by Goebbels in a powerful demonstration of his mastery of propaganda. The details were carefully approved by Hitler. All the representatives of pre– and post–Weimar Germany were there. This, Putzi thought, was "reaction" in full regalia. It also appeared to mark a turning point in Hitler's attitude. When he spoke of the "heroic Weltanschauung which will illuminate the ideals of Germany's future," it seemed to Putzi as if he were abandoning traditional Christian morality in favor of something new and more savage. The influence was pure Nietzsche. Despite the setting, though, it seemed Frederick the Great was no longer Hitler's hero. His place had been taken by Napoléon.

HIS MASTER'S VOICE

"The inspired sense of the art of the possible which had characterized the great Prussian king became submerged in the limitless lust for universal power of the Corsican," Putzi recalled later.

Two days later, when the deputies met for their first working session, the scene was set for the passage of the Act for the Removal of Distress from the People and the Reich—otherwise known as the Enabling Act—which was to provide the legal basis for Hitler's dictatorship. With the Reichstag building in ruins, deputies met instead in the Kroll Opera House. A giant swastika flag hung over the back of the stage; units of the SS cordoned off the building; lines of brown-shirted SA men stood inside. In a two-and-a-half-hour speech, Hitler laid out the reasons why his government needed absolute power—and ended by warning those who opposed him of the perils of resistance.

Despite the standing ovation, Hitler could not automatically count on the two-thirds majority he needed. Initially, the Catholic Zentrum party wobbled, but the Nazis were able to win them over during a recess with empty promises to guarantee civil and political liberties. The Communist deputies had all been taken into custody, leaving the Social Democrats alone to speak out against Hitler's plans. Their defiance was brave but futile. The bill was passed, 441 votes to 94; the requisite three readings took only a few minutes. As Göring announced the result, the jubilant Nazis rushed to the front and sang the "Horst Wessel Lied," which had been recently adopted as their anthem. Later that evening the bill passed the upper house, the Reichsrat, which was already completely under Nazi control, by a unanimous vote.

The Reichstag had effectively voted itself out of existence. "An historic day," commented the *Völkischer Beobachter*. "The parliamentary system has capitulated to the new Germany. . . . The great undertaking has begun. The day of the Third Reich has come."

Nearly all the constitutional restraints on Hitler had been removed. His power was not yet quite absolute, however, even though the other political parties had been banned and the trade unions eliminated. Putzi, like many other similarly minded conservatives, was reassured to see that many of the pillars of the old establishment, such as the Reichswehr, the foreign ministry, and the civil service, still remained. So, too, did President von Hindenburg. Putzi now naïvely expected the "agitation" to diminish rather than increase and reassured himself that a number of safeguards still remained. Not for the first time, however, he had completely misunderstood Hitler's intentions. Far from slowing down, Hitler was pushing his revolution at a faster and faster pace and no longer listening to those of his advisers who counseled moderation. The whole thing, Putzi felt, took on the air of a Grand National steeplechase; there was no chance to hear what one jockey said to the other as they approached hurdle after hurdle.

In the weeks and months that followed, every sphere of political and social activity was to be brought under the Nazis' control in the continuation of the process of Gleichschaltung. Violence against the Jews and the Communists was intensified. On March 22, the day before parliament reconvened, the first concentration camp was opened at Dachau, outside Munich. It was far from a secret installation; Himmler even called a press conference to announce its opening as a holding center for Communist functionaries and other left-wing opponents of the regime. The Nazis were rapidly building their apparatus of terror.

10

DINNER was set for eight o'clock on April 27, 1933, at the Berlin apartment of Louis P. Lochner. As bureau chief of the Associated Press, America's largest wire service, Illinois-born Lochner was eager to establish close relations with influential figures in the new regime. He and his aristocratic German wife, Hilde, also clung to the somewhat naïve hope that the Nazis' relations with the rest of society could be improved if they saw at close hand how the people they vilified were, in reality, honest and upstanding citizens. For this reason, they began organizing social occasions that brought together members of both groups.

The first Nazi guinea pig in Lochner's experiment was to be Putzi. Lochner—or Louis P., as he was known to his fellow newspapermen—was not risking much: Putzi was as atypical a member of the regime as it was possible to find and already had a wide circle of American, British, and other non-Nazi friends. Among the others on the eclectic guest list were General Wilhelm Groener, who had become anathema to the Nazis when, as minister of defense, he had ordered the dissolution of the Brownshirts; Kurt Sobernheim, a prominent Jewish banker; and Julius Curtius, a former foreign minister and cabinet colleague of Brüning's. The party was rounded off by George Messersmith, the U.S. consul general.

Putzi enjoyed such invitations. As the man who controlled media access to the new chancellor, he was in a powerful position and relished the status that it gave him. Dinners like this one were the perfect mixture of business and pleasure. There was one problem, though—

what to wear. Germany was rapidly turning brown, as more than one million people joined the party in the first few months of 1933 alone, swapping their civilian clothes for Nazi Party uniforms. Putzi reluctantly accepted that it would be expedient to follow suit. Inevitably, though, he decided to do so on his own terms. Hitler had given him permission to draw shirts and trousers from the party's clothing store, but Putzi considered the SA's dun-colored uniform a monstrosity. He therefore sent for a length of the best chocolate-brown gabardine from a London tailor and had it made up into a uniform with delicate little gold epaulettes. This dinner was to be its first showing.

Putzi had given the uniform a dry run that afternoon when he went to the Hotel Adlon to fetch his old friend, Hamilton Fish Armstrong, the editor of *Foreign Affairs*, and take him for an interview with Hitler. Armstrong was staggered at what he saw.

"Why, Putzi," he exclaimed. "I've never seen you in uniform before. How magnificent."

"Yes, it is rather good, isn't it?" Putzi replied. "Don't tell anyone, but it's English stuff. That does make a difference."

Hitler, by contrast, was appalled. "You look like a Turkish whore," he declared.

The reception Putzi received that evening was even more dramatic. The dinner was a black-tie affair; one by one the guests arrived, the men in their tails and their women in evening dress. The Groeners, Curtiuses, and Sobernheims were not in the habit of mixing socially with Nazis, but Lochner had warned them Putzi was on the guest list and they had not appeared concerned. By 8 PM everyone but Putzi had arrived. The hosts waited, wondering what had happened. Fifteen minutes later, just as Hilde Lochner was about to give the signal to open the dining room, the parlor door was suddenly flung open. In burst what Lochner described as a "huge, towering bulk of humanity in high boots and brown uniform."

Frau Groener winced and Frau Curtius stood aghast. Lilli Sobernheim, a short, plump woman almost as round as she was tall, whispered, "The Gestapo," and nearly fainted. Locher was equally surprised, not least because Putzi had hitherto made sarcastic remarks about the official Nazi uniform and had never been seen in one. Nothing if not well-bred, Putzi turned immediately to the hostess and apologized profusely for his late arrival.

"My butler simply could not find my evening clothes. So at the last moment I had to put on my uniform," he said.

No one believed such a story, of course. For Lochner, it was clearly Putzi's retaliation for being invited to a party with critics of the new regime. "One up for Hanfstaengl," he thought. "Rather clever." Putzi later confirmed that, as his host suspected, the uniform had been made specially for the occasion.

As Lochner started to make the introductions, he was concerned that Putzi might greet the others with the Nazi salute. He need not have worried, for his guest was ready to play the gentleman, clicking his heels in the traditional German manner when introduced to General Groener and bending almost double to kiss the hand of Frau Sobernheim. It was Putzi's turn to be surprised, however, when he turned to her husband.

"Herr Doktor, I believe you and I are related," the Jewish banker told him with an impish glint in his eye. Putzi immediately flashed crimson at the embarrassing suggestion that he might have Jewish blood, but quickly composed himself.

"How interesting! What do you mean?" It turned out that a Jewish cousin of Sobernheim's had married one of Putzi's Aryan cousins. As the rest of the party chuckled at the spectacle, the pair went into a huddle to discuss this apparently strange relationship in greater detail.

After dinner, Lochner managed to maneuver Groener and Putzi into a corner of the smoking room. Putzi apparently did not hold Groener's campaign against the SA against him and later came over to Lochner excitedly. "That man Groener is quite different from what I thought he was," he said. "He's so nice that I've invited him to have dinner with me sometime in my home."

"All my guests are nice," Lochner retorted. "The trouble with you Nazis is that you have such strong prejudices against anybody who isn't of your ilk."

"There ought to be more evenings like this," Putzi concluded enthusiastically.

In the months that followed, Putzi became an increasingly regular sight on the Berlin cocktail circuit. Among those whom he encountered was Martha Dodd, the impressionable young daughter of the American ambassador, William E. Dodd, who arrived with her father in July 1933. Putzi was distinctly unimpressed by the ambassador, a Southerner. A bookish and self-effacing history professor, he "teetered round self-effacingly as if he were still on his college campus," and was the "last person in the world who could have any effect on the German people." Putzi's sentiments were more than just the product of personal dislike.

Despite his growing identification with the Nazi cause, he continued to take a great interest in the way his "other" homeland was perceived in Germany. To his mind, Dodd was completely the wrong man to be its ambassador.

Putzi would argue later that, given Hitler's contempt for such "professorial types," the Americans should have sent some hard-boiled businessman who had the force of Theodore Roosevelt and was not afraid of straight, strong talk. Putzi also thought Dodd had made a serious mistake by taking over an old palace on the Pariser Platz for the embassy and not even bothering to do up the façade. These were the kind of accommodations you would have expected of a minor state like Yugoslavia, not of the United States of America, Putzi argued. They should have rented a building five or six times bigger, brought over a fleet of Cadillacs and Packards, and staffed the embassy with "strong and resolute men and lots of handsome robust women—preferably the Mae West type!" William C. Bullitt, a close associate of Roosevelt's who had just been appointed the first U.S. ambassador to the Soviet Union, agreed. The American embassy in Berlin was of a scale that would befit a country of the size and importance of Honduras, he told the president. "It is not a good stage setting for dealings with gentlemen who conceive of themselves as Parsifal and young Siegfried."

Putzi was especially scornful of Dodd's behavior during a secret two-hour meeting that he arranged for him with Hitler. Convinced that the Nazis were not taking Washington seriously enough, Putzi urged Dodd to try to impress Hitler with the scale of American military power and make clear to him that Washington would inevitably become involved in any future world conflict. To his great disappointment, Dodd, speaking in German, lost himself in pedantic and dreary detail and sounded "as if he had a hot potato in his mouth." Indeed, his enunciation was so poor that Hitler complained afterward to Putzi that he scarcely understood a word Dodd said, and making use of his gift for mimicry, he proceeded to do a cruel impression of his American visitor. Such meetings only served to further convince the Nazi leadership that "America was nothing to be feared and need hardly be taken into account as a serious enemy."

Dodd's glamorous blonde daughter was quite another matter, as far as Putzi was concerned—and she reciprocated his interest. They had met soon after Martha's arrival, when she was taken by Quentin Reynolds, the *Collier's* editor and correspondent, to a party thrown by one of the British journalists. Putzi made his usual late and dramatic entrance. Martha was fascinated by her first glimpse of a man who, she had been told, was the "artist among the Nazis, erratic and interesting, the personal clown and musician to Hitler himself."

"He had a soft, ingratiating manner," she recorded in her diary, "a beautiful voice which he used with conscious artistry, sometimes whispering low and soft, the next minute bellowing and shattering the room." Thanks to his powerful physical presence, indomitable energy, and never-ending talk, he could exhaust anyone and "out-shout or out-whisper the strongest man in Berlin." She concluded, "Bavarian and American blood produced this strange phenomenon. He could never have been a Prussian and he was proud of it."

His punctuality was also anything but Prussian. As Martha was quick to learn, attention-seeking Putzi had a habit of turning up after the other guests. That October, she threw a birthday party. He came roaring in after midnight, much to the delight of a princess who had been bored and only stayed on for the sake of meeting him. He met her on the way out and lured her back in again, and after a drink, he started playing several songs on the piano with his usual exuberance. He left soon afterward amid a mixture of wild gestures and shouted praise of everything and everyone in the house—including "Papa" Dodd, as he jokingly referred to Martha's father.

Martha was also at the receiving end of one of Putzi's more bizarre schemes. Hitler's sex life—or rather apparent lack of it—had been one of Putzi's concerns for some time. He was convinced that the growing violence and danger in Hitler's personality and ambitions were linked to an imbalance in his private life and had been on the lookout for a suitable woman with whom to pair him. One day, the telephone rang for Martha at the embassy. It was Putzi.

"Hitler needs a woman," he informed her rather grandiosely. "Hitler should have an American woman—a lovely woman could change the whole destiny of Europe. Martha, you are that woman."

Martha thought at first she had fallen victim to Putzi's usual horseplay. But she detected an underlying seriousness to his intent and was, in any case, excited at the prospect of meeting Hitler. Although critical of those around the Führer and of the system he was creating, she remained convinced he was a "glamorous and brilliant personality who must have great charm." Martha chose her clothes carefully; if she had been appointed to change the history of Europe, she noted wryly afterward, then she should dress at her most demure and intriguing best with a veil, a flower, and a pair of very cold hands. German men, she had come to understand, liked their women to be attractive appendages who were seen and not heard.

Putzi took her to the Kaiserhof, where they met Jan Kiepura, a young Polish singer also due to be introduced to Hitler that day. Kiepura was the first to be taken over to meet him once he had sat down at the next table, surrounded by his usual entourage of bodyguards. The two men had an animated conversation, apparently about music. Martha's audience was an altogether more strained affair. After Putzi had whispered a brief explanation in Hitler's ear, she went over and remained standing as he stood up and kissed her hand. Putzi must have forgotten to warn Hitler that Martha barely spoke any German, because when he murmured a few words to her, she barely understood what was said and beat a hasty retreat. They stayed at their respective tables for some time afterward, Martha aware of Hitler occasionally giving her curious, embarrassed stares.

As she and Putzi left afterward, he was his usual boisterous self. But she was not in the mood for his extravagant, senseless talk. She was trying to reconcile Hitler's role as one of the most powerful men in Europe with what she had encountered close up: an unobtrusive, dull, and even gentle and self-conscious man who seemed shy and uncomfortable in meeting people "above him in station or wealth." Only the burning, hypnotic, pale-blue eyes gave a sense of something far more powerful—and frightening.

Even if Hitler was not interested in Martha, Putzi was not immune to her considerable charms. According to his son, Egon, she was also one of a number of women with whom his father had an affair.

Later the same evening, Martha held a small party for some friends. One of the guests, Hans Thomsen, the foreign ministry's man in the chancellery, was appalled when the hostess went to the phonograph and put on the "Horst Wessel Lied." Thomsen thundered that such an anthem glorifying the martyr to the Nazi cause was "not the sort of music to be played for mixed gatherings and in a flippant manner." Putzi found the whole thing hugely amusing. "Yes, there are some people like that among us," he told Martha. "People who have blind spots and are humorless—one must be careful not to offend their sensitive souls." He was certainly not one of them himself.

Putzi's ironic attitude toward the Nazis also made an appearance before Prince Louis Ferdinand of Prussia. Von Ribbentrop had tried to woo him to the Nazi cause, but he refused. The prince nevertheless took a liking to Putzi. "His Bohemian life style and his sympathy for

America formed the basis for our friendship," he said later of their first meeting, in 1933. "He was a kind person, even though lots of people considered him slightly mad. In any case, he saw the whole Nazi hurly-burly like a theatre."

In the spring of that same year, Putzi arranged a meeting for him with Hitler. The prince, who as a young man traveling in America had taken a job at the Ford factory in Detroit, was treated to a forty-minute mono-logue by Hitler on how much he admired the American carmaker and his success in turning the automobile into "an instrument for uniting the different classes." Although somewhat bemused by the encounter, the prince was forced to admit that he sensed "a certain magnetic force emanating from him."

Putzi was also making a name for himself abroad, especially in Britain, to which he traveled often. One British lady subject to his charms was Diana Mitford, the daughter of Lord Redesdale, and a renowned society beauty. Diana and her five sisters and one brother were well-known and colorful members of the British establishment, who mingled easily with some of the country's most prominent writers, thinkers, and artists. Diana was also close to Winston Churchill. Married five years earlier at the age of eighteen to Bryan Guinness, one of the richest young men in Britain, she was now on the verge of leaving him: her new love and future husband was Sir Oswald Mosley, who was already gaining notoriety as leader of the British Union of Fascists.

Diana met Putzi during the spring of 1933, at a party in London given by one of the Guinnesses' cousins. Putzi had been playing the piano in the drawing room when she came in, but he promptly stood up and began regaling fellow guests with his description of the new German state and its leader. He left her in no doubt that Hitler "was everything in the world to him, as leader and as friend."

All that Diana knew about the Nazis was what she had read in the British papers, and that principally concerned the party's hatred of the Jews. Putzi was indignant when she asked him about their treatment.

"Oh, the Jews, the Jews, that's all one ever hears in London," he shouted. "People here have no idea of what the Jewish problem has been in Germany since the war. Why not think for once of the ninety-nine percent of the population, of the six million unemployed? Hitler will build a great and prosperous Germany for the Germans. If the Jews don't like it they can get out. They have relations and money all over the world. Let them leave Germany to us Germans."

Putzi boomed on in similar fashion all evening. Diana had met many drawing-room communists before who "breathed fire and slaughter," but he was her first "drawing-room Nazi." She was fascinated, especially when Putzi promised to introduce her to Hitler if she came to Germany. "You must all come to Germany," he told the guests. "You will see with your own eyes what lies are being told about us in your newspapers."

That September, Diana decided to take him up on the offer. The upheaval in her private life meant that she was keen to get away from London. Her younger sister, Unity, also wanted a break. The timing was fortuitous. When the two women tracked down Putzi, he told them a party rally was being held in the Bavarian city of Nuremberg to celebrate the Nazis' accession to power. He offered to take them along with him—and hinted that he might make good on his promise to introduce them to Hitler.

The two women were impressed by what they saw. The streets of Nuremberg's Old Town were packed with hundreds of thousands of men in military uniforms; there were swastika flags in many of the windows. The rally itself was spectacular. Albert Speer, then a young architect, was in charge of designing the set, which he crowned with a golden spread eagle one hundred feet high. Leni Riefenstahl, the celebrated filmmaker, helped him with the special effects. Most striking of all was the sheer sense of jubilation among the crowds. Diana spoke of a feeling of "excited triumph" in the air. When Hitler appeared, "an almost electric shock passed through the multitude." It was, she wrote, "thanksgiving by revolutionaries for the success of their revolution. They felt the black years since their defeat in the war were now over and they looked forward to a better life."

Putzi was the perfect host, showing the sisters around during the entire four days of the event and taking them to all the parades. He was wearing the same distinctive dark brown uniform that he had premiered at the Lochners', but to Diana's amusement he was sporting breeches and riding boots instead of the trousers favored by the other members of the Nazi leadership. Unity, in particular, wanted to meet Hitler, and asked Putzi two or three times a day when they would have a chance.

Putzi finally agreed to take them to the Hotel Deutscher Hof, where Hitler was based during the celebrations. On the way there, though, he expressed concern about their heavy makeup, which did not match the Nazi conception of beauty.

"You mustn't wear lipstick," he told them. "The Führer doesn't like it."

Diana dutifully accepted the proffered handkerchief and wiped it off, but Unity refused. "I couldn't possibly do without it," she said.

They continued to the hotel anyway and waited in the lobby as members of Hitler's entourage came past to judge whether they were worthy of an introduction. Finally, Hess came down and said Hitler was too busy to see them. Putzi was in no doubt that Unity's makeup was to blame.

For both women, however, those few days in Nuremberg were to change their lives. Diana went back to Britain convinced of the need to establish links between Mosley and the Nazi leadership. Unity was so impressed by this vision of the "new Germany" that she managed to persuade her parents to let her stay in Munich to learn German. Desperate to meet Hitler, she would go every day to the Osteria Bavaria restaurant in the hope that she might find him there. She sat there having lunch or coffee, sometimes with a friend, more often on her own, waiting for him—placing herself such in a position that he invariably had to walk past her, and sometimes talking loudly or dropping a book in order to attract his attention.

It finally paid off. When Unity met Hitler in 1935, she wrote a long letter to her father beginning: "Yesterday was the most wonderful and beautiful day of my life." She felt so happy, she wrote, "I wouldn't mind a bit dying." From then on, Unity befriended Hitler and became a regular visitor to the Braun Haus. Theirs appears to have been a purely platonic relationship, even if Unity may have wished otherwise. According to Putzi, Hitler cultivated Unity for her "snob value" but was never interested in her sexually—"she could just as well have been a bathtub with the water overflowing."

A number of other prominent Britons were also impressed by Hitler, even if few were as obsessed with him as Unity was. David Lloyd George, the former British Liberal Party leader and World War I prime minister, was among them. When Putzi visited him in Britain, Lloyd George presented him with a signed photograph of himself to take back to Berlin. On the back was the inscription "To Chancellor Hitler, in admiration of his courage, his determination and his leadership."

—

NOT every foreigner succumbed to Putzi's charms. Quentin Reynolds, the *Collier's* correspondent, found him superficial and two-faced. "You had to know Putzi to really dislike him," he said. Indeed his first impression, when he went to present his credentials at the Foreign Press Department, was of a likable fellow. A compulsive and amusing talker with an ingratiating manner, Putzi went out of his way to be cordial to Americans—a great contrast to the hostility of most other Nazi officials. When Reynolds asked during one of their early meetings about the chance of an interview with Rudolf Diels, the Gestapo chief, Putzi quickly obliged. The next day, he sought out the American at Die Taverne to tell him it was all arranged.

Putzi tried to ingratiate himself on a personal level when Reynolds's servant, Martha, ran afoul of the Nazis: every morning, when the postman brought the mail he would click his heels and greet Martha with *"Heil Hitler"*—which was rapidly becoming the customary form of address. Martha, a pink-cheeked young woman, would reply with equal determination, *"Grüss Gott"* (May God Be with You)—the traditional greeting of her native Bavaria. Such defiance of the new regime could not go unnoticed for long, however. One day, two brown-uniformed storm troopers, one of them fluent in English, knocked on the door and told Reynolds his servant had been reported as someone unfriendly to the regime and they were taking her to SA headquarters for questioning. Reynolds immediately called Putzi and told him what had happened, making sure the two storm troopers could hear him.

Putzi did not disappoint. "Let me speak to one of those nitwits," he said, and when the phone was passed to the English-speaking member of the duo, he let rip.

"Have you nothing better to do than to annoy a simple peasant girl who works for the representative of the great Hearst organization?" he roared, forgetting Reynolds actually worked for *Collier's*. "If you ever bother her again, I will complain personally to Ernst Röhm and he will take care of you."

Putzi's intervention had the desired effect. Mopping his brow, the senior SA man promptly apologized to Reynolds for the misunderstanding. Shortly afterward, the postman was transferred.

Reynolds soon came up against a far less accommodating side of Putzi, however. Perhaps because of the journalist's poor command of German and relatively scant knowledge of the country, Putzi believed he would be able to influence what he wrote far more than others, like Lochner, who had already watched the Nazis at close quarters for several years. And so, when the two men ran into each other in the bar of the Adlon Hotel about a month after Reynolds had arrived, Putzi congratulated him on not having written anything about the Nazis' supposed mistreatment of the Jews, which, as he told everyone else ready to listen, was little more than anti-German propaganda. This was not to last long, however. It soon became clear to Reynolds that the picture Putzi tried to sell him of the Nazi regime did not square with what he saw with his own eyes.

This was demonstrated dramatically when Reynolds stopped over in Nuremberg on his way to the Salzburg Music Festival with Martha Dodd and her brother, Bill; quite by chance, he became one of the first foreign correspondents to witness the horrors of the Nazis' anti-Semitism firsthand. Arriving at their hotel just after midnight, they caught a glimpse of a torchlit parade through the city. As happy, laughing crowds lined the streets, the swastika banners of the parade came into view. In the heart of the march was a woman who was half supported and half dragged by two six-foot storm troopers. Her face was white with powder and her head shaved. Around her neck had been hung a placard that read: "I wanted to live with a Jew." The woman, named Anna Rath, they learned, had made the error of trying to marry her Jewish fiancé despite the ban on marriages with "Aryans."

When Reynolds filed his story, it was splashed all over the American press—earning him plaudits from his bosses and a dressing-down from Putzi. When he got back to Berlin, he found a note ordering him to report immediately to his office.

Putzi was livid. "There isn't one damned word of truth in your story!" he shouted. "I've talked with our people in Nuremberg and they say nothing of the sort happened." Reynolds soon silenced him by revealing that he had two unimpeachable witnesses with him in Nuremberg, both of whom would back his story.

There was nothing Putzi could do. But soon afterward, he got his revenge, albeit in a bizarre way. Reynolds's parents were visiting Berlin and he threw a lavish dinner party for them to which Putzi was invited. As usual, Putzi soon sat down at the piano and began bashing out a few harmless German ditties. Hearing Reynolds translate for his mother, Putzi turned to her and announced he would play her one of his compositions, which had words in English. He then proceeded to serenade the unfortunate woman with a foul Nazi song in which "Jews, Catholics and Negroes" were singled out as the enemies of the Third Reich. Reynolds was in no doubt that this was Putzi's way of getting back at him for his Nuremberg report and had to restrain himself from hitting him. Luckily, Putzi was called away soon afterward to go and play some Liszt for Hitler in the chancellery. Reynolds accompanied him to the door to see him off. Controlling his temper masterfully, he said: "Never come to my house again, you louse."

While it took Reynolds some time to see through Putzi, others, like Bella Fromm, a Jewish society columnist for Berlin's *Vossische Zeitung*, took an instant dislike to him. An "absurd-looking giant," he accompanied almost every phrase with violent gesticulations of hands "of almost frightening dimensions" and drove every point home with a jerk of his "strangely distorted head," she wrote after meeting him for the first time at a party. Putzi, loved by the party members much as a court jester is loved, was "Nazi-struck," she declared. "He has neglected family and business for years to follow the trail of his master like a faithful hound." When Putzi boasted of how he would play the piano for Hitler late in the night to help the Führer when he was suffering from bouts of insomnia, Fromm could not prevent herself from retorting, "Who cares?"

Fromm was also angered by the extent to which Putzi remained an apologist for Nazi policy well into 1933. "All the rumors about the persecution of Jews and the mistreatment of Catholics are cheap lies and absurd tattletales," he told her at a tea party at the Italian embassy that March. It was a similar story a couple of months later when they ran into each other at the glamorous Rot-Weiss-Ball. Putzi was enchanted by a Jewish friend she had with her. "You should go to the anthropological institute for a consultation," he told her. "I think it is absurd that you should be Jewish. Your skull has the perfect Aryan formation."

Fromm had another taste of Putzi's anti-Semitism in May of the following year at a farewell party held by Ambassador Dodd for Messersmith, the departing U.S. consul general.

"All this excitement about Jews," Putzi complained. "Messersmith is one. So is Roosevelt. The party detests them."

"Dr. Hanfstaengl, we've discussed this before," Fromm retorted. "You don't have to put on that kind of act with me."

Putzi was beginning to soften his tone. "All right, all right," he conceded. "I have lots of friends in the United States, and all of them side with the Jews too. But since it is insisted on in the party program . . ."

As they parted, Putzi offered her a fruit drop. "Have one," he told her. "They are made especially for the Führer." Before popping it in her mouth, Fromm was horrified to see that it was decorated with a swastika.

Putzi scarcely attempted to conceal such anti-Semitism from visiting journalists and other official visitors, especially those who sought an audience with Hitler. Will Moore, an American whose brother had studied with Putzi at Harvard, found him a "ruthless example of a ruthless government" when he ran into him during a visit to Berchtesgaden. "He advocates the complete crushing of all Jews and the extermination of Communists and criminals rather than burdening the state with their upkeep," he said.

Another who experienced such anti-Semitism firsthand was Robert Bernays, a British journalist and Liberal Party politician, who had come to Germany to look into the Jewish question. Aware of the regime's acute sensitivity to criticism, he had been careful not to take part in any anti-Nazi demonstrations or do anything else that might put him on any German blacklist before he arrived. Putzi seemed to him the best entrée to the Führer and so he sought him out. But Putzi was suspicious of Bernays and was convinced he was Jewish. In fact, as Bernays wrote later to Tom Clarke, the editor of the *News Chronicle*, his great-grand-father had actually been a German Jew, but had fought at the Battle of Leipzig—which might have made him an honorary gentile. Since then, he had "generations of parsons on both sides of my family."

Putzi rang up the British embassy in Berlin to learn more about his visitor.

"Who is this Mr. Bernays?" he demanded. "It is a Jewish name. We call it Bernice here."

"I don't know what you call in Germany," replied a secretary, who knew the visitor personally. "But in England, it is pronounced like it is spelled—Bernays."

And so Putzi agreed to see him. Their meeting did not go well. After a few minutes of sparring, Putzi launched into a tirade against the Jews, whom he described as guests in Germany who had abused their posi-tion and must go. "Your press, your law, your finance, your politics are all controlled by the Jews," he thundered, before launching into a crescendo of abuse. "Go and tell your Jewish friends."

Bernays struggled in vain to convince Putzi that it was not just "his Jewish friends" but the entire House of Commons that was appalled not just by Hitler's campaign against the Jews but also by his attacks on civil liberties and a revival of the militarism that had provoked the First World War. "Can you wonder that we are angry and downright alarmed?" Bernays asked.

Putzi was having none of it. Although he conceded that the perse-cution of the Jews had been more ferocious than necessary, he told his skeptical guest that it was important to understand that the events of March 1933 had been "a revolution, not a change of government." The real enemy was communism—something that the people of Britain could never understand because the country did not even have a single Communist MP.

"What is the alternative to Hitler?" he demanded. "Communism." Hitler, he said, had the powers of "organizing and inspiring," rather like Britain's David Lloyd George, and would cooperate with anyone "to meet Communism and war." Putzi also claimed to be deeply concerned about the strength of anti-German feeling in Britain; to illustrate his point, he picked up a copy of *The Sphere*, a British magazine, showing an effigy of Hitler at Madame Tussaud's Waxworks in London, daubed with red paint. "Is that the way to establish good relations?" he demanded.

Bernays could already see that his chances of obtaining an interview with Hitler were dwindling with each minute he spent with Putzi, but he thought he might as well ask anyway. Bending the truth slightly, he had described himself as a "nationalist" MP, but when Putzi asked him the name of his party's leader, he knew he was sunk. He toyed for a moment with pretending it was still David Lloyd George, but admitted the leader's name was Herbert Samuel—thereby confirming Putzi's suspicion that the whole thing was a Jewish provocation.

A few days later, a friend of Bernays's ran into Putzi and asked if he was arranging the interview for him.

"Do you think that I am going to get an interview for a sow of a Jew?" Putzi asked him.

Putzi, meanwhile, was continuing to satisfy his other important role in the party as Hitler's pianist, ready to come to his side whenever he was needed. "Putzi was to Hitler what harp-playing David was to Saul," commented Louis P. Lochner of the Associated Press. "He eased der Führer out of his frequent fits of depression with his piano playing." As a result of the curious hours that Hitler kept, however, such a summons could come at any time. A typical incident was one evening when Putzi was holding a *Bierabend* (beer party) at his home for some diplomats, government officials, actors, writers, and several foreign correspondents. At 1 AM, when the party was in full swing, the telephone rang. It was Hitler.

"What are you doing, Hanfstaengl?" he demanded. "Are you too tired to come and play for me?" Putzi left the party and hurried to the chancellery.

Hitler looked drawn and tired. "Play anything," he said.

Putzi proceeded to work his way through a selection of favorites, from Puccini and Verdi to Schumann, that he knew would relax Hitler. He would normally, of course, have played some Wagner, too, but considered it inappropriate given the lateness of the hour. It had the desired effect; when Hitler looked so relaxed he was ready to sleep, Putzi left him and went back to his party.

It remained a matter of continual astonishment to Putzi why Hitler seemed so keen on his playing. Others who heard him at the keyboard were struck more by the vigor and sheer volume of his playing than by his virtuosity. "He always left the piano crumpled and exhausted, not to mention himself and his listeners," Martha Dodd said of one of his performances at a party she held. "And the rooms of the embassy reverberated with sound for days afterward."

There was nevertheless something about Putzi's music-making and character that especially appealed to Hitler. Putzi liked to tell the story of how a virtuoso Italian pianist had once come to play for Hitler.

"Now do you still like Hanfstaengl's playing after hearing that man?" a friend asked Hitler laughingly.

"I would rather hear Hanfstaengl play a hundred wrong notes than hear that man play one right one," Hitler retorted.

11

LATE one evening that summer, Hitler called and invited the Hanfstaengls to join him at his house in Berchtesgaden for a week. Putzi declined, saying he had too much to do in Berlin, but suggested that Helene and Egon go without him. Hitler agreed. He was still fond of Helene and the prospect of a week alone with her—or at least without her husband—was appealing.

It was shortly after midnight when Hitler's car arrived for them. They were driven to the Nazi leader's sumptuous apartment on Prinzregentenplatz, where he and a few of his entourage were waiting. They finally set off at about 1:30 AM in two identical open-top Mercedes-Benzes. Egon and Helene were in the first one with Hitler. It was not until daybreak that they finally arrived at Haus Wachenfeld. Mother and son were both put up in the upstairs guest room, from which they had a magnificent view of the valley beyond. The next day Hitler took pleasure in taking them around. He even showed them his own relatively modest first-floor room, which, like the rest of the house, was furnished in the simple *Landhaus* country style. Other than the bed, there was only a small writing table and a few bookshelves.

Egon, who had recently persuaded his reluctant father to allow him to join the Hitler Youth, saw a lot of Hitler over the next few days. He and Helene regularly ate with him and other members of his entourage. Hitler, Egon recalled, was rather gracious—at least by his usual standards. Normal conversation was not usually his forte; he would listen or, more commonly, preach. But when he sat at the table in Berchtesgaden he would behave like an ordinary host, even though he was reluctant to talk about anything but automobiles, engines, the size and performance of various ships, and other such technical subjects.

Although Egon and Helene were the only guests given the privilege of sleeping in the house, it was full during the day with other Nazis who lived in surrounding hotels and *Pensionen*. Göring was one of the most frequent visitors; he and Hitler would walk around a small patch of grass, talking. Seated on the veranda, Egon would pick up snatches of conversation that gave a chilling insight into the nature of Nazi rule: on one occasion, for example, he heard Göring boasting about how he had just signed twenty death warrants.

Once, Egon walked over as Hitler was standing alone on the veranda, looking toward Salzburg. In the distance some houses and what appeared to be a castle were just visible.

"Look, boy, that's Austria over there," Hitler said suddenly.

"You were born there, Herr Hitler, weren't you?" Egon said.

"Yes, I was—in Braunau on the Inn. It's a really beautiful country."

"Why don't we drive over and visit it—it's only a short way up," Egon suggested.

Hitler smiled. "We will, someday. It's really a shame that they don't belong to us. But they'll come home into the Reich someday."

———

ALTHOUGH Putzi mingled with ease with foreign diplomats and journalists, his relations with other members of Hitler's entourage remained poor. He had naïvely hoped that Hitler, on coming to power, would have ditched Wilhelm Brückner, Julius Schaub, Heinrich Hoffmann, Sepp Dietrich, and the other members of the "dreary crew" whom he had come to despise during the various election campaigns. To his horror, they continued to form Hitler's inner circle even after he moved into the chancellery. Considering Hitler to be "theirs," they formed a wall around him to protect him from influences they felt deviated from the party line. Their attitude put Putzi in mind of an old comedy by Gerhard Hauptmann called *Schluck und Jau*, set in the seventeenth century. In the story, a duke comes across a couple of drunken tramps while he is out on a hunting trip with some friends and, as a joke, brings them back to his castle and puts them in his bed. When they wake up, they are told they are the duke and his chamberlain, and, to everyone's amusement, they come to believe it. For Putzi, Brückner and the others were Hauptmann's tramps.

Putzi was even more concerned about the growing influence of Goebbels, who as propaganda minister gradually replaced Rosenberg in the role of his nemesis. Putzi had long been suspicious of this "mocking, jealous, vicious, satanically gifted dwarf," whom he saw as the "pilot-fish of the Hitler shark." Goebbels's earlier admiration for Putzi had also long since given way to suspicion. Putzi believed Goebbels had never forgiven him for an occasion when he had become one of the few people to see his crippled foot without a shoe. He would also mock the way that Magda Goebbels addressed her husband by the pet name of *"Engelchen"* ("little angel" or "cherub"). "Magda calls out 'Engelchen,' but who should come round the corner but the old black devil himself, club foot and all," Putzi would comment.

Such remarks necessarily got back to Goebbels, who manifested his hatred for Putzi in the pettiest of ways. On one occasion, Putzi and Hitler dropped in to Goebbels's apartment to discover he had just been presented with a grand piano. Hitler immediately asked Putzi to play; Goebbels, although inwardly seething, faked approval. This went on for months until Putzi arrived one day to find the instrument had been put deliberately out of tune. He didn't play there for Hitler again.

The two men's mutual distrust only intensified after Hitler came to power. Putzi was convinced his rival wanted to add the foreign press to his growing propaganda section. Goebbels appears to have seen Putzi as little more than a minor irritant and was beginning to tire of his sarcastic humor and less than total devotion to the cause. Yet far from trying to appease him, Putzi embarked instead on a collision course. It was an unequal struggle. Putzi may have openly nicknamed his foe Gobbespierre—in a mocking comparison with Robespierre, the French revolutionary leader—but the propaganda minister was one of the most powerful men in the new regime and it was a serious tactical error to cross him.

One of their first clashes was over a film. Ewers had brought out his promised book on Horst Wessel at the end of 1932, to loud acclaim from the Nazi leadership, and after Hitler came to power, he decided to turn it into a film. Putzi agreed to compose the music and also to act as assistant producer. Filming began on the streets of Berlin on July 6. The emphasis was on authenticity: many of the roles were played by Wessel's former comrades in arms—some of whom got badly carried away when they reenacted their brawls. A scene depicting one of their fights with the communists in a beer hall ended with the destruction of twenty-three tables, two hundred and seventeen chairs, and a hundred and seventy-three beer glasses, as well as the breaking of eleven teeth.

When a rough cut of the film was ready, they showed it to Hitler and photographer Heinrich Hoffmann. Both were impressed. So, too, was a small group, including Hjalmar Schacht, the president of the national bank and a close friend of Putzi's, who were invited to a private screening on September 20. The gala opening in the Capitol Cinema in Berlin on October 3 was described by Hearst's International News Service as "the most important premiere for the German film industry of Fall 1933." Putzi, already living way beyond his official salary, was delighted. Given Wessel's prominence in the Nazi pantheon, the film was almost guaranteed to be a hit at the box office.

They had not reckoned on Goebbels, however, who resented such an intrusion onto territory he considered his own. Indeed, it is difficult to think of a better demonstration of the poverty of Putzi's political judgment. Goebbels waited until the film was due to open nationwide on October 9, Wessel's birthday, and then suddenly banned it on grounds that it did not do justice either to the figure of its hero or to the National Socialist movement. The film, he claimed, "endangered the vital interests of the state and Germany's image." Matters were not helped by the involvement of Hanns Heinz Ewers, who remained a controversial and scandalous figure despite his professed enthusiasm for the Nazi cause. Putzi was now faced with a substantial loss. He appealed to both Goebbels and Hitler, but to no avail. In the end, Goebbels allowed the film to be shown—but only after twenty-seven cuts had been made. In the ultimate indignity, he insisted it should not even carry Wessel's name. It was renamed *Hans Westmar*.

Putzi's only consolation was the music. The musical climax of the film was "Deutsches Largo," the funeral march he had composed for his daughter, Hertha. Hitler was so impressed after hearing it at the first Nuremberg rally that he decreed it should continue to be played in subsequent years. In *Triumph of the Will*, Leni Riefenstahl's film of the first rally, the march can be heard being played by a brass band as Hitler and other leading Nazis pass through the ranks of tens of thousands of members of the Deutsche Arbeiterfront (German Labor Front), standing to attention, their polished spades glinting in the sunlight.

Putzi's work with the press did not bring much consolation for his cinematic failure. Before coming to power, Hitler had been willing to listen, albeit often grudgingly, to Putzi's insistence on the importance of projecting a positive image of the movement abroad. The situation had now changed. Hitler was pressing on with his "revolution," largely oblivious to the concerns of the rest of the world. The Nazis had swiftly turned much of the domestic media into loyal and unquestioning servants of the new regime and expected the Berlin-based foreign correspondents to toe the line too.

Increasingly, the Nazi authorities would read the stories that reporters cabled to their offices and return unsent those deemed harmful to the regime. They also singled out individual journalists they considered especially hostile. In March, Hearst's International News Service had been forced to withdraw its correspondent, Edward Deuss, after the Nazis took exception to some of his pieces. Several months later, Edgar Mowrer, who had angered the regime with his book, *Germany Puts the Clock Back*, and various critical articles, was eased out of the presidency of the Association of Foreign Press Correspondents.

To some extent, Putzi went along with such actions, but appeasement was not always the case. In March 1933, for example, Kurt Lüdecke, another of Putzi's foes, who had been lured back to Germany by Hitler's accession to power, wrote a cable, in Rosenberg's name, to the *New York Evening Post*, complaining about several articles that H.R. Knickerbocker, one of the most prominent of the resident American correspondents, had written about Nazi atrocities. Lüdecke claimed they were slanderous and demanded the journalist's recall. The newspaper stood by its man, however, and Knickerbocker appealed to Putzi for help. Putzi was happy to oblige, not least because of the opportunity it gave him to do some damage to Lüdecke and also to Rosenberg. After consulting with the American embassy, he went straight to Goebbels and together they took the matter to Hitler. Knickerbocker was allowed to stay—and Lüdecke was punished with a short spell in jail.

——

AS the Nazis' foreign press chief, Putzi undoubtedly shared a degree of moral responsibility for the regime's crimes. There is no doubt too, that he was an anti-Semite who saw in the Nazis the only salvation for his country. Yet he disagreed strongly with much of what was being done. Sometimes he would say or do nothing; on other occasions he would speak out against abuses. More often, though, he would try, in a more subtle way, to smooth out its worst aspects. His successes were at best minimal.

One of his greatest shocks was the trial of Marinus van der Lubbe, Georgi Dimitroff, and the others accused of burning down the Reichstag. Almost immediately after the fire, Hitler had changed the law to make arson a capital offense. Putzi had only vaguely followed the proceedings, but he was as surprised as everyone else when the Supreme Court dealt the Nazis a serious blow that December by acquitting all the defendants but van der Lubbe. It was only when Putzi read the official record of proceedings, though, that he saw the extent to which the choice of witnesses and the evidence they had given bore the mark of official influence. Indiscreet as ever, he shared his misgivings with some colleagues, saying he thought the whole thing damaged the reputation of the Third Reich abroad.

Hitler seems also to have realized in retrospect that the Reichstag trial was a mistake. "It was Hitler's first and last try at Russian-style monster trials," Putzi said. As the Führer complained to him one day over lunch, the judges had failed to grasp that at stake in Leipzig had been "questions of interests of the German state, not hair-splitting of Roman law." Hitler made it clear that judges would be guided in the future by "the interests of the movement and not abstract legal forms." He was as good as his word. Summary courts were introduced for all political crimes other than high treason, and a new People's Court was also established, with retrospective powers and looser requirements for evidence. "The need for factual evidence in many cases is due to the erroneous reasoning of the jurists, and therefore should be eliminated," the Nazis argued. "The guilt or innocence of a man is to be determined by whether or not he is dangerous to the existence of the State."

After their acquittal, Dimitroff and the others were due to fly to Russia. But there were strong rumors that Göring was plotting to have them killed before their plane could take off for Moscow. The trial had received a lot of attention in the American and British press and Putzi knew their deaths would be a public relations disaster. He hatched a plan with Göring's press chief, Martin Sommerfeldt, a decent man just as concerned about the regime's image abroad as he was. Sommerfeldt argued that the only way to dissuade his contrary boss from doing something was to have the foreign press claim he was about to do it. Thus, if they wanted to stop him having Dimitroff killed, all they needed to do was to have a story appear warning of such a plan.

Putzi turned to Louis Lochner for advice. The journalist was willing to help, but after discussing the matter with Ambassador Dodd, he realized that he might endanger the Associated Press's relations with the German government by accusing Göring in print of plotting a murder. They decided instead to make use of a young correspondent from Reuters, the rival British wire service, who had just arrived in town and could be excused for not knowing the rules.

The next day, Lochner and Putzi took him to the bar of the Adlon Hotel, and when Sommerfeldt dropped by, apparently by chance, they steered the conversation toward the plot. Sommerfeldt was suitably indignant at such a slur on his boss, and when the Reuters man asked for a denial, he was happy to give him one, provided it was attributed to a "reliable source." That evening the story ran on Reuters and Sommerfeldt sent his boss a copy. Göring was livid at first, but his temper cooled when he saw himself described as a soldier and a gentleman, and he happily released an official denial of the "horrible rumor" circulating. As a result, Dimitroff and two of his fellow Bulgarians made it safely to Russia.

Putzi's efforts to influence foreign policy were less successful. He made such an attempt in October 1933 at a time when tensions were growing between Hitler and Mussolini, the Italian Fascist leader. As the exponents of similar philosophies, the two men should have been natural allies. But relations between them were cool, especially over Austria, which was sandwiched uncomfortably between its two large and rapacious neighbors. Hitler was already starting to talk of Anschluss—annexing his homeland and adding it to the German Reich—while Mussolini wanted to maintain Austria's independence. In what clearly went beyond the competence of a foreign press spokesman, Putzi drew up a nine-point program to improve German-Austrian relations and had it delivered to the Austrian embassy. But when the Austrian ambassador contacted Konstantin von Neurath, the foreign minister, to discuss Putzi's suggestions, he knew nothing about it and complained to Hitler; he, in turn, was furious and reprimanded Putzi.

Putzi was undaunted, and early the following year, armed with a letter of recommendation from his close friend, Italian ambassador Vittorio Cerruti, he set off to Rome to visit Mussolini. It was not only a matter of trying to improve relations between the two dictators. Putzi had a personal motive, too, to see if he could persuade Mussolini to agree to a screening of his film, *Hans Westmar*, in Italy. This time, though, Putzi did not attempt to go behind von Neurath's back. The foreign minister thought the visit an excellent idea.

Putzi had little trouble securing an audience with *Il Duce,* but his reception was cool. Mussolini was not convinced Putzi was really coming on Hitler's behalf and showed little interest in his film. Putzi was at his persuasive best, however, and convinced him to allow a private screening at the Villa Torlonia. The film clearly had the desired effect, as, shortly afterward, Mussolini agreed to a second meeting in his office. This time, the atmosphere was much warmer. According to Putzi's subsequent account of their encounter, he shared with his host his concern at the poor state of ties between their two countries, especially over Austria. "Relations between our two countries are bad," Putzi told him. "It seems to me entirely wrong that these difficulties should exist between our two Fascist states."

Finding Mussolini even more receptive than he had hoped, Putzi then put forward his suggestion. Why not invite Hitler on a visit to Italy—say, to the Palazzo Vendramin in Venice, where Richard Wagner had died? What better place could there be for a meeting between two Wagner lovers? To Putzi's delight, Mussolini agreed. He also signed a photograph of himself and dedicated it to Hitler.

Putzi's joy was short-lived, however. Hitler was distinctly unimpressed when Putzi returned to Germany and boasted of his freelance diplomacy. Hitler questioned whether Mussolini's remarks really constituted an invitation, as such: although he could not help but be impressed by the signed portrait when it was produced in a fine silver frame. Putzi was convinced that Hitler simply did not want to give him credit for paving the way toward such an important breakthrough in foreign policy.

Putzi was also trying to influence policy at home, which in his eyes was taking an increasingly unwelcome direction. The dark goings-on within Gestapo headquarters and in the newly established concentration camps especially appalled him. Putzi's efforts often came in the form of helping out individuals in trouble with the regime. In the case of violinist Fritz Kreisler, who was listed as non-Aryan and stripped of his belongings, Putzi arranged for the foreign office to release his property. He also claimed to have secured the release of a number of people from the concentration camps, among them the British wife and child of a socialist member of the Reichstag who had fled Germany.

Putzi and others in the conservative camp, such as von Neurath, Schacht, Gürtner, and General Walther von Reichenau, continued naïvely to believe that Hitler could still be persuaded to see reason and moderate his policies. Of the group, Putzi was virtually the only one who still enjoyed almost daily access to the Führer, and they all agreed he should remain in his post. As he told one American visitor that year, he considered it his role to "restrain and try to civilise the new regime. . . . It was wild and violent but . . . it could and would quiet down and become more reasonable."

Putzi said later, "It was the experience of power that turned Hitler into an unrestrained sadist. . . . In the course of 1933 I gradually realised that the devil had got into him." In reality, the devil had entered Hitler long before.

Some contemporaries, like George Messersmith, also questioned how genuine Putzi's commitment was to the conservative cause. For the American consul general, Putzi was an opportunist, pure and simple, who despite his affable exterior was often working to undermine those whom he professed to be his closest friends. "He is constantly trying to give the impression to Americans, to correspondents, and to foreigners that he is a conservative and really out of sympathy with many acts of the party, but in fact this is merely a pose," Messersmith wrote.

Whatever the true nature of Putzi's feelings, he not only supported the Nazi regime but also continued his campaign of trying to sell it to the rest of the world. In a New Year's message to America on December 31, 1933, Putzi compared Hitler to President Franklin D. Roosevelt, both of whom, he said, were "self-made men." "That is, Roosevelt made himself by conquering an infirmity of the body, Hitler by conquering the infirmity of the German people."

Although considerable articles in the foreign press had been devoted to Hitler and his policies, the Nazi leader as a person remained an enigma to foreign readers. The first anniversary of his accession to power was rapidly approaching, but the interviews he had so far given had all been dry question-and-answer affairs, whose content had been vetted by the Propaganda Ministry. No one had been permitted to conduct a personal interview, which would have given some insight into his character. Lochner suggested to Putzi that he would be the man to do one. Putzi saw his point immediately. He knew how the American media worked.

The meeting was arranged for early February the following year. Lochner was given fifty minutes with the Führer. Hitler, dressed in the brown uniform of a Nazi storm trooper, was seated behind a desk in the right-hand corner of his spacious office as the American entered. He walked halfway across the room and greeted Lochner affably, motioning to a sofa. He and Putzi, the only other witness to the conversation, sat on straight-backed chairs. The interview, conducted in German, was wide-ranging. At one point, according to Lochner, Hitler's "face darkened and his voice grew hard." At other times, he found him using "crisp, precise words" or "pausing for a moment to reflect, then speaking quickly"; or, "speaking in a voice that vibrated with emotion, his jaw became firmly set, his index finger pointed straight at me."

Putzi was impressed with the result: he liked this kind of personalized interview and was convinced Hitler would approve too. He was wary, however, of sending a copy to the Propaganda Ministry because he was convinced that they would eliminate any personal references. When Lochner gave him a German translation of the article, Putzi decided to wait for his moment.

"I'm going to keep the manuscript in my pocket until I can place it directly in the Führer's hands," he told Lochner. "I want to make sure he is in a good humour when I hand it to him."

Putzi was as good as his word: a month later, the interview was approved.

—

ONE of the strangest projects with which Putzi became associated at this time was a book, *Hitler in der Karikatur der Welt* (*Hitler in the Caricature of the World*), which came out in September 1933. Putzi had become obsessed with what he considered the way in which the foreign press misunderstood and misrepresented Hitler and his policies. The political cartoons especially rankled. With his little mustache and the lock of hair falling across his forehead, Hitler was a gift to cartoonists; the result, understandably enough, was often hostile. Putzi decided to counter this by publishing a selection of the most critical of these cartoons—and then refuting each one with a description of the truth. He claimed as inspiration Hitler's idol, Frederick the Great, who once ordered that a pamphlet that was critical of him should be put on display so that as many citizens as possible could read it.

In his introduction to the book, Putzi lavished praise on Hitler as "an unbendable pure man of will and action," determined to build a better future. By publishing such "derisive and insulting" pictures of Hitler, he said it would be possible "to demonstrate the misproportion between invention and truth," until the glaring contrast between reality and what was written became apparent to all. "What is the miserable tin kettle music of the world press compared with the almost counterpoint-like consequence of the political actions of the Führer and the symphony of his successes?" he demanded.

The book begins with the cartoon "Hitlers Einzug in Berlin," from the April 1, 1924, edition of *Simplicissimus*, which Putzi had shown Hitler in Landsberg, depicting him riding on a charger through the Brandenburg

Gate. It follows with a selection of other caricatures, many of them from the German press, but also from some American, British, and French newspapers. Although varying in mood, they are a familiar mixture of Hitler's mustache and swastikas. Underlying them all is the simple message that Hitler and the Nazis mean violence and war.

One from the *Daily Express* of March 4, 1933, satirizes the intimidation of voters ahead of the election the next day. In it, the unfortunate voter must first pass through a swastika turnstile, walk past a row of Hitler supporters with their right arms outstretched, and then climb stairs between two tank treads to cast his ballot in a box. Putzi's attempt to counter it is feeble, to say the least: "The author of this caricature neglects to mention the fact that elections in Germany are decided by secret ballot which prevents any influencing of the result," he writes. Another cartoon, from *The New York Times* of April 2, 1933, shows Hitler leading Germania—the female figure that depicts Germany—by a rope, past a sign that says "To the Dark Ages." Putzi responds with a quote from an article in the *Daily Mail* in July 1933, by the paper's owner, Lord Rothermere, praising Germany's good fortune in having Hitler as its Führer. And so it went on, with more pictures of Nazi book-burning and various depictions of Hitler, either sitting perched on the top of a spiked Prussian helmet or riding a bucking bronco called Germany.

It is difficult to determine how effective the book was in helping the Nazi cause. Looking at it decades later, the cartoons and caricatures themselves leave a far stronger impression than Putzi's often rather lame refutations. It nevertheless appears to have sold well, and in September of the following year the same publishers brought out a follow-up entitled *Tat gegen Tinte*, also compiled by Putzi. It was a similar collection of gentle humor and biting satire, only this time arranged thematically under headings like "Hitler der Friedensstörer" (Hitler the Troublemaker), "Hitler der Terrorist" (Hitler the Terrorist), and "Hitler als Kunstreaktionär, Kulturunderdrücker und Rassepolitiker" (Hitler as Cultural Reactionary, Suppressor of Culture, and Racist Politician). This time, though, Putzi provided rather longer and more tedious commentaries, packed with statistics about everything from agricultural production to the rise in the number of weddings, to explain how misguided the criticisms were. In order to reassure any of the party faithful who were worried that they might have stumbled across some subversive literature, it also carried the reassurance in large type: "*Dieses Buch würde vom Führer und Kanzler durchgesehen und genehmigt*" (This book was read through and approved by the Führer and Chancellor).

12

IN 1934, Putzi received an invitation to attend his Harvard class's twenty-five-year reunion. It would have to be cleared with Hitler, and Putzi hesitated, waiting for the right moment to make his request. The chance came one afternoon when he was sitting in his office and received a call from Otto Dietrich, Hitler's press chief. Hitler was taking tea in the Kaiserhof Hotel and no one was there to sit with him. Although disappointed to be reduced to the role of "Reich's stopgap," Putzi reluctantly agreed to join the Führer. The hotel lounge was already filling up when he arrived. He found Hitler sitting in his favorite corner of the palm court, near the mock Hungarian orchestra. Word that the Führer was in residence always spread quickly—most probably, Putzi suspected, with the help of the waiters who earned tips by telephoning around the information. The clientele was less than high class; most of those present that afternoon were overdressed women in furs and with too much French perfume, keen to get a glimpse of their leader. They were a long way from the ideal of German womanhood—a teetotaler without makeup—preached by the Nazis, but this did not stop Hitler from eyeing them carefully as they walked past.

Assuming that Hitler wanted light relief, Putzi steered the conversation toward music, the subject that had always united them. As they talked about Strauss waltzes and Wagner, Hitler occasionally beat time to the music with his hand. Putzi became bolder, asking Hitler whether he would agree to his idea of going to Venice to meet Mussolini. Hitler said he was too busy to leave Berlin. Convinced that his pet project was

getting nowhere—and that his presence as an intermediary was therefore not required—Putzi broached the subject of the reunion.

"If that is the case, Herr Hitler," he said, "you will not be needing me
here. Have you any objection to my taking a short trip to the United
States?"

Hitler looked at him suspiciously. "What do you want to do there?
Sell that film of yours?"

"No," Putzi replied. "This year is the twenty-fifth reunion of my
Harvard class and it is more or less a point of honor to attend. It would
be a good opportunity to talk to old friends; some of them are very
influential by now. I may even see President Roosevelt."

It all proved far easier than he had expected; Hitler said he had no
objection. And so began a chain of events that almost certainly saved
Putzi's life.

———

HARVARD University puts especial emphasis on the part it plays in the
lives of its alumni from day one after graduating, not just through fund-
raising but also through an alumni relations program that has long been
the envy of almost every other university in the United States. Former
students regularly subscribe to the *Alumni Bulletin*, join the local
Harvard Club, give to the Fund Council, vote for overseers, and attend
class reunions. Strenuous efforts are made by the secretary to keep track
of addresses; even the handful that appear to have been lost may not have
given up completely on the college. Of all the reunions, the twenty-fifth
is probably the most important, as it falls at a time when most alumni
are in their mid- to late forties and at the height of their careers. The
twenty-five-year reunion class is expected to present the university with
a donation large enough to cover the difference between what they paid
for their education and what it cost Harvard to provide it.

Hanfstaengl was not merely to attend the celebrations, however. The
class secretary, Dr. Elliott Carr Cutler, an eminent brain surgeon who
was to be chief marshal of the alumni at the commencement,
announced that he had chosen Putzi to be his aide, which would mean
he would have to wear a top hat and morning coat and carry a baton.
Despite the obviously private nature of the visit, Putzi would be the
highest-ranking Nazi to visit America since the party had come to
power. Many who had watched with horror the events unfolding in
Germany were appalled.

The American press immediately sensed a story. "Any Harvard alumnus returning to Cambridge, Mass., in June for commencement can learn all he desires to know about Adolf Hitler through Dr. Ernst Franz Sedgwick Hanfstaengl, the German chancellor's personal liaison officer with the British and American press and one of his most intimate friends," wrote *The New York Times* on March 29. Putzi told the newspaper he was looking forward to the reunion "with the greatest anticipation." He said he might also bring along a copy of his film, *Hans Westmar*, which he had already shown to Mussolini and notables in Stockholm. "That film can show better than any words of mine what we Nazis stand for." He said he would accept Cutler's assessment of five hundred dollars as a contribution to the class reunion fund, but would have to place the equivalent in reichsmarks in a German bank for the use of Harvard students coming to Germany to complete their education. Putzi, the newspaper noted in a short report from Cambridge, was "extremely popular among the members of his class and Harvard would not object if the class of 1909 wanted to watch his film."

The next day, *The Harvard Crimson* published a letter from Benjamin Halpern, a student at the Harvard Graduate School of Arts and Sciences. In the letter, headed "Heil Hitler," Halpern, who was Jewish, criticized Cutler's decision to invite Putzi and said he would stay away from the commencement ceremony. "It seems a very extraordinary thing indeed that he [Cutler] should be allowed to select his aides at will or perhaps from among the highest bidders without any control from the administrative offices," Halpern complained. The newspaper noted that many other Jewish alumni shared his concerns. Although it published the letter, the *Crimson* did not share its sentiments. "To object to the presence of a Harvard man among other Harvard men in any capacity, on purely political grounds, is an extremely childish thing to do," it said.

One evening shortly after the initial *Crimson* articles, as Putzi was practicing an especially tricky Chopin étude in his home in Munich, he received a call from Cutler, warning him about the growing press campaign. Putzi said it would be better not to come at all; Cutler suggested a compromise—he should come in a private capacity rather than as his aide. Putzi agreed, but in order to calm passions, they decided to give the impression to the press that he would be staying away.

And so, on April 5, *The New York Times* ran a story on its front page quoting Cutler as saying Putzi would not be attending after all. No reason was given, but the surgeon said he stood by his decision to invite him. "In selecting Hanfstaengl for the post of aide, it seemed to me that

Harvard alumni who have always stood for the fundamental principles of a university, the right of free speech and the toleration of all beliefs, might properly welcome this graduate back," he said. Harvard president James Bryant Conant, who was spending the week in New Hampshire, declined comment on the affair, but Halpern, the letter writer, was delighted. "Hanfstaengl as the representative of a government which considers the intellectuals the dirt of the earth and free speech a rank poison has no place at such an event as a Harvard commencement," he told the newspaper. "His presence could only arouse strife and discord and help to break down the traditions of tolerance for which Harvard stands."

Almost three weeks later, Putzi weighed in with an interview with the Associated Press, which was picked up by a number of papers. He proclaimed himself to have been "flabbergasted" by the controversy over his appointment and made it clear that he was extremely unlikely to attend after all—even though he did not rule it out completely. "To find myself in the midst of a heated Harvard controversy, which extends even to Congressional circles, is the more surprising as Harvard since time immemorial has stood for freedom of opinion," he declared. "I would love to attend and I certainly will do so if my duties here permit. As I am overcrowded with work, the chances are none too good. As for propaganda, I never made propaganda and never shall. Scores of classmates and other American citizens whom I don't even know are asking me to come."

Even if he was unable to attend in person, Putzi was still keen on making his mark on the event. And so, on May 24, he wrote to Conant with another suggestion. He proposed creating a "Dr. Hanfstaengl Scholarship," which would "enable an outstanding Harvard student, preferably the son of my old classmates, to study in Germany in any field of art or science." Six months of the year-long scholarship were to be spent in his hometown of Munich or "Germany's cultural centre" as he described it. This was intended to repay in part the "incalculable advantages" that his time at Harvard had given him, both in terms of knowledge of America and the world and of the "spirit of discipline and fair play inculcated on the sporting fields of Harvard."

The letter was made public two weeks later. After tipping off a few selected reporters, Putzi walked into the ancient banking house of Delbruck, Schickler & Co. and wrote out a check for twenty-five hundred reichsmarks (one thousand dollars) to the order of Conant. "This represents a scholarship I am offering to some Harvard student to be selected by President Conant," he told the teller. "The student can use the money for a semester's study in Munich and another semester anywhere else in Germany." Asked by one of the reporters whether this meant he was no longer planning to attend the reunion, he replied with an Italian proverb: "*Qui vivra verra*"—literally, "He who lives will see." *The New York Times* reported that a decision on whether or not to accept the money would be taken when Conant met the Harvard Corporation a few days later.

The controversy over Putzi's potential visit reflected the turbulence of the time not just at Harvard but in America as a whole, which had been turned upside down, first by the Wall Street crash and recession, then by FDR's New Deal. For those looking beyond the borders of the United States, probably the major preoccupation—and the greatest unknown—was Hitler. Opinion was becoming increasingly polarized between his apologists—or those who were at least prepared to give the nascent Nazi regime the benefit of the doubt—and those who rightly saw in the movement's anti-Semitism and bullying tactics the tragedy to come. There were fears, too, of war.

There was the same dichotomy of views about Hitler within the microcosm of Harvard itself. Matters were further complicated by a traditional commitment to freedom of speech and a fierce loyalty to alumni, regardless of what they had done since leaving the university. The National Student League, which was in the forefront of criticism of Putzi's visit, had organized a number of protests against Nazism and Fascism and tried to organize a general walkout on classes by students and professors to protest against the trend toward war. There were many, however, who dismissed the dictatorships as little worse than misguided. Professors suggested Hitler's regime would not last, while articles by Mussolini frequently appeared in the *Crimson* without even generating controversy. In an editorial on May 17, 1934, the newspaper noted the strong opposition aroused at Harvard by the student league's activities and urged reform and a period of introspection. "Not only have they failed to put their program across, but their attempts to do so have diverted attention from their purposes," it complained. "Claiming freedom of speech, they are apparently unwilling to let Mr. Hanfstaengl come here and say what he pleases."

▬

ON the evening of June 10, Putzi threw a splendid garden party at his home at Pariser Platz 3, in Berlin. Many of the Nazi notables were there, although the big three—Hitler, Goebbels, and Göring—did not attend.

Putzi, dressed in a dark suit, presided. Helene was statuesque in a flowing white evening dress. The timing was deliberate. The North German Lloyd liner, the *Europa*, the last ship that would have gotten Putzi to Harvard on time for the festivities, was due to leave later that evening, but Putzi had still not said for certain whether or not he was going. The significance of the event was not wasted on the American reporters who had been closely following the affair. On the bottom of page nine of *The New York Times* the following day was a small report noting that Putzi had stayed in Berlin, thereby passing up the last chance to go to the reunion.

Even as the morning editions hit the newsstands the newspapers were having to hastily revise their stories. Unbeknownst to the partygoers, Putzi's young assistant, Harald Voigt, was already in America making the necessary preparations for his trip. While his guests were still eating and drinking, Putzi, clad in a raincoat and dark glasses, slipped out of his house, caught a late train to Cologne, and from there took a mail plane to the French port of Cherbourg, where the *Europa* was making its last stop before setting off across the Atlantic. With him he had five large suitcases and three wooden crates, each of which contained a bust. One was of President von Hindenburg, which he intended to give to the United States Military Academy at West Point; the second was of Arthur Schopenhauer, the German philosopher, destined for the Harvard philosophy department; and the third was of Christoph Willibald von Gluck, Putzi's favorite composer, for the Harvard music department's "golden chapel."

The newspapers were forced to admit the following day that they had been duped. "Whether Herr Hanfstaengl's missing of the normal connections and his belated chase of the *Europa* was caused by indecision continuing until the last moment is a matter of conjecture," observed *The New York Times*.

The boat trip was pleasant and uneventful. Putzi was in civilized company far from the stresses of Nazi Germany and was able to relax. There was concern in Harvard, however, at his decision to attend, not so much because of fear of what he would do and say but rather about the use that opponents of the Nazis might make of the visit. The university, fearing a possible bomb attack on its controversial guest that might also harm innocent bystanders, discussed the impending visit with the governor of Massachusetts; he, in turn, consulted the state police. New York's Criminal Alien Squad was put on alert to watch subversives, on the grounds that "they know most of the radicals of prominence on sight." It was decided that a guard of detectives and uniformed patrolmen would protect Putzi when he landed. They would prevent any demonstration against him, escort him to his hotel, and accompany him anywhere he went in the city.

The American Jewish Committee and B'nai B'rith also tried to calm tensions. Their joint consultative council issued a statement. Although the council "abhors the policies of the Hitler regime" it urged "no discourtesy of any kind" be shown to Putzi. This was on the understanding that his visit was solely for the purpose of attending the class reunion. The German consulate general described his visit as purely personal and said he would not be officially received. A congressional committee investigating Nazi propaganda in America denied reports it intended to interview Putzi over his possible role in the Black Tom affair and other acts of German sabotage in America during the First World War. The State Department declared it also had no desire to question him.

With Putzi on his way, controversy flared up again in the press. One of the harshest attacks was penned by the prominent journalist Heywood Broun, in his column "It Seems to Me" in the *New York World-Telegram* on June 15. Like Putzi, Broun was an old boy of Harvard. This did not prevent him from denouncing the controversial visitor, whom he accused of "fomenting the cruel religious and economic persecutions going on in Germany." He predicted that the progress of "Hitler's agent" through America was certain to be marked by a series of bloody riots. For this reason, he declared that Putzi should be forcibly removed from the *Europa* on arrival and sent to Ellis Island as an undesirable alien. Hitler's "minstrel" should be greeted with "thunders of silence and mountain ranges of inattention," he said. Broun also claimed to have learned new details from some of Putzi's former classmates about his expulsion from the New York Harvard Club following the sinking of the *Lusitania*, which he said had been prompted by a fistfight that ended with the German lying unconscious on the floor. Nor did he have a good word for his piano-playing skills, commenting merely: "He plays very loudly. . . ." Broun concluded, "I think that Dr. Ernst Franz Sedgwick Hanfstaengl should be officially advised to play in his own backyard."

The Harvard Crimson, by contrast, rallied to Putzi's defense. It argued in an editorial that he should not only be extended the same greeting given others returning for their twenty-fifth anniversary, but also even be given an honorary degree "as a tribute to the position to which he has risen."

—

SATURDAY, June 16, 1934, dawned fair in New York. The weather forecast called for a high of 81 degrees. The front page of *The New York Times* reported the last-minute suspension of a steel strike by the Amalgamated Association of Iron, Steel and Tin Workers that was due to start that midnight; a bungled assassination attempt on Cuba's president, Carlos Mendieta; and confirmation that the American's president's tall, blonde daughter, Mrs. Anna Roosevelt Dall, was going to end her eight-year marriage to her New York stockbroker husband.

Hitler was also in the headlines, with the announcement that he and Mussolini, in a meeting in Venice, had agreed on "freedom for Austria," with the country's independence maintained at all costs. In Berlin, meanwhile, a retrial of those accused of murdering Horst Wessel in January 1930 ended with Sol Epstein and Hans Ziegler condemned to death by decapitation. The newspaper also carried a statement from Putzi's assistant, Harald Voigt, on an inside page, dismissing suggestions that his visit would lead to difficulties. If there were problems, he claimed they would emanate, "in my judgment, not from Dr. Hanfstaengl and not from true Americans." The newspaper claimed Voigt had been irritated by indications that Putzi's visit was not being taken seriously, chief among them the question of whether he would appear at the reunion in his famous "self-invented chocolate-colored uniform," which, it said, had earned him the nickname of "the Chocolate Soldier" in Berlin.

That afternoon, the *Europa* steamed into New York Harbor and docked at Pier 86, at Forty-sixth Street and the Hudson River. A crowd of fifteen hundred to two thousand demonstrators was waiting for Putzi, penned in behind police barricades. Many carried banners proclaiming "Oust Nazi Hanfstaengl," "Ship the Hitler Agent Back" and "Free Ernst Thälmann." Approximately one hundred uniformed police, backed by another fifty-six in plainclothes, were deployed to maintain order.

Putzi, meanwhile, was giving an impromptu press conference in the first-class saloon to forty journalists who had come on board with the quarantine and immigration officials. Those seeing him for the first time were struck by the sight of this tall man with a great shock of black hair. Dressed in a dark suit with subtle stripes, black shoes, light-tan soft shirt, and black tie with diagonal white stripes, he was, commented one observer, "the acme of self-possession."

Putzi was in a jovial mood. Musing on his time at Harvard and his regret at not having been back in America since 1921, he was at pains to insist that his visit was a purely private one. Hitler, he said, had been reluctant to allow him to come on grounds that there was "much work to be done" in Germany. But after missing both the ten- and fifteen-year reunions, he had been determined to come this time and had eventually won Hitler over. Asked to comment on Heywood Broun's demand for him to be interned on Ellis Island, he replied sweetly: "He's a nice boy, a very nice boy. I can't say why he doesn't want me in the country, but it is probably just class jealousy. He was a class ahead of me, you know." He also insisted, in vain, that people tended to call him "Hanfy" rather than "Putzi" these days.

The reporters tried to steer the interview onto meatier stuff, in particular the Nazis' growing mistreatment of the Jews. Putzi was equally determined not to respond. He made no secret of his anti-Semitism back in Germany, but was reluctant to be drawn into such contentious matters while in America.

"I am sorry, I can't answer that," he said. "That is a political question. Perhaps at some future date I shall have something to say. When will that be? Some years from now."

Putzi brushed off a Jewish reporter who tried to corner him later as he walked up to the sundeck, asking for five minutes of his time. "I should like to give you five million years," Putzi snapped back. Later, in a brief interview for the newsreels, he said simply: "The situation of the Jew in Germany is fairly normal." He then posed for photographs with a couple of former classmates who had made the journey across the Atlantic with him. At the request of the photographers, he also stood on his own, leaning against the ship's rail, with his arm raised in the Hitler salute.

The protestors had been working on the assumption that Putzi would be put off at a midtown dock— Pier 86. From there, it was thought, he would take a taxi to the 125th Street station of the New York, New Haven & Hartford Railroad and then board the 6 PM train to Boston. And so they swarmed around each car leaving the pier, to check whether Putzi was inside and booing a few unfortunate *Europa* passengers they mistook for him.

Putzi was still on board, though. Commodore Scharf, the ship's captain, invited him onto the bridge and handed him his binoculars. It was clear that Putzi had to avoid going ashore by the main gate and they paused to devise an alternative plan. At that moment, six young men in brand-new Harvard blazers and ties suddenly appeared on board. The most senior of them announced himself as Benjamin Goodman of the New York Police Department.

"President Roosevelt has sent a message to say that he hopes you will have a pleasant visit," Goodman said after presenting his pass. "We are here to ensure that there will be no incidents."

And so, together with the six men and his mountains of luggage, Putzi boarded the tugboat *William C. Moore*, which put him ashore at 125th Street. After dining at the Claremont Inn on Riverside Drive, he went on at about 7 PM to the Stork Club on East Fifty-first Street with Quentin Reynolds, who had left Berlin and was now working in New York for *Collier's*. The pair were entranced by Olive Jones, a "hostess-entertainer" at the club, and spent most of the evening listening to her piano waltzes.

"A decided talent," Putzi told her, as he leaned on the piano. "But you must practice five hours a day; three hours at the piano and two in retrospect."

Jones was equally taken by Putzi. "He's just a great big Don Juan," she told reporters. "He was so kind; he said I ought to go to Berlin to study music—and what d'you think? He said if I went to Berlin he'd personally supervise my career."

Putzi and Reynolds left at 11.30 PM and took the night train for Boston, which departed a quarter of an hour later.

Reynolds still had mixed feelings about Putzi after their clashes in Berlin. He was there in a professional capacity, though, in connection with a piece that Putzi had agreed to write for *Collier's* magazine. According to a German newspaper report, he also handed Putzi his fee: the considerable sum of two thousand dollars.

The essay, entitled "My Leader," which appeared on August 4, was that week's cover story. Highly personal in tone, it told of Putzi's life and how he became attracted to National Socialism. It also set out to present the "real picture" of Hitler, and dismiss the various "misunderstandings" that had arisen about him and his party in America and elsewhere abroad. The Germans, Putzi wrote, had been offered a clear choice between Communism and National Socialism. "One promised chaos, adherence to principles abhorrent to the German nature and virtual allegiance to a governing body of foreigners," he wrote. "The other promised stabilization of industry, the return of self-respect, the unification of all parties into one German nation and the eventual return of economic prosperity." Germany had chosen Hitler, which meant it "cast out the undesirable elements that for many years had been throttling my country." He went on to paint a glowing portrait of a nation fighting poverty and unemployment and whose people, once cowed and beaten, now marched down the streets, their heads held erect.

Although clearly tailoring his comments for an American audience, Putzi could not entirely refrain from a touch of anti-Semitism, accusing the Jews of having too enthusiastically embraced the role of "pacemaker for Bolshevism" and of having associated themselves too closely with the "rotten, disorganizing forces" feeding on the German body politic. The description of Hitler was predictably flattering: a "dynamo" with incredible reserves of energy, stamina, and patience, who regularly worked fifteen-hour days and had a personal life entirely beyond reproach. Like President Franklin D. Roosevelt, he had given Germany a "new deal," Putzi wrote. He concluded with a word of warning, however. "If misfortune comes we will face it," he said. "If we are hit, 'we will be hit in the face—not in the back,' for that is our heritage once taken from us but restored by Adolf Hitler."

The train from New York pulled in to Boston's South Station at 7.30 AM. Ralph Bradley, a cotton merchant and fellow member of the Naughty Nines, at whose home in Back Bay Putzi was due to stay, had climbed on board at his local station, greeting him with a cheery, "Hello, Putzi." A crowd of reporters was waiting at the station; so, too, were the superintendent of police, the assistant superintendent, twenty-nine uniformed men, a squad of detectives largely from the alien squad, and a number of Massachusetts state troopers—but, surprisingly, no communists, socialists, or anti-Nazis.

Bradley drove Putzi first to his home, where several other classmates were waiting. Then, it was on for lunch at Cutler's home in Brookline. They were joined there by Abbott Lawrence Lowell, who had stepped down the previous year after almost a quarter of a century as Harvard's president. He asked Putzi to explain Hitler's popularity. The reply was simple: With the war lost and the communists in charge of the streets, it was necessary to build things up again. The sheer number of parties in the Weimar Republic—as many as thirty-two—made decisive action impossible. They therefore all had to be rolled up into a single state party, with Hitler at its head.

"If a car gets stuck in the mud and begins to sink deeper and deeper and the engine stops, and then a man comes along and pours something into the works which starts it up again, you don't ask what it was he put in," Putzi told him. "You set to and get the damned thing out. It may only have been *Beigeisterungsschnapps*, a mixture of mother's ruin and exaltation, but it is enough for the time being."

"This whatever-you-called-it may be all right to start with," Lowell replied. "But what happens when the driver gets drunk on it?"

Putzi had no reply; he was already beginning to believe Lowell was on to something. That evening he held a press conference in the little garden in front of Bradley's house. The atmosphere was light-hearted, with Putzi launching into panegyrics on baseball and his love of gin. Asked who was the better orator—Hitler or Roosevelt—he replied: "That is like asking which is better in a storm—umbrella or overshoes," barely concealing his grin of satisfaction at what he considered a rather clever answer.

The journalists wanted answers to more serious questions and again their concerns centered on the plight of the Jews under the Nazis. Putzi was just as reluctant to give a straight answer as he had been on the *Europa*.

"I do not think it is good to discuss that question," he said. "It doesn't help Germany and it doesn't help the Jews." And with that he paused.

"But I will say this," he added in a phrase subject to different interpretations. "I will say that the Jew's situation in Germany is going to be normal before long." Some read a sinister meaning into his words.

Shortly afterward, the journalists left him in peace. When he went to sleep that night, the Bradley house was guarded by six policemen.

The following afternoon, Putzi attended a memorial service in the new university chapel for the Harvard dead of the First World War. He agreed afterward again to answer questions from the press. As the reporters crowded around him in a shady corner of Harvard Yard, a voice called out.

"What did you mean in your interview yesterday that the 'Jewish problem' would soon be restored to normal?" demanded Rabbi Joseph Shabow, also a Harvard alumnus. "Did you mean by extermination?"

Putzi was clearly offended. "Now, now," he replied. The session was quickly declared over.

After a few days with Bradley, Putzi moved northward to Beverly Farms and the home of another wealthy classmate, Louis Agassiz Shaw. He also managed to fit in a visit to a horse race and a trip to watch the Boston Red Sox play the St. Louis Browns. Putzi would have found it difficult to keep a low profile even if he wanted to. For his protection he had been allocated four state troopers, two of whom were Jews. All had been ordered to wear the alumni uniform of white flannel pants, sports jacket, and striped tie. In the end, they served as a shield not against protestors but against the army of reporters from New York and Boston who popped up at almost every stage of his visit.

That Wednesday came the climax of his trip, the Harvard parade. After several days of rain, the weather was warm and dry. The celebrations began at noon, when the seniors in their graduating caps and gowns and the alumni in their picturesque costumes gathered for lunch in the various houses of the university. Then, after lunch, Cutler, who was the chief alumni marshal, led the parade from the houses across Lars Anderson Bridge to the ivy-covered football stadium for the traditional confetti battle. It soon became clear that thanks to the huge publicity that accompanied his decision to participate, Putzi was to be the center of attention.

Leading the parade were the last few survivors of the classes of 1869, 1873, and 1878, tottering their way unsteadily forward. Then came the class of 1914, in white pants, orange polo shirts, and black caps; and those of 1919, wearing white pants, fancy blue tunics, and blue-and-white caps in the form of eagles. A group of them held aloft a placard that read:

1919
FOR CLASS PRESIDENT
MAX HANFSTANGEL
FOR CLASS VICE PRESIDENT
ADOLPH KEEZAR

Just how amusing Max Keezar, a popular Jewish merchant on Harvard Square, found this juxtaposition of the names was not clear.

There was worse to come: next into the stadium were the class of '24. Dressed in Bavarian peasant costume, complete with lederhosen, long socks, and dark green hats with feathers, they goose-stepped their way around the stadium, their right hands stretched out in Nazi salutes. Behind them they dragged a huge beer truck, labeled Harvard Beer and Ale, from which they dispensed beer all afternoon.

Then came the class of '09, which, some three hundred strong, was by far the biggest in the parade. They were preceded by five members of the class of '19, who carried the placard "Hanfstangel for President" and also gave the Nazi salute. Most of the Naughty Niners were wearing straw hats, dark coats, and white trousers. Putzi eschewed the class uniform in favor of dark soft hat, blue coat, and brown trousers. In his button hole was a red carnation. There was no goose-stepping or Nazi salutes for Putzi's class, although Putzi himself gave a few such salutes to friends he spotted. Finally came the seniors, who were graduating that day in their black caps and gowns.

After all the speeches were done, the seniors, alumni, and guests all rose to sing "Fair Harvard." Then, as the last strains faded out, the sky was suddenly full of multicolored streamers and tiny pieces of paper. The annual confetti battle raged for a full fifteen minutes before the crowd moved to Soldier's Field for the Harvard-Yale baseball game. Harvard won, three to two.

As Putzi was walking after the confetti battle, a smiling, plump man came over to him. He looked vaguely familiar but Putzi struggled in vain to recall his name. Halfway toward the middle of the stadium, he rather ostentatiously shook Putzi's hand; when the crowd saw him they roared their approval. Putzi only found out later that the man was Max Pinansky, Maine's first Jewish judge. The picture appeared a few hours later on the front pages of the afternoon papers and Putzi, who had taken absolutely no initiative in the matter, found himself hailed as a peacemaker. It was, he thought, "marvelous pro-German propaganda, worth a hundred interviews with Hitler." The response back in Germany was far less positive.

Putzi stayed away from the commencement the following afternoon. It was just as well. Members of the National Student League and other opponents of the visit kept up a steady protest throughout Conant's speech, drowning out his words as he thanked Cutler, who had just announced a gift to the university of a hundred thousand dollars from the class of '09. Then there was a sudden commotion. Two women, who had slipped into the Sever rectangle and taken seats there, suddenly threw off their shawls and looped chains to which they had handcuffed themselves around the chairs and the wooden platform on which they were sitting. They then tossed away the keys. On the backs of their dresses, which were now visible, anti-Nazi slogans had been sewn with red ribbons.

"Down with Hitler," read one. Another read: "Free Thälmann and Michaelson"—a reference to two of Germany's leading political prisoners. Police swooped in on the pair and quickly unfastened the chains. A piece of railing was torn away as the women were led off to the Fogg Art Museum across the street and then to Cambridge police headquarters. They identified themselves as Sheila Shugrue, age eighteen, and Nora Burke, age twenty, both of Cambridge.

There was more trouble later the same evening in Harvard Square. Charles McBride, twenty-one, also of Cambridge, walked into the square with a chain around his waist and locked himself to the iron fence around the yard outside Lehman Hall. Wearing a white sweatshirt with red lettering, "Free Thälmann," sewn on the back, he spoke for fifteen minutes, denouncing Hitler, Putzi, and the Nazi regime and accusing Harvard of disgracing itself by inviting Putzi to the celebrations. He was relieved by another twenty-one year old, Joseph Jacobs, from the Dorchester section of Boston, who continued speaking until the police arrived. A large crowd had already gathered and was blocking the traffic.

The police had been caught almost completely unawares. They had been watching out for demonstrations on Harvard property but had gone back to their stations when the ceremony ended. They finally arrived, and after borrowing a hacksaw from a nearby garage to cut McBride free, they took him and Jacobs to the station. The protest didn't end there, though. Another youth, claiming to represent the Marine Industrial Union, climbed a telegraph pole and began denouncing Hitler before climbing down and running off, throwing away the "Free Thälmann" sweatshirt. Some protestors then climbed on the shoulders of their friends and started haranguing the crowd, while others began handing out stickers that read: "Give Hanfstaengl a degree, Master of Torture, drive out the Nazi butcher, free Thälmann and all imprisoned anti-Fascists."

As the crowd reached two thousand, more police arrived on the scene, sirens blaring as they moved in. Every time anyone tried to speak, the police pulled them down and arrested them. Those arrested were charged with disturbing the peace, and seven of them also for speaking in a public place without a permit. As they sat in police headquarters that evening, they sang the "Internationale."

Putzi had missed all the drama; he had spent the day in the country. Later that evening he arrived in Cambridge and went to the alumni association headquarters in Wadsworth House, just off Harvard Square, unaware that anything untoward had happened. He left later for New London, Connecticut, where he was due to attend the Yale-Harvard boat race the next day.

Putzi spent the weekend on the North Shore with a former girlfriend who lived in Beverly Farms. Then, in the middle of the following week, he reappeared in Boston to dine with members of the German consulate. The press, which was closely following the visit, had another announcement to make. The following Saturday, Putzi was to attend the society wedding of the season, the marriage of John Jacob Astor III, America's wealthiest bachelor, and Ellen Tuck French in Newport, Rhode Island. Putzi was to be guest of honor at an informal prewedding luncheon to be given by Francis O. French, the bride's father, although some newspapers suggested that the bride's mother was not entirely happy about it.

The controversy over the invitation to Harvard, meanwhile, refused to die down. *The New York Times* published a letter, signed by a Robert Skliar of Washington, D.C., claiming that Putzi's presence made a mockery of the university's liberal traditions: "Can any liberal accept and defend a man whose fundamental activity consists in organizing, abetting and defending persecution and violence applied in Germany and to be applied in the United States when the day comes?" he wrote. "Dr. Hanfstaengl may or may not be a very charming person, but a university is no place for a man who devoted the best part of his lifetime to destroy intellectual freedom, humiliate the finest minds and burn the books they produced."

13

THE narrow streets around the old Trinity Church in the heart of Newport, Rhode Island, were packed. The wedding service was not due to start until 4 PM, but the people had already begun to gather during the morning, standing closely pressed in the street and on the sidewalk, apparently oblivious to the heat. From time to time the police would push them back to make way for the cars of invited guests, but they would soon surge forward again. Photographers clung to the iron railings around the graveyard and rooftops on the other side of the street.

This was the social event of the season, a high point in the calendar of America's most prominent families, known as the Four Hundred. That afternoon, the scions of two of the country's oldest and richest families were to be married. John Jacob Astor, twenty-one, was probably America's most eligible bachelor. His great-great-grandfather, a fur trader, had established the basis of the family's wealth and the work had been continued by his father, who lost his life on the *Titanic*, leaving a vast fortune to be shared between Jacob and his half brother, Vincent. Astor's bride, Ellen Tuck French, was only marginally less grand. Just eighteen, she was a granddaughter of Amos Tuck French and related to the Vanderbilts.

As with all the grandest of families, there was inevitably a whiff of scandal. The groom's mother, Madeleine, who was rescued from the *Titanic*, had caused a stir the previous November when she married Enzo Fiermonte, an Italian boxer, who at just twenty-six was only five years older than her own son. There were doubts until the last moment whether she would attend this wedding; in the end, she did make an appearance, dressed in a gown of blue organdy in cape effect with a large hat. Wisely, perhaps, Fiermonte stayed away.

The ceremony was replete with symbols of early American tradition. The church, a long, narrow, weather-beaten white clapboard building with a towering white steeple and gilded spire and weather vane, was little changed since it was built in 1726. The couple was to be married according to the ancient ritual of the Protestant Episcopal Church, whose worshipers came to New England with the first settlers.

Despite their enormous wealth, the emphasis was on simplicity. There was a marked absence of extravagant floral displays and gifts of expensive jewelry. Although the bride and groom received numerous gifts—including many fine pieces of china and silverware—they were, according to *The New York Times*, which put its report of the wedding on its front page the next day, "on the whole of the sort that any ordinary couple of moderate circumstances might enjoy."

Simplicity was a relative term, of course. Around two hundred and fifty people were invited, drawn from some of America's most patrician families. They had received invitations engraved, simply, by Tiffany of New York with the words: "Please present this card at Trinity Church Saturday the Thirtieth of June." A number of local parishioners had also been invited and were admitted by vestrymen who recognized them. The gate on the Church Street side was manned by Pinkerton detectives and local police who kept out gate-crashers. A plush red carpet had been laid from the gate to the door of the church. Inside the open doorway stood the ushers, resplendent in black cutaways, white waistcoats, gray striped trousers, high wing collars, lavender ascot ties, white gloves and spats, and black shoes. In their lapels they wore white carnations.

Putzi was one of the first guests to arrive that afternoon. Because of the intense heat many of the guests had opted for informal wear. A stickler for tradition, he was decked out in top hat, black coat, and striped gray trousers—one of the few people outside the bridal party to be thus attired. He paused for a moment for photographers.

When the bride arrived, a gasp went up from the crowd. A tall, slender woman, Ellen Tuck French was dressed from head to foot in white, with a gown of heavy ivory satin in princess style with a V-neck and pointed sleeves and a fifteen-foot train falling from the shoulders. Her reddish brown hair was discernible through a long tulle veil in coronet effect caught up with orange blossoms. She carried a bouquet of white orchids and lilies of the valley. She paused for photographers before walking through the churchyard and then through a side door of the church on her father's arm.

The ceremony lasted just nine minutes and was according to the modernized Episcopal ritual. The bride promised to love and honor, but not to obey, her husband. The bridegroom, dressed in black cutaway, striped gray trousers, and white ascot tie, was mopping his brow with his handkerchief because of the heat as he stood waiting at the altar.

Looking solemn, they posed for pictures in the bright sunshine outside the church, before boarding their Rolls-Royce, bound for a reception for three hundred people at their summer home, Mapleshade, on Red Cross Avenue. Champagne, salads, and sandwiches were served to guests under brightly colored umbrellas as a gypsy orchestra, brought in specially from New York, played. The couple slipped off quietly that evening for a honeymoon that was to take them to Vancouver and Seattle. They were spared the usual battery of rice and confetti after a small group of friends erroneously told the crowd they had already left by a back entrance. While private detectives stood guard, servants were dispatched to local wine shops for copious supplies of champagne.

———

JUNE 30, 1934, was destined to go down in history as more than just the day of the Astor wedding. Back in Germany, events were taking a dramatic turn. The crisis had been brewing for months. The euphoria that greeted Hitler's assumption of power the previous year had long since faded; the economy was slowing and the Nazi rhetoric of national renewal was not being matched by the provision of much-needed jobs. Although there was no overt opposition as such, discontent was growing.

Some of the nationalists allied with von Papen dreamed of turning the discontent to their own advantage, toppling Hitler and putting in his place a more conventional right-wing dictatorship. "We are partly responsible that this fellow has come to power," said Ernst Jung, a right-wing intellectual and one of Papen's speechwriters. "We must get rid of him again." On June 17, Papen had delivered a blistering speech, written by Jung, denouncing a "false personality cult" around Hitler and criticizing other aspects of Nazi rule. Goebbels immediately banned the speech from print, but it was too late to prevent extracts appearing in the *Frankfurter Zeitung*, one of Germany's leading newspapers.

More serious for Hitler was what to do about Ernst Röhm, whose SA was becoming a law unto itself. As the year went on, Hitler seemed to have become increasingly convinced that he should break with him, but did not appear initially to have decided how dramatic that break should be. Röhm's behavior had made him powerful enemies, and the conservatives were keen to see him cut down to size in the interest of restoring internal peace. When Hitler went to see Hindenburg on June 21, General Werner von Blomberg, the defense minister, made it clear that the Führer would have to act to curb the SA—or see the president declare martial law and hand power to the army. A number of leading Nazis, including Göring, Himmler, Hess, and Bormann, also wanted to see an end to Röhm. As a former Luftwaffe officer, Göring, in particular, likely would have sided with the army in any showdown with Röhm. Rumors, undoubtedly false, began to appear that Röhm and the SA were plotting a coup.

Hitler appears to have finally decided to take action on the evening of June 28, after he learned that Papen was due to meet Hindenburg two days later with the aim of constraining not just Röhm and the SA but also him. Action, when it came, was swift—and Hitler took personal charge. All SA leaders were told to attend a meeting in the Bavarian town of Bad Wiessee late in the morning of June 30; Hitler had already flown down to Munich at 2 AM. Some four and a half hours later, he arrived at Röhm's hotel with members of his entourage and a detachment of police. Pistol in hand, Hitler declared Röhm a traitor and had him arrested. Several others were taken with him to Stadelheim jail— among them Edmund Heines, the SA's chief group leader for Silesia, who had been found in a room near Röhm's in bed with a young man. Röhm was given a pistol and the latest special edition of the *Beobachter,* which had an article detailing the putsch he was accused of planning. It was hoped he would draw the appropriate conclusions and kill himself. He failed to take the hint and was shot. A number of other top SA officials were also executed. The massacre was not confined to the storm troopers, however. Among others killed during what became known as the Night of the Long Knives were leading conservatives such as Kurt von Schleicher, the former chancellor, and his wife, and Herbert von Bose, Papen's cabinet chief. Papen himself was placed under a form of house arrest. Although no definitive total figure of the number of dead was given, it was probably as high as two hundred.

PUTZI was unaware of the dramatic events unfolding on the other side of the Atlantic when he arrived in Newport that morning for the wedding. He had arrived in an old Ford from Beverly Farms outside Boston, where he had been the guest of Mr. and Mrs. Louis Agassiz Shaw. At the wheel was Nathaniel Simpkins, a young man related to an American aviator and former college friend of Putzi's, who had died in the First World War.

Putzi was bombarded with questions from waiting reporters about what was being described in first reports as an attempted revolution in Berlin. For one of the few times in his life, he was at a loss for words.

"I have no comment to make," he said. "I am here to attend the wedding of my friend's daughter. The wedding is more important than anything else today. I never mix business with pleasure, and today I stick to my program." His only comment was to point out that he had long known both the Astor and the French families. Col. John Jacob Astor, the groom's late father, had been one of his own family's closest friends. He went to a nearby hotel to study the newspapers.

He was still not much the wiser when he went after lunch to a friend's house to change into formal clothes. Later that afternoon, while he was in the church, an enterprising reporter crept in and crawled along the aisle to where Putzi was sitting, on the Astor side. What comments had Putzi to make, he demanded to know in a whisper, to reports that Röhm had been arrested for plotting to overthrow Hitler?

"Not here; later, outside," Putzi replied.

It was only the following day, when the full enormity of what had happened was becoming clear, that Putzi felt able to comment. "News that came to me on Saturday was news to me, but it was not entirely unexpected news," he said in a statement carried by several newspapers. "My leader, Adolf Hitler, had to act and he acted thus as always. Hitler has proven himself never greater, never more human, than in the last forty-eight hours. Hitler would possibly have been on his way out if he had not acted as he did; if he had not acted and saved the most precious thing in the world—his providential mission." As for those leading figures who had been killed, Putzi replied harshly: "There will be others who will fill their places." Germany, he claimed, was marching on to a bright future, and Hitler "has not only averted ruin for Germany, but for the entire civilized world."

Putzi insisted he was not worried about the events' consequences for himself and had no instructions to return home. His confidence hid concern, however, not just for his wife and son, who were still in

Germany, but also for what fate might await him if he went back. He sought the advice of von Neurath, the foreign minister, cabling him secretly via his contacts at the consulate in Boston. Von Neurath suggested he should return, and do so as soon as possible. Putzi already had a provisional booking on the *Europa* on July 7 and decided to confirm it.

This left time for some important unfinished business. The next day, he rolled up at Harvard in a taxi with his three busts, of Gluck, Schopenhauer, and Hindenburg. The university was deserted. Perspiring freely from the heat and the weight of the gifts, Putzi made his way to the music department. As he walked through its empty corridors, he came by chance across the department's chairman, the composer Edward Burlingame Hill, who had dropped in to his office to collect some things before leaving for his summer home in New Boston, New Hampshire. The timing was good: it was the two hundred and twentieth anniversary of Gluck's birth, and Putzi persuaded Hill to accept the bust.

Over lunch, Putzi boasted to Hill that he had written an orchestral suite in honor of Hitler.

"It has a military tempo, a revolutionary tempo," Putzi told him. "It describes the Nazi power."

In the course of their conversation, Putzi also sought to justify Hitler's brutality. "In all revolutions after a period of from three to four years there comes a time when the old revolutionary leaders must be replaced by constructive statesmen," he told his host. If Hitler had not come to power, "Germany would have gone red-bolshevist and Christianity would have disappeared overnight."

Despite his success with the Gluck, Putzi was unable to find anyone at Harvard prepared to take the Schopenhauer or Hindenburg; so, after a two-hour search, he consoled himself with a shopping trip. Still, he did not give up on unloading the remaining busts. On July 4 he left Beverly Airport aboard a chartered plane bound for West Point, the crate containing Hindenburg's bust on board.

The prestigious military academy did not often accept statues; but it had taken one of Maj. Gen. John Sedgwick, Putzi's great-grandfather, who had been killed in the Civil War, when his family presented it. The omens were not good, though. Col. Simon B. Buckner, Jr., the academy's commandant, had warned that final acceptance of the bust "will not be given until a lot of red tape is unraveled" and "it looks as though it will not be accepted." Putzi had to content himself with visiting the grounds to pay respects to his great-grandfather.

The Hanfstaengl family at home in the early 1890s.
(Bayerische Staatsbibliothek, Munich)

Putzi (far right) with his mother, sister, and brothers before the First World War.
(Bayerische Staatsbibliothek, Munich)

Villa Hanfstaengl in Munich, built for Putzi's parents in 1889. *(Bayerische Staatsbibliothek, Munich)*

Putzi as Gretchen Spootsfeiffer in *Fate Fakirs*, a Harvard show, in 1908. *(Life, Dec. 29, 1947)*

Putzi in America, February 1915.
(Papers of Djuna Barnes, Special Collections, University of Maryland Libraries)

During the 1920s with Hitler in Café Heck in Munich.
(Bayerische Staatsbibliothek, Munich)

Putzi (left) with Hitler and his entourage on April 3, 1932 during the presidential election campaign. (*Bayerische Staatsbibliothek, Munich*)

Putzi with his wife, Helena, and children, Egon and Hertha, shortly after Hertha's birth in 1924. (*Bayerische Staatsbibliothek, Munich*)

Putzi in uniform, with an unknown woman, at a Nazi party rally in 1936. *(Bayerische Staatsbibliothek, Munich)*

Putzi, at the piano, entertains Hitler (left), Helene Hanfstaengl, Magda Goebbels, Ernst Franz, and Joseph Goebbels (right) in the Goebbels' Berlin apartment on February 11, 1932. *(Bayerische Staatsbibliothek, Munich)*

Despite protests (above), Putzi went ahead with his visit to his 25th Harvard Class Reunion in June 1934 (below). He later became embroiled in controversy over his attempts to make a donation to the university. *(Bayerisches Hauptstaatsarchiv, Munich)*

Putzi with Unity Mitford during the first Nazi rally in Nuremberg, Bavaria, August 30 through September 3, 1933. *(Bayerische Staatsbibliothek, Munich)*

Putzi and his son Egon at work on the "S-Project" at Bush Hill, Virginia, during World War II. *(Bayerische Staatsbibliothek, Munich)*

Putzi testifies during "Denazification" proceedings in Weilhem, Bavaria, in January 1949.
(Ullstein)

Putzi relaxes at the piano at his home in Munich circa 1972.
(AP/World Wide Photos)

—

ON Saturday, July 7, 1934, the *Europa* set off from its pier at the foot of West Forty-sixth Street. After more than two weeks of unusually hot weather, the temperature reached 92 degrees in the shade in Central Park. A forty-piece band of the Friends of the New Germany played as Putzi climbed on board and gave the Nazi salute. The music was in honor of a seventy-strong party from a pro-fascist organization bound for Germany. A searchlight was trained on the ship's swastika flag.

Putzi could be excused for feeling a sense of trepidation as he left American soil. The unfolding crisis in Germany had continued to be front-page news over the previous few days. It also threatened to take on international dimensions, with Nazi claims that André Francois-Poncet, the French ambassador to Berlin, had been involved in the plot. The only consolation was that things appeared to be calming down; that morning, *The New York Times* reported that Hitler had called for a return to peace and quiet and, to set the tone, had left for a weekend in the Bavarian Alps. Even Papen, the vice-chancellor, whose position was still highly uncertain, was smiling when he was visited in his home. "My plans are not yet complete," he told an interviewer. "Everything is still unsettled." Under the truce, he was free to come and go, although his house was still guarded "presumably to protect him from hot-blooded Nazis."

Putzi still managed to be bullish when quizzed by reporters on the situation in Germany. "What happened really began a year ago and the consequences were a matter of maturing," he said. "Germany is coming down now to a condition of stability." As for the implications for the country's Jews, he replied: "That is a matter that will have to be found out." He also made light of his inability to dispose of the two busts. They were "just casts," he said, vowing to bring them back when he returned in November for the Yale-Harvard football game "and show them in two leading galleries."

The busts were not the only matter of unfinished business. There was also the question of the Dr. Hanfstaengl Scholarship that Putzi had tried to endow. The matter was finally decided that September, when a meeting of the president and fellows of Harvard University voted to reject it. President Conant wrote to Putzi afterward, thanking him for his generosity and explaining why it was not possible to accept his money.

"We are unwilling to accept a gift from one who has been so closely identified with the leadership of a political party which has inflicted damage on the universities of Germany through measures which have struck at principles we believe to be fundamental to universities throughout the world," he wrote. "Since your offer was made public and has been the subject of discussion, we deem it proper to make this letter public." It was accordingly released a few days later by the Harvard News Office and published in several newspapers.

Conant's move was applauded not just by the presidents of several other New England colleges but also by newspaper commentators. The *New York Post* said it "does Harvard honor" and the *Montgomery Alabama Observer* described it as "one more point scored for enlightenment in America." Joseph Brainin, a syndicated columnist, also weighed in: "The president of Harvard acted in the tradition of a great American institution of higher learning," he said. "He felt that the Hanfstaengl scholarship at Harvard would be a contradiction of all that great university stands for."

Predictably enough, one of the few notes of dissent was sounded by *The Harvard Crimson*, which claimed the refusal was scarcely in line with the liberal traditions of which Harvard was justifiably proud. "Hanfstaengl's offer was a friendly gesture, and it is regrettable that the Corporation could not have treated it as such, answering it in the spirit in which it was given," it said.

The legal repercussions of the "Hanfstaengl affair" were also dragging on. That October, the two women who had chained themselves to benches and fences in the Yard in June and had repeatedly interrupted Conant's speech with cries of "Down with Hanfstaengl" were fined fifty dollars each for their actions. In a courtroom packed with students, Conant had successfully pleaded for leniency. Another seven people—six men and one woman—were found guilty of disturbing the peace and speaking without permits, and were fined twenty dollars each and sentenced to six months' hard labor in the Middlesex House of Correction. The judge, George James, was almost apologetic. "I'm sorry to impose jail sentences," he told them. Six of the seven were pardoned after just one month and became Harvard heroes.

The scholarship affair was nevertheless to have a bizarre postscript two years later. In February 1936, Conant was forced to issue a public denial that he had asked Putzi to contribute to Harvard's three-hundredth anniversary fund. Putzi, in a mischief-making mood, had leaked the news that he had written again offering money to the university. Conant had sent a form letter to all sixty-seven thousand alumni proposing the creation of national scholarships and roving professorships. Although it was intended merely to solicit the "general sympathy" of graduates toward the proposals, Putzi interpreted it as a plea for funds and considered his inclusion on the list a sign that the university was ready, after all, to take his money. This time, he suggested ten thousand dollars to make possible ten years of study at the University of Munich for American students.

And so the controversy took off again, with all the same arguments being aired on both sides. To add to the confusion, *The Harvard Crimson* claimed in March 1936 that, contrary to what had previously been understood, Putzi had already contributed fifteen hundred dollars to the 1909 class fund and was determined to send a Harvard student to the University of Munich the following year "with or without President Conant." The whole affair was turning into farce. When a reception was held some time afterward to honor work done for the university by Art Wild, Harvard's publicity director, who was responsible for dealing with the controversy, he was presented with a rubber stamp with the wording: "The University has no statement to make regarding Mr. Hanfstaengl's offer."

PUTZI was uneasy during the voyage back to Germany. As the *Europa* passed through the English Channel he heard on the radio Hitler's speech to the Reichstag justifying what he had done. As the only man on board who knew personally so many of those involved, Putzi was incredulous at the explanation given. Most absurd of all was Hitler's claim to have been surprised and shocked by Röhm's homosexuality. Putzi recalled a blazing row between the two men during the Reichstag election campaign two years earlier when a journalist had published a detailed exposé of Röhm's private life, which had been splashed across some of the opposition newspapers. Equally absurd, he thought, was the claim of the French ambassador's involvement. The worst aspect of the affair, in Putzi's mind, was the arbitrary nature of the whole thing: Röhm and some of his followers were fairly unpleasant characters, but this did not mean it was right to shoot them without trial. Putzi could also, of course, only wonder whether he was making a terrible mistake by going back. Von Neurath had advised him to return, but the way things were going, how could he be sure he would not fall victim to a future purge?

When Putzi arrived back in Berlin, he found many of his friends and colleagues still in a state of shock. His old friend, General von Epp, was in despair and had only narrowly decided against leaving the country. At

Hess's liaison office, where Putzi's own office was located, the people "behaved as if they were chloroformed." Nobody seemed to know what was going on or, if they did, they did not dare share their insights with Putzi.

The most sensible reaction would have been to lie low for a few weeks; Putzi decided instead to go and see Hitler. He learned that the Führer was relaxing with the Goebbels family in the exclusive Baltic Sea resort of Heligendamm. After finding out the name of the hotel, he phoned and announced he was coming.

The hotel was almost deserted when he finally arrived. Hitler, he was told, was still up in his room, but Goebbels and his family were on the beach. When Putzi made his way through the pine trees to the sea, he felt like he had stumbled into a theatrical comedy mocking high society. There among the spotless row of beach huts was the Nazi propaganda chief, clad in his flannels. The hearty greeting he gave Putzi put him in mind of a "rich paterfamilias greeting an old family friend."

The mood changed sharply when Putzi went up to see Hitler in his room later. Looking up from daily press reports that Goebbels had prepared for him, he fixed Putzi with a hostile glare.

"So, there you are, Mr. Hanfstaengl," he said. "Haven't they done you in yet?"

The use of "Mister"—a reminder of his American origins—was an ominous sign; so, too, was the fact that he pronounced Putzi's name with an English s rather than the normal German sh sound.

"No, Herr Hitler, the communists in New York did not get me after all," Putzi retorted, showing him a sheaf of press cuttings. Among them was the photograph of his handshake with Pinansky, the Jewish judge.

"Nice friends you have," Hitler said. "What sort of propaganda is that for the party when the foreign press chief fraternizes with a Jew?"

When Putzi tried to explain the importance of the Jewish lobby in America, Hitler cut him short.

"Hanfstaengl, you ought to have been there," he continued. Putzi's thoughts immediately turned to the list of those executed on June 30.

"Have been where?" he asked.

"In Venice, of course. Mussolini would have been pleased to see you again."

"That was hardly my fault," Putzi retorted. "I kept in touch with you about it right up until the moment I left. . . ."

"I know, I know," Hitler replied. "But it was all arranged in a hurry at the last moment and by that time you had gone."

Putzi did not believe him for a moment, but did not press the point.

It was clear that the matter was closed as far as Hitler was concerned. In any case, his audience was at an end. Hitler's aides and other hangers-on came in and out, and they were all swept down to dinner.

Hitler's mood changed after they had sat down to eat. Suddenly he became jovial again and the reassuring *sh* was reinstated in Putzi's name—even though Goebbels, with his usual malevolent air, could not resist mocking him for the way he had crept ashore in New York rather than face down the demonstrators. There was something almost surreal about watching Magda Goebbels in her summer dress mingling with the other guests while the whole of Germany was "groaning under this atmosphere of murder, fear, and suspicion," Putzi thought. Indeed, the whole thing put him in mind of the Mad Hatter's tea party from Lewis Carroll's *Alice's Adventures in Wonderland*.

LATER that month, Putzi accompanied Hitler to the annual Wagner Festival in Bayreuth. Hitler's admiration for the composer was legendary. When a ceremony had been held in Leipzig in March the previous year to mark the fiftieth anniversary of Wagner's death, Hitler had eschewed his usual party uniform in favor of formal dress of a top hat, cutaway, and striped trousers. Of all the Wagner operas, *Die Meistersinger* was his favorite. There was hardly a ceremony that Hitler presided over where the overture to the opera was not played; Hitler was said to have seen more than two hundred performances of it. Putzi was happy to go to Bayreuth with him—if only because his presence at Hitler's side suggested that all was not lost.

It was on July 25, while the festival was under way, that Engelbert Dollfuss, the Austrian chancellor, was killed in cold blood. Theo Habicht, who headed the Austrian wing of the Nazis, had been plotting for some time against Dollfuss, but it is not clear whether Hitler actually gave the final command to pull the trigger. Whatever the truth, once the first reports came in, Hitler demanded more information. Putzi came up with the idea of calling Louis Lochner, the Associated Press's Berlin bureau chief, who had been sent to Vienna to report on the story. He begged Lochner to tell him the latest news and Lochner obliged by reading the stories he had telegrammed to AP. But Putzi wasn't going to get something for nothing.

"Okay, now I've told you what I know—what's the latest over your way?" Lochner asked him. Putzi did not disappoint.

To Lochner's surprise, he replied in a low voice, almost a whisper: "A certain very old gentleman in East Prussia is very seriously ill; we fear the worst."

It had become clear in April that Hindenburg was seriously ill, and Hitler was told privately that he would not last much longer. Then, in June, the president had retired to his estate at Neudeck in East Prussia. This was the first intimation that the press was given of just how sick he was, though, and Lochner immediately flashed the story. Goebbels denied it, but Lochner stuck by his report.

14

HINDENBURG'S estate in Neudeck, in what was then East Prussia and is now Poland, was a fine one, with a long feudal tradition of offering a warm welcome to visitors. The reception accorded Hitler's party was distinctly cool, however. Only Hitler and his adjutant Brückner were allowed in to see the dying president. Putzi, to his chagrin, was made to wait outside with Otto Dietrich on a bench near the outbuildings, without even the offer of a drink. Hitler said little when he emerged. They all spent the night at Count Dohna's Finckenstein estate, which had been the scene for part of Napoléon's romance with Countess Walewska. Although Napoléon's room was still as it had been in his day, Hitler declined an offer to sleep there.

The next morning, August 2, 1934, Otto Meissner, Hindenburg's cabinet chief, was in tears as he announced the president's death. In a statement the next day, Putzi thanked America for the tributes paid to him. "Such a true estimate of the character of a typical representative of what is noblest in German life cannot fail to improve the world's understanding of the true ideals of the German people," he wrote.

Hindenburg's death transformed the political situation in Germany in one stroke. He had been first elected president in 1925 at the age of seventy-eight, after the death of Friedrich Ebert, but despite his advanced years he stood again in 1932 as the only candidate who could defeat Hitler. Those who voted for Hindenburg had done so largely because they saw in him a bulwark against the lawlessness and brutality of the Nazis. The elderly president's advisers had been convinced that they could come to terms with the Nazis, however, and so had encouraged him to fire Heinrich Brüning, the leader of the Catholic Zentrum party, thereby paving the way for Hitler's appointment as chancellor. But rather than trying to control Hitler, Hindenburg had increasingly given him free rein, and did nothing as he stripped away the last vestiges of democracy and grabbed more powers for himself. Hitler nevertheless remained in awe of him; as Putzi noticed on a number of occasions, even a telephone call from the president was enough to have a profound effect on Hitler.

Hindenburg's death removed the last, albeit largely symbolic, obstacle to the completion of Hitler's revolution. On August 19, 1934, a plebiscite was held to give him absolute powers. Out of an electorate of 45.5 million, some 43.5 million votes were cast—38.4 million of them "yes." A mere 4.3 million people had the courage to vote against the proposal. "Those middle-aged Germans, doubtful of Nazi rule, apprehensive of the future, did not dare to express their fears by voting against the Leader," wrote one British observer who was touring the country at the time of the vote. "After all, what was the alternative, except anarchy and civil war and new horrors?" There was nevertheless something in the German mentality and in this loyalty to Hitler that could not be understood. "There are mysteries in the German mind we cannot fathom or understand. It is because of those mysteries that other people are uneasy and afraid."

It was part of Putzi's job to try to tackle that unease, at least as far as the foreign press was concerned. The Nazis' image abroad had been severely damaged by the brutality of the Night of the Long Knives; the American newspapers, in particular, were taking an increasingly critical stance. A chance to burnish Hitler's reputation soon presented itself in the form of William Randolph Hearst. The newspaper baron had set off that July on a tour of Europe with his mistress, Marion Davies, passing through Belgium and Holland and on to Bavaria, where he attended the Oberammergau Passion Play. Despite the political upheavals, Hearst was surprised to find Germany still as he remembered it: "picturesque and orderly." "Everybody is for Hitler," he wrote in a postcard to Julia Morgan, his architect. "We think he is a tyrant in America, but his own people don't think so. They regard him as a savior."

Hearst, who was on his way to take a cure at the baths at Bad Nauheim, was met a few days after the August plebiscite by Putzi, who flew down to Munich to have tea with him. Karl von Wiegand, Hearst's correspondent for Central Europe, warned his boss about Putzi, but

Hearst was not having any of it. He had known Putzi for forty years—as his father had before him—and he was a "good sort," he wrote back. Nor was it "a crime" that he liked to make a "little money occasionally for news features." Hearst's only real complaint about Putzi was that he was an extremist who might not be giving Hitler the best advice on how to treat not just the Jews but also the Christian churches.

On August 23, the *Beobachter* and the rest of the German press carried an article by Hanfstaengl detailing a "series of conversations" with Hearst. Their contents were picked up by a number of American newspapers. "The results [of the plebiscite] represent a unanimous expression of the popular will," Putzi quoted Hearst as declaring. "This overwhelming majority with which Hitler astonishes the world must, as we now learn, be accepted as self-evident and in a sense must open up a new chapter in modern history. If Hitler succeeds in pointing the way to peace and order and an ethical development which has been destroyed throughout the world by war, he will have accomplished a measure of good not only for his own people but for all humanity. Germany is battling for her liberation from the mischievous provisions of the Treaty of Versailles and for her redemption from the malicious suppression and encirclement to which she has been subjected by nations which in their avarice and short-sightedness have only shown enmity and jealousy over her advancement. This battle, in fact, can only be viewed as a struggle which all liberty-loving peoples are bound to follow with understanding and sympathy." Putzi concluded the article by saying that Hearst had promised to attend the Nazi party rally in Nuremberg the following month.

The media baron later claimed that most of the words attributed to him had actually been written by Putzi. He did not appear unduly concerned, though; as he wrote to Joe Willicombe, his secretary, he had tried to give an interview, but Putzi had "liked his own ideas better." Hearst believed such distortions were only to be expected and not much worse than what he had experienced elsewhere in Europe.

"When you are interviewed in Germany, don't imagine that what you have to say matters in the least," he told Willicombe. "The interviewer looks you over carefully, listens indifferently and then goes away and writes what he thinks will be pleasing to Hitler. I don't blame the interviewers. If they fail to do this they get their papers shut up for a week or so." The media baron nevertheless conceded that the final two paragraphs, in which he congratulated Hitler on his victory, were "mine and exact."

Putzi's claim that Hearst had agreed to go to Nuremberg was another matter. His guest was appalled at the revelation, although it was not clear whether he had not agreed to attend or simply wanted to do so incognito. Either way, Hearst ordered the editors of his American papers not to follow up the story.

Hitler wanted to meet Hearst, and Putzi tried hard to persuade the American to agree. But Hearst was reluctant and claimed to be unable to interrupt his cure. Davies, by contrast, was enthusiastic. "Mr. Hearst has no desire to meet Mr. Hitler. But I have," she told Putzi. So for three days she pleaded with Hearst to change his mind. In the end, Hearst sounded out his friend, Louis B. Mayer, the Hollywood studio boss; Mayer urged him to go ahead, saying he might "be able to accomplish much good" for the Jews. And so it was decided to hold a meeting in the chancellery in Berlin. Hitler agreed that Hearst could write it up and publish it afterward. Putzi arranged for a private plane to fly the newspaper baron from Munich to Berlin and went along himself as interpreter.

According to Hearst's account of the meeting, Hitler demanded to know why he was so "misrepresented, so misunderstood" in America and why its people were so antagonistic to his regime. Hearst did not pull his punches; the Americans, he told Hitler, "believe in democracy and are averse to dictatorship." Without referring to the Jewish community by name, he also spoke of a "very large and influential and respected element in the United States who are very resentful of the treatment of their fellows in Germany."

"But I am entirely a product of democracy," Hitler retorted. "I, as a private citizen, appealed to the people of Germany. I was elected to my office by a majority vote of the people of Germany. I presented my proposals, my policies, to the people of Germany. They endorsed those policies by more than a two-thirds majority."

And so the rest of the meeting went. Hearst, nevertheless, left the chancellery convinced that he had been "able to accomplish some good." Hitler, he wrote afterward to Willicombe, was "certainly an extraordinary man" whom the Americans underestimated at their peril. "He has enormous energy, intense enthusiasm, a marvelous faculty for dramatic oratory, and great organizing ability," he said, but added: "Of course all these qualities can be misdirected."

The meeting was also a great coup for Putzi, who boasted of his success in capturing the great Hearst. "I only had to convince him that we were interested in justice and he softened right up and went in to see Hitler," he boasted. "Hitler put on one of his acts—it is amazing how easy it is to impress these Americans."

Many in America were not so easily impressed—chief among them Dorothy Thompson. Her highly critical book, *I Saw Hitler*, published in 1932, still rankled the regime—even if her colleagues had ribbed her over the conviction with which she had written off Hitler's chances of coming to power. Appalled by his appointment to chancellor, she had kept up her assault on the Nazis. In July 1934, she had gone to Austria to gather information about the murder of Dollfuss; in the middle of the following month she arrived back in Berlin.

The day after Putzi's interview with Hearst was published, the regime had its revenge on Thompson. Some police officers went to the Adlon Hotel, where Thompson was staying, told her she was no longer welcome in Germany, and gave her twenty-four hours to leave—or be expelled. Thompson had little alternative but to comply. The next day, almost the entire Anglo-American press corps turned out to see her onto the Nord Express. She was in tears as they presented her with a huge bunch of American Beauty roses.

Thompson's expulsion was principally for publishing *I Saw Hitler*, but also for articles she had written on several other visits since the Nazis had come to power, especially those in which she criticized the mistreatment of the Jews. It was carried out on the basis of a retrospective law that made it an offense for a foreigner in Germany to express any opinion "detrimental to the interests of the Reich" or disrespectful of any of its officials.

Thompson was a prominent global figure and her enforced departure was seized upon in America and elsewhere as further evidence of Hitler's growing intolerance of contrary opinions. Frederick Birchall, the Berlin correspondent for *The New York Times*, feared that Hitler intended to "banish from Germany all foreign correspondents who do not fully regard Nazi doctrines as the height of political wisdom and are not willing to become mere echoes of Nazi propaganda." Other members of the media shared his concern. As Putzi should have realized, the whole affair turned into a public relations disaster, alienating many in America who had still been willing to give Hitler the benefit of the doubt. Ironically, for all her sadness at expulsion, the main beneficiary was Thompson; already a renowned journalist, she was turned almost overnight into a celebrity.

—

IN public, at least, Putzi continued to defend the regime. The day Thompson was expelled, *The New York Times* published a lengthy interview he had given Jane Grant, one of its writers, ten days earlier. Clad in a black alpaca suit, he rejected suggestions that he was somehow presiding over a "propaganda bureau for Germany." "I am here to dispense information sought by foreigners and members of the foreign press, not to thrust it at them," he told her. Somewhat unconvincingly, Putzi also tried to dispel suggestions that Hindenburg's death would lead to a dramatic change in course. "Hitler realizes that the power destiny has placed in his hands is possibly greater than that of any man in the world, but he also realizes that he has surely the most gigantic problems to solve in the world," he said. "This alone will protect him against any cheap, giddy and despotic interpretation of the power entrusted to him. Power is nothing; justice is all. There is no more humble, modest, self-controlled person in the world today than Adolf Hitler."

Putzi also spoke out in favor of the Nazis' policy toward women—including their being banned from politics and the attempts made to encourage them to leave the workplace. He spoke approvingly, too, of the campaign against nail polish and lipstick: "German men believe these things to be rather symbols of a modern inferiority complex on the part of the weaker sex, eternally haunted by the spectre of declining attraction and under-magnetism," he said. He also voiced approval for the government's policy of forced sterilization of the handicapped or others who did not meet the high standards demanded of Hitler's master-race-in-the-making. Germany was a country of "quality," not "mass," production, he said. "We cannot afford to have in our population even a small percentage of deficient children."

Despite such outward manifestations of loyalty, Putzi was clearly growing disillusioned. He had long been openly cynical about aspects of the regime and vocal in his criticism of his two ideological foes, Rosenberg and Goebbels. Indeed, he took pride in the fact that still no one in his office greeted each other with the "Heil Hitler" that was rapidly becoming de rigueur throughout German society. Yet what was tolerated as amusing eccentricity in the early days of 1933 was already downright dangerous eighteen months later. His distaste at Hitler's policies was reinforced by a growing sense of his own powerlessness and irrelevance. In subtle ways, he began to move increasingly toward open opposition.

One of those struck by Putzi's independence of mind was Edgar von Schmidt-Pauli, a conservative journalist and writer. He had traveled to Munich in 1931 to write a book on Hitler and the men around him and was favorably impressed—but later became critical and, like Putzi, probably only survived the Night of the Long Knives because he was away on a business trip to Paris. The writer, who met Putzi frequently in Berlin after the Nazis came to power, noted how he, too, was losing faith in the regime. They had several conversations in which Putzi expressed his outrage over the Nazis' lust for power and described some of the decrees they had issued as "idiotic." Nor did Putzi miss a chance to put in a bad word about Rosenberg and was becoming increasingly critical of Goebbels and even of Hitler. This was strong stuff, especially since Putzi admitted that he was already concerned about his own safety. Such was the ferocity and openness with which Putzi criticized the regime, that von Schmidt-Pauli began to avoid being seen with him in public.

A chance meeting at a reception one evening at the Italian embassy seemed especially perilous. As von Schmidt-Pauli and his wife were leaving after speaking to a number of leading Nazis, including Rosenberg, they came across Putzi.

"How can you speak at all to a fool like Rosenberg?" Putzi demanded. "He is not a fool anymore, but a criminal."

When Putzi launched into an equally loud denunciation of "the other criminals," von Schmidt-Pauli swiftly silenced him. His own position was already precarious enough without being associated with that kind of stuff. He wondered how long Putzi would last if he did not watch himself.

Others, too, were shocked by Putzi's outspokenness. Benno Jehle, who worked at Munich's Oberwiesenfeld Airport, was on duty one day in 1935 when Putzi landed aboard a JU 52. As he walked into the terminal, he was greeted with the usual cries of "Heil Hitler."

Far from acknowledging them, Putzi suddenly retorted in a loud voice, "Oh, do stop all that Heil nonsense."

The other passengers and staff who heard the outburst looked around uncomfortably at each other. But Jehle, who was opposed to the Nazis and was to flee to Switzerland during the Second World War, was impressed. When Putzi was unable to find a taxi to ride into town, he offered to drive him home. In the privacy of the car, Putzi launched into a tirade against the Nazis, criticizing, in particular, Hitler's decision to appoint the "incapable" von Ribbentrop as ambassador to London.

Putzi had never thought much of him—and certainly would have liked the job for himself.

Such indiscretions were not going unnoticed. Erika Schweickert, who headed the Humboldt Haus in Berlin, part of the German Academy of Exchange Services (DAAD), was struck by the critical tone Putzi adopted not just toward the Nazis' cultural policies but also toward the regime itself. "He used to say often that Dr. Goebbels and Rosenberg were his bitter enemies and that he was not being listened to anymore because of his words of warning," she recalled later. One day she had an ominous call from the Gestapo. "We know that you have been meeting Dr. Hanfstaengl and we would like to warn you against further meetings, because he is not considered politically reliable," she was told.

Putzi's relations with Hitler, meanwhile, continued to worsen. Part of the problem was undoubtedly his rivalry with Goebbels. Putzi had never liked the man whom he described behind his back as the "poisonous dwarf." After Hitler came to power, the two men clashed over Putzi's work with the foreign press, which Goebbels saw as part of his domain. Goebbels was a dangerous man to cross, however, as he had shown when he effectively sabotaged Putzi's film about Horst Wessel.

Putzi also began to clash even with Göring, until then one of his oldest allies among the leading Nazis. When Göring threw a birthday party at his home, which was known as Karinhall after his late lamented wife, Putzi told him off to his face for displaying works of art plundered from various German galleries. An indignant Göring first denied the accusation but then angrily retorted, "And what about it, then? At least people see the beautiful pictures if I put them on display." Putzi replied that many more would have seen them if they had been left to hang in their old places.

Putzi's son recalled an important Nazi function in the summer of 1934 in the Reichskanzlei in Berlin that he attended with his parents. Thirteen-year-old Egon queued up with the others present for the chance of shaking Hitler's hand, but when he finally reached him he was struck by the coldness with which he was treated. Perhaps because of his father's growing estrangement from Hitler, there was little of the friendliness of the previous summer in Berchtesgaden. Nor were matters helped by the manner in which his parents greeted Hitler: while the others present raised their arms to him in salute, declaring "Heil, mein Führer," Putzi simply said "Heil," while Helene gave the traditional Bavarian greeting of "Grüss Gott."

Alone of those around Hitler, Putzi made a point of never calling him "der Führer" and whenever he did the Heil Hitler salute, he invariably did so with a crooked arm rather than the more fanatical straight-arm gesture. When a formal form of address was required, he always used "Herr Reichskanzler."

On their way home, Helene mentioned Hitler's apparent displeasure at the way in which they had greeted him. Putzi merely complained, as he had before, that Hitler had not made good on his promise to dissolve the Nazi Party once he had seized power. Although only a small incident, it was typical of the way things were going. Increasingly, it no longer seemed a question of whether Putzi would break with Hitler but rather when.

—

PUTZI claimed, after the Second World War, that the final straw had been Hitler's discovery that his foreign press chief was trying to arrange a visit for a British member of Parliament to a concentration camp. "From that moment on, it was clear to me that Hitler had a bad conscience," he declared. But although this and other such manifestations of independence on Putzi's part may have played a role, there was another, more intriguing explanation for his falling out with the party. Indeed, his final break with the regime can be traced to a day in October 1934 when, as usual, he joined Hitler and his aides for lunch in the Reichskanzlei. It was then that the conversation turned to Kurt Lüdecke, and the anti-Nazi radio broadcasts he had started making from America.

Lüdecke was already a member of Hitler's entourage when Putzi first joined the movement, and Putzi had been immediately suspicious of him. Nothing had happened in the intervening decade to make him change his mind. Lüdecke had drifted away from Hitler in 1925 and moved to the United States, where he married an American woman. He had remained attracted by the Nazis, however, and as their popular support grew, he tried to find his way back into Hitler's inner circle, helped by his patron, Rosenberg. A few months after Hitler's assumption of power, Lüdecke was back in Berlin—demanding to be made press attaché at the German embassy in Washington.

Putzi had watched Lüdecke's return to favor with dismay, not least because of the renewal of his alliance with the odious Rosenberg. And so Putzi had set out to discredit both of them and began gathering compromising material. Rudolf Diels, the head of the security police, who was a personal friend, had been only too happy to help. It did not prove very difficult: Putzi's first discovery was that Rosenberg, a virulent anti-Semite, was having an affair with the daughter of a Jewish publisher. Equally intriguing was the discovery that Lüdecke's own account of his past had been largely fictitious and that he had actually been active as a black-mailer and a con man beginning in 1911. In particular, Putzi discovered that Lüdecke had earned himself several hundred dollars from black-mailing a German doctor in New York by threatening to report him for performing an abortion. Putzi duly passed the evidence to the appropri-ate authorities and shortly afterward Göring had both Rosenberg's mis-tress and Lüdecke jailed. Hanfstaengl built on his success by penning a lead article on the affair for the *New Yorker Staatszeitung*, the city's German-language newspaper, headlined "Lüdecke Arrested on Charges of False Pretenses and Extortion."

Hitler had intervened, however, and ordered Lüdecke's release, clear-ly hoping he would go straight to Washington to take up the post he had secured for himself. Lüdecke had instead decided to stay in Germany to clear his name and began to prepare a libel action against Putzi; his aim, he told Dr. Alfons Sack, a well-known lawyer, was to shed light on "a hot zone of Nazidom." There is little doubt that, thanks to his long association with the party, Lüdecke knew much about Hitler and his close associates that they would rather not see aired in public. Given his extensive experience with blackmail, he must have thought that by so doing he could oblige Hitler to back him more strongly. It was a dangerous game, however, and Rosenberg tried to persuade him to desist. Lüdecke refused, and on July 5, 1933, a week or so before the case was due to begin, he had been taken into protective custody—only this time on Hitler's orders.

There would be no early release this time. Lüdecke was taken first to Plötzensee Prison and then to Brandenburg concentration camp. During the run-up to the Night of the Long Knives, however, he had escaped to Switzerland and returned to America, where in the autumn of 1934 he began making broadcasts denouncing Hitler and his regime.

Putzi's dislike of Lüdecke was so strong and so widely known that when the subject of those broadcasts came up at the lunch in the Reichkanzlei that October, none of those present was surprised by his reaction.

"There you are, Herr Hitler," said Putzi, who was sitting two seats away from him. "I have warned you for the last ten years against hav-ing people of this type around."

He then began to describe the contents of the police dossier that he had compiled on Lüdecke, adding: "The whole movement has been tainted by allowing such people too much freedom. Now look at what he is doing. What else can you expect?"

Hitler was livid.

"It's all your fault, Hanfstaengl," he yelled at him. "You should have handled him much more diplomatically."

"How do you expect anyone to handle a man like that diplomatically?" Putzi retorted, beside himself.

It was, Putzi recalled, a very ugly and unpleasant scene. Hitler tried to cover himself by claiming that the police records were a case of mistaken identity, but Putzi was not prepared to back down.

"I will get them together again and show them to you," he insisted. "These facts concern him alone and everyone else knows it." The lunch party broke up in disorder.

It was a measure of Putzi's stubbornness that he did not leave matters there, but instead went off and began busying himself assembling the compromising material. He also continued to attend lunch in the chancellery. At one such meal a couple of days later, Hitler suddenly turned to him.

"Hanfstaengl, *Spielen Sie das Ding von Ihnen*—[play that thing of yours]," he ordered.

"Which one?" asked Putzi.

"Your funeral march," he said.

Even though it was not long since it had been played at the Nuremberg party rally, Putzi found the whole thing rather odd and felt a sense of foreboding. He nevertheless obliged.

He was working on his dossier and calling various people in the police courts. They quickly provided him the material, which he duly forwarded to Hess, Göring, and a dozen or so other people in the Reichsleitung (the German national leadership). A few days later, Putzi brought in the files and put them down in front of Brückner.

"The matter is under investigation," Brückner said, clearing his throat and looking embarrassed. "The Führer would prefer you not to come here for the next two weeks until a decision has been reached."

Putzi heard later that his files had been put on Hitler's desk, and when he saw their contents he swept them onto the floor in a rage and shouted, "I never want to hear about that matter again."

It was then that Putzi heard Lüdecke was working on a book. He was delighted at what he felt was the final proof he needed of his rival's malign intentions. Before he could learn anything more about its contents, there was yet another twist. Putzi had gone for a short vacation on the Tegernsee and when he came back found a letter to Hitler from Lüdecke—or rather from a committee of men who described themselves as Lüdecke's friends. It was the fourth carbon copy, so the text was faded. Its message was clear, though: in it, they claimed Lüdecke had gone to America because he had failed to get justice in Germany. They said he wanted fifty thousand dollars and if he did not get it by January 15 the following year he was ready to publish material about Hitler.

Putzi went immediately to the chancellery, brandishing the letter, but decided to discuss the matter with his aides rather than Hitler himself. He was in an ebullient mood; vindication seemed guaranteed. "I then waited and expected Hitler would say 'Heavens on earth, what have I done, this is a blackmailer,'" he said later. But if Putzi thought Hitler would take his side, he was to be bitterly disappointed.

Putzi could never understand why Hitler should be loyal to a man like Lüdecke. "This question I have asked myself very often," he said. "I cannot get rid of the idea that he has probably some blackmailing material."

Putzi never met Hitler face-to-face again.

15

THE King's Bench Division in London had seen its share of strange libel cases, but the matter before Lord Chief Justice Herbert on November 29, 1935, was stranger than most. That morning saw the first hearing of Ernst Hanfstaengl against London Express Newspapers Ltd. Like many such cases, it seemed to turn on a small detail.

The proceedings had their origin in an August meeting the previous year between Putzi and William Ormonde Thompson, a prominent left-leaning Chicago lawyer who was campaigning against human rights abuses in Germany. Thompson had long been interested in Germany; he considered its people the most highly educated in Europe and was surprised and a little chagrined about the turn of events after January 1933. His attention had been sparked by an article in *The New York Times* in May 1934, describing the establishment of the so-called People's Court to try cases of treason and acts against the state, and another the following month reporting the decapitation of Horst Wessel's killers. To someone used to the practices of the American legal system, it was all very strange and alarming. Thompson also wanted to see for himself the concentration camps being set up in Germany, because a number of articles had appeared in the newspapers claiming great cruelty there.

So, on August 1, 1934, shortly after Putzi had returned from America, Thompson set off on the steamship *Washington,* bound for France. After a few days in Paris, he went on to Berlin and checked into the Bristol Hotel. Thompson was well connected; a cousin gave him a letter of recommendation to Ambassador Dodd. He also sought out Junius B. Wood, an old friend who was the Berlin correspondent of the *Chicago Daily News*. Wood helped him secure a meeting with the head of the People's Court, but it was far from illuminating. They had only thirty minutes and no common language and the interpreter was not up to the job. The only consolation was that Thompson was allowed to watch proceedings normally open only to German reporters. He saw three communists being sentenced.

Thompson was still determined to visit a concentration camp, and Wood suggested he seek out Putzi. After a few fruitless visits to Putzi's chaotic office on the Wilhelmstrasse, they finally met on August 25. Their meeting began cordially enough, but Thompson soon steered the conversation toward his hope of getting permission to visit a concentration camp. For all his loyalty to Hitler, there is little doubt that Putzi shared much of his visitor's concern about what was really going on behind the walls of the camps. There were limits, however, to what he could agree to as a representative of the regime.

Speaking in what Thompson later described as a "perfectly gentlemanly way," Putzi replied he was not "running a tourist bureau to the concentration camps" and claimed that any such visit might interfere with plans being finalized to release fifteen thousand prisoners.

The conversation then turned to the continuing stories coming out of Germany of human rights abuses and other cruelty.

"Well, you have lynching, shooting, and kidnapping in the United States," Putzi told him.

These acts, Thompson said, were the work not of the government but of criminals. "In England there are no such occurrences." He added, "And yet, if anything, the English papers are stronger in their condemnation of what is going on in the camps than the American papers."

Putzi's earlier convivial mood gave way to anger. "God damn the Oxford professors," Putzi exclaimed, standing up. Then, according to Thompson's account of the affair, he walked around the desk and exclaimed: "I will send some of the goddamn swine over to them so they can burn down their Oxford."

And that was it; the two men spoke for a few more minutes but the interview was at an end. The whole thing had lasted barely half an hour. Putzi, by then calm and friendly again, showed Thompson to the door of his office.

It had become clear to Thompson that he would not be permitted to visit a camp, and so, three days later, he took a flight to Copenhagen.

Before leaving, however, he wrote a short article describing the interview with Putzi and his other experiences and circulated it among various newspapers. On August 29, the day after he left, the *Chicago Daily News* carried a story by Wood entitled "Lawyer Sees Liberty Gone from Germany." Several other publications picked up the story, among them *Time* magazine, which ran its own version on September 10.

Thompson's uneventful visit would have remained so if it had not been for Putzi's planned trip to London. On September 19, the *Daily Express* carried a brief article, of just a few paragraphs, on its front page headlined "Hitler's 'Putzy' [sic] Is Here," illustrated with a photograph. The article noted how Hanfstaengl, "intimate friend" of Hitler and the Harvard-educated head of the Nazi foreign press department, had come to London and was staying at Claridge's. Then came the problematic part.

"Recently, William Ormonde Thompson, one-time partner of the great American lawyer, Clarence Darrow, was shown through the Nazi People's Court by Dr. Hanfstaengl," it said. "According to the account in the journal *Time* on Sept. 10, when persistent lawyer Thompson started quoting the opinions of British jurists on the subject of Nazi justice, harassed Harvardman Hanfstaengl grew highly excited, and finally incoherent. 'Roared he "Damn those Oxford professors! I'll send some of our swine to burn down their Oxford!"'"

The *Daily Express* may only have been repeating what had already been published in America. But this, as every British journalist knows, is no defense under Britain's libel laws, which have long been among the toughest in the world. Putzi decided to sue—even though the entire case rested on just one phrase and on an account of a meeting at which only he and Thompson had been present.

Putzi flew to London on November 26, 1935, checking into the Carlton Hotel in Whitehall. Agnethe von Hausberger, his secretary, who was also to be a witness at the trial, joined him the next day. Putzi was in good spirits and "confidant [sic] that Lord B[eaverbrook, the *Express's* owner] who is a bluffer will back down."

At the trial, which opened four days later, Putzi was represented by sergeant-at-law Alexander Sullivan, who had made his name defending Sir Roger Casement, the senior British civil servant hanged in 1916 for trying to enlist German help for Ireland's doomed Easter Rising against British rule. The *Express's* case was argued by Sir Patrick Hastings, one of the highest-paid advocates at the British bar.

Putzi's position was clear. Although not denying the broad gist of his conversation with Thompson, he maintained his words had been slightly—but crucially—different. Having first pointed out how many people in the concentration camps had been sent there for attacking public buildings, he claimed to have said something to the effect of "What would the Oxford professors say if some of the communists burned down their Oxford?" It was an important distinction, for this version did not contain any suggestion of a threat. The *Daily Express*, nevertheless, denied that its article was defamatory and entered a plea of justification and fair comment on a matter of public interest.

Sullivan gave Putzi an impressive introduction. His client held a high position in the German civil service, he told the court, and was a member of a great Munich family that had a long connection with the art world and were pioneers in the art of photolithography. There was also a link, albeit tenuous, with the British royal family. Putzi was the godson of Duke Ernst of Saxe-Coburg Gotha, brother-in-law of Queen Victoria's.

Putzi was at his theatrical best when he took the stand. With a "pained look on his face" he denied making the comments attributed to him. "There was infinite injury in Dr. Hanfstaengl's voice as he testified today," commented *The New York Times*. "There was sadness in his manner at the suggestion that he ever lost his temper or did such a 'vulgar' thing as to call Communists 'swine.'" Putzi told the court the statement attributed to him could only have been made "by a man of violent and vulgar temper." "What hurt me most was the idea that somebody would say I would burn down the finest seat of learning in the Anglo-Saxon world," he went on. "It is just like saying I would burn down Goethe's or Schiller's house."

Thompson, who had agreed only with reluctance to cross the Atlantic to testify, stuck to his guns. Shortly before the case was adjourned for the weekend, he went on the stand and, under oath, declared Putzi had indeed told him: "Damn Oxford professors! I will send some of the swine over to them so they can burn their Oxford."

The *Daily Express* quickly realized it stood little chance of victory, and when the case resumed on Monday, the newspaper gave in and agreed to a substantial settlement. A triumphant Putzi went back to the Carlton Hotel and telephoned a press statement to DNB, the German news agency. He also began to gather together pictures of those involved in the trial to prepare a booklet about the case.

The same day, the foreman of the jury, Col. David Lynch, sent Putzi a handwritten note from his home in London's prestigious Portman Square. "I regret that I missed you when the case concluded as I would have greatly liked to congratulate you on your victory," he wrote, noting the "delightful holiday" he had just spent in Bavaria. "If you are remaining in London any time it would give me great pleasure if I might call on you. It would perhaps interest you to know what was the opinion of the jury on the whole matter." Lynch was not the only one in British society sympathetic to Putzi—and, by extension, to the Nazi cause. W. Perkins, one of the solicitors at Essex House, on London's Essex Street, who handled Putzi's legal affairs, wrote to him the following month of "my sympathies with your great movement."

Although Putzi did not win any damages, he was awarded costs as part of the settlement. He was determined to get as much as he could, and the bill he finally sent to Brown on January 23, 1936, after a number of promptings, amounted to 3,300 reichsmarks, with another £115 to cover incidental expenses incurred during his ten days in London. In the end he had to make do with just £203—including a mere £20 for his expenses at the Carlton Hotel.

INCREASINGLY estranged from Hitler and his entourage, Hanfstaengl now felt himself largely cut off from the man whom he had previously served so loyally. He nevertheless still continued to act as an apologist for the regime, as was exemplified by his appearance at the Nuremberg rally in 1935. In a speech for the foreign press, he was effusive in his praise of Hitler and the dramatic action he had taken—even though he personally no longer had access to him.

"Whoever does not understand the Germany of today—or does not want to understand it—will also not be able to understand coming events in Europe and in the whole world," Putzi declared. In what must have strained the credulity of his audience, he then tried to put the Nazis into a broader political and philosophical context, tracing the origins of their ideas back to Edmund Burke, the eighteenth-century English conservative thinker; Thomas Carlyle, the nineteenth-century Scottish essayist; and Americans such as Madison Grant, Henry Fairfield Osborn, and Lothrop Stoddard. He also poured scorn on those commentators who had claimed when Hitler came to power two years earlier that he inevitably meant war. "These prophecies have not been fulfilled and will not be fulfilled," he told his audience. "Germany is instead beginning to play a leading role in the great struggle between order and chaos."

Despite his effusive praise of the Nazis, the party continued to disappoint him, not least over his second venture into film. Goebbels had effectively sabotaged his first effort, about Horst Wessel; his second attempt was even more disastrous. It was entitled *Volk ohne Raum (People Without Space)* and was based on Hans Grimm's 1926 political novel espousing German colonial expansion in Africa. The film was almost entirely Putzi's creation. He wrote the screenplay, composed the music, and secured the financing through a considerable loan from the Bank der Deutschen Arbeit, the savings institution linked to the German Labor Front. But in August 1936, even before the film was finished, Goebbels banned it. The reasons for the ban were never spelled out, but Putzi saw it as yet another attempt by his rival to undermine him. It was also an enormous financial blow. With no chance of the film earning any money, he had to find a way of repaying the loan. To default would have further imperiled his position and laid him open to accusations that he had misappropriated the German workers' hard-earned money. In the end, the only way out was to mortgage his share of the family firm.

That December, when Putzi applied for two Nazi Party decorations, the Blutorden (the Order of Blood), which was awarded to those who had taken part in the 1923 beer hall putsch, and the Ehrenzeichen (the Badge of Honor), which was given to the party's earliest members, he was refused both. The party treasurer told him that Hitler had ordered a halt in the distribution of Blutorden, while he did not qualify for an Ehrenzeichen because he had not formally joined the party until 1931.

Putzi's alienation from the regime was now becoming public. Ambassador Dodd noted in his diary in November 1936 how Hitler had come to dislike Putzi and refused to see him. Far from toeing the line, however, Putzi was continuing to take chances. In particular, Dodd noted, he had gone to Paris a few days earlier, where he had given an interview about Roosevelt's reelection that looked almost certain to get him into trouble. "He simply indicated his admiration of the country where he would like to live if he could take any of his property with him," Dodd wrote. "I am wondering a little what will be said or done here when he returns. He is supposed to be very clever. I cannot quite say whether he is or is not." When writer Edgar von Schmidt-Pauli visited Putzi in his office one day, he found him a changed man, unsure of himself and speaking "like someone who believed he, too, would be locked up tomorrow."

The foreign press, too, chimed in on Putzi's marginalization. Joe Williams, writing in the *New York World-Telegram* in October, under the headline "Remember Hanfstaengl," sneered at the fall from grace of a man who had been "very palsy-walsy with Hitler." "Anyway, old Putzy is just another kraut-head in Germany these days. Either he has lost his touch at the piano or der Fuehrer has switched to the bazooka. Putzy who boasted of his power and position in the Nazi picture, didn't even have a ticket to the [Berlin Olympic] games. He wound up putting the bite on an American sports writer."

Putzi's personal life was also going badly. It had been more than sixteen years since he and Helene had met and married with almost indecent haste. The first strains had already begun to appear soon after their arrival in Germany. Helene was shocked by what she found there and the primitive nature of their first home. Life had improved with their move to Pienzenauerstrasse, but other problems had remained. Their relationship had not been helped by the relocation of Helene's mother to their home. The long illness and eventual death of their daughter, Hertha, had added a further strain. They nevertheless remained together, but Putzi was a difficult husband. Eccentric and idiosyncratic, he was also extremely self-centered and selfish. He was often unfaithful, while his sex life with Helene was largely unsatisfactory. After Hitler's assumption of power, Putzi spent an increasing amount of his time in Berlin, while his wife stayed behind in Munich with Egon. The couple's gradual drifting apart came to a head in the spring of 1936; Helene had simply had enough.

Putzi initially refused to accept a divorce and was equally unwilling to pay alimony. In the end, though, he agreed to both. The terms of their divorce were agreed to and signed on May 12. Putzi was to give Helene a one-off payment of three thousand reichsmarks, followed by three hundred reichsmarks a month tax-free for the rest of her life—or until she remarried. Helene did not move out immediately, instead staying on until August 18. "I better leave you now when you are okay rather than later when things might be bad," she told him. She was, presumably, referring to the banning of *Volk ohne Raum*, which happened the same day.

According to Egon, however, it was not Putzi's many infidelities but rather his lack of consideration for his wife outside the bedroom that eventually ruined their relationship. "My parents got divorced not so much because of the many affairs of my father but because he was so inconsiderate," he recalled more than half a century later. "He would say 'I shall be home for lunch at 1:30' and then it got to 2:30 and he would arrive with two unaccounted guests. And this, of course, put a tremendous burden on my mother and on the cook. It culminated one day when he did not turn up for lunch at all and two days later he phoned his wife from Paris. This is what my mother couldn't stand."

Shortly after her divorce, Helene Niemeyer began an affair with Hans Trausil, a poet she had met through her husband. He seemed to offer all the qualities she missed in Putzi; it promised to be the great love of her life and they moved in together in a house at Armberg on Lake Starnberg that she bought with the money from her divorce settlement. As Helene rather openly revealed to Egon several years later, the attraction appeared, to a great part, to have been physical. "My mother experienced her first orgasm with Trausil," Egon said. "My father had been a lover of the type 'wham-bam, thank-you-ma'am,'" he said. Egon believed the affair had begun only after his parents were separated; this may not have been the case, however. Putzi's diary for 1936 contains a number of references to a "Herr T"—almost certainly Trausil—whom he blamed for causing his problems with his wife.

Soon after Helene moved out, her friend Emmy Streck met Hitler at a reception in Berlin. He immediately asked after Helene. When she told him about the divorce, he suddenly blurted out: "Well, I'll have to send her a telegram right away and wish her luck!" before thinking again and quickly adding: "No, that wouldn't do, after all." Hitler concluded with the observation: "Frau Hanfstaengl is one of the few real ladies in Germany."

——

LATER that summer, Putzi took Egon for a trip on Lake Starnberg. High on the hills above them was the village of Aufkirchen, the black onion-shaped dome of its church glinting in the sunlight. Everything was still; the silence was disturbed only by the sound of faraway laughter from boys and girls bathing near the shore.

Putzi suddenly turned to his son. "It's nice and quiet here, and we're alone," he told him. "Boy, listen to what I say and don't forget a word of it. Things are not well. We all believed in the movement, didn't we? I'm still trying to believe in it. But I've found a lot of foul corruption here and there. There are many despicable individuals, criminals and perverts to whom Herr Hitler listens. At the rate we're going, we'll have war—a war in which England and America will be against us. It's dangerous for Germany and for the world. The country is in a foul state internally. I ascribe that mainly to the blackguards who are sitting firmly entrenched behind official desks in Berlin and elsewhere. I've tried, God knows, to get at Hitler and warn him."

Ever the optimist, Putzi still clung to the hope that things might improve. There was the danger, though, that the Nazis might turn on him, forcing him to flee. He hoped Egon would decide to follow him into exile, but if so, the boy should not tell anybody—not his best friend or his girlfriend or even his mother, who was now living in Bavaria on her own but, as an American citizen, was in no danger. Nor should he attempt some "Hollywood-style" escape by skiing down the opposite side of a mountain to Austria; it would be far better just to take the train. They agreed to use the codeword "Perhaps"—the name of their little sailing boat. If Egon received a message telling him to have *Perhaps* painted or repaired, it would be the signal for him to take immediate steps to leave.

Egon was to recall that conversation for many years afterward. It opened his eyes to many matters and prepared him for the crisis that was to come. Neither he nor his father were ready, however, for how soon that crisis would come, nor for the strange form it would take.

BEHIND ENEMY LINES

16

AS so often before, it began with a phone call and a summons from Hitler. Putzi's fiftieth birthday, February 11, 1937, was only a few days away, and he was in the library of his home in Munich, working on a speech for the two hundred and fiftieth anniversary of the birth of George Washington. The party Putzi held every year to mark Washington's birthday had become a fixture on the Berlin social calendar—almost anyone who was anyone in the American expatriate community was there, together with some carefully selected Germans.

Fritz Wiedemann, another of Hitler's adjutants, was on the line. "You are urgently requested to come to Berlin at once," he said. "Flight Captain Baur has been instructed to bring you by special plane from the Munich airport." Putzi had been trying for some time to resolve his dispute with Hitler over Lüdecke, but he was not sure whether this summons was a good sign or bad. Orders were orders, though, and he had no alternative but to comply.

The promised special plane failed to turn up; Nazi Germany was not always as efficient as it has since been portrayed. So, the next morning, Putzi took a regular Lufthansa flight instead and was in his Berlin office by noon. He found a note from Wiedemann asking him to report to the Reichskanzlei at 4 PM. Wiedemann had commanded the company in which Hitler had served as a messenger during the First World War. Putzi found him agreeable, if slightly narrow-minded. The two men nevertheless got on well. At their meeting, Wiedemann came straight to the point:

Hitler wanted him to fly to Spain immediately to help out the German journalists who had gone to the country to report on its civil war.

Putzi was indignant. "Suddenly such an important thing," he said sarcastically. "You are nice people; tomorrow I am fifty years old and you send me to Spain on my birthday."

Wiedemann was not to be swayed. "Why don't you comply with these measures, Hanfstaengl," he suggested in a friendly manner. "Many of us miss having you here quite a lot. If you succeed in this mission, the Führer will no doubt want to have you back here again. Your influence would be very valuable."

Wiedemann was unable to reveal any more about the mission, except that it was top secret. After warning Putzi not to say a word about it to his secretary, Wiedemann told him to go across to the Ministry of Propaganda, where he would be filled in on the technicalities by Ministerialrat Berndt, one of Goebbels's advisors, who headed the press department. Putzi was struck when he arrived in the ministry by how pleasant everyone was to him, right down to the girl doing the typing.

Berndt had only scant information to add to what Wiedemann had already told him, however: the Nazis were concerned that German correspondents in Spain were not able to get as good frontline access as their American counterparts enjoyed. The problem, he said, appeared to lie with a certain Captain Bolin; it would be Putzi's job to change his attitude toward the Germans. He would fly to Salamanca and stay in the Grand Hotel, which had been taken over by the Nazis as the headquarters of a bogus commercial organization called HISMA, to which Putzi would be attached.

To Putzi's disquietude, Berndt then began talking about the dangers of Spain and the possibility of being shot down. He also asked Putzi to give him two photographs as soon as possible so he could make him a false passport. It was all beginning to sound rather strange.

"How long will I be away?" Putzi demanded.

"About five or six weeks," came the reply.

Putzi was appalled. He knew five or six weeks could easily turn to three or four months. He had already reconciled himself to missing his fiftieth birthday celebrations; setting off for all that time without being allowed to put his affairs in order was completely out of the question. At the very least, he needed to get some more suitable clothes together for the trip. Wiedemann was unyielding, though.

"We have had a lot of trouble arranging this flight," he told him. "You must depart here tomorrow afternoon at four. You will be picked up at three by a car, which will take you to the airport. By that time I shall have fixed your papers and all the formalities."

So Putzi called his housekeeper, asked her to send some things from Munich, and began hastily to pack. That evening, he ran into Karl Heinrich Bodenschatz at a party at the Finnish embassy. A former World War I flying ace who had served with the legendary Baron von Richthofen, Bodenschatz had become Göring's adjutant in 1933. He greeted Putzi warmly. He already knew about the mission and told Putzi what a great opportunity it gave him to restore his relations with Hitler. Bodenschatz also asked him to go and see Göring the next morning before leaving.

Putzi found Göring in great form; although their once warm relations had cooled in recent years, all seemed forgotten when he greeted him.

"What are they doing with you?" Göring demanded.

"Don't you know?" Putzi retorted.

"They are sending you to Spain."

"Yes, tomorrow is my fiftieth birthday and my old mother has invited me and the boy, and I have to call this whole blooming thing off."

"We cannot help you, you have to go," Göring told him. To Putzi's surprise, Göring also asked him to look out for some other things for him. "If you hear of any minerals, you understand."

That only added to Putzi's sense of disbelief, not least because he did not know Spain at all and did not speak the language.

"Isn't this funny, you give me a job to look for quicksilver and copper and things that you need up here in Germany; at the same time I am meant to look after German correspondents on the entire front from Gibraltar up to I do not know where. This is two jobs; I would rather have yours."

Göring was insistent. "No, Goebbels and the Führer want it, you had better do Goebbels's job," he said. "And on the side do it for me and look out for what you hear and any discoveries, you understand— report them to me." Göring then made a few heavy-handed jokes about keeping away from Spanish women if he did not want to catch venereal disease, and their meeting was over.

Nothing Göring had told Putzi had eased any of his misgivings. If the mission was as important as everyone was trying to make out, then surely the Führer would have wanted to see him? But maybe even this, too, could be explained away. The whole thing, he tried to convince himself, must be a clumsy attempt at reconciliation. "It was my fiftieth birthday and knowing that Hitler had been more or less in a fix with me and it is very hard for him, surrounded as he is with all my enemies, I thought that is probably his technique to get me back into grace again by sending me to Spain and then being able to call me back two months later and say 'Did I not tell you Hanfstaengl was a fine man?'"

In any case, he had little choice. Before leaving, he placed a call with Agnethe von Hausberger, the secretary in his Berlin office, telling her that his orders had changed suddenly and that he was going to spend his birthday with his family in Bavaria.

—

ON the morning of February 11, Maj. Gen. Karl von Schoenebeck, the commander of the test stations in Rechlin-Müritzsee, had received a call from Bodenschatz. He was told to make available a JU 52, with night-flying equipment, for a "special mission." A pilot named Frödel was put in charge of the plane.

That afternoon a car arrived at Putzi's apartment to take him to the airport. There were two other people in the car: a man from the Propaganda Ministry, who appeared to be called Neumann, and a rather scruffy young man in a camel hair coat with a camera around his neck who introduced himself as Jaworsky. To Putzi's distaste, the pair of them spent most of the journey talking about the horrors of the Spanish Civil War in the most lurid details. Their car did not drive south toward Tempelhof Airfield, but instead set off westward toward the military airport at Staaken. At Adolf-Hitler-Platz they picked up Berndt, who gave Putzi his fake passport. It was in the name of Ernst Lehmann, whose profession was given as painter and decorator. Bodenschatz was waiting when they arrived at Staaken. Colonel Kastner, the commandant of the airfield, was also with them. Surprisingly, Kastner then produced a parachute and told Putzi to put it on. As Putzi fumbled with the straps and webbing, he was annoyed to see Jaworksy filming him. It was all rather off-putting.

When Putzi boarded the plane, he became even more alarmed. The seats were made of bare metal and some sixty to seventy hand grenades lay scattered on the floor. The prospect of spending many hours on board was not a welcome one. Jaworsky finally climbed in, too, accompanied by another man. Putzi was not introduced, but he put him down as a "real Gestapo-type." At last the door was bolted shut and the plane took off; as it rose into the air above Berlin, it was buffeted by strong winds. They had been in the air for only ten minutes when Jaworsky came back to Putzi's seat and told him the pilot wanted a word. And so Putzi walked forward, stooping because of the low ceiling, and sat down next to Frödel. The pilot looked him full in the face.

"Aren't you Dr. Hanfstaengl?," he asked.

"Of course," Putzi retorted. "Who else am I supposed to be?"

"I only know you as Ernst Lehmann, but I recognized you from pictures in the newspapers. What are your instructions?"

Putzi said all he knew was that he was flying to Salamanca. Frödel looked surprised. "You are not going to Salamanca," he said. "I am to take you over the Red lines between Barcelona and Madrid, where you are to parachute down."

"What are you talking about?" Putzi demanded. "I have been with Göring. Who has ordered this?"

"Bodenschatz," he replied. "It was in the plan when I opened it. Why are you getting so excited about this? Aren't you an agent?"

"Me, an agent?" Putzi said.

"Yes, they told me that you were an agent. You asked for this job, didn't you?"

"Well, I did not ask for it."

"You know Spanish, don't you?"

"No," Putzi replied.

Suddenly it began to dawn on Putzi what a fool he had been. This was a death sentence, there was no doubt about that, even if there would have been far simpler ways of carrying it out. What better way to eliminate one of the oldest—but most awkward—of the Führer's associates than with a heroic death on a secret mission? Putzi could even visualize the headlines in the *Beobachter* announcing his demise. Clutching at a straw, he tried to persuade the pilot that there must have been a misunderstanding. Why not land somewhere and phone Berlin to sort the matter out? Frödel refused; he had his orders and intended to stick to them. A few moments later, the Gestapo-type came back and Frödel asked Putzi to return to his uncomfortable metal seat.

Putzi was still sitting pondering his fate when, about a quarter of an hour later, one of the engines began to make a rattling sound.

"There's something wrong. We'll have to land and look at it," the pilot called out, giving Putzi what he took to be a meaningful look. He brought the craft down to land at Klein-Polenz, a small airfield tucked away in a pine forest between Leipzig and Dresden in southeastern Germany.

The airfield was deserted; all the mechanics had gone home for the night. So the group all went to the bar and Putzi ordered a round of vermouth. Frödel joined them a few minutes later; the plane could not be repaired until the morning, he told them. It had been decided that they would spend the night in Leipzig. A car would come in twenty minutes and pick them up.

Feigning airsickness, Putzi slipped away and put a call through to the dutiful von Hausberger, who was waiting in his office for instructions. She was appalled at what he told her. She said several foreign journalists had already called asking how he was planning to spend his fiftieth birthday, but she had stalled them.

"If someone asks for me, tell them I have phoned and will be spending my birthday at my mother's house in Uffing," he told her.

Putzi knew he had to seize his chance. After standing the group another round of vermouth, he slipped away again and set off down a country lane. A peasant woman with a cart told him there was a railway station a mile or so away, from where a train was leaving soon for Leipzig. Putzi boarded it just in time; as it set off and passed a level crossing a few minutes later, he caught a glimpse of Frödel standing at the gate. He also saw Putzi.

"We've been looking for you everywhere," the pilot called out. "Come to the Hotel Hauffe." He was too late. The train picked up speed and Putzi hurtled toward Leipzig.

As he sat in his compartment, Putzi pondered what to do next. He thought of going to Berlin to demand an explanation for his bizarre and heavy-handed treatment, but was wary. Of course, it could all have been a joke, he thought. But how would Hitler and the others react if he called their bluff? And if that was what they called a joke, what might they do if they were in earnest? If they had thought nothing of killing hundreds of people during the Night of the Long Knives, they could easily dispose of him. No, the only course of action was to leave the country and try to establish his position from the safety of neutral Switzerland.

Anyone watching Putzi as the train steamed into Leipzig's main station could be excused for thinking they had stumbled onto the set of a detective movie. He let the other passengers get off first, then climbed into another train waiting on the next platform and got out the other side.

Putzi found out there was a night train leaving for Munich in a couple of hours. There was still the matter of his luggage, though, which he had left behind. He suspected it might have been brought to the

Hotel Hauffe, together with the others' things, and took a taxi over there. He told the driver to stop and wait for him out of sight. Glancing furtively through the revolving door, he could see his bags standing next to the porter's desk. Fortunately, there was no sign of the other members of his party, and despite the danger of being spotted, he walked into the lobby, trying hard to affect a nonchalant air.

The porter, however, recognized Putzi and gave him a cheery "Heil Hitler, Herr Doktor." The other people in the party were expecting him and had already gone to the Auerbach Keller, he told Putzi, and offered to carry his bags upstairs. Putzi told him he had met a friend at the Astoria and decided to stay there instead and asked him to load the bags into his taxi. Before leaving, he left a note for Frödel, saying he had received new instructions from the Reichskanzlei and would see him in the morning.

And so he hurried back to the Leipzig station with his bags and took the night train to Munich. He was too nervous to sleep; he spent almost the entire journey looking out the window, ready to jump out if he caught sight of anything untoward. The train pulled into the city at Munich's main station at dawn on Putzi's fiftieth birthday. There was only just over an hour before the connection left for Zurich. Putzi hurried to the nearby Regina Hotel and called his sister, Erna, who lived in Solln, on the outskirts of Munich. He urged her to come as soon as possible because he had something urgent to tell her. He waited until the last moment, but she failed to turn up and reluctantly he boarded the train without meeting her. Three hours later it crossed the border at Lindau. After traversing a narrow tongue of Austria, he had reached Switzerland and freedom.

It is difficult to explain how Putzi was able to slip away with such apparent ease. As Egon subsequently noted, only a small number of people seem to have been in on the plot against his father. In what appeared a stroke of luck, the three men responsible, Hitler, Goebbels, and Göring, spent that evening at the Berlin Philharmonic, where Wilhelm Furtwaengler was conducting. Immediately after the concert, Hitler boarded a train for Munich, while Göring left for a hunting trip in Poland. The Gestapo evidently thought Putzi was still somewhere in Bavaria, but did not bother to check on his office in Berlin or his house in Munich. Nor did they bother any of his friends with questions or make the slightest attempt to trace his son.

"They hoped that Father would eventually waver and come out of hiding," Egon believed. "Then they'd snatch him and everything else, without creating too much attention. If this liquidation had succeeded as planned, Father would probably have been accorded the extreme honor of a state funeral with all the trimmings—and Hitler might have patted me on the head again and told me that my father was a fine man, who died in the execution of his duty toward the fatherland, and that I could do nothing better than take after him."

The Nazi newspapers marked Putzi's fiftieth birthday with fulsome praise. Putzi, the *Beobachter* noted, was a member of one of the oldest Bavarian families, dating back to 1350; since 1931 he had been Hitler's "permanent companion." It noted the books he had written and pointed to his renown as a composer who had written the well-loved marches "Deutscher Föhn," "Jugend Marschiert," and "Deutschland Trauert." His latest work, it stated, was the monumental "Volkschoral Hymne an das Deutsche Erbe." The tone was very much that of an obituary.

——

SO what exactly had happened? The plan for Putzi's "mission" appears to have been hatched a few days earlier over lunch in the chancellery. Every afternoon, sometime after 2;30 PM, members of the leadership would eat with Hitler in his bright, airy dining room. Those especially in his favor would be invited to sit around the main circular table, which had room for fifteen. Hitler would take one of the dark red leather seats on the window side. The remainder would sit at one of the other four smaller tables. Hitler nicknamed the gathering the Restaurant zum Fröhlichen Reichskanzler—literally the "Merry Chancellor's Restaurant."

The meal itself was always simple: plain meat, potatoes, and vegetables, washed down with mineral water, bottled beer, or cheap wine, but because of Hitler's appalling timekeeping, it could often drag on until well after 4 PM. Attendance was important, however, not only to demonstrate closeness to the Führer but also to obtain an insight into his thinking. The daily lunch served both as a channel for Hitler's henchmen to keep abreast of his changing views and as a chance to throw out a bait that might allow them to be granted a personal audience.

Goebbels was one of the most frequent guests and knew how to turn the meals to his advantage, planting jokes which made Hitler roar with laughter but which, more often than not, were intended to demolish his rivals in the struggle for power. Putzi was among the victims of his vicious tongue. Goebbels had long been jealous of Putzi's close ties with Hitler and, according to Albert Speer, the armament minister, never missed an opportunity to blacken his name. "Goebbels began casting aspersions on Hanfstaengl's character, representing him as miserly, money-grubbing, and of dubious honesty," Speer recalled of the luncheons. "He once brought in a phonograph record to show that Hanfstaengl had stolen the melody for a popular march he had composed called 'Der Föhn' from an English song."

The final straw was when the subject of the Spanish Civil War came up and Goebbels told those at the table that Putzi had "made adverse remarks about the fighting spirit of the German soldiers in combat there," Speer said. "Hitler was furious. This cowardly fellow who had no right to judge the courage of others must be given a lesson, he declared." A few days later, Putzi was ordered to fly to Spain.

"All the chapters in this story elicited great merriment at Hitler's table—all the more so since in this case Hitler had plotted the joke together with Goebbels," Speer continued. "But when word came a few days later that the missing [foreign] press chief had sought asylum abroad, Hitler became afraid that Hanfstaengl would collaborate with the foreign press and profit by his intimate knowledge of the Third Reich."

A bizarre role in the affair may also have been played by Unity Mitford. Putzi's connections with Unity and her sister, Diana, had intensified since he had taken them to the first Nuremberg rally. In early 1935, the *Hausmeister* at the Braun Haus, a former army major, had come to Putzi's sister, Erna, asking for help in finding lodgings for Unity, who had come back to Germany to study the language. The *Hausmeister* did not speak any English, Unity still barely knew any German and he was at his wits' end knowing what to do with her. Erna, almost fifty and childless, took Unity, almost thirty years her junior, under her wing and invited her to stay in her comfortable turn-of-the-century wooden house in Solln. Although Unity spent a lot of time away, she kept her clothes, books, and photographs there for the next four years. Erna, who like her brother was extremely well-connected, provided an entrée to Munich's haute-bourgeoisie. She also arranged singing lessons for Unity.

Putzi himself did not like Unity at all; even her anti-Semitism became too much for him. "She spent her time snooping. She hated Americans, and she was a fanatical Jew-baiter, always on about it, boring me with the Jews," he recalled. "She corroborated Hitler in his asininities; that was her chief failing at a critical moment." Putzi nevertheless felt he should keep on her good side, if only because Hitler was clearly so attracted to her. He suspected that, with her sister married to Sir Oswald Mosley, Unity dreamed of going one better and marrying Hitler.

She was also notoriously indiscreet—a quality that Hitler soon learned to use to his own advantage as she moved closer and closer into his inner circle. She used to spend a lot of time at the British consulate in Munich and could be the perfect unwitting conduit if Hitler wanted something to get back to the Foreign Office in London. "Hitler knew that if he wanted something broadcast he had only to talk in front of Unity," recalled Winifred Wagner. "That he told me himself."

Such indiscretion worked in both directions, however. Germany had become a dangerous place, where one careless word could easily seal someone's fate. While most of those around Hitler behaved themselves accordingly, Unity would unthinkingly repeat gossip that she had heard to Hitler, often unaware of the disastrous effect her indiscretions might have. Erna tried in vain to make her more careful, accusing Unity of acting as if "the party were an operetta."

Putzi's "mission" may have been partially a result of such indiscretion. Some time earlier he had taken Unity and Egon, by then fifteen, out in his boat on Lake Starnberg. As they rowed, Putzi reminisced about how tough it had been to live as an enemy alien in New York during the First World War and how, if another war came, he would much rather spend it alongside his comrades in the trenches. He then, as usual, began criticizing the malign influence exercised by Goebbels, Rosenberg, and all the others around Hitler. Unity was appalled; if he thought that way he should no longer be the party spokesman, she told him.

Putzi stood his ground, professing his loyalty to the Führer and saying that it did him no good to be surrounded by yes-men. The damage had already been done, however. Unity was fiercely loyal to Hitler and all those around him.

"Father, this woman really hates you," Egon told his father after she had gone. "I saw it in her eyes."

Putzi may have paid for his careless words shortly afterward when Unity visited Berlin with her sister, Diana, and cousin, Clementine Mitford. Hitler invited the women to dinner with him in the Reichskanzlei and later they all watched a film together. Afterward, the conversation turned to Putzi, and Unity appears to have recounted some of what was said during the boat trip. According to this version of the story, it was then that it was decided to send Putzi on the flight—although it was made clear that he would never actually be made to parachute out of the plane and would be allowed to land back in Munich after flying around harmlessly for a time. "He plans a wonderfully funny joke on Putzi," was how Unity put it in her diary.

The whole thing may have been little more than a joke to Unity—or to Goebbels—but there seems little doubt that the mission was intended by Hitler as a serious warning to Putzi that he should toe the party line a little more conscientiously or else face the consequences. Putzi certainly saw the whole thing as a serious attempt to kill him—and continued to believe it for the rest of his life.

"A joke is supposed to end humorously and not degradingly," he recalled later. "They should have landed and then Bodenschatz should have come out with a cake, with burning candles, and say, 'Hanfstaengl, the Führer sends his best regards to you, we will have dinner with him tonight.'"

——

PUTZI began his exile in style, staying at the Hotel Baur au Lac, which was, as it is now, one of the most exclusive and expensive in Zurich. He checked in as Dr. Franzen and took a room on the top floor. One of his first actions was to summon Erna. He then shaved for the first time in thirty-six hours and at 6 PM, completely exhausted, lay down on the crisp linen and went to sleep. "God how tired—and Zurich outside the window with new clear church bells to lull you to sleep," read his last diary entry for his birthday.

Erna duly arrived the following afternoon. She had taken Putzi's gradual fall from grace badly and his exile only worsened matters. Not only could it have damaging consequences for the family firm, it would also, by extension, harm her own position. As they sat together in his comfortable hotel room, she listened incredulously to the story of his flight. She could not accept, as Putzi did, that Hitler had intended to kill him and thought her brother was suffering from a nervous breakdown. And so she hatched her plan.

Through a friend, they had a connection with Carl Jung, Freud's former partner. Now in his early sixties, he was still practicing in his native Zurich. Erna was convinced that Jung could help her brother; in the meantime, she could help herself by spreading the word in Berlin and Munich that Putzi was sick and being treated. She could not tell Putzi himself, of course; he would have been outraged at any suggestion that he was suffering from paranoia. But Erna had found a neat way around this as well by suggesting to her brother that he *pretend* to be sick. On

February 16, Putzi had the first of his consultations at Jung's home in Küssnacht. It must have been a fascinating encounter. Although Putzi went back the next day, they did not continue further. Jung warned him it would be unwise to pretend to be his patient.

Putzi kept his head down, spending most of his time in his heavily curtained room, where he also took most of his meals. Occasionally he would wander along the lake or gaze in the windows of Zurich's art dealers. Back in Germany, rumors were growing about his fate. The Washington birthday party was only a few days off. This year's guest list was as glittering as ever. Besides prominent Americans such as Ambassador Dodd, Col. Truman Smith, and Rev. Stewart H. Herman, Jr., of the American Church in Berlin, it also included Germans such as Dr. Hugo Eckener, Prince Louis Ferdinand of Prussia, and the German ambassador, Heinz Dieckhoff, who were seen as friends of the United States. A few days before the party was due, those on the guest list received a call from von Hausberger, telling them it had been canceled. She did not give a reason.

On March 13, the *Daily Telegraph* of London ran a story claiming that Putzi had been expelled from Germany and his press office "liquidated." Some reports claimed he was in Spain, others that he was in Britain, the newspaper said. It was understood, though, "that he was recently denounced and thereupon required to leave the country." *The New York Times*, too, picked up the story; it noted that Putzi had formerly been one of Hitler's closest friends but said relations between the two men had been deteriorating over the preceding two years. The cause of the breach was variously described as jealousy and internal dissension among Hitler's other friends.

The story rapidly took off. The next day, the American press carried a report from Berlin stating that Putzi was hiding out in the Alps rather than carrying out a supposed secret mission to Spain. Before leaving just over a month earlier, it noted, he had declared: "I am afraid there is something phony about that special mission of mine." Friends were quoted in the report as saying he had departed on secret orders from Hitler, with whom he had been out of favor for some time, but had not gotten any farther than Switzerland. There was also speculation that Joachim von Ribbentrop, the German ambassador to Britain, had wanted Putzi to be moved to another job where he would not be able to criticize the work of his embassy.

Such newspapers reports, although edging toward the truth, were nevertheless speculation. A German government spokesman said he knew nothing of Putzi's location or future plans. Von Hausberger would say merely that the foreign press office "was in the process of liquidation." Nor was Putzi's family able or willing to shed any light on the affair. Erna said she believed her brother had gone on a secret mission for Hitler but did not know where he was. His mother said she had expected him to come and see her on his birthday but had received a letter from him the following day in which he said he had left on a mission. "The goal is secret," he wrote, adding that she would hear from him later, when he was free to talk. "Since then we've heard nothing whatever of him."

To add to the mystery, the Propaganda Ministry issued a communiqué the next day announcing that Putzi's bureau was in the process of being dismantled because it had become superfluous; its head was traveling abroad and would be assigned to "artistic duties" when he returned, likely in two or three weeks. Other rumors had Putzi on vacation or official business in Moscow, Spain, or even New York.

Louis P. Lochner, the Berlin bureau chief of the Associated Press, was intrigued by the affair. He was among those who had been invited—and then uninvited—to Putzi's Washington's birthday party. In a society where disappearances were becoming all too common, he was curious to find out what had happened to his old friend. He received his answer two days later at a cocktail party given by Martha Dodd. Lochner and some of the other guests were talking about Putzi's mysterious disappearance, when they were interrupted by Lt. Cmdr. Harry Guthrie, the U.S. naval attaché, who had overheard their conversation.

"There's nothing mysterious about Hanfstaengl," Guthrie said. "Why, I ran into him at the bar of the Hotel Baur au Lac in Zurich only yesterday; I've just returned from there."

Lochner sensed a scoop. Although he was the only journalist in the group addressed by Guthrie, there were others at the reception and there was a danger that they might pick up the story. He left as quickly as possible without attracting attention and tried to telephone Putzi in the hotel. Whatever had really happened to his friend, he reckoned his natural curiosity would get the better of him and he would take the call. His hunch was correct.

"How did you find out I was here?" Putzi demanded.

"Never mind," Lochner replied. "You know as well as I do that a newsman does not reveal his sources. The main thing is that I know where you are. That's today's big story, plus anything you want to tell me about your reasons for fleeing."

Putzi urged Lochner to take the next plane to Zurich, where, he said, he would tell him the whole story. Lochner demurred; he felt he had already gotten the facts he needed. And in any case, if any follow-up was needed, he could always ask his colleagues from the Associated Press bureaus in Berne or Geneva to go and see Putzi. In the meantime, Lochner recalled, Putzi instructed the hotel to tell any callers from Berlin that "Herr Doktor is not in."

The next morning the American press carried Lochner's story. Putzi, it reported, had expressed surprise that the world had been hunting for him. "I am taking a vacation and going daily on outings. I expect to return to Berlin after Easter," he was quoted as saying. Informed that his office had been closed and an announcement made that he would receive an academic assignment, he declared: "I am now fifty years old and have for some time been waiting to get back to my historical studies. I am glad if that will be made possible."

The regime in Berlin, meanwhile, was stirring. It is not clear at what point precisely that Hitler learned how badly their joke had backfired. Indeed, he and Goebbels probably initially believed Putzi would come home of his own accord after a few weeks away. But more than a month had now passed and Putzi was still in Switzerland. He had let little slip about his intentions, but the Nazi leadership knew he could be a loose cannon. As one of the few people who had been close to Hitler since the early 1920s, Putzi was literally the man who knew too much. Given his literary ambitions, it was likely that he might record his reminiscences in a book.

By 1937, as the Nazis' aggressive policies drove the world closer and closer to war, Hitler should have had more important things to worry about than the prospect of a few revelations from a former aide. The whole thing was potentially embarrassing, though, and he and the men around him were keen to avoid a scandal. Putzi had to be persuaded to return to Germany.

The Gestapo sent several messages to Putzi, urging him to come home. They were all ignored and another approach was clearly required. And so, on March 20, the liveried porter in the Hotel Baur au Lac announced the arrival of a certain Herr Bodenschatz. Putzi was astonished. But Göring's adjutant was relaxed and the mood warm and convivial. The whole thing, he insisted, had been nothing more than a joke, to which Putzi had, unfortunately, overreacted, and he suggested he return, saying he had nothing to fear. To emphasize his point,

Bodenschatz even gave Putzi a letter signed by Göring. It was written in the familiar *du* form.

Dear Hanfstaengl,

According to information received by me today, you have been in Zurich for some time and have no intention of coming back to Germany. I presume that the reason for this is your recent flight from Staaken to Wurzen in Saxony. I assure you that the whole affair was only intended as a harmless joke. We wanted to give you an opportunity of thinking over some rather over-audacious utterances you have made. Nothing more than that was intended.

I have sent Colonel Bodenschatz to you, who will give you further explanation in person. I consider it vitally necessary for various reasons that you come back to Germany straightaway with Bodenschatz. I assure you on my word of honor that you can remain here amongst us as you always have done in complete freedom.

Forget your suspicions and act reasonably.

With comradely greetings
Heil Hitler
Hermann Göring

In a postscript, he had added by hand: *I expect you to accept my word.*

Putzi was not convinced. If it was all a joke, he asked, why had his office been closed, his staff dismissed, and an arrest order issued for him?

"It is just the idea of joking and was meant to give you a little fright," Bodenschatz insisted.

It is funny that I should need three ministries for a little fright," Putzi replied. "And it is very funny that the pilot tells me that we are going to Barcelona and that you are using the taxpayers' aeroplanes to make such really unnecessary jokes. If that is a joke, then why didn't the pilot tell me?"

"Don't talk about the pilot," Bodenschatz said. "Everything he said was rehearsed before the plane took off."

Putzi still had not been won over. "Since when has Lufthansa and the aviation corps in Germany had such marvelous actors that they can improvise such things as the pilot said to me?"

Bodenschatz did not have an answer.

For the time being, Putzi's main concern was for the safety of Egon, who had just turned sixteen and was at boarding school in Starnberg, just over thirty-five miles southwest of Munich. Putzi knew the Nazis could easily use his son as a hostage to force his return and realized he would have to play for time. He said he needed to think things over, and Bodenschatz proposed going to the Swiss Alpine resort of Arosa for a couple of days before coming back for his answer.

Putzi decided to try to speed up Egon's departure. Since their conversation on the lake, his son had known he might have to flee the country; and soon after his arrival in Zurich, Putzi managed to get word to him, telling him to make preparations to leave. He also warned him not to give any impression of undue haste, since this could give the whole thing away. The situation had obviously changed, though, as a result of the publication of Lochner's story. So, the day before Bodenschatz's visit, Putzi had telephoned the school's director, who passed on the message to his son telling him to attempt to leave for Switzerland that weekend.

There was a problem, though. Egon realized, to his horror, that he did not have a passport. Under normal circumstances, he would have just gone to Munich to get one, but he was afraid that hindering instructions would have been sent through from Berlin. He was in luck, though. He was formally a resident of Starnberg and so was able to go to the Bezirksamt there instead. As a minor he needed the permission of his parents for such a document and wrote to his father asking him to send it to him.

This process was still going on when Bodenschatz returned to Zurich two days later for his answer. Putzi had sent Egon the necessary note, but they needed more time to get his passport and so he decided to drag out the negotiations with Bodenschatz. He did so by denouncing Goebbels as the most probable agent of his misfortune and demanding to know how Göring's guarantee would protect him from the vengeance of the "little doctor."

Bodenschatz was beginning to lose his composure. "We cannot keep things quiet forever," he told Putzi. "The foreign press people in Berlin are already starting to ask all sorts of awkward questions. If you won't see reason, things might become very unpleasant for your family."

Putzi was not ready to be threatened in that way. "Tell your boss to get any idea of hostages out of his mind," he said. "If I hear that one of them has been as much as threatened I shall publish everything I know about the whole Nazi regime. All my records have been in places of safety for some time and I can tell you even the little Herr Goebbels won't come out of the closet for weeks." Upping the stakes, Putzi also demanded a written apology, ideally from Hitler himself. The Nazi leader had humiliated him badly, he said, and "must understand that I will need a very long time to come to terms with this joke."

Part of this was pure bluff; although Putzi had a few documents with him, most of his papers were still in Germany, and, despite his efforts, he had not yet succeeded in getting them out. Bodenschatz did not know this, though.

"Very well," replied the envoy, who had clearly exhausted his negotiating mandate. "I will report back to Göring and call you from Berlin. There must be some way of settling this."

The Nazis clearly had not anticipated such resistance. But three days later Bodenschatz was back again, and this time he tried a different, more conciliatory line. Although confirming that Putzi's office had been closed down since he left, he offered him an important position under Göring and said he could name his own salary. The arrest warrant against him had also been withdrawn. He gave Putzi until Easter to accept the offer—or face the consequences.

Putzi was not swayed; after the visit, he had telephoned Starnberg and found that, even though the note he had scribbled for his son fell short of the documents required, Egon had managed to persuade an elderly official working in the Bezirksamt to issue his passport. If all went well, the boy would soon be on his way to Switzerland.

Indeed, that morning, after drinking some Cinzano to try to steady his nerves, Egon had boarded a train bound for Zurich. The journey to the border town of Lindau proceeded smoothly, but when the train stopped there, the frontier police began to work their way through the almost empty compartment. Egon crossed his fingers as the guard walked toward him. The guard stared for a few moments at his passport and then handed it back to him. He then demanded to look into his bag. Inside lay some towels and a picture of Hitler. The guard bent down to examine the dedication:

To my young friend Egon Hanfstaengl
Most cordially, Adolf Hitler
Berlin, March 24, 1932

Egon's heart missed a beat. Why had he been so foolish as to bring it with him, he asked himself. The guard straightened himself up and looked at Egon.

"Did the Führer really sign that himself?" he asked in some amazement.

"Sure he did. My father brought it to me," Egon replied.

"*Donnerwetter* [that's a bit of all right]. But why are you taking it with you like that?"

"Well, you know, it's not everybody has such a picture. Besides, I want to show it to my aunt in Zurich. I'm going to spend my vacation with her—haven't seen her in a long time."

Impressed, the guard told him to close his bag. The boy's ordeal was not over yet, however. The guard demanded to know how much money Egon had with him. He told him he had about forty reichsmarks.

"I'm sorry, boy, but I can't let you across with more than ten marks," the guard said. "That's the law."

At this stage Egon would happily have thrown the money out the train window, but the guard suggested he send it to someone by money order. "Then you show me the slip and I'll let you through," he said.

Egon ran into the station in search of the telegraph office. The only person he could think of was his elderly aunt Hedwig in Munich. So he sent the thirty reichsmarks to her. He made it back to the train just in time to show the guard the slip before the train pulled out of the station.

"I'm glad you made it," the guard said. "Have a good trip and enjoy yourself."

Egon sat down in his window seat and waited; the last mile to the border seemed to last an eternity. But then came the sign: "Grenze-Österreich." They had reached the Austrian border. The Austrian border guards showed little interest in him and had only a cursory look at his passport. The train continued, but it took only a few minutes to cross the narrow tongue of Austrian territory and then there was the sign for the Swiss border. The Swiss official did not say much either; like his Austrian counterpart, he was happy with a quick check of Egon's papers.

Egon had to struggle to contain his joy. He was out, more by blind luck than anything else, but he was free nonetheless. He was also dead tired and ravenously hungry. But there was nothing to do but wait. So he kicked off his shoes, sat back in his seat and waited impatiently as the train meandered its way through the Swiss countryside toward Zurich.

It was almost midnight when his train finally pulled into the station. Egon spotted his father immediately. Dressed in his oldest country clothes, he towered above the other people waiting and seemed to shift from one foot to another as he tried to catch a glimpse of those emerging from the train. Even though exhausted, Egon couldn't resist playing a trick on his father. Sneaking around his back, he waited until everyone else had gotten off and then surprised him.

"*Herrgott* [Lord God]," Putzi exclaimed. "*Herrgott*, fellow you made it! I've met every train from Munich for two days and now you're here at last."

They walked from the station down through the Bahnhofstrasse to the hotel. Zurich was almost completely blacked out; the city was holding an air-raid practice. After leaving Egon's things in Putzi's room on the top floor, they set back out again and went to the Bahnhofrestaurant Zur Enge. Despite the lateness of the hour, Egon managed to devour a steak and heaps of salad. It was almost 2:30 AM when they finally went back to the hotel. He slept through most of the next day.

With Egon's arrival, Putzi had severed a vital link with Germany. Now there no longer seemed a point in remaining in Switzerland. A new, though no less dramatic, phase in his life was about to begin.

17

PUTZI left Switzerland for London on April 1, 1937. The date was chosen consciously—it was the birthday of Bismarck, the Iron Chancellor. Money was beginning to be a problem, though, and he had to borrow one hundred Swiss francs from a friend. He and Egon took a second-class compartment to Calais and then crossed the English Channel to Dover by ferry.

Putzi's arrival was noted by Britain's Special Branch, a division of the Metropolitan Police. "Ernst Hanfstaengl, German, well-known as a Nazi press propagandist, arrived at this port from Calais at 1.15 PM today. He was allowed to land for two to three weeks in order to visit friends. He gave his future address as Bayswater Hotel, London." The description was concise: "Age fifty; occupation 'writer'; height six foot four inches; powerful build; broad shoulders; hair and eyes, brown; complexion, pale; clean-shaven; large features. Wearing grey trilby hat; dark grey suit; blue shirt and collar; brown tie; dark grey overcoat; black shoes." His son, Egon, the report noted, was accompanying him and would stay at the same address.

Putzi may not have had much money, but he was determined to spend what little he had left in style. After using his last coins to tip the waiter on the train to London, he hailed a taxi when they arrived at Victoria Station. Egon, who was aware of the parlous state of their finances, was horrified at the extravagance, but his father told him not to worry. Perhaps in order to cover his tracks, Putzi told the driver to make not for the Bayswater Hotel but instead for Claridge's, one of the most expensive establishments in the city. He asked the doorman to take care of the fare and took a cheap garret room normally used by staff. The next few days were spent avoiding the newspapermen who had heard rumors of his arrival in London. Egon would be sent to survey the lobby for "enemies," and they would enter and exit the hotel by a small side entrance.

Money, or rather the lack of it, was to be the defining feature of Putzi's next two years. A man with lavish tastes, he showed little inclination to change his ways. Soon after arriving, he enrolled Egon at St. Paul's, one of the most prestigious private schools in London and engaged a personal secretary, Elizabeth Downing, and a housekeeper/cook. The challenge was finding a way of paying for all this, while at the same time continuing his complicated negotiations to return to Germany. Journalism was one possibility, although potentially hazardous. The days were long past when Putzi could expect to be paid for the kind of pro-Hitler piece he had written for *Collier's* three years earlier. The mood in the press had changed: in demand now were critical articles about the Nazis containing salacious details about Hitler and his entourage. Yet writing such a piece would mean a clear break with the regime and Putzi was not yet ready for that; a part of him still dreamed of returning to Germany. For the time being, at least, he had to bide his time.

There was another way of making money, though, and it presented itself unexpectedly a few days after his arrival. When Putzi called Mary von Gersdorff, a friend from Berlin, she mentioned that the latest edition of *Cavalcade*, a British magazine, contained a "nasty article" about him. The story, dated March 27 and headlined "Clash," gave a poignant description of Putzi's exile in Zurich and mused on the reasons for his departure from his homeland. The magazine claimed he had upset von Rippentrop, of whom he had always been jealous, by planting stories in foreign papers suggesting that he was about to be moved from his post as ambassador to Britain. Von Ribbentrop had then gotten his revenge. Putzi, the magazine said, "was told that the time for him had come to leave Germany. Hitler's loyalty was at an end." As he wandered lonely and despondent, "Putzy [sic] wondered why his friend Hitler had not come to the rescue, felt his chances were growing smaller every day."

Putzi was delighted at von Gersdorff's find. He would have to consult with his lawyers, of course, but if they agreed that the *Cavalcade* article was libelous, a legal action could provide a useful source of much-needed funds. Equally important, it would give him leverage against Berlin; he could make it clear to Hitler that if he was to bring a case against the magazine, then he would have to reveal the true sinister circumstances of his flight. The article, he told von Gersdorff, "is invaluable to me and my lawyers and forms a superb platform for all we are intending to do." Kenneth Brown, his lawyer, agreed and an action was launched.

The day after Putzi first learned of the *Cavalcade* article, Brown replied on his behalf to the letter that Göring had sent him in Switzerland. "It is now apparent that the public in and outside Germany is being led to believe that I am prevented from returning to Germany for reasons which are discreditable to myself and I have no intention of standing for this," Putzi wrote. If his name could not be cleared in any other way, he would sue newspapers that spread "obnoxious and untrue reports," describing in the process how and why he had left Germany. In such circumstances he could not be expected to return home for the time being.

The Nazis were still keen to lure Putzi back, though, especially because of his intimate knowledge of Hitler dating back fifteen years and the potentially embarrassing use that he could make of it. And so, on April 12, Bodenschatz was sent to visit him in London. Putzi was in no mood to change his mind, however; indeed, the opposite was true. The *Cavalcade* report and other stories elsewhere meant that his departure from Germany was now a public matter—making some kind of formal apology all the more necessary in his eyes. Bodenschatz was unyielding too. He did not bring with him any new concessions, only an ultimatum: Putzi had five days to return to Germany. If he failed to do so, he would be treated as an emigrant and, ominously, "other agencies" would take over the case. The next day, Bodenschatz left.

Putzi refused to be cowed. The day the ultimatum expired, he moved not to Germany but to a new rented home in Maida Vale in West London. He also wrote to friends back in Munich asking them to take personal effects from his house there and put them in safekeeping.

Goebbels was livid, not least because he had been largely responsible for the "joke" that had prompted Putzi's flight and was now backfiring. As he made clear in an entry in his diary the day after the Bodenschatz visit, the entire affair was inching toward acute embarrassment. "Hanfstaengl is in London. He is threatening revelations," Goebbels wrote. "A swine . . . I never considered him anything else. . . . If he starts speaking his mind, it will put all the other émigrés in the shade. Once we get him, we must arrest him very quickly. And never let him go."

Yet despite Bodenschatz's attempt to portray his visit as Putzi's last chance, Berlin was not yet ready to give up. A few days later, Göring sent over Fritz von Hausberger, the husband of Putzi's secretary, to warn him that he would be considered a traitor and dispossessed if he did not return home. The former Austrian army officer had been given instructions to persuade Putzi to come back and offered him no fewer than seven different jobs. His wife, eager to see her boss return, also tried to put pressure on Putzi's sister, Erna, to persuade him to reconsider. Then, on May 8, Herbert Stenger, staff leader of the Verbindungsstab (Liaison Staff), arrived with the usual mixture of promises and threats. Even Putzi's mother, Katherine, became involved when she took advantage of a visit to Britain two months later to reiterate to her son Göring's invitation to return home. Putzi's aide, Voigt, had an attempt too. But Putzi refused to listen to any of them.

Soon afterward there was good news on his court case. On July 7, *Cavalcade*'s owners formally apologized to Putzi for suggesting that he was "guilty of conduct that was discreditable to himself." Although the details were not announced, they agreed to pay him two hundred and fifty pounds in damages as well as costs. Putzi was delighted and fired off a statement in which he described his victory as a tribute to British justice. He also contacted Louis Lochner, the AP Berlin bureau chief, and urged him to get the story into the German-language papers of Switzerland and Austria that were read by the Nazi leadership. Putzi was convinced that his victory would help his quest for an apology from Hitler. But if the Nazi leader and his cronies were impressed, they kept it to themselves.

However welcome the two hundred and fifty pounds, Putzi could not live by legal judgments alone. Nor was he receiving any money from the family firm in which he had been obliged to give up his shares. He instead set to work on his memoirs, and on July 19 he signed contracts with publishers Hamish Hamilton in London and Harper and Brothers in New York. To help his research, he fired off letters to antiquarian bookshops in Munich in search of material on Hitler's rise to power. He wanted, in particular, a book of his collected speeches, a secondhand copy of *Mein Kampf*, and a complete set of back issues of the *Beobachter*. This was clearly going to be a serious work, which would rely on more than just his memory. Bizarrely, Putzi also ordered books in German about Oliver Cromwell. To avoid arousing attention back in Munich, he often wrote in English, signing himself

Ernest Sedgwick. He also engaged Robert Wölfle, who owned an anti-quarian bookshop near Munich University, to catalog his library and other personal effects that he had left behind during his hasty flight.

Putzi, meanwhile, was becoming a nonperson in Germany. An exchange of letters between the tax office and the Gestapo, dated March and April 1937, that were to emerge only after the war, made it clear that he would be arrested if he ever returned to Germany. On the orders of Martin Bormann, it was ruled that "Herr Dr. Hanfstaengl not be mentioned anymore in publications of any sort. . . . This measure is to be carried out absolutely as a party-internal matter so that it does not become public." The order continued, "I also request you to consider how it would be possible to withdraw his books and compositions from sale in a discreet way, without attracting attention." In Putzi's absence, a Reichsfluchtsteuer—a tax for leaving Germany—of forty thousand reichsmarks was also imposed on him.

Things were beginning to change, though. And again the cause was Putzi's old nemesis, Lüdecke. Ever since moving to America and start-ing his propaganda broadcasts, Lüdecke had been threatening to reveal everything he knew about the Nazi leadership. In November he did so: his book *I Knew Hitler: The Story of a Nazi Who Escaped the Blood Purge* was published in the United States to considerable success. A British edition did not come out until 1938, but Putzi was able to have his first glimpse at the book late that month at the British Museum. The book, which ran to more than seven hundred pages, was very similar to one that Putzi himself could have written—and in fact did write after the war. Starting with his own first meeting with Hitler in 1922—just a few months before Putzi's—Lüdecke went on to describe the growth of the Nazi movement up until the Night of the Long Knives and his own bizarre relationship with it.

Putzi himself earned only a few snide references. After claiming cred-it for introducing him to the movement, Lüdecke noted how he swiftly became "Hitler's admirer-in-chief" and a sort of social secretary whose "comfortable and cultivated home was unquestionably the first house of the kind to open its doors to Hitler." He also mocked Putzi for his "eccentric manners" and "grotesque features." But although hinting at the tensions between them, Lüdecke failed to describe how his long-running feud with Putzi had helped precipitate both their downfalls.

Publication of the book had contradictory effects on Putzi. On the one hand, he felt vindicated; now that his old rival's break with the regime was final, there could be no further obstacle to his own rehabilitation. At the same time, though, it appeared to cast a shadow over his own plans to write his memoirs. As rumors grew that he too was intending to put pen to paper, so too did speculation that he would follow Lüdecke down the path toward exile from the party.

Putzi was still unsure of what to do; before taking any further action he needed to know for certain the reason for what had happened to him and who was responsible. Part of him wanted to cling to the idea that "the joke"—if that is what it was—had been perpetrated by Goebbels and some of his cronies but not by Hitler himself. This, in turn, explained his reluctance to rush into print with his book. If he published all manner of compromising material about Hitler and it turned out that the Nazi leader had known nothing of the conspiracy, then he would have felt very foolish. Putzi also hesitated because of rumors that Goebbels was in disgrace over an affair that he was having with Lina Barowa, a glamorous Czech actress. If his great enemy was about to be forced out, then it could only be beneficial to his own case.

As Putzi saw it, it was ultimately all up to Hitler. If the Nazi leader could be persuaded to write a letter apologizing for what had happened, then Putzi could deposit it with his lawyers in London and be in a "relatively strong position to force my point of view through." But this meant he had to be careful not to blemish his record as a loyal supporter of the regime.

IT was at about this time that another event from the past came back to haunt Putzi. Almost two decades had passed since the end of the First World War, but some outstanding property claims between Germany and America still remained unresolved. Matters were complicated by allegations that Germans who had been living in America at the time had been involved in various acts of sabotage—chief among them the explosion on Black Tom pier in July 1916. A number of corporations that had suffered losses as a result—including the Lehigh Valley and Canadian Pacific railroads, which served the pier—wanted compensation to be paid out of German property confiscated by the U.S. Alien Property Custodian during the war. A Mixed Claims Commission, comprising one American, one German, and one independent umpire, was appointed in 1922 to investigate the various incidents prior to April 1917. But by 1938, it still had not completed its work.

Putzi had been dragged into the affair in 1934 when James Larkin, an Irish-born dockworker and Labor Party leader who had spent the war in New York, filed an affidavit accusing him of having spied for the Germans. Larkin, active in the Socialist Party of America, claimed Putzi had been one of the official agents in and about the port of New York "charged with the supervision of the destructive operations from 1915 onward." As a result of these allegations, Putzi had only narrowly avoided being subpoenaed by a House Committee looking into German activities in America during his visit to Harvard in June 1934.

Whatever the truth about the spying allegations, Peaslee & Bingham, the lawyers acting for the Lehigh Valley Railroad, suspected that Putzi had valuable inside knowledge of what had been going on within New York's German community during the war. The fact that he was now living in exile in Britain also suggested that he might be more willing than other Germans to give evidence. On March 11 they sent his lawyer a telegram saying that they understood he might be in America and wanted to consult him for "possible valuable service." They promised to cover his traveling expenses and "reasonable compensation for his time." In a follow-up telegram ten days later, they said they wanted to know whether Putzi was willing to corroborate testimony by Larkin that the two men had met in New York in April 1916 and discussed matters relating to Germany's activities there. Even if Putzi was not prepared to file a formal affidavit, then at least his knowledge about what had gone on and about recent false defenses in litigation could be decisive, they wrote. Confidentiality was assured.

Putzi, as ever, wanted to weigh all the options; his growing debts and dearth of possible sources of income left him little alternative. Therefore, while continuing to make encouraging noises to Peaslee & Bingham—not least to try to find out how much they were prepared to pay—he also approached the German embassy and told them what was going on. The affair appeared to present him with a golden opportunity to prove his loyalty to Berlin, not just by refusing to testify for the Americans but by taking the stand for Germany instead. He also hoped he could extract some money from Berlin for his pains.

His strategy succeeded—but only to a point. Göring, who also had become involved, wanted Putzi to testify for Germany and promised sufficient funds for his trip. But the Nazis balked at Putzi's attempt to use the case to extract a formal apology for the manner of his departure. They were apparently also staggered by his demand for more than a thousand pounds to cover attorneys' fees and various costs, as well as a first-class round trip ticket to New York.

On March 29, 1938, Ernst von Weizsäcker, the German state secretary, wrote to the German embassy in London, on behalf of von Ribbentrop, warning Putzi to lower his demands. "If H. [Hanfstaengl] is inclined to anticipate and demand 'satisfaction' with his return to Germany, that is a basis upon which nothing further can happen," he wrote. The best Putzi could hope for was to go back home and live quietly, without becoming involved in politics. If he did so loyally, then he could conduct "an unmolested existence."

Putzi was caught in a difficult situation: to testify for the Americans would certainly have been his most lucrative option—an important consideration since, as he noted in his diary on April 1, he had just two pounds in his pocket and still had not paid Elizabeth Downing, his secretary. He was reluctant, though. He saw the case as a total invention and considered Larkin a perjurer. To have testified for the Americans would have meant a final break with Berlin. Also, whatever his feelings, the case was against imperial Germany, to which he still felt loyalty, and not against the Nazis, an important distinction in his mind. There was the matter of his word, too, for he had discussed the matter with von Weizsäcker and von Neurath in late summer 1936, when he was still living in Germany, and assured them he would testify according to the truth.

On April 8, Putzi left aboard the *Ile de France* for the six-day voyage to New York. He was inclining to the German side, but still not completely decided. His visit was a far more subdued affair than the trip to Harvard four years earlier. Then he had been at the height of his powers and influence; now he was a mere exile caught up in a curious matter that remained obscure to the outside world. Putzi's arrival nevertheless caused a stir in the local press and he was understandably cautious. Harry Meeker, an old New York friend, and his wife, Muriel, heard he was coming and went to meet him when the ship docked. Seeing Meeker making for him in the distance, Putzi immediately assumed he was a reporter and dodged him. Muriel eventually caught up with him.

Putzi's first stop was at the Harvard Club, where he had arranged to meet Dr. Paulig, a diplomat at the German embassy. During that and subsequent meetings, Paulig helped him draft an affidavit in which he denied any link with the German military during the First World War and any involvement in "destructive operations" directed against the

American war effort. It was agreed that he would travel to Washington on April 26 to sign and swear to the final version of the document.

In the meantime, Putzi found time to revisit some of his former haunts. He stayed for several days at the Meekers' home at 163 West Eighty-eighth Street and repaid their hospitality by taking them to eat at Voisin's, on Park Avenue, and Longchamps, on Seventy-eighth Street and Madison Aveune. They also made a trip to the Metropolitan Museum of Art. As well as meeting other old friends, Putzi visited the site of his old shop on Forty-fifth Street and what had been his residence at 4 Christopher Street—which to his chagrin had been turned into a parking lot. Much of the time the press was on his trail; he was forced to make a swift exit through the kitchens after he thought he had been spotted during one of his visits to the Harvard Club. On another occasion, he contemplated escape across a roof. The Meekers found the whole thing terribly amusing. "We had a good laugh when we read about the city being searched (in vain) for Dr. Hanfstaengl, while we were taking it easy in the center of things," Meeker recalled later.

Yet despite all the time he had spent with Paulig, Putzi was still not sure whether to sign or not. To the frustration of the German embassy, he decided to give himself more time. Two weeks later he returned to Britain—without having put his signature to the document.

Putzi's American trip had a bizarre postscript. Among those newspapers and magazines that wrote about it was *The New Republic*. On April 27, 1938, the day he left New York, it carried an article entitled "Undesirable Refugees." The magazine wrote: "We are heartily in favor of the suggestion that the United States extend its hospitality to political refugees from other countries, but this does not lessen our dislike of two recent ones." The first of the pair was Gerardo Machado, the former president of Cuba, a "bloody-handed dictator" whose police had murdered at least three hundred and fifty of his political opponents. The other was Putzi. "Dr. Hanfstaengl was famous as Hitler's boyfriend until he became the victim of a palace intrigue," the magazine added. "Political sanctuary is supposed to be for the victims of persecution, not the persecutors themselves."

This was exactly what Putzi needed—or so it seemed. Still flush with the success of his action against *Cavalcade*, he saw the chance of a second victory. This case appeared to have far more potential. Not only was it a clear libel that should earn him substantial damages, but since the charge was as insulting to Hitler as it was to him, it appeared to provide another means of leverage with Berlin. Had *The New Republic* been a British publication, Putzi could have taken advantage of Britain's tight libel laws to sue there, and would likely have won easily. Unfortunately, though, *The New Republic* was published in New York.

There was another path to vindication, however. British libel law also allowed for the possibility of suing those who disseminate a libel— which could mean any shop that sold an offending publication. There was one important proviso, though, in that a shop could not be expected to be familiar with every word of every publication they sold. The onus would be on the person bringing the action to prove that the vendor was aware of the libelous content of the publication and went on selling it regardless.

With this in mind, Putzi hatched his plan. On May 11 he called a friend, Doris Alberta Lynch, who lived on London's Gloucester Place. "If you are near a bookstall where you can buy a copy of *The New Republic*, I think it would interest you to see something in it about me," he told her. He suggested she buy the magazine at Selfridges, a leading department store. Just over a week later, Putzi's solicitors wrote to Selfridges, warning them against selling the particular edition of the magazine containing the alleged libel. The shop had stocked only one copy of the magazine—and had already sold it to Lynch. The shop's foreign newspapers department was nevertheless warned of the problem and told not to supply any more copies of the offending issue.

Putzi waited for a month and then on June 21 asked Elizabeth Downing, his former secretary, to go to the store and try to buy a copy of the same magazine. To avoid arousing suspicions, he told her to buy another thirteen back issues as well. Putzi was in luck, for the assistant on duty forgot about the legal warning and took the order. On August 12, all fourteen copies were duly delivered to Downing. This gave Putzi the basis for his case. Selfridges, he could argue, was continuing to distribute copies of a magazine that contained a libelous slur on him, despite having been specifically warned not to do so.

In the meantime, Putzi was also working on the other part of his plan to involve Berlin in the case. He wrote to Herbert von Dircksen, who earlier that year had replaced von Ribbentrop as German ambassador to Britain. Different versions of the letter in both English and German exist in Putzi's papers, but the sentiment in each is the same. He enclosed with it a copy of the offending issue of *The New Republic,* which he claimed circulated freely in Britain as well as in America.

"You will admit that the terminology Hitler's Boyfriend [Hitler's *Lustknabe*] constitutes an outrageous libel on the private life of the

Führer," Putzi wrote. "At the same time, the characterization constitutes an unbearable insult of my person." It was unfortunate, he went on, that the whole affair was bound to become entangled with the Black Tom sabotage trial at which Lüdecke, the "well-known homosexual black-mailer," was almost certain to be allowed to appear. "What steps, be it in a way of protest by the government or a law action [sic] does the German government intend to take in order to defend and fortify my moral character as a credible and honest witness and thereby to enable me to do my duty towards the truth and towards my country?" he demanded.

All this time, British authorities remained puzzled about what Putzi was doing in the country. It was obvious to MI5, the domestic intelligence service, that he had fallen into disfavor with the Nazi regime, but it was not clear whether this was the result of a personal dispute or of a more fundamental ideological disagreement. "One thing is certain," read a report by "our representative in Berlin" dated February 8, 1938. "The Party had heard that he intended to publish a book and that he was in possession of certain documents the . . . publication of which would cause inconvenience to Germany."

The agency nevertheless continued to watch him closely, monitoring his contacts with his numerous friends in London and noting his negotiations with Hamish Hamilton, the publishers, to write his book. They were also intercepting his mail, which included a number of chatty letters from Unity Mitford. Putzi, they realized, was in frequent contact with the German embassy in London. One letter, dated February 23, from the air attaché, revealed that some matter apparently relating to him would soon be put before Hitler for his attention; then on June 3, he received a letter from Dircksen inviting him to come and see him at the embassy ten days later. More baffling for MI5 was an anonymous letter dated June 14—written in French and posted in Italy—noting that Erna had sent her brother a special warning not to try to come and see her as he would face "extremely dangerous difficulties" at the border. Despite such intriguing snippets, the British authorities were still baffled. "We know very little beyond this about his activities," concluded a letter to Major V. Vivian of the secret intelligence service, dated July 27.

The Black Tom and the Selfridges affairs were, meanwhile, becoming increasingly intertwined with each other—and Putzi was determined to use his leverage over the first to draw the Nazi regime into helping him out on the second. On November 4, Kenneth Brown wrote a letter to Hjalmar Schacht, the president of the Reischsbank, who had always been sympathetic to Putzi, enclosing copies of the two cables he had been sent that March by Peaslee & Bingham from New York. They were, he said, "further evidence of the loyalty my client has shown to his country." Brown described to Schacht how Putzi had refused such "bait from the opponents of Germany," but had instead immediately placed his evidence at the disposal of von Weizsäcker and gone to New York to provide the material for an affidavit.

Brown's attempt to portray Putzi as a loyal Nazi was undermined to some extent by his ultimate refusal to sign the affidavit. But the lawyer had an explanation for that, too: Putzi had declined for the simple reason that he would not be considered a fit witness while the libel was still outstanding against him. Brown also bemoaned the lack of help or even advice that the Germans had provided his client. "One would have thought that those who were responsible for the conduct of Germany's suit in America would have appreciated the importance of a witness (whose evidence the opponents at any rate regard as essential) having his character and prestige cleared and established," his letter concluded.

18

AS the year 1939 dawned the world was only a few months from war. In March of the previous year, Hitler had seized Austria—in what the Nazis called the Anschluss—realizing his dream of uniting the land of his birth with the Reich. Buoyed by the ease of his success, he had then turned his attention to Czechoslovakia. Outright military conquest had initially appeared out of the question, but the three million ethnic Germans who lived in the Sudetenland offered Hitler an easy way of destabilizing the country and weakening its defenses. Far from standing up to the Nazis, the other European powers were ready to make concessions. The Czechoslovak state, created at Versailles, was seen by many even in Britain and France as an artificial construct; an editorial in *The Times* of London on September 7 urged that it simply be given to the Germans. The matter was resolved—in a fashion—at the Munich Conference on September 29 at which Britain, France, and Italy agreed that the Sudetenland be ceded to Germany the following month.

A few days later, Hitler crossed the Czech border in a four-wheel-drive Mercedes and his troops marched in to a tumultuous welcome from the local German community. Such was the dread of war in Britain and France that when Neville Chamberlain, the prime minister, arrived back in London waving a piece of paper that he said would ensure "peace in our time," he was hailed as a hero rather than accused of giving in to the Nazis. There was an outcry when Winston Churchill began a speech in the House of Commons with the words "We have sustained a total, unmitigated defeat."

The concessions made at Munich merely whetted Hitler's appetite and heightened his contempt for the spinelessness of Britain and France. On October 21, he gave the order for the "liquidation" of the rest of Czechoslovakia and the seizure of the Lithuanian port of Memel, now known as Klaipeda. A month later, he added a postscript ordering preparations for the taking of Danzig.

At home, Hitler was also trying to mobilize the German people and prepare them psychologically for war. Taking advantage of the assassination of a German diplomat in Paris by a Jewish exile, he began to stoke further the fires of anti-Semitism. On the night of November 9— later to be known as Kristallnacht because of all the windows broken— rampaging mobs throughout Germany attacked Jews in the street, in their homes, and at their places of work and worship. At least ninety-six Jews were killed and hundreds more injured; more than a thousand synagogues were burned; almost seventy-five hundred Jewish businesses were destroyed; cemeteries and schools were vandalized; and thirty thousand Jews were arrested and sent to concentration camps.

It was not long before Hitler turned his attention to what was left of Czechoslovakia, using the same tactic to destabilize it as he had with the Sudetenland—encouraging a minority to revolt. This time he used the Slovaks as his instrument. On March 14, under pressure from Hitler, they declared independence; at talks in Berlin in the early hours of the next morning, Emil Hacha, the elderly and frail Czech president, was offered a choice—either accept "German protection" or see his country invaded. He had little choice but to buckle under. Hitler, meanwhile, was already looking to his next target—Poland.

From his home in West London, Putzi had been watching events with concern. Egon's eighteenth birthday was approaching and he was in his last year at St. Paul's. Putzi wanted his son to follow in his footsteps and study at Harvard; this would also have the advantage of taking him away from the increasingly threatening situation in Europe. So on January 28 he made an application to the American consulate general in London for Egon's passport.

Putzi's own plans for the future were less certain. He was spending most of his time reading and working on his book, but was not yet ready to publish it—since to do so would mean burning his bridges with Hitler. He was, as he admitted later, "waiting until the last possible moment." The idea of accompanying Egon to America was certainly attractive. Yet despite everything that had happened, the lure of Germany was also strong. Like many of his countrymen, Putzi saw nothing wrong with the Anschluss even if he was shocked by the way the Nazis behaved afterward. The same was true of the annexing of the Sudetenland. Putzi was appalled, however, by a speech that Hitler made a few days later in Saarbrücken. Far from behaving magnanimously in victory, Hitler came across as brutal and ignorant. Putzi blamed his attitude on the influence of von Ribbentrop, the former ambassador to Britain, who had taken over as foreign minister in February 1938 from the more civilized von Neurath.

Putzi was to claim later that this was a turning point, but even at this late stage, it seems, a personal written apology from Hitler would have been enough to make him return to Germany. "If I felt it was the old Hitler talking to me and not the Führer, and I think if I felt that the human creature I once knew had been reflected in his letter, I would have said possibly this is my duty to go back," he recalled later. It was not only the hope of reconciliation that inspired him. Implausible as it sounds, he claimed later that he was still hoping for an "opportunity for the reformation of Hitler."

Complicating matters was the continuing parlous state of Putzi's finances. He had been paid five hundred pounds as an advance from the publishers Hamish Hamilton, and supplied them the first installment of his book, which covered the period up to his first meeting with Hitler. (If he went back to Germany, he would have left the manuscript with Kenneth Brown, marked "To be burned in case of my natural death and to be published in case of so-and-so.") But apart from the damages he had been awarded in the *Cavalcade* case, the advance was all he had earned since coming to Britain. To make ends meet, he had been reduced to borrowing two thousand pounds from his solicitors against likely revenue from the book and any articles, but he had no immediate way of repaying the loan. A lot was resting on the outcome of his libel case against Selfridges.

———

ON Thursday, May 18, 1939, the case of Hanfstaengl v Selfridges and Co Ltd began in the King's Bench Division of the High Court in London. Mr. Justice Atkinson presided. Putzi had the impression from the beginning that the judge and jury were against him.

Erich Sachs, Putzi's counsel, opened his case with a description of his client's background and character. Putzi, he told the court, had been born into a Munich family of high repute; one of his godfathers was the duke of Saxe-Coburg, and a brother-in-law of Queen Victoria. The family firm, for which he had worked, was also well-renowned. Although not denying how close he had once been to Hitler, Sachs stressed that their friendship had since waned. Indeed, Putzi was a moderate man, whose views were "not in alignment with the practice of the Nazi Party with regard to such things as concentration camps and religion."

Proving that the wronged party has a reputation that can be damaged is an important part of any libel action. Yet this was not the issue at stake here, for Putzi was trying to stop the dissemination of *The New Republic* in Britain rather than pursue its American publishers, which necessarily focused attention on his motive and methods. "What is your object in bringing this action, to clear your character or to make money?" demanded G.D. Roberts, one of the Selfridges barristers, during cross-examination. Putzi, somewhat disingenuously, insisted that his motives were not financial, although he added that he did not want to have damages "that are in the way of an insult."

Putzi nevertheless faced an uphill struggle in convincing the jury that he was not guilty of what Roberts described as "a dirty trick." Roberts told him, "Not a soul in England would have known of the article in the paper if you had not brought this action." Putzi's action, he claimed, was a purely artificial one in which he had manufactured evidence of publication by tricking and trapping Selfridges into supplying a copy of a back issue of a weekly magazine purely in order to start a legal action. How could Putzi demand damages if the only publication—the sale to Downing—had been provoked by his own agent provocateur?

The case appeared doomed from the start. Nor could Putzi, as one of Hitler's closest sympathizers, expect to count on much sympathy from the jury; attitudes in Britain toward Nazi Germany had changed radically in the four years since he had won his action against *The Daily Express* and even in the two years since his victory over *Cavalcade*.

The judgment was handed down the next day: the court ruled that there had been "no publication." That is, regardless of whether or not Putzi's description as "Hitler's boyfriend" was libelous, Selfridges could not be accused of distributing the article that contained the offending phrase since the only copies of that edition of the magazine sold in Britain had been to Putzi or his agents.

Putzi had hoped the case would be his financial salvation; instead, it threatened to precipitate his downfall. Not only did it fail to bring him any damages, he was also obliged to cover both his own and Selfridges' legal costs. Such an order came with the full authority of the courts. If he failed to pay, his British residence permit could be revoked and he would effectively be expelled.

The setback spurred Putzi to action; it was not yet clear how large the costs would be, but it was certain they would run to hundreds of pounds—which was hundreds of pounds more than he had. The only solution to his financial woes was a lucrative deal with the press. At the same time, his legal defeat had also removed an important psychological barrier to his writing. As Putzi saw it, Hitler's failure to come to his assistance meant that the Nazi leader was responsible for his financial woes—entitling Putzi, in return, to dish the dirt on him in print. The same day the judgment was handed down, he began to contact magazines interested in printing his story.

Putzi was ready to sell his story to the highest bidder. The most promising prospect seemed to be *Collier's* magazine, for whom he had written in 1934. He contacted Quentin Reynolds at the magazine in New York and offered him a ten- to twelve- thousand-word article at a dollar a word. There was also the possibility of combining this with a deal with the *Daily Express*, which was ready to pay him five hundred pounds for six articles to be published at the same time in Britain as *Collier's* appeared in America.

Negotiations continued through June. To Putzi's delight, *Collier's* seemed ready to take a much longer piece of twenty-five thousand words at the same generous dollar a word. But on June 29, just before the contract was due to be signed, the magazine had a last-minute change of heart and decided on only one shorter article instead. All was not lost, though. At a breakfast meeting the previous day, Bill Hillman, the London representative of Hearst magazines, had told Putzi that *Hearst's International-Cosmopolitan*, *Collier's* arch rival, might be interested in three four-thousand-word articles at the same one dollar a word. Putzi promptly got down to work writing a synopsis for *Hearst's International-Cosmopolitan* and sent it off. Time was pressing; Brown had just written to him warning that Selfridges was demanding four hundred and twenty-five pounds in legal costs. Although Brown had managed to have one hundred and forty-five pounds disallowed, this still left Putzi with two hundred and eighty pounds to find.

Putzi's synopsis was clearly not what *Hearst's International-Cosmopolitan* had expected, and a few days later Hillman told him that Herbert May from the magazine would come over to help him produce a new synopsis. In the meantime, Putzi was continuing to explore other possibilities. On July 11, the Fleet Street office of King Features

Syndicate Inc. sent Putzi a brief synopsis of a series of three pieces they wanted him to write for them. It was to include not just his own story and his role in Hitler's rise but also "Hitler the man as Hanfstaengl has known him" and "Personal sketch and anecdotes of Hitler's intimate tastes." Nothing came of the deal.

Whoever Putzi ended up writing for, it was clear that the kind of critical material expected of him would mean a final break with Hitler. Yet he continued to regard his memoirs as nothing more than an insurance policy. Paradoxically, even as he was negotiating to tell all to the highest bidder, he was still putting out feelers, through Josef Thorak, Hitler's sculptor, and various other intermediaries in Berlin, about a possible return to Germany. On May 27, he had even sent Göring a telegram boasting that he had "defended the Führer's honor in the trial" and demanding that he send over Bodenschatz to talk to him before he took a "fundamental decision" the following week. Nine days later, when he still had heard nothing, Putzi followed it up with a letter in which he warned that he would soon be forced to carry out an "extensive presentation to the public of events and people since 1923." He continued, "A further delay is impossible. . . . Before the final decision, I appeal one last time to the sense of justice and great-heartedness of the Führer."

Göring did not reply. Such thinly veiled attempts at blackmail were not going down well in Berlin. The Nazis were still determined to bring Putzi back, though, and decided to enlist his sister's help. According to Erna's account, Hitler invited her to tea in his apartment in the Prinzregentenstrasse and asked her to persuade her brother to return. The meeting appears to have gone well and Hitler even declared that he was ready to help reach an understanding with Putzi. Erna was wary, however. It was not clear whether she then deliberately set out to sabotage the whole thing or whether she was just trying to extract the maximum benefit from the situation. Either way, it had a disastrous effect. Apparently without even discussing the matter with her brother, she went away and compiled a list of conditions under which he would be prepared to come back to Germany—including a sixty-thousand-mark annual allowance, which Erna would collect for him. She asked Unity Mitford to take the letter to Hitler.

Unity dutifully obliged a few days later. Tracking down Hitler as usual in the Osteria Bavaria, she told him she needed to see him alone on a private matter and he invited her to his flat. As they sat having tea, she handed him Erna's letter, apparently unaware of the contents. Hitler was livid. After reading just a few sentences, he grew extremely angry, denounced Putzi and his sister as money grubbers, and burned the letter with a candle. He also ordered Unity to stop living with Erna immediately; staying just one day longer was completely impossible, he told her. Since she now had a flat of her own there was no excuse not to move into it. Bizarrely, Hitler even offered to buy her furniture for the living room—even though she was getting a generous allowance from her parents.

Unity left the meeting frightened and shocked. She took Hitler's warning so seriously that she was reluctant even to meet Erna again. She instead went to see Pinky Obermayer, a mutual friend, and asked her to pass on the message for her. That evening she cleared her things out of Erna's house in Solln and spent the night at a hotel. Late the next day she left for England.

Putzi was appalled when Unity called to tell him what had happened. "Erna ruined it all," she told him. "Everything would have come right except for the proposal to transmit the pension."

Putzi immediately tried to disassociate himself from Erna and stepped up his campaign for rehabilitation, this time sending Thorak a letter to pass on to Hitler. His efforts were barely more successful than those of his sister, though. The first text was rejected because Heinrich Hoffmann, Hitler's photographer, who had also been drawn into the affair, deemed its tone too imperious. Putzi then came up with a more obsequious version, which was shown to Hitler and reportedly met with a favorable response. The same stumbling block remained, however—Putzi insisted he would return to Germany only if he first received a written personal guarantee from Hitler. Such a letter—which he would, of course, have lodged outside the country—would have allowed him to return with honor and prevented Hitler from turning against him. "If he had sent a letter, a miracle might easily have been done," Putzi said later. "That was my belief, call it foolish if you like."

Egon, for one, was appalled by his father's naïve attitude and pointed out that even a personal letter from Hitler would be far from an absolute guarantee of his safety. "You are foolish, Papa," he told him. Putzi was ready to take the chance, though. "If the big top dog writes to me then I will risk it, even though I possibly risk shooting later on," he said.

The "top dog" was showing no inclination to write, however, and time was running out. On August 4, Putzi received a bankruptcy order, together with a summons instructing him to appear in court twelve days later.

One last hope was Winifred Wagner, the mistress of Bayreuth, who was one of the closest women to Hitler. Born Winifred Williams in South Wales, she had been sent as an orphan to Germany before the First World War and had married the composer's son, Siegfried. He died in 1930, however, and she had run the Wagner Festival almost single-handedly since. Hitler's love for the composer was one of the defining features of his life and the annual festival one of the highpoints of his year. When he stayed in Haus Wahnfried, the grandiose house built by Wagner, he was at his most informal. Winifred, for her part, did her best to cultivate him. She had been drawn to him before he came to power and became an even more fervent supporter after 1933. She was one of the few people still to call Hitler "Wolf"—his secret name during the early years.

Winifred had sent Putzi an invitation to visit her in Bayreuth during the festival and watch a performance of *Die Valkyrie*, apparently at Hitler's bidding. Although no promise was made of the Nazi leader's protection, Winifred made it clear that Putzi would be at liberty in Germany and that Hitler was "very friendly again." Putzi should come back and everything would be all right, she said. It was an encouraging sign. Winifred was the "last possible chance to get at the man Hitler and not at the Führer, not at this uniform and all that," he wrote. "I wanted to get at the old Hitler again." Yet even the "Hitler of Bayreuth" could not be entirely trusted, and Putzi still wanted his letter.

Discussions, meanwhile, were continuing on the magazine deal. On August 10, Putzi, Hillman, and May finally met. Putzi handed them a plan for three pieces, each of five thousand words, at the same fee of a dollar a word—with a thousand dollars to be paid on signature. It was agreed that they would sign a preliminary contract on August 14—just in time for Putzi to pay off his court debt. The final binding contract was to be signed twelve days after that.

Before the *Cosmopolitan* meeting Putzi had telephoned Winifred in Bayreuth, who told him she had been assured that it would be safe for him to come back. There was still no letter, of course, but she promised to try to persuade Hitler to write one. A few days later Putzi did receive a telegram—but it was from Martin Bormann, the Reichsleiter, rather than Hitler. Bormann acknowledged the message sent through Winifred and gave Putzi further assurances that he could return without fear to Germany, where he would be given a suitable position. He also made it clear that the German embassy in London would cover all his debts.

On August 18, Putzi decided to clear up the matter once and for all and again called Wagner. He reached her during a performance of *The*

Flying Dutchman. He had told his skeptical son to listen in on their conversation on the extension. "Egon," he had told him, "Frau Wagner is quite incapable of lying to me, because she likes me."

Putzi and Wagner had a long talk, during which she was insistent that he return.

"Did the gentleman in question really promise me?" demanded Putzi, reluctant to speak Hitler's name. "What did he promise me?"

"You come back and he will write you a letter," she assured him.

Putzi insisted that he should receive the letter before leaving Britain, but there was little Wagner could do. Hitler was not due to come back to Bayreuth until August 24—several days after Putzi's bankruptcy deadline would expire.

That same evening Putzi received a letter from Hitler's Berchtesgaden office, signed by Bormann. Written in a slightly exasperated tone, it restated the previous offers, but did not offer anything new. The end had been reached; a break now seemed inevitable.

On August 18, Putzi sat down and wrote to Bormann what was intended to be his final letter. The only man able to undo the "debasing events" of February 1937 was the Führer, he wrote, but Hitler's failure to provide him with the undertaking he wanted had made it impossible for him to make an honorable return to his homeland. "I see myself obliged to postpone my return to another time and to take the clarification of my affair into my own hands," he concluded.

A week later, Putzi bought Egon's ticket for America. The next day, August 26, he signed the definitive contract with *Hearst's International-Cosmopolitan*. The die was cast. After more than two years of maneuvering, Putzi had finally broken with the Third Reich.

19

THINGS were looking up for Putzi. After long negotiations, on September 1, 1939, he signed a contract to write a five-thousand-word article on "the character and inside story" of Adolf Hitler for *Hearst's International-Cosmopolitan,* for the considerable sum of five thousand dollars. Hearst had an option for another two pieces on the same terms. Putzi was paid four hundred and fifty dollars immediately, with the promise of another two thousand and fifty dollars thereafter and the remaining twenty-five hundred dollars on completion. The timing was unfortunate, to say the least. At a quarter to five that morning, fifty-three divisions of the German army under Gen. Walther von Brauchitsch cut through Poland's frontier at several points. Within a few hours they had penetrated deep into the country; Hitler's blitzkrieg had begun.

Egon was booked to sail for North America the next day on the Canadian Pacific Liner *Empress of Britain.* Putzi saw him off and went back home. He intended to follow his son across the Atlantic a few months later, but had first to wind up his affairs. His plans were quickly changed by the events in Poland. Later that day, as Putzi was getting down to work on his article, there was a knock at the door. Two policemen were waiting outside.

Nearly seventy-five thousand Germans and Austrians were living in Britain at the time, among them some fifty-five thousand Jews and other predominantly left-wing opponents of Nazism who had fled their homelands since Hitler came to power. Although the loyalty of most was in no doubt, British authorities identified two thousand as potential security risks, either because they were thought to form part of German espionage networks or else because they were avowed National Socialists. It was decided to detain them immediately.

Putzi was near the top of their list. The policemen took him to Bow Street Aliens Office, where he was registered and allocated the serial number E.Z. 281247. His home was searched and a large number of letters and other documents, most of them in German, were found. The police locked the two safes and a filing cabinet and sent the keys to the superintendent of the Special Branch of the Metropolitan Police. Putzi, meanwhile, was taken to the Olympia Exhibition Centre, a short distance from his home in West London, where a makeshift detention camp had been set up.

Covering nearly an acre and with seating for nine thousand people, Olympia was the largest roofed arena in Britain, and probably in Europe. Opened at Christmas 1886 with the gigantic Paris Hippodrome Circus, the imposing redbrick and stone building had been used since to stage everything from Buffalo Bill's Wild West Show to the Royal Tournament annual military display, as well more conventional trade fairs like the Ideal Home Show. Appropriately enough, it had also been the setting for a number of meetings of Oswald Mosley's British Union of Fascists—including one in June 1934, at which Jewish and other antifascist hecklers were brutally beaten by gangs of Mosley's Blackshirts. A radio exhibition had been held there until the day before the detainees arrived; now in place of the exhibits there were rows of simple beds.

The forty-one men collected together in Olympia were a diverse group. Putzi's past association with Hitler meant he was undoubtedly the best-known among them, but there were also a number of prominent journalists, businessmen, and other pillars of Britain's German community. All had been detained because they were considered security risks. In what was to become a leitmotif of British government policy, however, no attempt was made to discriminate between supporters and opponents of Hitler's regime or even to segregate them from each other. Thus, virulent pro-Nazis who happened to be in Britain at the time were mixed in with Jews and others who had been forced to flee Germany. In one of the more grotesque examples of this policy, Bernhard Weiss, the Jewish former assistant police chief of Berlin, who had left after the Nazis seized power, was detained alongside Captain Schiffer, the man said to have signed his arrest warrant before himself fleeing after the Night of the Long Knives.

On September 3, Putzi and the others were called into the main hall shortly after 11 AM. Lieutenant Colonel Buggaley, the commander of the center, informed them that Britain and Germany were now at war and that they were henceforth regarded as enemy aliens. They were thus transformed from detainees into internees and told to elect a leader to represent them with the British authorities. They chose Weiss. Although the Nazis among them would have preferred Schiffer, they realized that it would go down better with their captors if they chose a Jew.

That afternoon, the ranks of the largely middle-class internees were swelled by the arrival of the thirty-seven-man crew of the *Pomona*, a German freighter that had been shipping bananas from Jamaica on behalf of a British company and had been impounded after it docked in London. The mood among the internees, who had been hitherto split fairly equally between Nazis and anti-fascists, quickly changed. The officers started greeting each other with the Hitler salute and made anti-British and anti-Semitic remarks, emboldening the Nazis among the original forty-one.

Egon, by this time, was heading toward the mid-Atlantic. The *Empress of Britain* had been only six hours from Cherbourg when war was declared, but he and the others on board were only told the news several days later. The ship was crowded and many people had to sleep on the squash courts. The windows were painted black and everyone carried their life preservers at all times in case of attack. In the days that followed, he became increasingly worried about the fate of the father he had left behind.

When it was announced that they would be landing in Quebec in twenty-four hours, Egon suddenly remembered the Hitler Youth uniform he had brought with him and feared the reaction of Canadian customs officials if they found it. He decided to keep the leather pants, but knew the distinctive brown shirt would have to go.

That night he unpacked the shirt, rolled it up into a bundle, and made his way to the high deck at the stern. The moon shone brightly and the deck was deserted. He unwrapped the bundle and had a last glance at the uniform, with its swastika armband and the insignia on the shoulder: Bann 325 Gefolgschaft 13. Then he tossed it as far as he could and threw the cap after it. He watched it getting smaller and smaller before it finally hit the sea below. He paused for a moment, turned back to the deck, and prepared for his new life in America. On its return trip the ship was sunk by German torpedoes.

—

THE detention center in Olympia was intended as only a temporary holding center and on September 5, Weiss was given the order to prepare his group for departure. At 10 AM the following day, Putzi and a number of the other internees were marched to the nearby Addison Road station in West London where a special train was already under steam. The barrage balloons over the city were glittering in the sunshine like rows of silvery clouds as the group headed out of the station.

The train followed a circuitous route, heading first northwestward in the direction of Liverpool, and then cutting eastward across central England past Cambridge, before dipping back southward again. The internees had not been told where they were going—whether in Britain or overseas—and each change of direction prompted new theories. It was after 5 PM when they finally arrived at their destination: Clacton-on-Sea, a popular seaside resort on the windswept Essex coast, normally a mere one and a half hour ride from London. After lining up on the platform, they were marched off into town. The baggage followed by truck. Crowds of locals began to walk with them, but seemed curious rather than hostile. After several days locked up in Olympia, the internees enjoyed the warm evening breeze.

Their new home was to be Butlin's Holiday Camp. Billy Butlin, a South African showman who had come to England to make his fortune, had rightly seen the potential for mass tourism in a new law that guaranteed all workers paid holidays, and in April 1936 he had opened a camp in Skegness, in Lincolnshire, on the east coast. The Clacton camp had followed in June 1938. It was an immediate success. Its capacity, initially for four hundred people, was soon increased to three thousand. The day war was declared, Butlin was informed that both camps were being requisitioned by the armed forces and was ordered to rehouse his campers elsewhere. The following Monday, the army took over the camp in Clacton, while the navy commandeered the one in Skegness. Both were surrounded with barbed wire and searchlights were fitted.

The Clacton camp was made up of rows of identical brightly colored wooden huts—or chalets as they were known—surrounded by neat flower-beds. Beyond, spread over some twenty-eight acres of land, lay golf links and grassland. The sea, visible from parts of the grounds, was less than one hundred yards away. Each hut measured ten feet by ten feet and had a lightbulb, a pair of beds with springy mattresses and good-quality white woolen blankets, and a basin with a cold tap. The camp also boasted an open-air swimming pool, an arcade of shops, a dancing pavilion, tennis courts, a football ground, and facilities for riding and golf. As one internee put it, "Everything the exuberant imagination of a bank clerk could dream of for a holiday with his girlfriend was provided and catered for."

Unfortunately for the internees, the best of the facilities were out of reach. Although the last of the paying guests had left only the day before, the barbed wire laid across the camp barred access to the sports grounds and the main dining hall. Internees were allowed into both only when accompanied by guards.

Life was comfortable enough, though. For the first weeks there were only eighty internees in the camp and the weather was unseasonably warm. The men were not required to work and spent most of their time socializing in the sunshine or playing tennis, football, or volleyball. Those with a little money to their names did not even have to clean their own huts or do their own laundry. Such work was carried out by the *Pomona* crew in return for tobacco. With the excuse of toothache, internees were allowed into town under escort to visit the dentist. It was not difficult to persuade the soldiers guarding them to arrange a detour to a local pub.

Incarceration necessarily brought its frustrations, though. The camp was run by members of the Essex Regiment, some of whose officers and men clearly took pleasure in imposing petty restrictions on the internees and in punishing those who broke them. The men were barred from smoking after dark, for fear they might give a signal to enemy planes, and were not allowed razor blades, in case they used them to menace the guards or cut their way out through the perimeter fence. After several weeks, they were also required to do "fatigue work," such as cleaning the officers' mess—despite protests that this was against the Geneva Convention. Their numbers grew, too, and within a few weeks, there were more than three hundred people interned there.

Of just as much concern to many of the inmates was the growth in tension between the Nazis and the anti-fascists, which had worsened considerably since their time in Olympia. Captain Sievers, the *Pomona*'s ardently Nazi commander, soon forbade his men to work for Jews or others such as Putzi who had fled Germany. The Nazis became more assertive with each advance that Hitler's armies made in Poland and started attacking and beating the Jews. The anti-fascists wrote letters to the camp commander and various British authorities to protest and demand that they be separated from the Nazis, but their requests repeatedly fell on deaf ears.

Putzi had little interest in the sports facilities on offer in Clacton. Like many of his fellow internees, he was outraged at being incarcerated in such a manner without charge or trial and directed all his efforts to securing his release. There was some cause for optimism. Soon after he was brought to the camp, the British government announced the setting up of one hundred and twenty tribunals, which would be tasked with studying the cases of all enemy aliens in the country. They were to be placed in three groups: Category A, who were deemed unreliable and would be immediately interned; Category B, whose reliability was not absolutely certain and who would be subjected to certain restrictions; and Category C, who would be allowed to continue their lives as before and even be permitted to work in the civil defense corps and armament industry.

The tribunals were not due to start their work until October 2, but Putzi quickly began putting together his case. He had a number of powerful friends in Britain. Between them, he and his lawyers began compiling a list of those who could lobby on his behalf or else serve as character witnesses in front of a tribunal. They included Sir Robert Vansittart, the government's chief diplomatic adviser, and David Margesson, a member of Parliament.

On September 26, Putzi wrote a "humble petition" to the Home Secretary appealing to be released. In the nine-page letter he gave an account of his life and final falling-out with Hitler. Although he admitted to having continued links with the Nazi regime after leaving Germany, he insisted that he had since made a complete break with Berlin—citing a letter he wrote to Hitler on August 18, 1939. He also noted that he had signed a contract with Hearst to tell his story and included a copy as proof. "Your petitioner respectfully submits that so far from his release from internment being a danger to the State it would release to the United States of America and the rest of the world information of incalculable value as propaganda against the present Nazi regime at the very time when the Neutrality Declaration question in the United States hangs in the balance," he wrote.

British authorities were in the meantime continuing to study Putzi. A few weeks after he was detained, two Special Branch officers had returned to search his house. Much of what they had found looked certain to complicate his case. Among the large number of documents and correspondence retrieved was a copy of the letter Göring had written

Putzi while he was in Switzerland dismissing his departure from Germany as the result of a "harmless joke"; another from Unity Mitford, dated February 7, 1938, from Vienna; and transcripts of conversations between Putzi, Unity, and her sister, Diana. In one, Diana claimed that she had admitted helping Unity, her friend, Captain (Fritz) Wiedemann, and A.H.—obviously Adolf Hitler—in the perpetration of the "harmless joke." There was also the letter from Martin Bormann, dated the previous month, assuring Putzi that he could return to Germany.

Although Putzi had been closely watched since his arrival two years earlier, intelligence documents, since declassified, show that MI5 and the Special Branch had never convinced themselves of why he had come to Britain nor of what his intentions were. The outbreak of war made it all the more important to establish where his true loyalties lay. Leonard Ingrams—described in one such document as "the brother of the Ingrams who is our security officer at Aden"—asked and was granted permission to see Putzi in the camp in Clacton.

Ingrams, who said he had known Putzi for a considerable time, wrote up his impressions for Capt. Guy Liddell at the War Office on September 25. His mission had been threefold: to find out if Putzi was in touch with any organized opposition to Hitler in Germany; to see if there was anything Putzi could do to destabilize the situation in his homeland; and to solicit any advice Putzi could offer the Allies on how to pursue the war.

Putzi did not tell Ingrams anything he did not already know, however. During the interview, he laid great emphasis on proof he could provide that the Nazis had tried to kill him—which, as Ingrams wrote, was not really proof at all. To the objection that he was a patriotic German and undoubtedly interested in a German victory, Putzi retorted that there was no such thing as a patriotic German, "the inmates of the camp being sufficient proof that there is no unity in that country." Putzi, Ingrams concluded, was "a man of great personality and his present circumstances affect him probably more than they would the average person. On the personal side, he complains of wet feet and a shortage of food and I think he looks rather distressed. He would like me to send him some cheese. Would that be permitted?"

Liddell forwarded the letter two days later to Vansittart, but pointed out that the chances of his being released were slim: "He may have changed a lot since I last saw him, which was immediately after the Nazis came into power. He was then in a very excited and irresponsible state. Although I liked him personally, I had the feeling that he was the kind of person who might do anything. I feel that he is fundamentally German and must remain so," he concluded.

The newspapers, meanwhile, also got wind of Putzi's internment. An article in *The New York Times* on October 4 said of him: "Under other circumstances, Ernst Franz Sedgwick Hanfstaengl might have passed jovially but not conspicuously through life. He was the best of companions. He played the piano, he sang, he told stories. It was always not hard to think of him as touched with a fanatic madness. A naively amiable man, weak enough to be swept off his feet by authority and power, perhaps he deserved no worse fate."

British authorities were not yet ready to give up on Putzi. The same day the article appeared, he had a visit from a captain who had been sent by the commandant of the camp to sound him out on the kind of help that he could provide the British war effort through publication of his memoirs in America. Putzi's response disappointed his captors. Although he was prepared to play some role in anti-Nazi propaganda, he said he was unwilling to make a direct personal attack on Hitler. He also emphasized his conviction that, in drawing up any message to the Germans, "the destruction of Hitlerism must not mean the rehabilitation of German Jewry." It should instead be "blonde Englishman speaking to blonde German," he said. "Pro-Jewish propaganda, in the present state of German opinion, would be a fatal mistake and adverse to the understanding we were trying to create between the British and German peoples and the overthrow of the Hitler regime."

A report written on Putzi's interrogation by the Special Branch six days later reveals the struggle he faced in convincing his hosts that he had really finally broken with Hitler. "Hanfstaengl was at manifest pains to evade inconvenient questions, an impression which was later fortified by blatant contradictions and deliberate untruths," his interrogator wrote. "His sincerity is in grave doubt and I consider that his protestations of hatred against the Nazi regime and his professions of sympathy for this country should be accepted with extreme caution." The report's conclusions, recorded on October 18, were damning: Putzi had been sympathetically disposed toward Germany and the Nazi regime right up until the outbreak of war and had refrained from publishing his book for fear of burning his bridges there. Indeed, if it had not been for his insistence on receiving an apology from Hitler, he would probably still be holding high office in the Nazi government.

British intelligence services would have been even warier of Putzi if they had known that German authorities had been continuing their efforts to persuade him to return home, even after the outbreak of war. In a sign of the importance still attached to Putzi's case, Hitler had given an order on September 5 to the Swiss embassy in Britain, which represented German interests, to contact him. Even if Putzi was not prepared to go back to Germany, then he should at least consider going to the Netherlands instead, Hitler said. The Swiss refused to carry a message that they deemed political, so the Germans had to try through the Dutch instead. Their efforts were to no avail; it was only when Hitler was alerted to the publication of a story in the *Daily Express* revealing Putzi's internment that he understood why he had not responded to their call.

——

THE internment program was controversial from the start. While the more jingoistic sections of the British popular press contrasted favorably the conditions enjoyed by the internees with the horrors of Hitler's concentration camps, there was no doubt that many inmates suffered considerably. Husbands and wives were separated and internees were often housed in tents without mattresses. They were also refused the right to read newspapers, listen to the radio, or receive letters, and were unable to discover what had happened to family members. There were several suicides. Humanitarian groups argued in vain for an improvement in conditions, despite winning the support of several MPs and prominent backers such as the writer H.G. Wells.

To many critics, the most shocking aspect of the policy was that many of those interned were either loyal British subjects or else foreigners who had fled from Germany or Italy precisely because of their involvement in the struggle *against* Nazism or fascism. The British authorities nevertheless continued to treat pro-Nazis and anti-fascists alike, rejecting appeals by Weiss, among others, for the two groups at least to be physically separated from one another. Indeed, according to Alec Natan, an ardent anti-fascist internee who wrote an account of his experiences in detention, the Nazis were often treated better because the British government was worried about retaliation against its citizens who were interned in Germany.

Putzi found himself in an uncomfortable position. Although he could have expected something approaching hero status among the Nazis because of his past closeness to Hitler, the manner of his departure from Germany mitigated against him. Nor did he fit in comfortably with the anti-fascists, especially the Jews. They, in turn, were understandably suspicious of a man who had been instrumental in the Nazis' rise to power. Putzi was left, as a result, in a kind of no-man's land between the two—a fitting enough place given his own mixed feelings toward the leadership in Berlin and the war. Whatever his misgivings about the Nazis' excesses, Putzi's quarrel with Hitler was essentially one of honor, and once hostilities were under way he found it difficult, as a patriotic German, to hope for a British victory.

Fellow inmate Natan, who was fascinated by Putzi, was struck by these contradictions in his character. Putzi, he noted, had not abandoned the ideology of National Socialism and still stuck firmly to many of its original points, blaming Goebbels and Rosenberg "for the mess that led to war." Hitler himself he could hardly bear to mention: a clear sign of the bitterness he felt at having fallen out with his old friend. Natan found Putzi equally inconsistent when it came to the Nazis' policies toward the Jews. Although not an anti-Semite a priori and a critic of the "nonsense" of the Nuremberg race laws, he strongly opposed the mass influx of eastern Jews into Germany that had occurred since 1917. Bizarrely, Putzi appeared to see himself as the leader of a coming Fourth Reich, "which will avoid mistakes made by his predecessors and might even attempt to inoculate democratic principles into its ideology." For Natan, this was pure self-delusion. Everything Putzi had attempted hitherto had ended in failure, Natan concluded, and if he was so determined to be the focus of attention, he would be better off employing his talents in the concert hall than in politics. Neither, however, was an option for the time being.

Putzi did not remain long in Clacton. In early October, the weather began to change: the autumn sunshine gave way to storms and heavy rain, and the huts began to fill with water. It became clear to the British authorities that the camp would be unsuitable for human habitation over the winter, and the internees were told that they were being moved south. Their departure date was set for October 16. Those who could afford to pay four shillings and sixpence—just under a quarter of a pound—a day were transferred to the relative luxury of an A-class camp in Paignton, in Devon, on the so-called British Riviera, where they were promised better food and more comfortable accommodations. Those who did not have the money—which, to Putzi's considerable chagrin, included him—were told that they would be sent to Seaton, about thirty miles east along the Devon coast. Again, no attempt was made to separate the Nazis from the anti-fascists. As the men marched off to the

Clacton railway station that morning, the strains of "Land of Hope and Glory" and "God Save the Queen" mingled with German patriotic songs.

Putzi's new home was a Warner's holiday camp, a down-market and cheaper rival of Butlin's, which drew its clientele largely from the lower middle class. To the dismay of the internees, conditions in Seaton were far less agreeable than in Clacton. The camp's owners had removed most of the fixtures and fittings before handing it over to the War Office, leaving little more than two rows of huts with simple beds. When the internees arrived, they did not find a single chair, mattress, or pillow. Most of the mirrors were broken, and the taps leaked.

The food was also far poorer than in Clacton. One of Putzi's few satisfactions in the weeks that followed was catching eels that swam in the swampy ground through a hole in the floor of his hut. He did not care much for them himself, but there were plenty of takers among his fellow inmates—who polished his shoes in return. The miserable English winter was also setting in. One of the inmates compared their conditions to a Nazi concentration camp: "*Dachau war besser*—[Dachau was better]," he declared.

Putzi's moment came on October 30, when he appeared before the Home Office advisory committee that was considering appeals against orders of internment. It was sitting in Burlington House in Piccadilly, which now houses Britain's Royal Academy of Arts. Putzi was brought up from Seaton to London the previous day. The five-member panel was chaired by Norman Birkett, a prominent lawyer who, after the war, was one of the British judges at the Nuremberg war crimes tribunal. The questioning, which lasted for more than three hours, was intensive, spanning Putzi's entire career with Hitler. It also covered in great detail his behavior since coming to Britain and his negotiations with the Nazis. The tone was civilized.

Putzi had already presented the committee with a long petition setting out his case; he had also included character witness testimony from ten members of parliament and other prominent members of the British establishment, such as Vansittart. During the hearing, he attempted to portray himself as a decent German nationalist who had become increasingly disenchanted with the Nazis as the full extent of their appalling plans became clear and who had fled the country after Hitler tried to have him killed. His intensive contacts with Hitler's aides until just weeks before his detention counted against him, however. The committee was also concerned that, for all his professed revulsion at events in Germany, he had made clear that he would have happily gone back and worked for Hitler as late as summer 1939 in return for a written personal apology. His insistence that the only reason he wanted to do so was to exert a moderating influence on Nazi policy cut little ice. The committee found him "vain, conceited and rather irresponsible."

Any decent counsel would have advised a different defense; Putzi, however, was not permitted one, nor was he allowed to confer with Brown ahead of the hearing. Indeed, it seems that a letter he wrote to his solicitor was deliberately delayed by the authorities.

On November 9, G.P. Churchill, the committee's secretary, wrote up its conclusions in a document marked *Secret*. "The inference is irresistible that Hanfstaengl was not, in principle, opposed to the Hitler regime but, on the contrary, was anxious and willing to be reconciled and to take his part in a position of power, if personal apologies for the incident of 1937 had been tendered," he wrote. For this reason, he concluded, the committee's members voted unanimously against Putzi's release. "They would be uneasy, to say the least of it, if this man, once so powerful in Nazi circles and up to a very late hour anxious to be powerful again, were at liberty at this time."

Putzi was disappointed by the ruling, but not surprised. "Because I replied to his [Birkett's] decisive question whether I wanted to go back to Germany with 'yes' the committee decided in favor of my continued stay there," he wrote.

Five days later, Putzi and a group of other internees were moved again, this time to the horse-racing track at Lingfield Park, in Sussex. All in all, it was a great improvement over Seaton. Those inmates who were paying for their upkeep were housed in the members' rooms, while Putzi and the others were shown to the grandstand. The glass roof kept out the wind and rain, and the central heating proved effective throughout what was to be a hard winter. The internees were also pleasantly surprised by the kindness with which they were treated by the camp's commandant, Major Ayres, and his staff.

Brown, meanwhile, was continuing to lobby on Putzi's behalf. On November 20, he formally petitioned the advisory committee for a new hearing; his client's inability to confer with him before the case meant he had been denied the legal advice which was his right, he claimed. The Home Office was not swayed. On December 1, Putzi received a letter telling him he would continue to be interned. Putzi took the rejection of his appeal badly—especially since many of those interned at the same time as him were already being released. According to fellow inmate Alec Natan, he began increasingly to suffer "fits of hysteria" that poisoned relations with the other internees. "He began to shift his position in becoming an eternal grumbler and malicious gossip-monger," Natan wrote of Putzi. "Violent anti-Semitism, too, got the better of him." To the horror of many of the anti-fascists, Putzi also played a leading role in a strange pagan celebration that the Nazis held to mark the winter solstice, which ended with the singing of the "Horst Wessel Lied" and the German national anthem around a bonfire on the racetrack.

Early in 1940, Putzi was transferred to another camp, at Swanwick, in Derbyshire, which had already acquired a deserved reputation as a hotbed of Nazism. Some of the anti-fascists suspected the camp's commander of having Nazi sympathies. Jews and other critics of the regime were regularly attacked—often under the eyes of their guards, who did little to intervene. "Don't get excited," one British officer reportedly said after witnessing such an incident. "It is just like a public school, where the newcomers always get beaten up as a sort of initiation."

It was all too much for Putzi, who had hitherto straddled the pro- and anti-Nazi camps. That April, he finally found himself pushed into the ranks of the anti-fascists after refusing to join in festivities to mark Hitler's birthday. As a result he was subject to frequent harassment and made himself even more unpopular by interceding on several occasions on behalf of some of the Jewish inmates. Cornered one day by five or six Nazis in a washroom, he spread his gigantic hands and warned his assailants that they might succeed in killing him, but at least one would remember him for the rest of his life because he would lose an ear in the process. They decided not to risk it.

In May, Putzi's ordeal ended. After a number of appeals, he was allowed, to his great relief, to return to the relative comfort of Lingfield. He found a piano there and formed a piano quartet with three of his fellow inmates.

During Putzi's time in Swanwick, the question had arisen as to whether to allow him to write an article about Hitler. British authorities were in favor, especially since it was felt that it could have considerable propaganda value. The Home Office, however, insisted that he could do so only from captivity. There could be "no question of releasing this man who is probably the most dangerous of all internees," it said.

20

PUTZI was due for yet another move, and this time it was to be across the Atlantic. The war was going badly for Britain in spring 1940. Hitler's armies seized Norway and Denmark in April; then in May, they attacked the Low Countries and France. The end of the month saw the forced evacuation of British forces from the beaches of Dunkirk. On June 14, the Germans entered Paris; eight days later, a Franco-German armistice was concluded at Compiègne and the northern half of France occupied by the Nazis.

British fears of a German invasion were growing, as was concern about the role that might be played by resident foreigners. Stories of the assistance that the Nazi invaders had received from fifth columnists in the occupied countries added to the fear of the "enemy within." On May 12, the *Observer* reported how many of the Reichsdeutsche living in the Netherlands, furnished with special passes, had awaited the arrival of the German parachutists. Two days later, the *Daily Express* noted how "poisoned chocolates and wine, spies disguised as priests and postmen and housemaids, every kind of trick to sap confidence and cause confusion has been used by the Nazis."

Winston Churchill, who succeeded Neville Chamberlain as prime minister on May 10, was determined to prevent Britain from suffering the same fate. One of the first moves by Anthony Eden, secretary of war in his new coalition government, was to announce the creation of a civic guard, the Local Defence Volunteers—later to be known as the Home Guard—to repel potential invaders. During the weeks that followed, machine guns were brought into position in Whitehall, signposts removed from roads to confuse invaders, and the police and military given the right to enter houses they suspected of containing equipment used to make signals to the enemy.

At the same time, calls were growing to round up all the "B" and "C" category enemy aliens who had hitherto been permitted to stay at large in Britain. "Would it not be far better to intern all the lot and then pick out the good ones?" demanded Colonel Burton, a Conservative member of parliament. Faced with a concerted campaign by the right-wing press, the government acted. During May, some three thousand enemy aliens living within a twenty-mile coastal strip running from Scotland in the north to Southampton in the southwest were interned. Then all "B" category aliens—around three thousand men and thirty-five hundred women—were taken in too. "Country Saved from Fifth Column Stab," declared the *Daily Herald*. Even this was not enough for some; on June 21, the government decided to intern all those in "C" category as well.

As far as the authorities were concerned, incarceration of aliens was a distinct improvement on leaving them free to wander around Britain, where they would be in a position to commit acts of sabotage. But it was feared that even those in camps could be liberated by advancing German troops and serve as a fifth column. A decision was therefore taken by the War Cabinet to select some seventy-five hundred of the most potentially dangerous men and "export" them out of harm's way to Australia and Canada.

Putzi was among those chosen. He set off from Liverpool on June 20 aboard the *Duchess of York*, the first of three ships due to sail within a few days of each other. As with their previous moves, the internees had been kept completely in the dark as to where they were going. It was only when their train arrived in the port of Liverpool and they caught sight of the ship that they realized they would be crossing the Atlantic.

The crossing had little in common with Putzi's previous transatlantic voyages. Conditions on board the *Duchess of York* were miserable; the ship was carrying twenty-five hundred internees, more than twice her normal capacity. The journey provided Putzi with ample opportunity to ponder the dramatic slump in his fortunes. After eight days at sea, the ship made it safely to Quebec. Those internees on board the second vessel, the *Arandora Star*, also bound for Canada, were not so fortunate. On July 2, a day after leaving Liverpool, the vessel was torpedoed and sunk by a German U-boat off the west coast of Ireland. Some 682 of the 1,571 German and Italian refugees on board lost their lives.

Despite the disaster, the British government pressed on with its policy of transferring internees across the Atlantic. A total of more than thirty-five thousand prisoners of war and Japanese-Canadians were to be interned in Canada during the course of the war. They were housed in twenty-six main compounds and dozens of smaller camps. Among the three camps on the remote and inhospitable shore of Lake Superior was one set up in an empty factory in Red Rock, Ontario. It was here that Putzi was brought.

The inmates were thousands of miles away from the battle between the Royal Air Force and the Luftwaffe that was to rage in summer 1940 in the skies above Britain. Life at Red Rock was tough, however, especially once the tough Canadian winter set in and the temperature plunged well below freezing. Putzi spent much of his time reading. His tastes were eclectic: besides studying history, philosophy, and literature, he also read the Bible simultaneously in English, Greek, Latin, French, German, and Dutch, comparing the quality of the translations. Later he also tackled the Koran. His letters home reveal nostalgia for the beauty of the Bavarian Alps and the Munich he had known as a child. Relations with most of the other inmates were no better than they had been in the camps in Britain, however. The predominant sentiment at Red Rock was pro-Nazi—so much so that a representative from the British Home Office sent out to Canada to interview those who claimed to be opponents of the Nazi regime did not even bother to go there.

Even though Putzi had yet to speak out publicly against Hitler, the nature of his departure from Germany placed him in an awkward situation and he and other opponents of the regime were often threatened by the "ultra-Nazis." Matters were not helped by an interview that Egon gave the Canadian press in September in which he said he was happy his father was "as far as away as possible from possible death at the hands of the Nazis." Putzi sent his son an indignant letter: "I had to finally convince them that you had probably been misquoted and that you must have referred to the now happily eliminated possibility of my being killed by some German torpedo or air raid bomb," he wrote.

Putzi may have been far from Britain, but he was not forgotten. In November, five months after he had crossed the Atlantic, Charles A. Smith, London editor of Hearst's International News Service on Fleet Street, wrote to the Home Office pointing out that Putzi was still under contract to write his article for *International-Cosmopolitan*. Smith asked for permission for Putzi to do so and for his papers to be returned. In a letter the next month, Smith noted that "the article contemplated would have tremendous propaganda value from the British point of view insomuch as it would attempt to expose Herr Hitler." Smith offered to send the Home Office copies of the contract.

The British were wary, but the following month, "after very careful consideration," they agreed to return Putzi's things. The Special Branch handed them over to Putzi's solicitor, Kenneth Brown, two days after Christmas. They included four Collins "Paragon" diaries, four loose-leaf notebooks, two diaries, various special passes for the German Reich, letters, documents, and a German passport, No. 141.R.611/36, issued in Berlin on February 2, 1937, in the name of Ernst Lehmann.

The following February, Hearst's London office asked Brown to have the documents sent to Canada. Brown carefully sorted out the most sensitive material from the rest to try to speed the process, but the Home Office was dragging its feet and refused permission to send some of the documents; they included dossiers on Winifred Wagner and Göring and another containing correspondence with Unity Mitford. The Home Office claimed to be sympathetic to the plight of the American publishers, but noted that the problems they faced were "an ordinary business risk if one publishes articles by prominent Nazis as Hanfstaengl, who are obviously likely to be interned if they remain in this country or to be put to death if they return to Germany." They also insisted that anything Putzi wrote be sent back to the censors in Britain to be approved, even if it was based on information obtained in North America. It was not until July 1941—almost eight months after the first request was made—that the documents were finally released, and then only after Putzi's lawyers had personally lobbied Home Secretary Herbert Morrison.

BY early 1941, Egon, now well into his sophomore year at Harvard, was ready to make a decision of his own. On September 22, 1939, he had been among the students who passed through the registration hall to join the ranks of first-year students. The controversy that had raged so furiously during his father's visit just five years earlier had almost completely died down; his acceptance merited only a couple of paragraphs at the head of a list of "progeny of famed celebrities" who joined the '43 registration. He was still a newsworthy figure, though. As he was sitting at one of the long tables in Memorial Hall, filling out interminable forms, flashbulbs suddenly exploded around him. A series of newspaper interviews followed.

Egon had inherited some of his father's penchant for being the center of attention, and he rather enjoyed it—even if he had to keep reminding himself that the interest was not in him but in Putzi. It was difficult not to be impressed, however, especially when he looked down at a discarded newspaper in a Boston subway car and saw his own face staring back at him. Inevitably, the attention died away after a few days, leaving him to resume normal student life.

On February 2, 1941, the day before his twentieth birthday, Egon enlisted in the U.S. army. Since he was not yet of age he needed a letter from his mother, Helene, who had left Germany and gone back to New York before the war began in Europe. She willingly provided it. Pearl Harbor was ten months away and there was still an extraordinary degree of isolationism at Harvard. Egon was struck by the number of people at the university who believed that this was a purely European war in which the United States would not make the mistake of becoming involved. Egon was nevertheless convinced that America would sooner or later join the Allied side. For this reason, given his parentage, he felt he had to show his cards.

At farewell celebrations in the International House, where he lived, Egon assured his friends he was "purged of the ideas which were on the way toward making me a Hitler barbarian—and I feel swell." He planned his first day in the army as a birthday present to himself. "This is an age of violence, not of scholars," he added. "I am enlisting in the army tomorrow to defend a way of life that is directly opposed to the ideologies of Hitler and his gangsters."

Egon had long wanted to become a pilot, and as part of his training in the Hitler Youth, he had been among a group selected to study aerodynamics and learn how to fly. It would be ironic if he became an air pilot engaged against Germany, he declared, because "when I was a youngster living in Germany, Marshal Göring congratulated me on my marksmanship and said I'd make a fine soldier. If I ever did, I'd be a good one to bomb Munich because I know the place so well. I'd bomb everything but the art galleries, the churches, and the breweries. No, on second thought, I'd bomb the breweries, because if there's anything that would make the people of Munich revolt it would be to deprive them of their daily liter of beer."

The newspapers seized on his decision. "Putzi's Son Will Say 'Uncle Sam' now instead of 'Uncle Adolf'" read the *Daily Record* under a photograph of Egon swearing his oath of allegiance to become a cadet in the U.S. Army Air Corps at Gunter Field in Alabama. Another newspaper carried a photo of him having his tonsils examined at the army induction center on Columbus Avenue where he reported the next day at 9 AM for his medical examination. News of his decision also reached Germany. Putzi's old rival, Goebbels, noted the event in his diary. "Hanfstaengl's son in the US army. Like father, like son."

In the months that followed, Egon was often called upon as an expert on Germany. One day he was told to go to post headquarters and report to the office of the public relations officer. Waiting for him were two journalists—one from the local newspaper, the *Montgomery Advertiser*, and another from the Associated Press. They wanted to know his views on Hitler's deputy, Rudolf Hess, who had arrived in Scotland on May 10 on a mysterious solo flight. It was the first Egon had heard of the story, but once he was handed a sheaf of wire-service reports he was happy to speculate on Hess's possible motives. He spoke of Hitler's original liking of Britain as a "brother nation" and about his deputy's incurable romanticism when it came to politics. He also mused about Hess's unhappy marriage—noting that his wife had often confided in Helene Hanfstaengl about her marital woes. The next morning Egon was startled to see a headline in the newspaper blaming Hess's flight on his desire to escape from his domineering wife.

No one thought to consult Putzi, who was still incarcerated in Red Rock. As the person outside Germany who probably knew Hitler's deputy the best, Putzi was convinced that he was the only one who could throw any real light on what had inspired Hess's decision. Putzi was certain Hess had fled because he feared for his life and had a number of suggestions for how the British could have exploited the situation to confuse the Nazi leadership and extract more information from them. They could, he suggested, have reported erroneously that Hess had crashed off the Orkneys or that he had landed in southern Ireland, thereby exposing that country's relations with the Nazis. Putzi could think of other equally provocative rumors that could have produced revealing reactions from Berlin. Instead, the British had simply announced Hess's arrival. The incident, he felt, had been treated with "incredible stupidity."

Putzi was not completely forgotten, though. In February 1941, most likely in response to the publicity generated by his son's enlistment in the army, he had received a birthday card from Pat Burton, a Harvard classmate. "American friends have just learned of your amazing whereabouts," Burton wrote. "Just why you should be there is inconceivable. Surely, as the father of an American soldier, you have a right to appeal to our government for entry into the U.S. where you lived so long as a respected member of the community. Keep your chin up!" Included with it were some newspaper clippings about Egon's nascent military career.

That November, *The New Yorker* also commented on Putzi's fate: "Ernst Franz Sedgwick (Putzi) Hanfstaengl, Harvard '09, has been somewhat shouldered aside by current events and some people may not even recognize the name as that of Adolf Hitler's onetime publicity agent, ghost writer and private pianist," wrote the magazine's celebrated Paris correspondent, Janet Flanner, under the title "Putzi's Progress." "His acquaintances around town, who shall be nameless, but who are legion, think he's making out okay. He maintains as steady a correspondence as the Canadian censors permit. Recently, he asked one of his girlfriends here to send him a pair of heavy black Oxfords, size 12-D and a copy of Racine's *Phèdre*. This would indicate a life of bookish solitude, broken by healthful strolls. French literature, Racine in particular, is a new enthusiasm for Putzi, who used to speak the language very badly. One of his first requests was for a French grammar and a Larousse and now, after a year's study, he pronounces Racine a marvelous mind. A peaceful, harmless existence for a fellow supposed by some journalists to be one of the half-dozen men who know the truth about the Reichstag fire."

By the time the *New Yorker* article had appeared, Putzi had moved on yet again. In October, the Red Rock camp had been closed and its inmates divided up. Putzi had hoped to be sent to a camp for non-Nazis—not least because he had been among a group of inmates who had signed a petition two months earlier in which they formally disassociated themselves from Hitler's Reich. To his horror, he was taken instead to Camp "Q" in Monteith, northern Ontario, where the atmosphere was even more stridently pro-Hitler. His group's reception was predictably harsh, as they met with abuse at roll call and shouts of "*Emigranten raus*" ("emigrants out") when they went to eat. They were also threatened with publication of their names in *Das Schwarze Korps*, an SS publication in Germany. They only had to endure it for just over a month, however; in late November, Putzi was sent to Fort Henry, in Kingston, Ontario.

Fort Henry was an imposing and inhospitable place. The original fort had been built during the war of 1812 to serve as a defense from attacking Americans. Probably the most effective work of defense ever built in North America, it was situated in the perfect place to guard the outlet to the St. Lawrence River and the Kingston navy yards. The strong limestone fortification had fallen into disrepair, but work was started on restoring it in 1936. On its completion two years later, the fort was turned into a museum. As difficult to escape from as it was to get in to, it had become an internment camp for German prisoners of war and "enemy aliens" upon the outbreak of war.

Putzi's quarters were damp and had a ceiling only six feet high, which prevented him from standing upright except during exercise periods. "Conditions were so bad that the commandant couldn't even look us in the face when he lined the prisoners up to count them," Putzi recalled in a newspaper interview after the war. "He counted feet and then divided by two to check his totals. That camp was so bad they finally closed it down." His fellow prisoners included "a Polish baron who had managed the North German Lloyd office in London, having become a German citizen after losing his estates in the First World War, the captain of the *Bremen*, some members of a circus, including clowns and dwarfs, and an eccentric and amusing individual who had a garter tattooed on his leg."

ON December 7, 1941, Japanese planes launched a surprise attack on U.S. warships in Pearl Harbor. Roosevelt declared war on Japan and Hitler responded by declaring war on America. For Putzi, this meant his break with Nazi Germany was now complete. His homeland was at war with the United States and his son was fighting on America's side. Ten days earlier, he had written a letter from the camp to *Collier's,* offering to write them an article. It was written in a scrawling hand on a page taken from an exercise book and addressed to Bill Hillman, who had left Hearst newspapers to become *Collier's* foreign editor in 1939. Unbeknownst to Putzi, Hillman had since moved on again to become a radio news commentator.

War between the Third Reich and the U.S.A. is at best a matter of weeks. When that happens, my only son, Egon Sedgwick Hanfstaengl who is Sergeant in the U.S. Air Force, and now at Macon, Georgia, will be facing the Luftwaffe.

In spite of my still being kept prisoner and consequently, to my profound regret, unable to speak and write, as a free man, a free author—which would have been far better propaganda—I must regard the outbreak of war as the zero-hour for ending my silence in regards to Hitler and Germany. Methinks it is the least I owe to my good son and his comrades in arms: to do everything within my weak power to help destroy the Hitler-regime and end this war as early as possible.

With a view to this, I suggest your coming here to talk matters over. Following the signing of a contract, I would be free to dictate the desired article, for you to take along . . . All would be done within 48 hours. Bring typewriter.

Au Revoir,
Yours sincerely,
Ernst Hanfstaengl

P.S. As I do not know whether you are in New York or not, I have written a similar letter to Quentin Reynolds to make sure to reach one of *Collier's* staff.

The letter was never forwarded to Hillman. On the top of a copy of the letter he had kept, Putzi had added later in red ink: "I received no answer to this."

DIVIDED
LOYALTIES

21

ON March 2, 1942, a black limousine drew up at the gates of Fort Henry. Inside were John Franklin Carter and his wife, Sheila. They had come to see Prisoner 3026. In order to make the visit, Jay Pierrepont Moffat, the U.S. envoy to Canada, had been required to seek special permission from Prime Minister Mackenzie King. Carter had met Putzi a decade earlier, during the 1932 election campaign, when he turned up in Berlin bearing a message from Franklin D. Roosevelt. That did not make Putzi any less surprised to see him again. His surprise only grew when he heard what his unexpected guest had to offer.

Carter was one of the more colorful characters in Roosevelt's entourage. He was also one of the best connected, with extensive contacts in business, media, and the diplomatic service across the world. Born in Fall River, Massachusetts, in 1897, he studied at Yale and then moved into journalism, working briefly for the newly launched *Time* magazine before moving to *The New York Times* and then becoming Washington correspondent for *Liberty*. His personal connection with the future president had begun shortly before the 1932 election, when he was invited to Hyde Park for lunch.

Roosevelt had been impressed by the breadth of Carter's contacts and after his victory asked him to become involved in foreign policy liaison and to come up with ideas for reorganizing the State Department. Carter went on to work as an adviser to Henry Wallace during his time as agriculture secretary and at the same time continued his career in journalism—starting a syndicated column, "We the People," which he wrote under the pen name of Jay Franklin—and published several books. He was also active in a campaign to have Roosevelt elected for a third term in 1940.

By the time the United States joined the war, Carter had another role, too. In early 1941, he had suggested to Sumner Welles, the undersecretary of state, the creation of a small, informal, secret intelligence-gathering unit answerable directly to the president. The suggestion was a timely one. American intelligence-gathering, especially abroad, was a mess, with responsibility shared between the FBI, the Army's Military Intelligence Division, and the Office of Naval Intelligence, whose paths were forever crossing. There was so far nothing equivalent to Britain's foreign intelligence service, MI6, which had been set up more than thirty years earlier. The foundation of such a service was to be laid that May, with the appointment of William J. "Wild Bill" Donovan to the new post of coordinator of information. The organization he created was formally transformed in June of the following year into the Office of Strategic Services (OSS), which, in turn, would be replaced in 1947 by the Central Intelligence Agency.

Even after Donovan's appointment there was still plenty of scope for Carter and his unit. His role, as it developed, was a wide-ranging one; although his main function was political analysis, he would also evaluate new weapons, troubleshoot military bottlenecks, and monitor other intelligence operations on behalf of the president. As Carter put it: "The overall condition was attached to the operation by President Roosevelt that it should be entirely secret and would be promptly disavowed in the event of publicity." Carter's journalistic career provided an ideal cover. After just a few months in operation, he already had eleven agents on the payroll of his still unnamed organization. Eyebrows were being raised, too, at the speed with which he was spending his way through money funneled into the operation via the State Department.

Putzi had made a lasting impression on Carter during their meeting all those years ago and Carter had watched the German's subsequent career. He could not help but be intrigued, therefore, when he learned that someone with such intimate knowledge of Hitler and his cronies was now living so close to American soil. The immediate pretext for his visit to Fort Henry was a letter Putzi had written two weeks earlier to Cordell Hull, the U.S. secretary of state. In the letter—a similar version of which he had also sent to Canadian authorities—Putzi had offered his services to the Allied war effort, proposing that he analyze German propaganda broadcasts and prepare and even broadcast counterpropaganda of his own back to his homeland. Carter immediately saw the potential benefits this could provide to his fledgling information-gathering network, and on February 10, he went to see Roosevelt about making use of Putzi.

"What on earth do you think he could do?" the president asked.

Putzi, he replied, "actually knows all these people in the Nazi government; he might be able to tell you what makes them tick."

Roosevelt did not need much more convincing. When it came to intelligence, given a choice between dry facts and statistics or juicy personal details, he always preferred the latter. At the same time, the president also instinctively understood the dilemma that Putzi, as a German, would face in working against his native land. Far from being a traitor, he would instead be doing his bit for the creation of a "new" Germany. "You can tell [Hanfstaengl] that there's no reason on God's earth why the Germans shouldn't again become the kind of nation they were under Bismarck," he told Carter. "Not militaristic. They were productive; they were peaceful, they were a great part of Europe. And that's the kind of Germany I would like to see. If he would like to work on that basis, fine."

And so, a few weeks later, after calling J. Edgar Hoover, the FBI director, to let him know what he was doing, Carter set off to Ontario to see Putzi face-to-face and sound him out.

It was a strange meeting. After more than two years in several different internment camps, Putzi was a shadow of the ebullient self he had been when Carter last met him in 1932. He had also lost considerable weight and was suffering with his teeth. Sheila Carter was so shocked at the sight of him that she offered Putzi the bouquet of violets she was carrying. When he described his life in the camp, she burst into tears.

The purpose of Carter's visit was to determine how serious Putzi's offer of help had been and learn what he was prepared to offer. A plan was also already forming in his mind in which the German would play a central role. "Legally, you are British property, but there might be a possibility that the Canadian government would hand you over to the U.S. government for safekeeping for the duration of the war," Carter told Putzi. "In which case, you would come to Washington."

Putzi was delighted at the prospect of liberation from the discomfort of the camp. He was also flattered by the personal involvement of Roosevelt. Inevitably, his mind turned to the years immediately before the First World War, when he had amused himself at the piano of the

Harvard Club in New York while the then-senator had been taking breakfast. Just as his piano playing had been central to his relationship with Hitler in the intervening years, so Putzi fantasized about playing for Roosevelt again. In fact, he even convinced himself that his musical abilities might have played a role in sparking the president's interest in the project. "I doubt in no way that today he [Roosevelt] still often thinks back to the Harvard Club anno 1912/1913—and has the idea to take from A.H., so to speak, his former pianist," he wrote in his diary.

Although Carter had Roosevelt on board, he still had to obtain British approval for the project. Churchill and the Foreign Office were not enamored of the idea of their most prominent Nazi internee, after Hess, working for the Americans. They were not convinced that he had severed his last links with Hitler and his regime and thought he might even be a Nazi agent. But Carter was determined to press ahead with his plan—regardless of what he saw as British sabotage—and enlisted Roosevelt's help to put pressure on London.

The president, in turn, called in Welles. The undersecretary of state was also intrigued by the plan, not least because of the insights he knew Putzi must have gathered while he was at Hitler's side during the Nazi Party's formative years. Even if the British government was right to suspect that he had not entirely severed his relations with the Nazis, Welles thought it would be worth interviewing him to see what light he could shed on the inner workings of the leadership. He explained the situation to Lord Halifax, the British ambassador to Washington, and arranged for him to see Carter. Halifax cabled the Foreign Office in London for instructions.

"I have been approached unofficially regarding Dr. Ernst Hanfstaengl, who is at present interned at Fort Henry in Canada," Halifax wrote to his political masters. "United States authorities are anxious to arrange for him to be transferred to this country as they think they could make use of him. I understand that the President is acquainted with this matter and approves this request. Please let him know as soon as possible whether Hanfstaengl's release may be authorized. United States authorities are anxious that no publicity should be given to this."

The Foreign Office wrote back to say it wanted more time, although it noted in passing that the Home Office would "in no circumstance be prepared to release him if he were in this country. . . . In any case it seems essential that we should know what they propose to do with him if released. . . . We should not wish to haggle over a request approved by the President, but our own experience of Hanfstaengl is that he is eccentric and unreliable."

Carter also faced resistance from the FBI and the State Department, both of which were wary of his fledgling intelligence-gathering organization. Edward A. Tamm, Hoover's number three at the FBI, was especially suspicious of Carter's motives. Noting that Putzi was writing his memoirs and several American magazines were competing for the rights to them, he suspected Carter of planning to make money out of publishing them himself. The bureau was also skeptical about how the arrangements would work in practice.

Under Carter's plan, Putzi would stay in a house in, say, Washington or Baltimore and be "paroled" to the FBI; an agent would then call once or twice a day to check up on him, but otherwise he would be free to get on with his work. Carter received a frosty reception, however, when he went to discuss the proposal with Tamm. As far as the FBI was concerned, if Putzi were to work primarily for Donovan's organization, then they should be in charge of his security and of supervising him. If it were up to the FBI, Tamm told him, they would "treat him like any other potentially dangerous prisoner and keep him under a constant twenty-four-hour-a-day guarded detention." And anyway, they would not do anything without specific instructions from the president. Apparently taken aback by his response, Carter decided to have Putzi quartered instead in a restricted area at an army base.

On April 22, some six weeks after their first meeting, Carter went back to Ontario to see Putzi. He had good news—both Roosevelt and Welles had finally approved the arrangements. Putzi would be flown to Washington, have dinner at Carter's house, and then be transferred to a nearby fort. Although he would formally be under military surveillance, he would enjoy the freedom of the grounds and be treated as an officer on parole. Carter also held out the prospect of a piano.

Putzi agreed immediately. He was delighted at the idea of moving to a place where he would not only be treated with some respect but also could get on with his writing. He had been trying for several weeks to work on the article he had promised *Hearst's International-Cosmopolitan*, but was finding it hard going. The authorities had proved accommodating up to a point; the camp's commandant had helped him obtain some reference books and he was allowed a room away from his cell where he could work for several hours a day. There was a limit to their hospitality, however: Putzi's request to have his working hours extended was refused and he despaired of ever finishing. Relations with the more ardent of the Nazis among the prisoners had also become so tense that he often feared for his safety. As far as he was concerned, the sooner he could leave the camp, the better. But that depended on the British and they were not yet quite ready to give in.

One of the many arguments that London used against Washington's employing Putzi was the claim that he was a homosexual—which was considered at the time as an obstacle to intelligence work because of the potential for blackmail. Carter turned for advice to Clare Boothe Luce, the beautiful playwright wife of Henry Luce, the publisher of *Time* magazine, whom he had known since they were classmates at Yale. She came up with a bizarre plan. Why not put Putzi's sexuality to the test by sending Gerald Haxton, Somerset Maugham's secretary and paramour, to see him? Haxton, who had spent two years as a prisoner of war in Germany during the First World War, would be able to speak German with Putzi. He also had a reputation for being completely unscrupulous. Maugham's wife—who had to share her husband with Haxton—had once said of him: "If he thought it would be of the faintest advantage, he'd jump into bed with a hyena."

And so Haxton was dispatched to the camp. Putzi passed the test with flying colors. When Carter went to see him the next day, he found him furious. "I wish you'd get rid of this man," he told him. "One of the things I couldn't stand about Hitler was all the fairies he had around him. I don't like fairies."

Many in London nevertheless remained dubious about the whole project. But, as one Foreign Office official wrote, in view of Roosevelt's personal interest and the conditions under which he would be held, "we, although sceptical about their finding Hanfstaengl of any use, do not feel we can object to the experiment."

Under the terms of the deal, outlined by Halifax and confirmed by Carter in a letter to the British embassy on May 26, Putzi would be flown to Washington, D.C., accompanied by a reliable agent of the American government, and be housed in a military installation at Fort Belvoir, south of the city. He would not be permitted to leave or receive visitors without special permission and would remain under surveillance twenty-four hours a day. If he proved to be useless or detrimental to the Allied cause, he would be sent back to Canada. British authorities would also be allowed to benefit from any information he provided.

The mission was to be kept completely secret too. There would be no publicity and Putzi would be known during his stay as Ernest

Sedgwick, taking the name from his mother's American antecedents. He would also not be released until the end of the war lest he betray what he might have learned regarding political warfare methods.

On June 23, Sir Ronald I. Campbell, minister at the British embassy in Washington, wrote to Carter confirming the arrangement. He could not resist expressing his doubts about Putzi a final time, however. Attached to the letter was a memorandum describing the British authorities' own dealings with him and the various complaints they had about him—ranging from his persistent lying during questioning to his apparent determination to be personally reconciled with Hitler right up until the outbreak of war.

"I must tell you frankly that the British authorities view the proposal to make use of Hanfstaengl with considerable misgivings," Campbell wrote. He concluded by insisting that the Americans stick to the conditions of the deal and ensure that Putzi not become a focus of attention for anyone apart from those who had a professional interest in him. "I think we all agree about the danger of confusing anybody's mind at this time into the belief that there are good and bad ex-Nazis," he said.

The next day, FDR sent a brief note to Welles authorizing a plane to be sent to Canada to bring Putzi secretly back to Washington. "What do you think?" the president wrote. "I cannot handle this except to give my approval of his coming to Washington if everybody else has agreed. It is all right to bring him in an Army plane but he must satisfy himself as to his safety while here." A few days earlier Carter had asked for funds to cover the operation. He thought he should be able to keep the total cost below a thousand dollars.

Quite why Roosevelt gave his backing to the project in the face of such steadfast British objections remains a matter of conjecture. Despite what Putzi thought, their old friendship—or rather acquaintance—does not appear to have played much of a role. As an intelligence source, Putzi also left a lot to be desired; there was no doubt of the closeness and length of his relationship with Hitler, but the British, who had questioned him at length, felt they had good reason to distrust him and were deeply suspicious of his political views. His motives for helping the Allies were also far from disinterested; it was, after all, his ticket out of Fort Henry. The president had a large number of other sources of information about Nazi Germany, so why make use of this one?

Part of the reason lay in Roosevelt's preference for tapping as many sources of information as possible. Distrustful of the kind of intelligence he obtained from conventional channels, he frequently gave the same task to a number of agencies and made use of information provided by a number of unconventional individuals. Vincent Astor, the hugely wealthy half brother of John Jacob Astor, whose wedding Putzi had attended during his visit to America during 1934, was one of his free-lance gentleman spies. William Bullitt, ambassador first to the Soviet Union and then to France, also entertained and informed the president with a regular stream of long letters that bypassed the usual State Department channels. Even though the responsibility for intelligence-gathering was being increasingly concentrated in Donovan's new organization, the president had no intention of changing his ways.

Putzi, as an enemy alien, was obviously in a different category from people like Astor or Bullitt, but he nevertheless suited the idiosyncratic pattern. Roosevelt was also attracted by the kind of information that Carter led him to believe Putzi could provide—quirky intelligence, rich in personal details, that would add a human dimension to the dry and factual material he was already receiving through other channels.

Nor was Putzi to be confined to merely providing background information. Carter assured Roosevelt that he would also be able to play a far more proactive role in Allied propaganda, giving advice on the kind of information that would especially resonate with ordinary Germans and writing his own scripts to be broadcast back to them. As Carter put it: "He was a guide to what might have been done to win the German people away from Hitler and break him up and get the political peace rather than a military obliteration."

Underlying this was the more fundamental question of how the Nazi regime could be overthrown. In the early months of 1942, the prospects of rapid military victory over Hitler seemed slim. Germany had already overrun much of Europe, and Roosevelt knew he faced a struggle in con-vincing the American people to make the economic and human sacrifice necessary for an invasion of Western Europe. The idea that not just the French, Dutch, Czechs, and other occupied peoples but also the Germans themselves could be incited to rise up and overthrow their Nazi oppres-sors was therefore an attractive one to the president. It would still mean the defeat of Hitlerism, but at a far smaller economic and human cost than from outright military conquest. This, in turn, put a premium on the kind of psychological warfare able to identify and exploit weaknesses in the Nazi system. In the case of the Germans, this meant making a dis-tinction between ordinary people and their leaders. In their propaganda broadcasts, the Allies therefore had to make it clear they blamed Hitler and his henchmen—rather than the population as a whole—for the aggressive and murderous actions being carried out in the name of Germany.

The policy was a contentious one, even from the start, and was bound to lead to further friction with Britain. For Churchill, the Nazi aggression was not something alien imposed on the German people, but rather a phenomenon that had its roots in Prussian militarism. Merely getting rid of the leading Nazis would not, therefore, solve the fundamental problem—especially if, as seemed the most likely scenario, they were overthrown in a palace revolution by another group of people implicated in the regime's past crimes. Indeed, according to this argument, with every month that passed, ordinary Germans also further forfeited the right to be considered victims. As British foreign secretary Anthony Eden put it in May: "The longer the German people support and tolerate the regime which is leading them to destruction, the heavier grows their own responsibility for the damage they are doing the world."

22

ON June 30, 1942—the eighth anniversary of the Night of the Long Knives—a U.S. agent called at Fort Henry and flew Putzi to Washington. It was a beautiful summer day. They went straight to Carter's villa. It was almost enough to wipe out the memory of the three miserable years he had spent in the camps. Carter also had a pleasant surprise for Putzi. Waiting in the next room was Egon, who had risen to the rank of sergeant in the U.S. army since enlisting just over a year earlier. The last time Putzi had seen his son had been in September 1939, when he had put him on the ship for Canada just before being interned. Putzi broke down and wept at the sight of him.

A few weeks earlier, Egon had been given an inkling that they were going to meet. It was eighteen months since he had joined the army and his initial exuberance had long since faded. After signing up, he had been sent to recruit camp at Montgomery, Alabama, the cradle of the Confederacy. The United States was not yet at war and the reaction from the locals was hostile. "We were not well received," he recalled. "There were signs on some cafes—cup of coffee five cents, soldiers ten cents. Or no dogs or soldiers allowed."

This all changed overnight after the Japanese attack on Pearl Harbor. Yet Egon was still frustrated. He dreamed of being a pilot, and should have been in a good position to become one, especially since he had signed up voluntarily months before the draft. There was one fundamental problem: only officers could become pilots, but Egon was barred from going to the school for officer candidates because of his father's Nazi past and the doubts this cast on his own reliability. The order to bar him, he learned later, had been imposed on the instructions of no less than Major General George Veazey Strong, assistant chief of staff, military intelligence (G-2). It was against this background that Egon was told one day that he was to travel to Washington on a special mission. It did not take him long to realize that it must have something to do with his father.

Although Carter was in overall charge of what was to be known as the S-project—the *S* came from *Sedgwick*—it was decided that Putzi's principal interlocutor and supervisor would be Henry Field, a middle-aged Oxford-educated anthropologist and Middle East expert, used by Roosevelt whenever he needed a discreet individual for unconventional tasks. Field took an almost immediate dislike to Putzi; his first impression was of "a tall, ungainly German with unruly hair and features suggesting mild acromegaly. An unpleasant-looking character with a forceful personality."

If anything, Putzi's relations with his hosts at Fort Belvoir got off to an even less promising start. The morning after he arrived at the camp with its colonial-style buildings, he was invited for breakfast by General Max, the commandant. Things seemed to be going well. Max had studied in Heidelberg in his youth and spoke some German. After they had finished eating, he invited Putzi into a neighboring conference room and asked him how he thought the war was progressing. On the wall was a large wall map of Europe and Africa running from John o' Groat's to Cape Town. Putzi immediately strode over to it. The whole world was waiting for the Americans to set up a front in Europe, he said, but it would inevitably end in disaster, for the Germans were already in control of large stretches of the French Atlantic coast, ensuring that resistance would be fierce.

"The only place I would have in mind is not in Europe at all, but here," Putzi continued, pointing at Casablanca with a long, forceful finger and speaking as if he were addressing a large audience. "Here is the weakest spot."

Max was flabbergasted. "Why down there in Morocco?" he demanded.

"Well," Putzi replied. "It is, after all, the best placed, safest landing point for your reserve troops and reinforcements. You will be able to take possession of North Africa and roll up Italy in no time."

Putzi did not have a chance to explain any more, however. While he was still talking, the general stood up abruptly and stormed out, leaving his puzzled interlocutor lost for words. Putzi, who rightly did not consider himself much of a military strategist, thought he had been doing little more than stating the obvious. Unbeknownst to him, however, he had predicted what was to be the United States' first military operation in the Atlantic theater. U.S. and British strategists were finalizing plans for what was to be known as Operation Torch, a series of landings near Casablanca and on the Mediterranean coast of Algeria, from where they would begin the liberation of North Africa. Although planning had already been going on for six months, the operation was not due to start until November.

Putzi was immediately ordered back to the officers' bungalow in which he, Field, and a U.S. army sergeant were to live. He was told he could only have exercise after dark, the sentries outside were immediately tripled, and Egon was sent away.

Everyone concerned was eventually absolved of any blame for Putzi's uncanny military predictions, but not before the matter had been put before Roosevelt. Carter was unfazed by the whole incident. "It was just Hanfstaengl using his brain," he assured the army.

The bungalow, which had six rooms, was surrounded with trees and was dark and gloomy. To Field's annoyance, Putzi insisted on the two lightest rooms for himself—one as a bedroom and the other as a study. He was still not happy, though, and when Major Bittenbender, a cavalry officer at the base, paid a visit, he bombarded him with complaints about both his quarters and the fact that he was only allowed out after dark. Bittenbender, flashing with anger, reminded him he was only a prisoner.

"I won't stand any trouble from you, just remember that," Bittenbender said as he walked out to his car. Putzi had to content himself with muttering a few insults in German. Field thought it fortunate that the major did not recognize which animal he was being likened to or understand Putzi's comments on his ancestry.

Field and Putzi had lunch alone that day; they spoke of Field's student days and the many trips he had since paid to Germany. The conversation reminded Field of two people who had met casually while on vacation. That afternoon, Field compiled a list of reading materials and reference books that Putzi said he needed. He also asked for a shortwave radio with which he could listen to German broadcasts. Field picked everything up in Washington. To his distaste, he also had to buy underwear, socks, and shoes for his charge, although nothing seemed to fit him properly. Putzi meanwhile signed a statement giving his word of honor to Carter, as a representative of the U.S. government, that he would "scrupulously observe all regulations and restrictions which may, from time to time, be established by the American authorities for the security and secrecy of my sojourn in the United States." The parole could be withdrawn by either side with a week's notice.

Putzi soon settled down to work. Field was something of a radio ham and once he got the receiver up and running, Putzi was told to listen to the main German stations and write memoranda on Nazi propaganda broadcasts, emphasizing their strengths and weaknesses. His comments were read by the psychological warfare experts, who would also occasionally write back asking for his opinion on specific questions. Putzi was fascinated by the subject, and even Field had to admit he worked hard at it.

Putzi was an awkward internee, however, and his joy and gratitude at liberation from the horrors of the camp in Canada quickly faded. From the start, he made life difficult for his guard—an army sergeant brought in to prepare and serve dinner who, to Putzi's distaste, was black. The sergeant was terrified of him.

"I've never seen anything like this prisoner, such mean eyes and what a temper!" he told Field one evening when Putzi was out for a walk with two armed guards. "I'm afraid he may try to kill me tonight."

Field tried to reassure him, but he, too, was wary of Putzi—especially since both he and the sergeant were unarmed. A few hours later, as he passed the open door of Putzi's room, Field caught sight of the handle of a revolver poking out from under his pillow. Appalled, he telephoned Bittenbender, who arrived in a jeep, accompanied by four armed soldiers carrying rifles with fixed bayonets. As the four surrounded Putzi, Bittenbender demanded to know where he had obtained the gun.

"I presumed you stupid Americans would never find it," Putzi told him. "I bought it in Canada from another prisoner."

"We're not as stupid as you think," Bittenbender retorted. "We know the Nazis quite well. I shall report this to the general and see what disciplinary measures he wishes to take. I want to tell you that we have orders not to kill you, but no orders forbidding physical punishment. If I have any more trouble with you, you will receive a bayonet in the leg and a beating. We will stand no nonsense from you. Is that quite clear?"

Putzi's manner changed at once. "Yes, sir," he replied, and the major left with his soldiers.

About half an hour later, the sergeant emerged from the kitchen with a tray holding two bowls of soup. Putzi, who was facing the door, shouted out as soon as he caught sight of him.

"*Schweinehund,*" he said, adding in English: "I will never eat anything prepared by a black man. I never have and never will." Then, at the top of his voice he shouted, "You're a lazy black bastard."

The sergeant ran to his room and pulled the chest of drawers against the door. Another call to Bittenbender was required; he arrived a few minutes later with the same four soldiers.

Putzi, Field felt, was enjoying every minute of it. "Good evening, gentlemen," he said. "I'm sorry that you were disturbed from your more serious duties. This Negro sergeant is an abominable cook, a dreadful sergeant, and lazier than anyone I have ever seen.

"Do you blame me, gentleman, for shouting at him?" he continued. "If you would stick a bayonet mildly into him, it might wake him up a bit."

The unfortunate sergeant, who had emerged from his room, stood cringing in his fatigue clothes. Then, with bayonets fixed, the soldiers made Putzi stand against the wall. Bittenbender told him that if he continued to refuse to eat what had been prepared for him, he would simply go to bed without dinner. Already tiring of his prisoner, he warned that any further outbursts would be treated much more severely.

Soon afterward, there was a crunch of gravel on the path outside and Col. Richard Lee, the second in command, swept into the room.

"I refuse to discuss the matter with you, Dr. S," he said. "You have been warned not to commit a nuisance on this post. If I have any further complaint about your behavior, I shall treat you as a Nazi would understand. Your exercise privilege is revoked for forty-eight hours pending an investigation."

Putzi had no alternative but to give in. He recognized military authority when he saw it and disappeared into his room, muttering vengeance.

Field slept badly and when he went in the middle of the night to the kitchen to fetch some water, he saw the sergeant sitting bolt upright at the table, terrified that he was going to be attacked if he slept. Putzi won a victory of sorts, though. Before lunch the next day, the black sergeant had been replaced by a white one.

That was still not the end of it. Putzi had been ordered not to look out from behind the shades of two windows that were facing a neighboring cottage. It was hot and one afternoon he could not resist the temptation to open the window and saw an army captain's wife hanging laundry on a washing line. He shouted at her in German and she ran terrified into her home. Immediately she telephoned her husband and told him there was a madman in the building next door. The colonel came to hear of the incident and again went around to castigate Putzi.

By September it had become clear to Carter and others involved with the project that Putzi could not stay much longer at the fort. It was not just because of his awkward behavior. The camp also had a stockade nearby that housed other Nazi prisoners. They considered Putzi a collaborator and traitor to their cause and the camp staff had tried to keep his presence there secret from them. But, after a few months, word reached them that a high-ranking Nazi traitor was living in their midst, with good food, comfortable accommodations, and use of a radio. The commanding general was worried that they might riot or even try to murder Putzi, and he became even more anxious to be rid of him.

The decision was taken, therefore, to move Putzi to a secluded private accommodation. It was up to the unfortunate Field to find somewhere that fit the bill. He began to do the rounds of the real estate agents, but after two weeks he still had not succeeded in finding anywhere suitably remote. It was then that Lee had a suggestion. Why not try Bush Hill, a secluded property deep in the countryside about twenty-five miles outside Washington, beyond Alexandria? Lee remembered playing there as a child; coincidentally, he recalled that it belonged to a distant cousin of Field's.

Field dimly remembered Emily Gunnell, and her sister, Mary, and set off to take a look. After a long cross-country drive, he drove into a lane through thick woods of third-growth oak, maple, and beech, down a long hill and across a rickety wooden railroad bridge. The road, declared one person who drove down it, was "probably the worst in the eastern United States." It continued through a pair of gateposts beneath a splendid holly tree and circled to the left. The drive was so thick with tall weeds and overgrown bushes that Field was forced to abandon his Ford and continue on foot.

The house was a substantial but run-down brick-built affair that looked as if it had not been touched since the 1850s. A steep flight of stone steps led to the veranda, which ran the width of the main block. Beyond lay what had once been the slave quarters; it was now filled with tools, documents, and odd souvenirs. There were also stables and garages overgrown with weeds. All this was set in around a hundred acres of woodland.

Field was pleased to see that the windows were open and the house looked occupied. Pushing his way through the bushes, he came to a porch where a white-haired old woman was rocking in the late-summer sunlight. Her eyes were closed. She woke up with a start when Field asked after his cousin and called her name. A few minutes later, Emily Gunnell appeared at the door.

"I haven't seen you since you were a baby in Oakland," she told him. "Do come in."

Lee's suggestion had been an inspired one; the two women had been trying for a long time to rent out Bush Hill and move to a milder climate. Emily Gunnell revealed that she had been praying for a miracle just minutes before her cousin arrived on the scene. Now God had granted it. Half an hour later, Field had rented the house. There was no mention of Putzi, of course. He told them their home was to be used as a radio listening post by the Federal Communications Commission.

The two women expressed their willingness to move to a hotel without delay. Before packing up, they asked Field for advice on what to do with half a dozen antique limousines parked at the villa. He suggested they scrap them—and they dutifully did as they were told—losing themselves tens of thousands of dollars in the process.

Once the women left, preparations were quickly under way to prepare the house for its illustrious resident. Rustic kitchen appliances were replaced by an electric stove, and a new refrigerator was procured. Coal- and wood-burning stoves were installed in those rooms without fireplaces. Tons of coal were obtained through official channels. There was no time to deal with the decor; the main living room was worn, with rotten brocade peeling from the walls and drooping over the portraits of the owners' early-American ancestors. The other dozen or so rooms were barely in a better state.

In October, once the new arrangements had been personally approved by the president, Putzi left the fort behind him and moved to Bush Hill. His military hosts could not have been more delighted to see him go.

"The transfer of the Man Nobody Knows took place to the satisfaction of all concerned and the new operation is already started," Carter wrote to Grace Tully, Roosevelt's secretary. "I have never seen happier faces than at Fort Belvoir when the Commandant was formally relieved of responsibility for a project which was unfamiliar to his Army experience."

——

PUTZI soon got back down to work in his new home. Armed with a powerful Hallicrafter shortwave radio with which he could listen to broadcasts from Germany, he began writing reports, his analysis of the news coming out of Berlin informed by his personal knowledge of Hitler and those closest to him. From the beginning, Carter took a close interest in the project, visiting Bush Hill often to put questions of his own to Putzi or to relay others from Roosevelt. To Field's great distaste, though, he was given the job of looking after Putzi on a day-to-day basis. Apart from the two of them, the household consisted of George Baer, a distinguished Jewish artist whom Putzi had met once in Schwabing before the war, and his American wife. A cordon bleu chef, she spoke German and, as well as providing excellent food, was expert at handling Putzi's ill-tempered outbursts. The household was completed by three military guards.

The routine was the same day after day. After breakfast, "Dr. Sedgwick" would sit down in his study and switch on his radio. He would listen to the main German news broadcasts, taking detailed notes in German, with the occasional English word or phrase. He would also read *The New York Times* and *The Washington Post*. Then after lunch and an hour spent resting or reading, often about Frederick the Great or Oswald Spengler, he would sit down to write up his memorandum, usually running to four or five hundred words. In it, he would analyze German propaganda, look for weaknesses in it, and suggest retaliatory attacks. Field also encouraged him to conclude with a question that would be embarrassing to the German high command if included in American propaganda, such as what had happened to the pornographic drawings made by Hitler and why his revolver was in Geli Raubal's hand when she was found dead in his apartment in 1931.

Every afternoon, Field would read the handwritten memorandum, making sure it was legible, and take it back to his office in Q Building of the Office of Strategic Services. He never needed to correct Putzi's English, which was excellent, thanks to his Harvard education. Four original copies and one carbon were made. The carbon was filed, while the others were destined for Grace Tully, to the attention of the president; for Welles; for Donovan; and for Carter. The next morning at ten o'clock, Field would deliver them all to Carter in the Press Building; he would pass them on, often with a brief note for each of the other three recipients.

The routine was changed, however, whenever Hitler spoke. The State Department would notify Field of an impending broadcast and he, in turn, would telephone the news through to Bush Hill, using a pay phone for security. Equipped with a highly sensitive headset, Putzi would listen to Hitler's speech, taking notes as he went. According to Field, it was often a difficult and disturbingly emotional experience for Putzi. As soon as Hitler finished speaking, he would stand up and start pacing around his office like a caged animal. For the next hour or so, as he wrote up his notes, silence would reign—interrupted only by occasional loud outbursts in German. Whatever the hour, these reports were immediately couriered to Carter. They were also passed to the psychological warfare departments of both the OSS and the State Department, which wove some of Putzi's comments into disinformation radio OSS programs, broadcast into Germany through a BBC transmitter in the Weald of Kent. Occasionally one of Putzi's points would hit home—especially the questions at the end of the broadcast. Official German radio was soon obliged to admit that a high-ranking former Nazi was now working for the Americans.

Roosevelt was keen to try out America's new intelligence asset. In one of his first questions, he asked Carter to obtain Putzi's suggestions on the best way for America to appeal directly to the German people, over the head of the Nazi regime. Putzi suggested waiting until victory in North Africa and then having Eisenhower, Marshall, or another high-ranking military officer address German soldiers and their families to point out to them that all their sacrifices had been in vain. There was a real possibility, he argued, that the whole army could be turned against the Nazis and overthrow Hitler—instead of "nursing a 'stab-in-the-back alibi' as after Versailles."

Just over two weeks later, Putzi was asked by the president for his opinion on recent changes in the German high command prompted by the appointment of Gen. Kurt Zeitzler as chief of the general staff. Putzi claimed that Hitler was becoming increasingly paranoid about a possible putsch against him from within the upper echelons of the army and was afraid the tenth year of his rule, which would soon be upon him, could be his last. The appointment of a Himmler loyalist such as Zeitzler was therefore the sign of an "all-out eleventh-hour decision" by Hitler to Nazify the Reichswehr, root and branch, and to "exclude, prophy-lactically as it were, all real and imaginative Juntas, sabotage-plots, intrigues and separate peace-moves emanating from the German con-servative opposition." In short, it represented "a clear victory of Himmler over the quasi-aristocratic Göring wing of the Party," he wrote. "Himmler, and Himmler's Gestapo, represent Hitler's final argument. Beyond Himmler there is nothing but fate—and the last mad throw of the political desperado."

Sometimes, British intelligence would ask permission through Welles to come and question Putzi. Although this was permitted, Field was under instructions never to leave anyone alone with his prisoner. On one occasion, Field took him for a question-and-answer session with a panel of his fellow anthropologists in a basement room at the Department of Justice. The academics had not realized what they were letting themselves in for. Putzi, with his rapier-sharp mind, made mince-meat of their tedious and rather obvious questions. The whole thing put Field in mind of a Nobel Prize winner forced to talk politely to a group of teenagers.

Although impressed by Putzi's intellectual gifts, Field did not warm to him personally. It was, he recalled two decades later, a "hideous assignment." Putzi became more and more temperamental and his "inexcusable behavior" drove away the staff who were there to look after him. "He demanded more variety in his food, less static on his super Hallicrafter, more books, less prickly woolen underwear and more freedom to roam," Field wrote. On one occasion this meant fetching an entire twenty-volume set of *Der Grosse Brockhaus* encyclopedia, which Field had to carry back from New York squeezed into his berth on the train. Even when he was not at Bush Hill, he was always at Putzi's beck and call, twenty-four hours a day.

To add to Field's burden, Putzi also began to suffer from chronic tooth problems—a result perhaps of the poor conditions in his various internment camps. And so the two of them would set off in Field's old Ford for the dentist on I Street. It was decided that they would attract less attention if they did not take anyone else with them. There was little danger of Putzi escaping; he was too conspicuous to hide for long and knew he would be sent back to Canada if caught. Most important was to keep the mission secret. Putzi was almost recognized on at least one such trip; on another, their car was followed by a group of journalists before Field succeeded in shaking them off. Field was also always having to take calls at home from reporters demanding to know Putzi's whereabouts.

In the early hours of one morning, Field had an emergency call to come right away to Bush Hill. When he arrived, there was pandemonium. Outside Putzi's office, an American sergeant, who was chief of the guards, was lying dead drunk on the floor. Baer and Field lifted him onto the sofa to sleep it off. Baer claimed Putzi had deliberately plied him with wine to get him drunk. Putzi was roaring with laughter and pointing at the sergeant. "That's the U.S. army for you; they can't win any kind of war," he declared. Field asked Putzi not to give alcohol to his guards again.

Although unaware of such goings-on, the British still had misgivings about the project, not least because of the continued transatlantic dispute over how narrowly—or broadly—the enemy should be defined. In their speeches during the spring and summer, Roosevelt and members of his administration were still making the distinction between the German people and their leaders. To Churchill, however, any attempt to absolve ordinary people of blame for the activities of the Nazi regime smacked of weakness and appeasement. In the eyes of the British government, Putzi was merely encouraging his hosts along this unwelcome path. Some of the information and recommendations he provided, especially his urging of efforts to inspire a military coup against Hitler, was felt in London to be especially unhelpful. So, too, was his rabid anti-Communism. Putzi was showing "signs of becoming increasingly dangerous in the advice which he was giving on Germany," Campbell at the British embassy wrote to Carter. The whole S-project, he said, "contains many elements which, both directly and indirectly, would prove detrimental to Anglo-American and Anglo-Soviet relations."

London, therefore, continued its efforts to undermine the project. About three weeks before moving Putzi to Bush Hill, Carter had written to the British embassy telling them what was planned and asking them urgently to respond. The embassy forwarded the information to London, but when the time came for the move, the Americans had not heard anything back and Carter had pressed ahead regardless. It was only some six weeks later that he received what he considered a rather offensively worded letter from Campbell stating that the Home Office absolutely refused to consent to the new arrangements, which by then were already in effect and working well. Campbell also wrote to Welles dismissing Putzi's reports as "entirely useless from the point of view of both psychological warfare and intelligence" and demanding that he should remain in America only on a one-month trial basis.

Carter was appalled at yet another example of British duplicity. As he saw it, Putzi's living conditions were perfectly in accordance with the "essence" of the original agreement, in that he was still being held under armed guard and was incommunicado. After discussing the matter with Welles, he told Campbell that the president had approved the arrangements and firmly suggested that the British government not pursue the subject any further. Carter was all the more put out by Campbell's admission that the British government did not intend to make any use of Putzi, but simply wanted to deprive the Americans of his services and liquidate the whole project.

Putzi's one-month trial came and went and Carter called Britain's bluff. Indeed, he was heartened by signs that some in London seemed to appreciate his efforts. On November 20, Carter wrote to the president to inform him that on the previous day, British intelligence had "congratulated him on the value and form of the reports from Dr. Sedgwick" and had urgently requested more of the same. With his own career and reputation riding on the project, Carter was also full of praise for his charge's work. Putzi, he said, had found a reference in a speech made by Hitler in a beer hall on November 8 that made clear the Nazis' plans to invade Spain and capture Seville and Gibraltar. Putzi, Carter wrote to Welles, recalled "many conversations in which Hitler pointed out that from Berlin to the Volga was the same distance as from Berlin to Gibraltar and that Germany needed to secure both intervening areas to be unassailable in Europe." This had been promptly referred to Welles, who had taken prompt action to offset it.

Such talking up of the S-project was probably not unconnected with Carter's attempts to secure some more money. It was already costing four thousand dollars a month—a not inconsiderable sum. Carter wanted another five hundred to cover extra expenses for road repair, well digging, an electric line, medical care, and other incidentals connected with housing Putzi at Bush Hill and utilizing his knowledge.

Carter was already beginning to wonder, however, how long the project could be kept secret. The British embassy in Washington had leaked news of Putzi's presence to several newspapers in a clear attempt to sabotage the whole project. Although none had yet published the story, it seemed only a matter of time, not least because of the piece Putzi had long been working on for *Hearst's International-Cosmopolitan*. Rather than allow the news simply to leak out, Carter wondered whether it would not be better to capitalize on the whole thing and announce it instead.

Roosevelt was alarmed. The administration's apparent harboring of a prominent former Nazi in a country house just outside Washington was potentially embarrassing and could lead some to question its commitment to the total defeat of Hitler's regime. The issue was all the more sensitive because the president was already under fire for agreeing to a deal under which Jean-Francois Darlan, a notorious Vichy collaborator, had been appointed head of the civil administration in North Africa in return for supporting the Allied invasion that had begun with Operation

Torch. Samuel Grafton, an American columnist, even coined a name for this and several other such cases: he called it Darlanism.

Roosevelt summoned Carter and told him to "make a quick deal with the editor of *Cosmopolitan*." On January 4, 1943, Carter was pleased to send the president a note telling him that he had done just that. Under its terms, the magazine agreed to withhold publication of the article until February 1; in the meantime, the administration would announce Putzi's presence on January 28 to tie in with extensive propaganda plans to mark the tenth anniversary two days later of Hitler's accession to power.

Carter made good use of the month's grace period he had won. He contacted a number of leading journalists—among them Dorothy Thompson; Walter Millis, the foreign editor of the *New York Herald-Tribune*; and the State Department correspondents of the Associated Press and United Press wire services—to explain to them the facts of the case. Putzi, he assured them, was "devoid of political or diplomatic significance in terms of German political life." He was also careful to deny any parallels between his role and that of Darlan. In return for being let in on the story, they agreed to be bound by the embargo.

Carter's press statement, released at midnight on January 28, was short and to the point. After a brief biography of Putzi—which emphasized his various American connections, from his education at Harvard to his son's service in the U.S. army—he described how he had been transferred from Canadian to American jurisdiction and was "actively cooperating with American intelligence representatives concerning certain aspects of the Hitler regime and the Nazi movement." It would not, however, "be compatible with the public interest at this time to disclose details of his present location or the precise nature of his services to this Government," he said.

The American media accepted such assurances willingly. The front pages of the newspapers were still dominated by accounts of the Casablanca Summit earlier that week attended by FDR and Churchill and by the successful Russian counterattack at Stalingrad. Putzi was hardly big news in comparison. An Associated Press report made it clear that he was "under guard, not a U.S. agent" and had provided much useful information. A well-informed government source—presumably Carter—confirmed that Putzi had been questioned "at length and very carefully" and had "volunteered a lot of information about the Nazi party, the leaders of the party and the personalities around Hitler." Trying to downplay the significance of the operation, the source pointed out that since Putzi was regarded as a "rather unstable genius" and had been out of touch with Germany for at least five years "he hasn't been consulted on anything of importance."

In a sign of the secrecy that had surrounded the whole operation, this report was the first that the Alien Enemy Control Unit of the Department of Justice knew about Putzi's presence in America. Its director, Edward J. Ennis, wrote to Hoover the next day, requesting his precise whereabouts and asking whether the FBI had any information suggesting that he might become "an alien enemy security problem." Hoover wrote back to reassure him that all was well.

While the press reported Putzi's presence in a neutral manner, the FBI's files contain a number of letters from ordinary Americans—some apparently recent refugees from Nazi Germany—appalled at the idea that such a close associate of Hitler could now be working for U.S. authorities. "As a proven enemy of democracy and of all human rights he ought to meet mistrust from the Government," wrote one especially harsh critic, whose name had been blacked out. "I cannot believe that the State Department is about to have any confidential relations with this man."

Regardless of such complaints, Carter congratulated himself that the release of the news had been "well-handled and well-received." Indeed, he was so pleased with his own performance that he wrote to the president the next day describing how he had won over the media through a series of one-to-one briefings with carefully selected reporters and editors. The methods, he suggested, could serve as a blueprint for future press relations, especially for the State Department, whose officials had a reputation among journalists for being aloof and never taking them into its confidence.

The British government was far less accommodating: in what seemed to Carter yet another attempt by London to cause trouble, the British embassy in Washington wrote to Welles the day before the press release was published, demanding the return of Putzi to its custody. Carter was furious. In a detailed eight-page memorandum to Roosevelt, he praised Putzi's cooperation, which he said had proved "useful rather than important," and demolished the British argument that they had somehow been kept in the dark about his movements. Their objections were about more than just Putzi, he told the president. The British were trying to secure for themselves a monopoly over political information and contacts with Europe and the Near East and were determined to "repossess Putzi in order to supply an object-lesson of their de facto supremacy in this field."

Carter argued that Putzi had lived up to his end of the bargain, in good faith and to the best of his ability. Forcing him to return to Britain would be "unjust and inhumane"—and possibly also life threatening, especially if he was put back in a camp where the prisoners were policed by Nazi terror gangs. Carter's conclusion was clear: "There are good reasons, in my judgment, for a quiet, temperate and good-humored refusal to submit to what seems to be a rather arbitrary demand," he wrote. Roosevelt heeded his advice.

A few weeks later, the March 1943 edition of *Cosmopolitan*, containing Putzi's article, appeared. Among its more sensational claims was that Hitler's niece, Geli Raubal, had not died at her own hand but had instead been shot by Hitler because she had fallen in love with her Jewish Viennese singing teacher. "Geli died by a bullet wound from Adolf Hitler's revolver," Putzi wrote. "Afterward Hitler, in sudden panic, sent for Hermann Göring and Gregor Strasser, a party leader. Strasser left grim-faced. Hitler's hatred of him dated from that moment. Strasser had refused to call it an accident." The article also claimed that, after the murder, Hitler worked his way through a "succession of blondes" from stage and screen who were told by Joseph Goebbels, the propaganda minister, to foster Hitler's "mother complex." It was all slightly racier stuff than what Putzi was sending to Roosevelt, although undoubtedly rather less accurate.

Despite such publications, Putzi's name disappeared from the press in subsequent months. His presence continued to be a source of fascination, however. The following April, the FBI was approached by United Artists on behalf of Charlie Chaplin. Chaplin had already finished *The Great Dictator*, his film about Hitler, and the studio did not explain what it wanted from Putzi. In any case, it was told that it would be "impossible to secure his services at this time."

23

DURING his time at Fort Belvoir, Putzi had already begun to lose interest in writing his routine propaganda reports. Field provided a solution. In addition to his regular work, Putzi was to prepare a detailed personal report on Hitler. With the help of a U.S. government psychologist, a list of questions was prepared and Putzi sat down to write about Hitler's strengths and weaknesses, his foibles and abnormalities, and attitudes toward everything from music, art, and literature to religion and women. He took to his new assignment with enthusiasm; for days he covered page after page of yellow foolscap. Field's secretary then typed up each section until a fifty-page double-spaced manuscript was completed. Although arranged in slightly haphazard order, it made fascinating reading. The two men then sat down together for several days to put all the material into a logical sequence.

FDR's secretary, Grace Tully, thought the president would be interested in the memorandum, so a beautifully typed copy was bound in a black cover and delivered to the White House. Tully was right. Roosevelt, who much preferred personal tittle-tattle to dry intelligence, was fascinated and named it "Hitler's Bedtime Story." He also loaned his copy to Harry Hopkins, his longtime confidant and unofficial adviser on foreign affairs, and to several other aides. The final version, dated December 3, 1942, ran to sixty-eight pages. In it, Putzi attempted a full analysis of Hitler's character, behavior, and influences. The tone was critical and vastly different from the eulogies of his beloved Führer he had penned just a few years earlier.

Predictably, perhaps, Putzi found the roots of Hitler's later actions in his childhood—in his violent and abusive father and a "hysterical-eyed mother" who occupied the central position in his whole "erotic genesis." While an adolescent, Hitler's lack of formal education was responsible for his enduring distrust of those he termed "the professor type." He was, however, gifted from childhood with an extraordinary power of speech and read widely—and was especially attracted by outstanding examples of rhetoric and historic epigram. When reading great lives he was always attracted to the "demagogic, propagandistic and militaristic" rather than the contemplative side.

Hitler's heroes were various, although they had in common a preparedness to use supreme force to achieve their goals. Thus, Oliver Cromwell was admired for his beheading of King Charles, while Field Marshal Blücher was praised for the determination with which he led Prussian forces against Napoléon. Napoléon, himself, had increasingly become a kind of role model, Putzi claimed, surpassing Frederick the Great, an earlier hero. Hitler admired in Napoléon his revolutionary spirit and anti-conservative, anti-capitalistic, and anti-bourgeois attitudes. He was especially impressed by the way Napoleon had progressively molded the French in his own image and wanted to do the same with the Germans.

Putzi said Hitler used to claim to have received a command "from another world" to save Germany while he was in the hospital in Pasewalk in the fall of 1918. Hitler's view of himself had changed over the years, however. At the beginning of 1923, he would refer to himself as "the drummer marching ahead of a great movement of liberation to come." This meant a greater leader was to come one day—which went some way to explaining the subservience he showed toward Ludendorff and the other members of the military caste. Ten years later the drummer had become the Führer and Nazi historians had even gone so far as to deny that he had ever used the term. If he had been referred to as "the drummer" at all, they claimed, it had been by his enemies who wanted to belittle his chances of supreme leadership. John the Baptist had been transformed into the Messiah, but Hitler's conception of the Messiah was not "Christ crucified, but Christ furious—Christ with a scourge."

Putzi also wrote in detail about Hitler as a person—and a curious picture it made. Meticulous about his personal appearance, he would never remove his coat in public, no matter how warm he felt. Nor would he allow anyone to see him in the bath or naked. His tastes were

Spartan: almost completely vegetarian, he gave up smoking soon after the war began. Following his incarceration in Landsberg, he also rarely drank either. It was this ascetic side to Hitler's nature that was responsible for the growing distaste he felt for the epicurean Röhm, who was renowned for his love of lavish dining and fine wine. Although robust physically and able to work long hours, Hitler was completely uninterested in either indoor or outdoor games, could not swim—indeed he was very much afraid of the water—and only occasionally walked. His only exercise was public speaking and he would be bathed in sweat after a major speech; he would only be happy and restful when he had talked himself to the point of swooning from exhaustion. Perhaps as a result, he slept badly—always going to bed as late as possible and then invariably taking a sedative.

Music was one of Hitler's chief diversions, serving the triple function of isolating him from the world, relaxing him, and then spurring him into action. *Tristan* was a favorite and if he was facing an unpleasant situation then he liked to have the *Meistersinger* played to him. Sometimes, too, he would recite entire passages of the text of *Lohengrin*, which to Putzi's astonishment he appeared to have learned by heart. Besides Wagner, Verdi, and certain pieces by Chopin and Richard Strauss, he also enjoyed gypsy music, rhapsodies, Liszt, and Grieg. He disliked Bach, Handel, Haydn, Mozart, Beethoven, and Brahms. He was also keen on movies—especially those banned in Germany, which Goebbels procured for him and were shown in his private theater in the chancellery. Also played were films of political prisoners and executions. Vaudeville and the circus, especially tight rope and trapeze acts, were favorites too. "The thrill of under-paid performers risking their life is a real pleasure for him," Putzi wrote. He did not care much for wildlife acts, unless there was a woman in danger.

Hitler's sex life was even more of a mystery to Putzi, even though he had observed him at close range for years in a way probably no one else had. Putzi speculated, as others have done—albeit without any concrete evidence—that Hitler may have become infected with venereal disease during his time in Vienna from 1909. There was also little doubt that Hitler had been exposed to homosexuality during his stay at the Männerheim Brigittenau, a Vienna hostel notorious as a place "where elderly men went in search of young men." Putzi did not feel he had ever been a practicing homosexual, however. "While the true Adolf Hitler is elusive to the diagnostician, there are certain facts which prove that his sexual situation is untenable and even desperate," he wrote. "There seem to be psychic if not also physical obstacles which make real and complete sexual fulfilment ever impossible. In general, what he seeks is half-mother and half-sweetheart." Thus unable to find satisfaction, Hitler would instead obtain release in addressing a crowd, which for him became like wooing a woman. Asked once by Putzi why he never married, Hitler replied: "Marriage is not for me and never will be. My only bride is my Motherland."

One of Hitler's stranger habits was his carrying of a whip—with which he would gesticulate when he was talking, usually somewhat bashfully, to women. Putzi was convinced that it played some kind of mysterious role in his relationship with the opposite sex. "All this wielding of the whip seems to be connected with a hidden desire on the part of Hitler for some state of erection which would overcome his fundamental sexual inferiority complex," he wrote. He wondered if it might have been prompted in some way by the memory of his sadistic, whip-wielding father.

—

THE portrait of Hitler was only one of dozens of reports that Putzi would write for the Americans. Documents in his files from the period give the flavor of the material that he was providing. In one six-page analysis entitled "The German Situation at the Beginning of 1943," dated January 4, he described the Nazis' attempts to rally the population in the aftermath of the successful Soviet counteroffensive at Stalingrad and the American and British advances in North Africa. "This has certainly not affected German morale and German prestige favorably," he wrote. Signs that the war was drawing into a fourth year would inevitably provoke comparisons with the First World War and its culmination in the "great collapse of nerves, the November Revolution of 1918"—something Hitler and his allies were desperate to avoid. For this reason, he, Goebbels, and Göring were increasingly trying to remind the people instead of the more heroic Seven Years' War and of Frederick the Great. Since Hitler had drawn the first parallel between the two conflicts in a speech in the Löwenbräukeller the previous November, he had made increasing allusions to the war. Such mentions, Putzi said, "constitute an obvious attempt on their part to accustom the masses to the idea of thinking in terms of seven rather than four years—of distant victory rather than imminent defeat."

For Putzi any such comparison between Hitler and Frederick the

Great was spurious. Not only was Hitler a "usurper who is constrained to buttress his government by oppressive quasi-police institutions," rather than a legitimate sovereign, his war aims were far more different: Frederick pursued only limited geographical goals, defined by Prussian soil and by safeguarding the future of the new Germany. Hitler's empire, by contrast, was "a geographic and ethnic monstrosity." Putzi also could not resist another sideswipe at Hitler—while Frederick stood for progress of thought, inviting men like Voltaire, Diderot, d'Alembert, Maupertuis, and other leading thinkers to his court, Hitler consciously avoided great scholars and "spends the bulk of his private time in the company of intellectual chauffeurs." Putzi was proud of his report. "As the above elaborations by no means exceed the knowledge of the average German, our information suggests their immediate use for propaganda purposes," he wrote.

Four days later, Putzi wrote a comment on Goebbels's New Year's Eve speech. He was not impressed: careful scrutiny of the original German text "proves beyond the shadow of a doubt that Goebbels has pulled the last stop of his big Wurlitzer-organ. . . . The various assertions, promises, etc., etc., having been disproved by the unexpected collapse of the German Caucasus—and Stalingrad—fronts will fatally boomerang back at Goebbels and the Hitler regime." Putzi predicted, "The beginning of the end is much, much nearer than most people believe. In all likelihood Goebbels will have definitely disappeared by the time we shall listen to the next German New Year's Eve speech. In the last analysis, this speech is . . . the open admission that the geopolitical gangster-philosophy has finally been checked."

On March 8, Putzi wrote another report on "the probable mode of exit of Adolph Hitler from the stage of history," in which he speculated—somewhat prematurely—whether Hitler might be tempted to commit suicide. His conclusion was that he might, if he ever found himself in a situation so bad that he had a "legitimate" reason to do so. Alternatively, he might seek a *Heldentod* (hero's death) at the front. "Hitler knows that in case of defeat there can be no Saint Helena for him," he wrote.

Putzi did not limit his contributions to such commentaries. After his portrait of Hitler, he turned his attention to his henchmen. A report on Himmler, dated April 23, 1943, described him as an overgrown child—"immature, enveloped and insensitive, blighted by the Great War and its aftermath." The key to understanding Himmler's psychology, Putzi wrote, was that he had originally planned to make agriculture and agronomy his career and therefore saw the world through the eyes of a simple farmer. "To him Germany is nothing but a big estate," he wrote. "His duty is to get results. What obstacles interpose themselves are treated either in the light of errors or sabotage—the former to be corrected, the latter to be dealt with as one deals with weed or vermin, by extermination. There is no hard feeling. It is merely part of the job. As a rule, farmers do not belong to the Society for the Prevention of Cruelty to Animals."

Himmler's true bride, Putzi claimed, was the swastika flag. This explained in part his approach to marriage: "He chose a wife, who being a Nobel Prize winner for Feminine Ugliness, represents no danger of becoming enthralled and depotentiated by too absorbing a domestic love-life." Indeed, Frau Himmler was "so impossible-looking, that she is never seen."

Such anecdotal stories clearly made interesting reading. Although it is doubtful how much operational use they were, Roosevelt had a considerable appetite for the kind of personal details that Putzi could provide. It came at a cost, however. In May, Carter asked for a further increase in his monthly budget from forty-five hundred to five thousand dollars. It was not just because of Putzi's medical bills—after expensive dental work he now needed his tonsils removed—but also as a result of a growth in the operation, which included the enlargement of Carter's New York office and the addition of the writer Henry Pringle to the payroll.

———

NOT all Putzi's reports were well received, however. Those who read his work were struck not only by his anti-Semitism but, even more, by his violent anti-Communism. This was highlighted by what was to become known as the Katyn Massacre. On April 13, 1943, the German government announced the discovery by its advancing army of the bodies of 4,421 Polish officers in a forest near Smolensk in western Russia. Shot in the back of the head and with their hands tied with barbed wire, the men were lying, layer upon layer, in huge ditches. The men appeared to have been made to stand or kneel on the edge of the mass grave. When the bullet struck, they pitched forward and fell in, thus saving their killers the trouble of burying them. The Nazis had immediately grasped the propaganda value of the grisly discovery. The Soviets, who had been so enthusiastically embraced by the West as an Ally, were the authors of this terrible crime, they announced. The Kremlin denied the charge, claiming that it was the Germans who had murdered the Poles and now wanted to discredit Russia.

Putzi had no doubt that the Russians were to blame and continued to point out in subsequent reports the all-too effective use that the Nazis were making of the massacre in their broadcasts to eastern Europe. "The sour truth remains that the Katyn story as put out by Dr. Goebbels proved and still is proving virtually unassailable," he wrote. "In this connection, it will be well to remember that nothing is better propaganda than the truth." If the Allies tried to ignore the whole thing, they would just make it worse, he warned. To any "non-Bolshevists" the "prospect of an allied invasion of the continent may well mean the collapse of the German dyke in the East and the subsequent flooding of Europe by the 'Bolshevist hordes,' with all the possibilities for further 'Katynization' on an unprecedented scale."

Such a view was necessarily unpalatable to Putzi's American hosts. There was little doubt that they, too, had realized the Russians had been to blame. Owen O'Malley, the British ambassador to the Polish government in exile, had admitted as much in a secret report to Winston Churchill who, in turn, came close to conceding Soviet responsibility for the massacre to Wladyslaw Sikorski, the Polish prime minister in exile. "Alas, the German revelations are probably true," Churchill told him. "The Bolsheviks can be cruel."

Yet the war had to be won, and the Western Allies desperately needed the Russians' help to defeat Hitler. Just over two weeks after the discovery of the bodies, Churchill was to send Stalin a telegram with fulsome congratulations for the "splendid speech" he made at that year's May Day parade. The truth about Katyn would have to wait. It was not until 1990 that the Kremlin finally came clean and Soviet president Mikhail Gorbachev formally laid the blame for the crime at the door of the NKVD, forerunner of the KGB. Two years later, after the breakup of the Soviet Union, Boris Yeltsin, the Russian president, handed his Polish counterpart documents proving beyond doubt that the massacre had been ordered by Stalin.

On other occasions, though, Putzi was just plain wrong—his judgment clouded by his intense hatred of Communism. On July 14, 1943, he told Carter that he expected Hitler to fall in about three months and this would be followed by a German revolution. He also took occasion to warn against the consequences of Katyn. The massacre, he said, had undoubtedly had a dramatic effect on public opinion in central and eastern Europe—something underestimated by American intelligence—which risked pushing "Poland into German arms again."

—

PUTZI kept talking to Field about Egon and how he missed him. After their brief meeting at lunch in June the previous year, Egon had gone back to his unit. He was still based in the United States, however, and when Field mentioned the matter to Carter, he came up with a plan: Egon would be brought to Bush Hill to become his father's military guard.

It was, as Egon described it later, a bizarre triple role. He was to be Putzi's bodyguard "both against possible danger from some crazy Kraut who might hate Father as a traitor, and against a possible incident staged by the British in order to discredit or terminate the S-project"; his prisoner-of-war guard "to keep Father from running away;" and his private secretary "to help him monitor the radio, compose his reports, type them etc." This anomalous position only enhanced Egon's sense of "being extraordinary." Field was impressed: Putzi's son was not only highly intelligent but also had a deep understanding of his complex father. Field also found him a far more agreeable character than Putzi.

Egon would help his father go through the transcripts made by the Federal Communications Commission and the microfilms of European newspapers they were sent and monitor the broadcasts from the Reichs Rundfunk. He also used his own knowledge and experience to help Putzi compose his reports. Egon noted his father's exasperation at being asked periodically to comment on claims that Hitler was dying. After he had been asked the same question for the fourth or fifth time, Putzi lost his temper: "Stop asking me that damn fool question," he told one of his interlocutors. "If and when he dies, I will tell you. I will have to, because you will certainly notice it then. That man is not just a figurehead; he is the kingpin and there will be tremendous upheavals; it won't go unnoticed."

Putzi had barely any more patience for the many senior officials who used to come and pick his brain. On one occasion, Egon heard him berating a major general in charge of psychological warfare for the fact that he did not speak German. "This is ridiculous," Putzi told his visitor in a raised voice during a meeting in the library, as Egon listened discreetly in the corridor outside. "I make you an offer: you come here twice a week and I will give you German lessons and inside of a few weeks you will be in a position to do the job you are now incapable of doing."

The general did not feel inclined to take the offer and stormed out of the building, barely acknowledging Egon's salute. Egon rebuked his father for treating a major general in such a way and practically throwing him out. "How do you expect to exert an influence, if you are going to use this kind of psychology?" he demanded. It was typical of his father, he thought. He always seemed to find a way to rub people the wrong way. People like Putzi were doomed to be "Cassandras," Egon concluded. "They will prophesy truly but will not be listened to. Their advice won't be taken because they preclude this possibility by offending their listeners to the extent where they can't judge the merits of what is being told them."

One afternoon, as Egon and Field were sitting on the veranda overlooking the garden, enjoying the hot sunshine, Egon suddenly interrupted Field's reverie with an unexpected proposal.

"The death of Hitler would shorten the war," Egon told him. "I believe I can kill him. I have unique qualifications." As Field listened, startled, Egon went on to outline a bizarre plan to assassinate the Nazi leader. He would go to Berchtesgaden, which he knew well from his childhood visits, at a time when he could be sure the Nazi leader would be there. There would then be two possibilities: he could either grab a rifle from a guard and fire at Hitler through the huge plate-glass window behind which he used to pace up and down at sunset. Or, alternatively, he could try to talk his way into the house, perhaps by telling the guards he was bringing a secret message from his father. "Once inside, I believe Hitler would be intrigued to see me," he said. "If I can get close enough to shake his hand, I can kill him." Egon was convinced he could survive long enough in the resulting chaos to claim prisoner status under the Geneva Convention as "an American sergeant acting under direct orders of enemy assassination from the commander in chief." Even if the plan failed, he was convinced it would severely upset Hitler's psyche.

Despite the outlandish nature of the proposal, Field was impressed enough to discuss it with Carter, who then forwarded it to the president. It came back with a curt refusal. It was not just the unlikelihood of success that promoted the rejection; Roosevelt apparently adhered to the ethical principle according to which one head of state does not try to assassinate another.

Undaunted, Egon came up with another suggestion shortly afterward. He pointed out that he knew details of the aerial defenses of Berchtesgaden, which he presumed would be the place to which Hitler would finally retreat, perhaps in order to stage some dramatic finale in the Eagle's Nest. Arrangements were made for him to instruct U.S. Army Air Force officers in the matter. There, with a pointer in his right hand, he stood in front of a sand table model of Berchtesgagen, complete with little model airplanes, and showed how it would be possible, with two squadrons of planes, to outwit the defenses and destroy the houses of Hitler, Göring, and the others. The Eagle's Nest, high above, would be left untouched because important records were kept there.

On another occasion, Egon described to Field his experiences in the Hitler Youth and how he had been taught as part of his training how to kill silently. OSS director Gen. William Donovan was so impressed when he heard about it that he had Egon give lectures to members of the OSS undergoing special training in the incongruously plush surroundings of the Congressional Country Club near Washington. Dressed in a camouflage suit and with his hands and face blackened, Egon—known for the occasion as Sergeant Martin—demonstrated several methods of silent killing, including strangling from behind with a piano wire and the other basic principles of night-fighting. Years later, a dignified Wall Street banker told Field how that day's lesson had saved his life, for he had been dropped behind German lines ahead of Patton's army and knew what to expect.

Inspired by Egon's time in the Hitler Youth, the U.S. authorities had another special task for him. On December 30, he was taken by Carter to the office of Leo Rosten, head of the domestic branch of the Office of War Information. There the two men urged him to write his memoirs "with special reference to the H.J." [Hitler Youth]. To most people, the idea of writing their memoirs at the age of just twenty-two would have seemed extraordinary. Such was the degree of press attention to which Egon had already been subjected, though, that he took it all in his stride.

In early January 1943, he picked up his pen and began to write. "I began, this day, to jot down a few guiding lines for eventual execution of 'my memoirs,'" read an entry in his diary on New Year's Day. The Americans also held open the tantalizing prospect of a film role: on January 12, Rosten called him in for a meeting with Lt. Col. Frank Capra, who mooted the idea of a small part acting in the second film in a series called "What Are We Fighting For." Egon was delighted at the idea; sadly, nothing came of it.

Progress on the book, too, was slow. Egon not only had to continue assisting his father, he also had to help look after Bush Hill, sawing up wood for the stoves, carrying in supplies, and pumping and carrying water whenever the Delco engine broke down—which was very often. The writing also did not come easily; Egon had wanted to write in the third person—à la Caesar—in order to achieve detachment, but was persuaded not to do so on the grounds that it would lack immediacy.

The project was not without controversy. Although Carter and Rosten were enthusiastic, General Strong was wary, in part because of a provision under army regulations against any soldier talking for publication about matters that might have direct or indirect military implications. He also claimed that it would violate the agreement with the British. Carter dismissed such objections, and the question of whether or not to publish became a subject of heated debate at cabinet level. Egon did not mind the confusion. In fact, he was becoming less and less enthusiastic about the whole project and welcomed the "Stop" orders that came from time to time as giving him an excuse to put off working on his manuscript. Eventually, on February 20, Henry L. Stimson, the secretary of war, took up the matter directly with Roosevelt. Carter, who was keen about the project, also discussed it with the president.

One day in early March, Carter summoned Egon, addressing him with a "contrived solemnity" that amused both of them. "Sergeant Hanfstaengl," he said. "The president has instructed me to convey to you his direct order coming from him in his capacity as your commander in chief—that you sit down and write your memoirs." On March 9, Egon began work in earnest. After taking a first look a week later, Carter proclaimed it "first-rate stuff."

Each page was taken to the OSS, where a typist would turn out several copies, one of which, Egon was led to believe, was handed to and actually read by Roosevelt. From time to time, Carter would encourage him with messages of interest or approval from the president. As a further sweetener, Carter told him *Reader's Digest* was interested in publishing extracts from the book for a considerable sum of money. Progress was swift. On June 1, the complete typescript was returned to Egon for proofreading and revision.

Carter was impressed with Egon's work. A week later, he wrote to Roosevelt praising it as "a very impressive document" that, after some further revision, could be effectively utilized for propaganda purposes. He also suggested that the president might like to meet Egon before he went off to "risk his life for this country." Roosevelt was happy to read the manuscript, but did not think it wise to meet "young Putzi." Egon himself was so tired of the project that the most he could bring himself to do was read through the draft. On July 8, he handed all 477 typed pages to Field and sat back to see what would happen. The manuscript was entitled *Out of the Strong*.

While Egon was finishing his book, Putzi was becoming increasingly preoccupied about his mother, who was by then well into her eighties. She had been writing to him regularly at his Fort Henry address, but the letters only got as far as the Office of Censorship in Washington. In September they were sent to the FBI, which, in turn, sent them to its laboratory to check for secret ink and the presence of codes and ciphers. They all, of course, tested negative. They were merely the outpourings of an elderly woman worried that she would never see her son again before she died. "Is there anything sadder for a mother than the separation which we must now suffer?" she wrote in one. "If I only knew how you are!" In another, she spoke of the "torture for all those separated from their loved ones who must remain without news of their welfare."

——

EGON'S real interest was not so much in writing his book as in his own military career. Despite his pleasure at being with his father, he had not joined the army to sit out the war in a country house on the outskirts of Washington. He wanted to go on active service, but Putzi's status meant Strong kept blocking it. Egon had inherited his father's determination, however, and on February 16 he had succeeded in having President Roosevelt sign a personal order allowing him to be sent to the front. But still he remained at Bush Hill.

On July 22, Carter telephoned with two pieces of good news. First, the manuscript was to be published: Henry Pringle, who had won a Pulitzer prize for his biography of Theodore Roosevelt and had recently been added to Carter's office, was appointed as ghostwriter and editor. After a few revisions, the manuscript was sent the following month to *Reader's Digest*. It was planned that it would also appear as a book. Of more interest to Egon, he was told that he was to be assigned to combat duties in the South Pacific. He would have preferred Germany, reckoning that he would be more useful there, but any assignment was better than remaining in Virginia.

On October 1, Egon made the last entry in the diary he had been keeping since he had arrived in Bush Hill: "*Packen—Abfahrt ins Blaue*" ("Get Ready—Departure for the Unknown"). Soon afterward, he happily set off for the South Pacific. Before leaving he gave Carter power of attorney over the disposing of the proceeds of his book. Egon did not get his hopes up. It was just as well, for despite Pringle's best efforts the book was never published. All the publishers they approached turned it down; one condemned it as a "particularly insidious form of German propaganda."

Egon was amused; looking back several years later, he regretted that he had been too young and weak to resist the temptation to write exactly what the U.S. authorities and American public would have wanted to hear. It was "a singular piece of good luck," he thought, that the book had never been published.

24

IT was a wet and miserable November evening as Alexander Sturm, recently graduated from college, drove his dark blue Lancia convertible toward Washington. He was on his way to his first job. He had been offered it that summer by Carter, but not told precisely what he was expected to do or how much he was going to be paid. That evening he was still very much in the dark: all he knew was that a hotel room had been reserved for him on F Street, not far from the State Department.

It was late when Sturm finally reached the hotel. His first impressions were not favorable. The room was so small there was barely enough space in it for its three pieces of maple furniture, let alone for Sturm and his two bags. Stepping out into the pouring rain, he sought solace in a meal of vichyssoisse and swordfish, washed down with a bottle of Niersteiner Spätlese 1934. As he walked back afterward to the hotel, he felt ready for anything. It was just as well.

The next morning, Sturm drove, as instructed, to Carter's house on Leroy Place. They went on together to a former school building that had been converted into a counterespionage headquarters. There, after much checking of papers and many signatures, the new recruit was introduced to a lieutenant named Neumann, who, he was told, would help improve his marksmanship. A lawyer by profession, Neumann listened approvingly as Carter outlined Sturm's assignment. It was all still rather vague; his main task, he was told, would be "to exercise tact." It was only as the pair of them set off again under a cloud-streaked pale blue sky, bound this time for Alexandria, Virginia, that Sturm at last learned the true nature of his work.

"Your immediate future," Carter told him, "is to be spent as body-guard and companion to Ernst Franz Sedgwick Hanfstaengl, otherwise known as 'Putzi,' formerly vice-dictator of Germany." Notwithstanding his overstatement of the importance of Putzi's previous role, Carter went on briefly to outline Putzi's life and background. For security reasons, he pointed out, his charge was to be known as Dr. Sedgwick or quite simply the doctor. And, with that, they drove on toward Bush Hill.

A smiling Baer opened the door to Carter and Sturm after they climbed the steep flight of stone steps and walked across the veranda. As they walked in, Sturm had his first glimpse of Putzi, as he emerged from a door opposite. He was clad entirely in khaki. The first thing that struck Sturm about him was his "hemispherical quality." He was not simply tall, but massive; straight black hair, parted in the middle, was forever falling in front of his eyes. Ever the perfect host, Putzi invited Sturm and Carter into the parlor where a few cubes of hardwood were burning on the hearth. A gray cat was curled up on the sofa asleep. The room was a strange sight: the tables and windowsills were covered with dusty piles of books, newspapers, and mimeographed reports. Worn and rotted brocade was peeling from the walls.

Putzi had been listening on his shortwave radio to a speech by Churchill, making notes with a steel pen, when they walked in. He turned and looked at Sturm approvingly. "He looks like Wagner's step-son," he said.

"A special service of the management," Carter replied.

Putzi said he would teach Sturm the German language and, in accordance with his liking for nicknames, announced he would call him Sturmi. He then gave Carter the latest installment of his weekly political critique, which would be relayed to the president. In it, he reviewed Hitler's most recent speeches, quoting notable phrases and describing at whom they were aimed. He also explained what they revealed about Hitler's state of mind. All of this was delivered in an excellent if deeply accented English. After taking coffee together, Carter and Sturm took their leave of Putzi and were back in Washington before noon.

Sturm spent the next week completing the formalities necessary before he could begin his assignment. He was again struck by the odd-ness and informality of the arrangements. His salary, he learned, was to be paid by Joseph F. Guffey, a senator from Pennsylvania who owed

Carter a favor. He was also given a card to the National Press Club, a check for twenty dollars, and a .38 caliber revolver in a left-handed holster. The gun had a strange history. It had originally belonged to Egon, who had carried it in addition to his government-issue automatic. But he had forgotten to take it with him when he left and his father had kept it on his radio table as a souvenir. One day, it was spotted by a Pentagon colonel who was suitably appalled at the idea of a prisoner like Putzi being armed. Since it was private property it could not be appropriated, so Carter took it into protective custody until it could be returned to its owner.

"Thus it happened," wrote Sturm, "that I was employed by a private citizen, paid by a senator to guard a state prisoner with a gun for which I did not have a license and which, like me, had no official status whatsoever." It could only get stranger.

Sturm began at Bush Hill on November 16, 1943. He and Putzi soon settled into a regular routine. Putzi would rise every day at 4 AM and read or write for a few hours. He worked in a study on the upper floor of the house. It contained a heavily loaded bookshelf and at least four tables covered with books as well as a few prints, reproductions, and other items of interest that he had found around the place. After breakfast, he and Sturm would repair to the parlor where they would listen to broadcasts from Berlin or, if there was nothing else of interest, music instead. At ten they would go for a walk in the woods, tramping along the paths and tracks deep in eclectic conversation.

Like the house, the grounds were untidy and neglected. This was such an affront to the sensibilities of one more used to the manicured grounds of Potsdam, Versailles, or Hyde Park that one December morning Putzi attacked the briars, nettles, and weeds that had taken over what had once been a huge lawn. After piling them all up, he then set fire to them, creating a huge bonfire. Baer's wife caught sight of the fifteen-foot-high flames and came running out of the house with a milk bottle full of water in her hand. Her alarm only added to Putzi's enthusiasm; by dusk, what had started the day as a jungle had been reduced to scorched earth.

In his reports early the following year Putzi continued to write about what were fast becoming familiar themes, chief among them the Nazis' continuing moves toward a rapprochement with the Church. Confirmation of this, he told Carter during a meeting that January, came from reports that Albert Speer, Hitler's chief architect, was drawing up plans for the rebuilding of churches destroyed by Allied bombing. Such attempts at repairing relations with the Vatican appeared to be linked with a broader attempt by the Nazis to convince not just the Germans, but also the Poles and other Europeans that Hitler's regime was the only defense against the atheistic Soviets. For this reason, Putzi argued, the Allies should try to convince ordinary Germans that they, too, were opposed to Russia's expansion westward, so they did not think that Europe's salvation from "Asiatic Bolshevization" depended solely on the Nazis.

In other musings that spring, Putzi cast doubt on whether Finland would conclude a separate peace with Russia and claimed that the Germans were praying for an early attempt at a second front, as they were confident that it could be beaten back with such heavy losses that it would dishearten the British and Americans. Putzi was also turning his attention to Germany's future. He argued that the Allies should turn the country into a federal state, with its capital not in Berlin but instead in another city such as Leipzig in the east or Kassel in the west. He was nevertheless pessimistic about the future of his native land. In one report in April 1944, he warned of the great difficulties of setting up an enduring democratic regime in postwar Germany. The Social Democrats and Liberals had both had their chance before the war, but had failed miserably, he claimed. For that reason, young people might well abandon Nazism as a failure, but would swing to the radical totalitarian left. Even though occupation by the Americans, British, and French would postpone such a regime, it would be inevitable once they withdrew. Joint occupation with the Russians would mean that any future government would necessarily follow the Soviet formula. "The Communist regime will appear as a spontaneous German movement," he declared.

While Putzi was pondering the future of Germany he was also becoming preoccupied with more mundane concerns. The Baers, who had been part of the project since the beginning, had been increasingly throwing their weight about and trying to reduce the domestic duties expected of them. The final sticking point came over the trivial matter of who was to wash the dishes. When Strum arrived, the Baers told him that this, along with cleaning the villa, was part of his duties. And this he dutifully did, until Carter visited one day.

"You don't have to wash dishes," Carter told him.

"You tell the Baers that," replied Sturm.

For a week they did as they were told, but when Carter returned for his next visit they gave him an ultimatum: either someone else would have to be found to do the dishes or they would leave. The dispute soon acquired a significance far greater than its import. When no solution was found, Field was brought in to mediate. Eventually, a compromise was found—a schedule was drawn up according to which they all took turns. But relations had been soured. The final straw came when Sturm went off to Washington one day and forgot to warn Mrs. Baer that he would not be back for lunch. One fine December morning a few days later, she and her husband walked out.

Putzi found the whole thing hugely amusing. After the Baers left, Sturm found him sweeping furiously in the kitchen and singing in a mock operatic falsetto: "Guests may come and guests may go, but I stay on forever." They were replaced by a retired army cook from County Court named McHugh. A lively little man with white hair and blue eyes, he had a weakness for the bottle and on several occasions when left unsupervised was found lying unconscious facedown on the kitchen floor. He was assisted by a heavily built Kentuckian from G-2 named Goranflo. In his early thirties, he was amiable by temperament but kept to himself much of the time—which convinced Putzi that he was spying on them. McHugh did not last more than a few months, however. He began to drink increasing amounts, and after Goranflo confiscated his whiskey supply, he began to smuggle alcohol into the kitchen by pouring it into bottles of food coloring. One day after lunch he went out for a walk and never came back. Shortly afterward he sent for his trunk. From then on, Goranflo and Sturm did the cooking, teaching themselves from a book entitled *Favorite Recipes of Congressmen's Wives.*

———

PUTZI was permitted to leave Bush Hill and go to Alexandria only for haircuts. Each time he was given a dollar and let loose in town; he was under orders to change barbers frequently so as not to arouse suspicion. Any change from the dollar he was allowed to keep; these he saved up and called his Escape Fund. Occasionally, his keepers would bend the rules. One evening in early 1944, they took him to the cinema for the first time to see the musical *The Gang's All Here,* with Carmen Miranda. Putzi was immediately struck by her, claiming that she reminded him of a Munich woman. In February they took him to the nearby battlefield of Bull Run; on another occasion, they went to the local bookstore where Putzi relished the opportunity to pore over the stock.

Putzi's joy at leaving the confines of Bush Hill was tempered by his dislike of traveling by cars. "Whenever I get into one of these things I take my life into my hands," he complained to Sturm as they set off in his Lancia. Indeed, the only thing he liked even less was airplanes—his aversion to them heightened by the flight in 1937 that had precipitated his departure from Germany.

Despite captivity, Putzi remained in high spirits. Sturm was struck by the multiplicity of impressions he did and by his sheer wit. When Sturm complained once that he was behind in writing his diary, Putzi told him not to worry. "Goethe was twenty years behind in his diary," he said. "It gave him that remarkable touch of prescience."

Two outsiders who came to see Putzi at the time recorded their impressions in detail. The first was Arthur Pope, the chairman of the American Morale Commission, who had known him since his Harvard days in 1905. Putzi, he noted, was resentful of his imprisonment, although not so much as a result of the personal discomfort but rather because he found it difficult to get used to being a "nobody"—as shown especially by the failure of the British to consult him over Hess. Putzi made it clear to Pope that he was equally contemptuous of what he saw as the way America had mishandled Hitler in the 1930s—starting with the choice of the despised Dodd as ambassador and compounded by Washington's repeated failure to make it clear that it would stand up against German militarism. The result, he claimed, was that Hitler was allowed to become convinced that, in contrast to the First World War, America would this time stay out of any conflict. Although fundamentally bitter and contemptuous of Hitler, he seemed to Pope to be deeply and permanently pro-German, taking a discernible satisfaction in news reports that the German line was holding. Pope also found him still "whacky about the Jews"; although claiming to have some Jewish friends, he remained resentful of their influence.

Jack Morgan, who spent a couple of days with him a week or so later to compile a report for the State Department, was convinced, by contrast, that Putzi was still Nazi-minded, regardless of the antipathy he felt for some of the leaders such as Goebbels. If the Nazi regime had tolerated any kind of dissent, then Morgan was sure that Putzi would have remained in Germany to play the role of "loyal opposition." This did not make what Putzi had to say any less useful; his ideas were what one might expect if he were "still in authority in Berlin and endeavoring to impress a foreign representative that all was well with the Reich."

Music, as always, provided consolation for Putzi. In the dusty front hall of the house, on a bare squeaky floor, stood an upright Steinway. It had been ordered and placed there on the direct orders of Roosevelt, who knew how important it was for his old acquaintance to be able to play. It was, however, somewhat out of tune. Field had been given the task of finding a good piano tuner, getting him approved by the FBI and the War Department and having him brought to Bush Hill. With all that bureaucracy to navigate, it took three months before a suitable man was found and approved. Field, who was in no hurry to do Putzi any favors, then waited another nine months before calling to arrange a visit. By that time, unfortunately, the piano tuner had died. Undaunted, Putzi nevertheless sat enthusiastically at the keyboard, playing music by Bach, Chopin, Beethoven, Schubert, Brahms, Wagner, and Strauss, as well as some of his own compositions.

—

ROOSEVELT'S sensitivity about publicizing Putzi's presence in the United States limited the opportunities for making use of him in active disinformation. There was no question of his making broadcasts to his countrymen in the same way that William Joyce, for example, was used by the Nazis to broadcast to his fellow Britons, who nicknamed him Lord Haw-Haw. Generally, the inside information that Putzi provided about Hitler's past or his relations with his lieutenants was incorporated anonymously into propaganda broadcasts. But Putzi was ready to play a more prominent role. The previous July, Carter had written to Roosevelt, suggesting the use of propaganda leaflets that would make explicit use of the fact that Putzi was in America. Despite the risk to his family and relatives in Germany, Putzi was keen to go ahead with it. Carter wanted a decision on the political aspects of the plan, which he said would involve "capitalizing on his personality in place of the present policy of suppressing any public or international references to Putzi." Roosevelt suggested that he discuss the whole thing with Bill Donovan, Cordell Hull, and Robert Sherwood, director of the overseas branch of the Office of War Infomation. The idea does not appear to have gotten off the ground.

Putzi was used in a bizarre way early in 1944 when Carter invited him to a dinner party on Leroy Place in Washington. Field drove him from Bush Hill in his old Ford. Putzi was wearing the blue suit that Field had bought for him in Alexandria; it did not have the cut or the style of the suits Putzi was used to buying in London, but it was decent. Putzi was exhilarated and full of questions.

"Who is going to be there?" he demanded. "Any of my Harvard friends? Will I know any of them? Do they all know why I am coming?" "Yes, they know why you will be there," Field replied. "Wait and see." Carter and his wife, Sheila, greeted Putzi at the door. "Dr. Sedgwick, we are so glad you could come tonight," said Carter. "Several of your friends are here to meet you, some from your Harvard days."

Inside were four couples, two young women, Putzi, and Field. It was agreed that no German was to be spoken and no reference made either to Hitler or the war. The conservation was to be about music, literature, Harvard, and other such light subjects. Although nothing distinguished Putzi from the other guests, he remained under constant surveillance. One of his guards was waiting on the table while another posed as the driver of a taxi parked across the street. The entire proceedings were also taped. By prior arrangement with the people next door, a small hole had been drilled in the wall and an FCC operator was sitting there.

The food and vintage wines were excellent, and Putzi, who relished any opportunity to be in the limelight, was soon deep in animated conversation with the other diners. By prearrangement, he began during the Baked Alaska to talk about music. Then after coffee and liqueurs, everyone moved into the drawing room where a Steinway grand on a white carpet awaited him.

Putzi did not need much encouragement to play. Before he sat down, Field lit two candles on either side of the music rack. He also pressed a white button underneath a microphone, which was resting on the piano between two candles. A tiny red light glowed, indicating that the tape in a secret recorder connected to it was running.

Putzi began by playing Debussy, quietly and beautifully. Then, gradually, the music became less light and frivolous, and he moved on to Hitler's favorites. At the same time, his mood changed: his expression became fierce, violent, and almost unrestrained. Field sensed he was projecting his body and mind to Hitler's great room with the long glass window in Berchtesgaden. "Now he was playing for der Führer."

Then, with what Field described as "almost cringing respect," Putzi began to address "mein Führer." His words sincere, emotional, and low-key, he begged Hitler to stop the war, warning that the Allies were intent on destroying their beloved homeland. Make peace at any price, he urged him, even if it meant total surrender. The music crescendoed to a climax and then stopped suddenly. Putzi stood up, trembling. He shook hands, thanked his hosts, and left the apartment.

Putzi did not speak during the entire journey back to Bush Hill with Field. The next day, he remarked on the good company, the excellence of the food and the wine, and the pleasure at seeing his old Harvard friends again. He said nothing more about the music, although Field knew he had discussed it with Carter.

The tape was sent to CBS, which then pressed thousands of copies of a single-sided phonograph record. Hundreds of boxes, addressed to Hitler, Göring, Himmler, Ribbentrop, and other German leaders, were dropped from U.S. aircraft over Germany, with instructions to deliver them unopened to their respective addressees. The music was also broadcast to Germany from an American transmitter in East Anglia. It is not known whether Hitler himself ever heard his former friend's exhortation. Himmler, however, was certainly aware of it. In one of his own broadcasts, he claimed "a well-known traitor to the Fatherland, now living abroad, was sending lies into Germany by radio and record." Anyone finding one of the records was ordered to destroy the parcel unopened. Field concluded that the dinner party had been a success.

BY the beginning of 1944, Carter was finding it increasingly difficult to keep things running at Bush Hill. As he saw it, there were only two ways of improving the situation: either bring the army or the FBI in to look after Putzi or else move him under an assumed name to a hotel or apartment house in Washington "to assure him of food and shelter." Carter was convinced that Putzi would be scrupulous in observing his parole, but was equally convinced that the British would be livid. Hoover continued to refuse to allow the FBI to become involved, however, and FDR suggested that the army should instead be put in charge of looking after him.

The next month, Putzi and Sturm came back from their walk one morning to find a large olive-colored car parked outside the house. Several colonels from the Pentagon had come, apparently to talk to Goranflo. They were accompanied by Neumann, who in the meantime had been promoted from lieutenant to captain. Putzi immediately saw a chance for advancing the project and invited them to stay for lunch. While Goranflo exercised his newfound culinary talents in the kitchen, Sturm served the vermouth, decanted the wine, and prepared the brandy and cigars.

Puzi was in sparkling form, stimulated by the presence of a new audience, and soon had the colonels in stitches. Before leaving, they accepted his offer to teach them German. It was decided that Tuesday dinner would be a good time to do so. After a not-so-subtle hint from Putzi, a private from G2 was sent to carry out all the chores—with the exception of cooking, for which Goranflo had by now developed a liking. The colonels were so keen on their German lessons that, soon afterward, they decided to take over the operation completely. Henceforth the S-project would be run by the Counter Intelligence Corps (CIC). Goranflo was given a staff of five, and Sturm, as an outsider, was informed by Carter that his services were no longer required.

A month later, Sturm went back to see Putzi on a social visit. He was staggered by what he saw. The paths had been raked, hedges had been clipped, dirty walls painted, and lawns had appeared from beneath the overgrowth. Cleanliness and order were everywhere. Carter, too, was impressed. Goranflo and his team were "energetic, adaptable and completely cooperative," he wrote. He was especially impressed by Goranflo himself, who had taken charge of the project at a most difficult moment and had "carried on with energy, good humor and complete willingness which are beyond praise."

Putzi, meanwhile, was continuing to make suggestions, some of which were eccentric, to say the least. One of the strangest was in May 1944, on the eve of D-day. Putzi proposed that a Hitler impersonator should make a speech telling the Germans that he had reached an understanding with the Allies for a joint operation to "hold back the Jewish hordes of Asiatic Bolsheviks from Europe." This fake Hitler, Putzi suggested, should make it clear that his first duty was to defend Europe from the Communists and claim that, for that reason, U.S. bombers would soon establish forward bases in Germany so the "forces of civilization" could conquer Russia. This way, so the argument went, rather than trying to repel the Allied invaders, the German forces would welcome them as reinforcements.

Carter liked the idea and passed it on to Elmer Davis, director of the Office of War Information. "Strange as it seems, this would appear plausible to the Germans and, if cleverly planted either via a fake Hitler or through some other official-sounding set-up, it might save lives and time," Carter wrote. It would have to be checked with the Soviet government, though, "to avoid possible misunderstanding."

Roosevelt was wary of the idea, however, and Davis swiftly dismissed it. Although he did not doubt that it would cause considerable confusion for a few hours, the consequences when the truth was known might backfire badly. "Confidence in our credibility would be gravely shaken and much of the effect of our propaganda would be permanently undone," he warned. Given that the Americans did not have their own disinformation radio stations, Davis said he had been obliged to discuss the matter with the British—who were equally opposed. The State Department, which was also consulted, was just as horrified, not least at how the Russians might react. "Even if the scheme were feasible, which we think is doubtful, it would be impossible to convince the Soviet government that it represented only psychological warfare," the president was told. "They and many other people in Europe besides the Germans would believe the suggested broadcast represented the secret policy of the United States and England."

—

ALL this time, the British government had been pushing to have the S-project terminated; Churchill himself had brought the matter up at the first Quebec Conference, in August 1943. FDR dug in his heels, however, leaving the British powerless. "The Prime Minister, in deference to the President's wishes, assented that he [Hanfstaengl] should remain under strict considerate treatment in the US," one internal British memorandum ruefully recorded. Indeed, if anything, such British efforts only increased Roosevelt's determination to hold on to Putzi.

It was becoming clear, however, that Putzi's usefulness—and, with it, that of the entire project—was drawing toward an end. With every month that passed, his insights into the Nazi leadership became more dated and thus of less value. Nor was he helped by his continuing anti-Semitism and the increasingly eccentric nature of some of his suggestions, such as the fake-Hitler speech. Field noted that he was becoming understandably upset at the massive bombing of his fatherland and writing fewer and fewer memoranda. Instead, he was devoting more and more time to a book he was writing on Frederick the Great. Putzi justified it on account of the increasing parallels being drawn by Hitler between the conflict and his hero's prosecution of the Seven Years' War. Field was not convinced, however. Relations between the two men, long poor, were getting even worse. Putzi was angry at the way Field kept needling him to write more reports. Field, for his part, found it difficult to hide his resentment that Putzi, with his servants and round-the-clock care, was living far better than he was.

More important, America's war aims had changed and the hopes of staging a palace coup in Berlin had faded. In a sense, the real change had occurred in January 1943 at the Casablanca Conference, when Roosevelt had rejected talk of any compromise by the Allies with their enemies and called for unconditional surrender. The Allied military successes in North Africa and the Russian victory at Stalingrad made this seem more possible. Any form of domestic rebellion against Hitler continued to be encouraged, insofar as it would undermine the German military machine, but it was no longer seen as a prime goal. Indeed, in speeches during the year, Roosevelt began increasingly to adopt the British practice of blurring the distinction between the Nazis and the German people as a whole. "When Hitler and the Nazis go out, the Prussian military clique will go with them," he declared on several occasions. "The war-breeding gangs of militarists must be rooted out of Germany . . . if we are to have any real assurance of peace."

Putzi failed to grasp this change of policy or at least failed to accept it, and continued to pin his hopes on a military coup against Hitler by the conservative forces that he had always admired. The old "Prussian Reichswehr-Junker set around Hindenburg, Groener and von Seeckt, . . . never really accepted the Austrian corporal, whose limitless schemes of expansion they distrusted and feared," he wrote in September. For this reason, he urged that American propaganda should contain some phrase that would make clear to the dissatisfied militarists that they were not being thrown into the same pot as the Nazis. Underlying this suggestion was Putzi's fear of Communism; if Germany were to be fought to exhaustion, he was convinced that the resulting chaos would culminate in the country's being turned into a Soviet republic. "This metamorphosis from swastika to sickle and hammer would take less time than certain experts seemed to believe," he said.

Roosevelt was increasingly reluctant to listen to such arguments, even though he did not yet see the need to sacrifice Putzi. By spring 1944, however, that was changing. Hitler was being forced on the defensive on all fronts. The Western powers were pushing northward through Italy while the Russians were forcing their way westward, regaining territory the Nazis had seized three years earlier. Then in June came the D-day landings in Normandy and the beginning of the liberation of Western Europe. With the total defeat of Nazi Germany now only a matter of time, the Americans were determined to fend off any peace initiatives from the Reich.

In this context, Putzi's advice was becoming increasingly irrelevant—nor did it come cheaply. Carter was now employing a total of twenty-five people and receiving ten thousand dollars each month from the

State Department to run the S-project and another, unrelated, operation known as the Bowman-Field Committee on Migration and Settlement— or the M-project, for short.

Ultimately, though, it was domestic concerns that were to deal the final blow. The campaign for the November 1944 elections was under way and Roosevelt had a tip-off from Carter that the British were threatening to make an issue of Putzi's presence on U.S. soil. In a sense, this would not have been anything new, as it had already been reported at the beginning of the previous year that Putzi was working for the Americans. The project had continued to be shrouded in secrecy, however, and Carter had subsequently made strenuous efforts to keep Putzi's name out of the papers. Roosevelt knew that a fresh burst of attention to the project—especially if the British succeeded in putting a negative spin on Putzi's role—would hand his enemies a potential propaganda weapon they could use against him.

Without any real arguments left for retaining Putzi, Roosevelt therefore moved swiftly to end the project. On June 28 he ordered that it be wound up with effect from July 1. Bringing Putzi to the United States had taken months of complicated negotiations; sending him home was far easier and quicker.

Grace Tully broke the news to Carter on July 7. He realized that it was futile to protest, but could not let the matter pass without a final appeal to Roosevelt. In a memorandum to the president later that day, he warned of his fears that if Putzi was sent back to an ordinary internment camp in Britain, he might face reprisals not just from British officials but also from fellow pro-Nazi inmates—especially once they learned about the help he had given the Americans and found out that Egon was a volunteer serving in the U.S. army in the southwestern Pacific. Carter also reiterated his concern that Putzi's treatment might dissuade other Nazis from coming forward to help the Americans.

Carter had little alternative but to bow to the inevitable, however, and began winding up the project. Five days later, he wrote to the British embassy pointing out that Putzi was at their disposal. He also offered to set up any interviews British authorities might want to have with him. The same day, he wrote to Grace Tully asking her to notify Maj. Gen. Jon T. Lewis, the commander of the Washington Military District, that he should hand over Putzi once the British had completed arrangements for his transfer.

No one had yet told Putzi, so, unaware of his own fate, he continued to write reports over the following weeks documenting the Nazi collapse. His mood was somber; he was at last convinced that the Germans were being beaten, and he feared for the future. But he also felt that thousands of lives were being thrown away by the Allies' insistence on pushing for unconditional surrender.

Putzi argued that America should turn its attention to defeating Japan before dealing the knock-out blow to Germany, fearing that Washington would be in too weak a position vis-à-vis Russia if it still had an Asian war to win. His gloom extended beyond the future of Germany to that of Europe as a whole. Within a year, he predicted, "the very name of Europe will have passed away and all that will be left will be 'Stalin-Asia.'" He also saw the failure of the plot by Col. Claus Schenk von Stauffenberg on July 20 to assassinate Hitler as leading to the liquidation of the last conservative elements in Germany and the transformation of the Nazi regime into "national communism." The German armies could probably hold out until 1945, he predicted, but there was no doubt that the "German goose is cooked." As for dividing Germany into three countries, as Sumner Welles had advocated, it would "lead to another Hitler twenty years later." None of this was the kind of intelligence Roosevelt wanted to hear, but even if it had been, it would have been too late to save Putzi from being sent back to Britain.

By mid-August, Carter was still waiting for word from the British. Army counterintelligence had informed the personnel guarding Putzi that the project was being wound up, but they still had not told their prisoner. Carter was sure that it was only a matter of time, though, before Putzi realized what was going on. There was another complication: Putzi had asked permission to see Helene, who was living in New York, to discuss matters involving Egon. Lt. Gen. B.W. Davenport, assistant secretary of the general staff, vetoed the request as "inadvisable and impracticable from the point of view of security." Since the army was now in charge of Putzi, Carter had to bow to their wishes.

On September 22, 1944, Carter came from the White House to see Putzi and broke the news that his mission was over. That afternoon, Putzi sat in the library at Bush Hill and pondered his fate—and that of his beloved homeland. Was he just to watch as Germany was turned into a "giant potato field," as had been suggested in the plan drawn up by Henry Morgenthau, Jr., Roosevelt's secretary of the treasury? One of the guards had left his loaded pistol in Putzi's bedroom by mistake and he contemplated suicide. No sooner was he about to start writing his farewell letters than he caught sight of an unopened letter from the Pacific. It was from Egon. Putzi could not go through with it.

Everything then happened much faster than anyone—even Carter—expected. The next morning, Putzi was taken to the Washington airport and put on the overnight flight bound for Prestwick, Scotland. During a stopover in Gander, Newfoundland, the plane took on a number of passengers, including a British general on his way home from Indochina. He took the window seat next to Putzi and the pair were soon engaged in animated conversation. As the plane landed, Putzi's guards were about to escort him off, when the band of a battalion of Highlanders appeared at the door to salute his traveling companion. It was, Putzi recalled, yet another of those "Gilbert and Sullivan interludes" with which his life had been so replete. He was formally handed over to British authorities at 10:30 AM on September 24.

Putzi's new hosts did not appear to have been expecting him. But he was put up for the night in the best spare room of the local police station and sent the next morning on a steamer bound for the Isle of Man, a tiny windswept island in the Irish Sea off the northwestern coast of England. There the same comedy was reenacted. Given the secret nature of Putzi's mission in America, no one there had been told he was coming either. The young guard who had accompanied him—and spent the entire journey being seasick—began to despair that he would never be rid of his charge. The German compound refused to take in Putzi, as did the Jewish one. He was therefore taken to the Japanese compound in Peel, on the west coast of the island.

The war, meanwhile, had already entered its final stages. After the D-day landings of June 6, 1944, in northern France, the Allies had advanced eastward, liberating Paris in August and clearing most of France and Belgium of German forces by that October. Then, on March 7, 1945, after smashing through the highly fortified Siegfried Line, they crossed the Rhine and swiftly overran western Germany. At the same time, the Russians were advancing from the east, entering East Prussia and Czechoslovakia in January 1945 and taking eastern Germany to the Oder. On April 25, the Western and Russian armies met at Torgau in Saxony. Five days later, Hitler bowed to the inevitable and committed suicide in his bunker beneath Berlin. The war in Europe was over. Germany's unconditional surrender was signed on May 7 in the French city of Reims and ratified the next day in Berlin.

Putzi watched the German collapse from the safety of the Isle of Man with mixed feelings. The dramatic nature of Hitler's demise had certainly come as no surprise to him. In the reports he had written at Bush Hill, he had predicted that the Nazi leader would be far more likely to commit suicide in the case of defeat than to suffer the humiliation of exile as Napoléon or Kaiser Wilhelm had done before him. Satisfaction that the war had ended "in the way [he] had so despairingly predicted" was tempered, though, with fears not just for his own future but also for that of his beloved Germany. Putzi had continued to cling to the hope that members of the German officer class would topple Hitler in a coup d'état long after the Allies had given up the idea as both unlikely and undesirable. If they had succeeded, he hoped, Germany's new rulers could have speedily concluded a peace with the Western Allies, and maybe joined them in fighting the Russians. Instead, his homeland had been forced into unconditional surrender—and half of it had been occupied by the Red Army. The fear, which Putzi expressed in his last report for Roosevelt the previous July, that Europe would be transformed into "Stalin-Asia" now seemed certain to become reality. The only small consolation was that his hometown, Munich, lay in American rather than Soviet hands.

Putzi was concerned, too, about the effect of the German collapse on his family. He was now allowed to write and receive letters, although they were often delayed for a long time. In what was probably the last letter to his mother, dated May 2, he reassured her about his living conditions. "Having learnt that Bavaria is now occupied by the U.S. Seventh Army, I make haste to let you know that I am well," he wrote. "I am interned at the above camp. From my windows I can see the Irish Sea all day long." He noted that Egon, who had just written to him from the Philippines, was doing well and had just gotten engaged to the only daughter of a New England bank president. He never saw his mother again. She died five days later.

Putzi remained at the camp until the summer of 1945, when he and his fellow inmates were shipped to Stanmore on the outskirts of north London.

CARTER had been away on a business trip to New York and only discovered that Putzi had been sent back to Britain on his return the next day. He was livid. In a brief memo to the president he condemned the army's action as "officious in the extreme." But it was too late. By definition, the departure of Putzi meant the end of the S-project. The episode did not dampen Carter's interest in intelligence, though. That September, he took great pleasure in forwarding Grace Tully a memorandum from the OSS praising the help he had given them with psychological warfare.

The president "might be interested to have concrete evidence as to the minor utility of some of my activities," he wrote.

In 1947, Carter sat down to tell the story of the S-project. Rather than trying to provide a factual account of the goings-on at Bush Hill he instead wrote up his experiences in the form of a fictional conversation between Roosevelt, Churchill, and Putzi. It was published as *The Catoctin Conversation*, under the pen name of Jay Franklin, which Carter used for his journalism.

Assessing the significance of Putzi's work for the Americans is difficult. The portrait of Hitler and the other such pieces of analysis are striking for the sheer quantity of personal information and the precise detail they provided. Although most are fascinating, it is difficult to see what operational use they could have been to the Americans. Many of Putzi's predictions also turn out to have been inaccurate, colored as they were by his own fanatical hatred of the Russians as well as by his desire to see the Nazi regime fall. On some occasions, though, notably with his realization that Stalin was responsible for the Katyn Massacre, he was proved correct. It was not Putzi's fault that the dictates of realpolitik prevented the Allies from acknowledging the truth and drawing the conclusions. Despite Carter's enthusiasm at the time for the S-project and unhappiness at its termination, he described it subsequently as nothing more than "picturesque and wildly funny, worth writing up from the point of view of the humor of it," but otherwise largely insignificant.

There is no doubting Roosevelt's personal interest, especially in the early months, when he not only read Putzi's reports but also put specific questions to him. If he never met Putzi or his son personally, it was to protect himself; he needed to maintain his distance from a project that was deeply controversial from its inception.

In an introduction he wrote for *The Catoctin Conversation*, Welles claimed Roosevelt followed the experiment closely; although apparently disappointed by the lack of detailed or concrete information, the president believed Putzi's reports had given the administration "a good deal of useful enlightenment as to the mental processes of the Nazi leaders," he wrote. Welles, who had been given a number of Putzi's reports, also found the information contained in them valuable, even though it was more useful from the standpoint of psychological warfare than from military intelligence. He was fascinated, too, by "what could be read between the lines." His conclusion: "The transcripts made available to me by Carter inclined me very definitely to the president's own conclusion that the project . . . had proved itself to be well worthwhile."

25

ON September 14, 1945, a Jewish-German inmate at the camp in Stanmore triumphantly presented Putzi with that day's copy of the *Daily Mail*. "You'll be released," he declared. "You're on the Gestapo death list." Under the headline "Britain Had 2,300 Marked Men," the newspaper quoted from Gestapo dossiers that had come to light revealing "Himmler's plan for 'liquidating' leaders in every field of British activity" had the Germans invaded in 1940. It claimed that the Nazis had drawn up a list of twenty-three hundred people—both Britons and Germans—whose arrest would have been "automatic" as part of their goal of achieving total subjugation of Britain.

The list, found in the Berlin headquarters of Reich security police by Allied investigators, was in neat notebook form, with the police file numbers of the wanted person appearing after each name. There were also extra pages for agents' notes and the results of their search. It appeared to have been originally compiled after the fall of France in 1940, but had been renewed yearly since. The list was led by Winston Churchill, Clement Attlee, and other British politicians, trade unionists, and newspaper editors. It also included a group of "prominent refugees." There, alongside Charles de Gaulle, Dr. Sigmund Freud—who had died in 1939—the novelist Stefan Zweig, and Czech president Eduard Benes, was Dr. Ernst Hanfstaengl.

It appeared to be the proof Putzi needed of his opposition to the Nazis. Convinced that it was his "get out of jail free" card, he showed it to the camp commander, who refused to pass it on. Putzi also managed to alert his lawyer, Kenneth Brown, who was equally unsuccessful in arguing that it was sufficient grounds for immediate release. Toward the end of the year, Putzi was moved to a camp set up at Beltane girls' school in Wimbledon, in south London.

Putzi asked to be transferred to the United States, but the Americans would not have him and the British wanted to send him to Germany. Then, by chance, at the beginning of 1946, he read in the newspaper that Eleanor Roosevelt had arrived in Plymouth. FDR had died the previous April, but Putzi knew his widow would still remember him. He wrote to her to plead his case, smuggling the letter out via the camp barber.

A few days later, Putzi was summoned to the commandant's office and handed a letter stamped "Opened by Censor." It was Eleanor Roosevelt's reply. It was clear that she thought Putzi was actually teaching at the school rather than interned there.

Dear Mr. Hanfstaengl,

I am so glad you are here in London. Could you let me know when your time permits to have tea with me at the hotel? Deeply touched by your kind appreciation for my husband,

Sincerely yours,

Eleanor Roosevelt.

Evidence of such high-level connections undoubtedly improved Putzi's treatment at the hands of his guards, but it did not bring about his release. Nor could he expect Harry S. Truman, Roosevelt's successor, to plead his case. On February 20, Putzi went on a hunger strike to protest against his planned repatriation. In a letter, reported two days later by the Associated Press, he claimed that sending him home would place his life in danger "from German underground fanatics." He pleaded instead to be allowed to join Egon, who had since been promoted to lieutenant and just returned to America from the Pacific after two years of active service.

Egon was also involved in an eleventh-hour appeal to the U.S. embassy in London to grant his father a visa. The same day that the AP report appeared, a family friend flew to Britain bringing with him affidavits in which Egon guaranteed that he would support his father if he were allowed to return to America. Time was running out, though;

Egon feared he could be deported within days. In an interview with *The New York Times* conducted in his room in New York's Hotel Chesterfield on West Forty-ninth Street, Egon said he was worried that Putzi would suffer because of the help he had given the American government during the war. If he were sent home, he said, "some Nazi or German nationalist might eliminate what he thinks is an absolutely black traitor."

Putzi's role in the S-project appeared to count for little with the Americans, however. In a statement issued on February 25, the State Department pointed out that no German had received a visa to visit the country since the beginning of the war and it was not going to make an exception for Putzi. That spring, he was taken back to Germany and placed in the former punishment and starvation camp at Recklinghausen.

Putzi's health was deteriorating sharply: his blood pressure wavered between 46 and 76 and his weight had sunk to just over one hundred and forty pounds. He was due to have been released on July 4, but the camp doctor opposed it on the grounds that he was too sick. Injections were used to raise his blood pressure to 100.

On September 3, 1946—almost seven years to the day since he was first arrested in London—Putzi was finally a free man again. He left the camp with fifteen reichsmarks and forty pfennigs for a third-class ticket to Munich and another five reichsmarks in travel expenses in his pocket. From there, carrying two heavy suitcases, he took a train to Tutzing and another from there to the house in Uffing.

—

PUTZI'S ordeal was still not over. Those associated in any way with Hitler's regime had to undergo a process known as denazification. Under the supervision of the victorious Allies, who now occupied Germany, a series of courts was set up. These went through each individual's records and, using a mixture of information submitted by the people themselves, official documents, and sworn affidavits provided by others, attempted to analyze the extent to which they had been involved in the Nazis' crimes. They were put into one of five categories—ranging from *Hauptschuldige* (the chief culprits) to *Entlastete* (denazified). The category chosen would be of considerable importance to the role he or she would be permitted to play in the new postwar Germany.

For Putzi, it was all unpleasantly reminiscent of the process he had endured in London after he was first interned. He nevertheless hoped that his actions since 1937—starting with his flight from Germany and ending with his involvement in the S-project—would be seen as out-weighing the help he had given Hitler in his early days and ensure him a place among the ranks of the denazified. His personal papers contain a sentence copied from Article Thirteen of the Law for Liberation from National Socialism and Militarism: "Exonerated are: Persons who in spite of their formal membership, candidacy or other external indica-tion, not only showed a passive attitude but also actively resisted the National Socialistic tyranny to the extent of their powers and thereby suffered disadvantages." Putzi clearly believed that this included him.

His defense was built on a number of elements. In detailed submis-sions made to the authorities, he tried to demonstrate how he had con-sistently tried to mitigate the worst of Hitler's excesses. He also tried to justify his occupation of the post of foreign press chief on the grounds that his place would have been taken by someone else far more radi-cal and fanatical if he had resigned. At home, for example, Putzi claimed to have tried to moderate Hitler's anti-Semitism, to have urged him to open the concentration camps to international inspection, and to have intervened personally to stop a plot to murder Dimitroff after he was acquitted of charges of involvement in the Reichstag fire; in foreign policy he said he had tried repeatedly to persuade Hitler against aggres-sive expansion to the east and alliance with the Japanese and to steer him toward establishing friendly ties with America. "As far as many of the things that I did not like about the Hitler movement were con-cerned, I comforted myself with the thought that these should be seen as teething troubles, as it were, that would disappear of their own accord over the years," he claimed. As proof of his determination to fight the regime while in exile, he cited his work on the S-project and the highly critical article about Hitler he wrote for *Cosmopolitan*.

All this, Putzi considered, constituted active resistance of the "National Socialistic tyranny" in the sense of Article Thirteen of the law. As far as the resulting "disadvantages" were concerned, he cited the seizure of his house on the Pienzenauerstrasse and other property by the Gestapo, the imposition of the forty-thousand-mark Reichsfluchtsteuer—the tax on fleeing Germany—and the stripping of his citizenship. His enforced departure meant that he had also been forced out of the family firm.

Putzi backed up his case with a mass of newspaper articles and var-ious other documents. A number of Germans also came forward to vouch for him: Harald Voigt, his former adjutant, testified how Putzi had repeatedly tried to persuade Hitler to ban *Der Stürmer*, Julius Streicher's virulently anti-Semitic newspaper; Edgar von Schmid-Pauli, a right-wing

Catholic writer who had run afoul of the Nazis, recounted how Putzi had often openly described Rosenberg and other leading members of the regime as "criminals," while Viktor Haefner, a former German First World War ace turned anti-Nazi, told how Putzi, often at risk to himself, had protected several Jewish inmates from attacks by ultra-Nazis when he was held at Fort Henry, even saving one who was lying on the ground and in danger of being trampled to death.

Carter offered to vouch for Putzi, telling Egon he would confirm that he had been in contact with his father on FDR's instructions since 1932 and collaborated with him "in the interests of world peace." He also tried to get Norman Armour, the assistant secretary of state, involved. The latter was not keen, although he let it be known that he might be prevailed upon to issue a statement on Putzi's behalf "in an actual emergency." In the end, Putzi made do with affidavits from Carter, Welles, and Eleanor Roosevelt.

——

THE hearing was set for 9:30 AM on Thursday, January 13, 1949. The courtroom in the Bavarian town of Weilheim was packed. The chief prosecutor, Manfred Frey, demanded that Putzi be classified as one of the chief culprits. Putzi, back in robust health again since his release from the camps, put on a theatrical performance, full of pathos and dramatic pauses, pacing up and down in front of the three-member tribunal. He described how after becoming Hitler's press chief, he had hoped that Hitler's propaganda was empty nonsense and that German bureaucracy would eventually win out. To his regret, he claimed, the bureaucracy had become Nazified and the Nazis had triumphed. To support his case, he produced the statements by Carter, Welles, and Eleanor Roosevelt.

Putzi easily won over his audience. The court's chairman ruled that he had "employed his powers to oppose National Socialism" and noted how during the Nazi period he had been stripped of his nationality and had his property seized. The fact that his post—that of foreign press chief—did not exist in the directory of Nazi positions (Amtsstellen) also counted in his favor as did his internment in Britain and work for Roosevelt. On this basis, he was formally freed of all charges of having been a Nazi and placed in category V—Entlastete (denazified). The audience—which included a number of foreign journalists, some of whom had known Putzi personally—was delighted by the judgment.

The case gave the press the opportunity to seize on his bizarre career and Putzi was again front-page news. "From internment camp to the White House," reported the Dutch paper *De Telegraaf.* "Hitler's foreign press chief became Roosevelt's advisor in psychological warfare." Putzi told another newspaper: "My aim was to establish an acceptable relationship between Germany and America. But it was hopeless given Hitler's shortsightedness and the stupidity of von Ribbentrop and Rosenberg." Aware that some at home might consider him a traitor for his role in psychological warfare while he was in the United States, he stressed that "from America, I was never involved in a struggle against the German people but only against their criminal rulers."

Despite the successful conclusion of his case, Putzi remained bitter that he had been forced to go through seven years of internment. "Have you ever heard of anything more ridiculous?" he asked Larry Rue, the veteran journalist from the *Chicago Tribune,* with whom he had lunched on the day of Hitler's abortive 1923 putsch. "Here I was a real fifth columnist in the Nazi Party, doing my best to keep it from adopting the cruel policies and ruthlessness that made it the object of hatred and contempt throughout the world. And I am punished for that."

Their interview was conducted in May 1954 in Mittenwald, a picturesque resort in the Bavarian Alps, where Putzi had gone to take a cure. It was all a far cry from their previous meeting: Putzi, who had put on rather too much weight, was on a starvation diet of potatoes, beets, and carrot juice, which allowed him to lose twelve pounds in three days and cured him of his rheumatism. Although he joined Rue for dinner in the restaurant of the sanatorium, he did not drink or eat anything.

—

BY the time he had been denazified, Putzi had reached the age at which most men think about retirement. He still had far too much energy for that. It was not immediately clear, however, what he could do or how he could earn a living. Business beckoned, but so, too, did politics, although the closeness of his earlier relationship with Hitler precluded his playing any important role in the postwar Bundesrepublik.

Putzi might have been expected to go back into the family art business, which was still run by his brother, Edgar. Although a founding member of the German Democratic Party and a staunch critic of Hitler, Edgar, four years Putzi's senior, had survived the Nazi era and the war largely unscathed. So had the family firm; it had been declared a *kriegswichtiger Betrieb*—literally a concern of importance to the war effort—and the technical expertise it had acquired in art reproduction was used for enlarging aerial photographs for the Wehrmacht. But relations between the two brothers, already poor from childhood, had deteriorated further during the long years in which Putzi had been Hitler's cheerleader and Edgar a determined anti-Nazi. Even in old age, they found it difficult to agree on anything—including art. "I won't even make an attempt to work with my brother," Edgar told Egon as relations with Putzi hit another low. "I would rather the firm went bankrupt." Indeed, for some time the two men communicated with each other only through their lawyers. A solution of sorts was eventually found, thanks to Egon, who had always gotten along well with Edgar and answered an appeal from both sides to come back from America and act as mediator. A family treaty was signed and Putzi was given back his shares.

Putzi did not play much of a role in the business, however, even after Edgar died in 1958 and it was taken over by Egon and his cousin, Edgar's daughter, Eva. According to Egon, his father railed against the modern art that they started selling; his son tried in vain to explain that consumer tastes had changed since the 1910s when Putzi had run the shop in New York. "The only thing we produced that he thoroughly approved of didn't sell at all, while the pictures he decided were no good and had no future sold rather well," Egon recalled.

One of Putzi's main priorities was the writing of his memoirs, which he had started working on in various forms in the late 1930s. The final impulse came from the writer Brian Connell. The two men had met several years earlier, and although Connell continued to write his own books, he remained fascinated by Putzi's story. In 1956, Connell went to see him in Munich to discuss how they could proceed. He finally spent two months with him, taping their long conversations. The result, combined with large amounts of material Putzi had himself compiled, formed the basis for a book, which came out in America and Britain the following year under the title *Hitler: The Missing Years*.

It was not a great commercial success; according to Egon, his father blamed the disappointing sales on the fact that the press was dominated by the Soviet Union's successful launch of the Sputnik. Egon's wife, who had worked in publishing, predicted that the book would not sell because the "I of the story is not sympathetic."

Harvard also continued to play a part in Putzi's life. Indeed in March 1953 he received a painful reminder that old animosities had not been forgotten, when Conant, the former Harvard president, visited Munich.

Putzi, who had learned of Conant's arrival from the papers, was unable to track him down, but was told by a waiter that his wife was having lunch in the Hotel Königshof with a group of German ladies. He sent over a dozen white roses accompanied by a note expressing his best wishes. A little later, to Putzi's horror, a "member of the German secret police" sought him out and returned the flowers with the explanation that Mrs. Conant did not want to meet him.

It was against this background that Putzi approached the preparations for the fifty-year reunion of his class in 1959. That spring, the usual requests were sent out for donations from alumni. The class of 1908 had stumped up a record $268,441 for its anniversary gift the year before, which its successor was keen at least to match. The reunion itself was set for June 8. Suddenly, the controversy of a quarter of a century earlier threatened to come back and haunt Putzi. "Hitler's Jester Plans a U.S. Visit" was the headline on an article in *The New York Times* of May 24, 1959. The report claimed that the one-time "piano-playing 'court jester' to Adolf Hitler" planned to attend the reunion as well as to give Harvard a second chance to accept the thousand-dollar donation that had been spurned in 1934.

"Business has been good in my art store and I might even make it $2,000," he was quoted as saying. "I am as clean as a hound's tooth for a visa to the States." This time would be different from 1934, he said. "I expect to have a swell time and get a warm welcome. Why not? I'm as anti-Nazi now as they come."

Putzi was appalled when he was sent the clipping a few days later. He had just written a letter to Hollis T. Gleason, the class agent, recounting the Munich incident with the Conants, which, he said, "made it painfully clear to me that there must still be much animosity toward me in certain Harvard circles." After seeing the report in *The New York Times*, he added a postscript: the interview on which the piece purported to be based had not taken place; the content was false and the general tone "manifestly spiteful." "I will not allow our 50th class day to be degraded into a field day for yellow journalism," he said. For that reason, he would not be attending and would not make even a symbolic donation. He nevertheless insisted that he would be happy to welcome any classmates to Germany, "un-annoyed by the shadowing efforts of any cliché-ridden reptile of the press."

Putzi's private life was no less stormy. To the horror of the rest of his family, he had fallen for Baroness Renate von Willich, a curvaceous aristocrat several years his junior. Von Willich—or Rehlein (little deer), as she was nicknamed—had first married the president of the biggest power works in Bavaria, bearing him two daughters. They had divorced and she then moved on to General Franz Ritter von Epp—the former Nazi *Statthalter* (governor) of Bavaria and Reich leader for colonial affairs, whom Bavarians rather cruelly nicknamed Chevalier d'Epp (Sir Stupid). That relationship had ended, too, and she moved on to Putzi, who later was jokingly to call her *Der Wanderpokal der Erotik*—the wandering cup of eroticism. The couple could just have lived together without marital ties, but Putzi was conservative by nature and they decided to marry. As divorcees, they had only a civil ceremony. In a small gesture of reconciliation with his brother, Putzi invited him to the wedding breakfast and asked him to be one of the witnesses.

The marriage was not an especially happy one and quickly took a heavy toll on Putzi's finances. Renate's daughters soon left their father and moved with her into Villa Tiefland, leaving Putzi to complain about having to satisfy their taste in expensive hats and clothes. When he tried sending their shopping bills to Renate's first husband, they were swiftly returned. Renate soon began plotting divorce. Bizarrely, the first inkling Putzi had that she intended to leave him came when she went to his friend, Hjalmar Schacht, the former Reichsbank president, and tried to prevail on him to persuade Putzi to bequeath her the house. For Putzi, it was the last straw. Shortly afterward, he summoned Egon and they went to a notary to sign the divorce papers. Bizarrely, his son cosigned the documents.

It was a decision both men would live to regret. As well as expensive tastes, Renate also had a good divorce lawyer, who succeeded in securing a highly advantageous settlement for her. By one calculation, some two-thirds of Putzi's income went toward her keep in his old age, obliging him to rent out part of his house to make ends meet. Nor would the financial demands end with Putzi's death; Egon's signature on the documents meant that he would continue to be responsible thereafter. To his dismay, Renate lived on well into her nineties, her taste for luxury undimmed by time. She was eventually declared not responsible for her actions, but not before many more unpaid bills had been sent Egon's way. His son, Eric, subsequently estimated that Putzi's decision to marry her had cost the family the equivalent of a substantial country house. "My grandfather was royally screwed," he said.

Helene had, in the meanwhile, also returned to Germany. After leaving Putzi, she had bought a house in Armberg on Lake Starnberg and moved into it with Trausil, who at first seemed the love of her life.

Before leaving for America, she had, at Trausil's suggestion, registered the property in his name; he warned her that it might be confiscated if it were registered in the name of a foreigner. This turned out to be almost as big a mistake as Putzi's divorce settlement with Renate. When Helene returned, in the mid-1950s, to reclaim the house, she received a cool reception from Trausil, who had taken up with another woman in the meantime.

Undaunted, Helene decided to stay in Gemany, settling in a small apartment in Munich. Her years of work in America had provided her with a pension, which, once converted into marks, was generous enough to provide a comfortable living. Even in her old age, she was always impeccably dressed and made-up. Unlike Putzi, she remained remarkably untroubled by the past: it is not clear whether or not she regretted the way she had saved Hitler's life when he fled to their home after the failed 1923 putsch. She could also console herself with the fact that she had never directly served the regime.

Relations with her former husband remained cool, however. Her decision to return to Putzi's native city inevitably meant that the two of them would come across each other at Christmas and other family occasions at their son's house. When they met they would give each other a peck on the cheek and engage in civil intercourse. Helene, in particular, remained reserved and there was never any chance of reconciliation.

Putzi was also haunted by a third woman—his World War I love, Djuna Barnes, with whom he had remained in touch sporadically over the years. Barnes had visited him for lunch in London in 1938, but he had upset her by making a pass at her. "It's always painful to have loved someone years back and find out what they grow up into," she wrote. "He was so much sweeter when I was twenty-three." Although the war had caused an interruption, they had remained in contact since. Putzi had sent her pastries and chocolates. She had fallen on hard times and he also offered her money on several occasions, but she had refused it. "He saved my life twice, first in the airplane and then when he didn't marry me," she told her friend Hank O'Neal. "It was not necessary for him to save me anymore."

In 1952, Putzi wrote her a letter: "'Old love does not rest'—it seems— and our early afflictions remain loyal to us throughout life." The letter was signed with "and a big hug from your old seducer Putzi." O'Neal noted that the only picture "with any color in her apartment was a post-card, 'Violets,' by Dürer," a memento of Putzi, which lay on the corner of her bureau.

IN 1970, at the age of 83, Putzi, still sprightly and alert, suddenly found himself back at the center of attention in his native land. The reason was the belated publication of a German edition of his memoirs. Entitled *Zwischen Weissem und Braunem Haus: Memoiren eines Politischen Aussenseiters (Between the White House and the Brown House: Memoirs of a Political Outsider)*, the book varied considerably from the earlier American and British versions.

One of the more telling of the additions is a section at the end in which Putzi bemoans the fact that no one accepts that the flight in 1937 that precipitated his departure from Germany was a serious attempt on his life. "The explanations were all the same," he said. "That I had misunderstood a rather heavy-handed joke and suffered a little from a persecution complex."

He had, it seems, long since come reluctantly to accept this point of view when at a cocktail party in 1965 he came across Major General von Schoenebeck, the former Luftwaffe officer who provided the Junkers JU 52 for the flight. To Putzi's delight, von Schoenebeck signed a declaration outlining what had happened and making clear that, as far as he was concerned, it was far from a joke. Putzi reproduced the letter in full in his book. He also cited a conversation with Dr. Sigismund Freiherr von Bibra, who had been German ambassador to Switzerland at the time. Von Bibra claimed a coded message had arrived in Berlin at the end of 1942 or early 1943 that declared: "Please, ensure that Dr. Hanfstaengl returns to Germany as soon as possible. Money is not important." This, Putzi felt, was proof that Hitler wanted to have his old friend back at his side as a "troubleshooter." He hastened to add, however, that he would have refused to return to that Germany "still run by that Gangster clique."

The book's publication coincided with a string of memoirs by other prominent figures associated with the Nazi regime who were ready to tell their stories now that enough time had passed since Hitler's fall. Putzi's book received mixed reviews, however. The influential weekly *Die Zeit*—required reading for Germany's liberal intelligentsia—condemned it as little more than an old man's belated attempt at self-justification. Putzi, it complained, was unable to separate the important from the trivial and any serious observations he had to make were "lost in a flood of trite anecdotes and gossip." The *Süddeutsche Zeitung*, in Putzi's native Munich, was a little kinder, but complained that, despite his proximity to Hitler during the early years, he had still been unable to explain the mystery of his rise.

In 1972, German television broadcast an hour-long interview with Putzi. He was in typically ebullient form, despite his advanced years. Seated much of the time at the piano, he visibly relished the opportunity to run through his old anecdotes all over again. Two years later, the interview was shown again. His father, Egon wrote, was "as excited as a retread bride."

Putzi also finally made it back to Harvard for a reunion in June 1974. Driving his son to distraction, he had been reluctant to commit himself to any itinerary, sowing confusion amongst those who had been due to meet him; at one point he appeared to have been lost completely. He eventually made it to his meeting of what was left of the class of '09. His powers of recollection fading and his stories slightly embellished, he gave a bizarre interview to *The Boston Globe* in which he described, among other things, how Hitler used to whistle along with old Harvard Hasty Pudding Club songs. "Hitler was a beautiful whistler," he recalled. "While I played, he'd recline and whistle the melody tremolo. How he enjoyed those Pudding Club scores." As for his subsequent life, he was philosophical. "What I have lived through is an enigmatic, grim, Gilbert and Sullivan farce," he declared. "You never know who is on your side, even in prison. Now at eighty-eight, I am a millionaire of time."

Time had run out for Helene in August of the previous year. It was, her son wrote, not an easy death—but "she bore it all with that undemonstrative stoicism which she had maintained throughout her life and which did not forsake her during the comforts of old age, the pains of illness, the final humiliations of organic disintegration."

Putzi himself—whom his son had taken to jokingly calling Learstaengl, or just K.L., after Shakespeare's tragic hero—was still going strong, writing and working on an enlarged and improved edition of his book. He also took great pride in his grandchildren—especially Eynon, the eldest, who had inherited his grandfather's musical talent, taking an impressive twenty-fourth place in the prestigious Tchaikovsky Competition in Moscow in June 1974.

The years were beginning to take their toll, however. On August 19, 1975, Putzi was admitted to Professor Dr. W. Hart's surgical clinic on Bertelestrasse in Munich, suffering from cancer of the thyroid. A week later, Hart operated on him for two and a half hours. Putzi spent a week in intensive care before returning to his regular room. Egon hoped it might be possible for his father to come home, even though they knew it would be a struggle to look after him. But he was fading quickly; soon he would eat only chocolate pudding and then he rejected even that. He remained as belligerent as ever, though, launching a tirade against his publishers for not reprinting his book and publishing one about Göring instead, and denouncing his nurses as communists and angels of death.

During one of Egon's daily visits several weeks later, his father proclaimed that his life was over and "demanded some form of euthanasia." The doctors were not ready to give up, though, and began to feed him intravenously—prolonging an existence that neither Putzi nor his family or friends wanted. The tug-of-death, as Egon called it, continued, but Putzi was getting weaker. On September 24, he lapsed into a coma and the doctors predicted he would die quietly within three to five days. But then the next morning he woke up at 6 A.M. and started calling for his newspapers, which he proceeded to read.

Death finally came on November 6. Putzi was eighty-eight. It was, wrote Egon, "a merciful relief for him and, indeed, all of us."

Putzi's passing was marked by only a short obituary in the German newspapers. His longevity had reduced him to a relic from an earlier age. The new generation of Germans had little desire to be reminded of the most inglorious era in their country's history. Born into the Germany of the kaiser, he had lived through the Weimar Republic, the horrors of the Third Reich and the Second World War, and the stability of the Bonn Republic. A child during the era of gas lamps and horse-drawn carriages, he had witnessed the first landing on the moon. Vain and self-centered, he had been drawn to Hitler as much by the glamor and reflected glory as by the Nazis' poisonous ideology. It was this love of the limelight that led him to stay too long at the heart of the regime and when the break came, it was inevitably on Hitler's terms rather than his own. Much of the discomfort that followed during the long years in internment was the direct result of his reluctance, even after he had fled Germany, to sever his ties with the Nazis. After that, inevitably, everything was downhill.

Putzi once described his political life as a "melancholic revue." In 1943, during a conversation with Sturm at Bush Hill, he summed up his frustration at the way things had turned out. "It is a terrible thing when you think you got on a bandwagon and it turns out to be a dustcart," he said. He had written his own epitaph.

ENDNOTES

Chapter 1

The account of Putzi's first meeting with Hitler has been taken from his various autobiographical writings, including Ernst Hanfstaengl, *Zwischen Weissem und Braunem Haus: Memoiren eines Politischen Aussenseiters*, München: R. Piper & Co., 1970, pp. 30–43.

Chapter 2

p.13. The work of . . . and marble, as well as glass, leather, and silk: *Villa Hanfstaengl in München*, undated, in Nachlass Hanfstaengl in the Bayerische Staatsbibliothek, Munich, Ana 405/39.

p.15. "Beneath the façade . . . expression in Beethoven's 'Pathetique' and Chopin's nocturnes": Ana 405/39, op. cit.

p.15. Edgar was also . . . "too many artistically minded adults": Ernst Hanfstaengl, *Hitler: The Missing Years*, New York: Arcade, 1994, p. 25.

p.15. The sergeant major ". . . within my weltanschauung": Ana 405/39, op. cit.

p.17. "When these noble . . . of the supposed elite": Loomis H. Taylor to Putzi, Feb. 26, 1958, Ana 405, op. cit.

p.18. "Get on the good side . . . Hotel Tourraine in Boston": Ana 405/39, op. cit.

p.19. He was remembered . . . "Harvard Club in New York City": *The New York Times*, Apr. 5, 1934.

p.20. He ordered beer . . . "Play us something, Hanfy": Charlotte B. Clifford, *Yankee*, June 1965. Her husband was a freshman and witnessed the scene.

p.21. "I think that he . . . time on his music": Hurlbut to Edgar Hanfstaengl, Nov. 21, 1906, quoted in David George Marwell, *Unwonted Exile: A Biography of Ernst "Putzi" Hanfstaengl*, Ph.D. dissertation, State University of New York at Binghamton, 1988, p. 35.

p.22. The generous final mark . . . he needed for his degree: Putzi's interview with John Toland, Sept. 2, 1971, in Franklin D. Roosevelt Presidential Library (FDRL), Hyde Park, New York.

p.22. They ran off when . . . some of his comrades: Ernst Hanfstaengl, *Hitler: The Missing Years*, p. 27.

Chapter 3

p.23. The gallery . . . he recalled later: Ernst Hanfstaengl, *Hitler: The Missing Years*, pp. 28.

ENDNOTES

p.25.   The two of them . . . she recalled later: Phillip Herring, *Djuna: The Life and Works of Djuna Barnes*, New York: Viking, 1995, pp. 67–73.

p.25.   On one occasion . . . dancing with her: Andrew Field, *The Formidable Miss Barnes*, London: Secker & Warburg, 1983, p. 61.

p.27.   "I have tried" . . . two decades later: Ernst Hanfstaengl, "My Leader," *Collier's*, Aug. 4, 1934.

p.28.   Putzi was suddenly afflicted . . . "at forward positions": Ana 405/23 quoted in Marwell, *Unwonted Exile*, p. 5.

p.28.   "I was engaged. . . all those German children?": Hank O'Neal, *Life Is Painful, Nasty & Short . . . In my Case It Has Only Been Painful & Nasty: Djuna Barnes 1978–1981*, New York: Paragon House, pp. 128–130.

p.29.   The women . . . better in bed than the men: Herring, *Djuna: The Life and Works*, p. 74.

p.30.   He admitted . . . "homesickness for Germany": Ernst Hanfstaengl, *Zwischen Weissem und Braunem Haus*, p. 8.

p.30.   Tellingly, Putzi was also . . . met only in 1917: *Badische Illustrierte*, Dec. 15, 1951.

p.31.   Putzi operated the gallery . . . his mother in March 1912: U.S. National Archives & Records Administration (NARA) RG 131/158/CM818.

p.31.   A report for the . . . his potential loyalties: Harry J. Jentzer, Feb. 21, 1917 in Ana 405, op. cit.

Chapter 4

p.34.   Putzi had been . . . "long, solitary, delayed life": Putzi to Kitty Hanfstaengl, May 12, 1920, Ana 405/45, op. cit.

p.34.   "He apparently seems to think" . . . that May: Putzi to Kitty Hanfstaengl, May 20, 1920, Ana 405/45, op. cit.

p.35.   Her father, Johann . . . a recent immigrant: Marwell, *Unwonted Exile*, p. 59.

p.35.   They expected . . . "regaining economic independence": Ernst Hanfstaengl, *Collier's*, Aug. 4, 1934.

p.35.   "The clock had stopped . . . ." he wrote later: Ernst Hanfstaengl, Hamish Hamilton, Ms 1/7, cit. Marwell, *Unwonted Exile*, p. 63.

p.36.   If Putzi wanted . . . by unanimous vote: Marwell, *Unwonted Exile*, p. 67.

p.37.   The pair worked . . . "Tolstoy's *War and Peace*": Ernst Hanfstaengl, *Hitler: The Missing Years*, p. 30.

p.38.   "Germany was a tame bear . . . didn't give a damn": Ernst Hanfstaengl, *Collier's*, Aug. 4, 1934.

Chapter 5

p.43.   There was undoubtedly something about Hitler . . . "when a student in polyglot Vienna": Ernst Hanfstaengl, *Hitler: The Missing Years*, p. 38.

p.44.   "Hitler's pot-pie needed a bit of upper crust," he recalled later: Kurt G. Lüdecke, *I Knew Hitler*, London: Jarrolds, 1938, p. 96.

p.46.   "Look at the portraits . . . ," Putzi told him: Ernst Hanfstaengl, *Adolf Hitler*, Dec. 3, 1942, p. 12.

p.46.   "He was an extremely . . . very marked histrionic talent": Putzi's interview with John Toland, FDRL, Mar. 18, 1971.

p.46. "It is imposing to think . . . will have to be brought up someday": Ernst Hanfstaengl, *Adolf Hitler*, p. 48.

p.47. A couple of years later . . . "hatred for its enemies": Letter to Alfred Rosenberg, April 2, 1925, in Archives du Centre de Documentation Juive Contemporaine, Paris, document LXII-1.

p.49. As Lüdecke put it . . . "open its doors to Hitler": Lüdecke, *I Knew Hitler*, p. 96.

p.50. "You must play . . . face the public": Ernst Hanfstaengl, "I Was Hitler's Closest Friend," *Hearst's International-Cosmopolitan*, March 1943.

p.51. "I authorize you . . . the German people." Ernst Hanfstaengl, *Adolf Hitler*, p. 44.

p.51. During the Second World War . . . "Frau Hanfstaengl," he said: Henry Picker, *Hitlers Tischgespräche im Führerhauptquartier 1941–1942*, Stuttgart: 1963, p. 165.

p.52. As for his appearance, it was "really quite pathetic": Helene Niemeyer, Notes, quoted in Marwell, *Unwonted Exile*, p. 84.

p.53. As *The Times* of London . . . "published in Bavaria": *The Times*, Sept. 7, 1923.

p.54. "The fact . . . the same for long": Egon Hanfstaengl, *Out of the Strong*, unpublished manuscript, 1943, p. 8.

p.54. As he recalled . . . "visiting prominent citizens": Ernst Hanfstaengl, *Hitler: The Missing Years*, p. 55.

p.56. "In 1923, it was an . . . and the press": *Münchener Post*, Nov. 11, 1930.

p.56. "To put it briefly . . . fragments in American slang?": Count von Treuberg to Hitler, quoted in Marwell, *Unwonted Exile*, p. 95.

Chapter 6

p.57. "That's right," . . . picking up the tab: *Chicago Sunday Tribune*, May 30, 1954.

p.58. The German currency . . . in a few hours: *The Times*, Oct. 12, 1923.

p.58. *The Observer* (London) . . . "with endless noughts": *Observer* (London), Sept. 9, 1923.

p.58. "My organization and I . . . to find us": *Christian Science Monitor*, Oct. 3, 1923.

p.58. "Swear you will not . . . Bring your pistols": Ernst Hanfstaengl, *Hitler: The Missing Years*, p. 91.

p.59. It was . . . "the spirit of international socialism": *Manchester Guardian*, Nov. 12, 1923.

p.60. "The national revolution . . . under the swastika flag": Joachim C. Fest, *Hitler*, London: Penguin, 1974, p. 183.

p.61. In his story . . . "to shoot any man opposing him": *Chicago Sunday Tribune*, Nov. 11, 1923.

p.61. "Better times . . . from shame and suffering": Fest, *Hitler*, p. 186.

p.62. The following morning . . . faced summary execution: *The Times*, Nov. 12, 1923.

Chapter 7

p.65. "Schmiedel . . . Could he be here?": *Neues Weilheimer Tagblatt,* Dec. 10, 1949.

ENDNOTES

p.66. "What do you think . . . for you to carry on": Helene Niemeyer interview with John Toland, FDRL, Oct 19, 1970.

p.67. Another pleasant memory . . . in his wardrobe: Egon Hanfstaengl, *Out of the Strong*, p. 3.

p.67. "What on earth . . . are well aware of this": Ernst Hanfstaengl, *Hitler: The Missing Years*, p. 113.

p.68. "Landsberg," noted *The Times* . . . "of the fortress": *The Times*, Nov. 14, 1923.

p.68. It put him . . . "to the South Pole": Ernst Hanfstaengl, *Hitler: The Missing Years*, p. 114.

p.68. The caricature became . . . "seemed impossible": Ernst Hanfstaengl, *Hitler in der Karikatur der Welt*, and *Tat gegen Tinte*, Verlag Braune Bücher Berlin Carl Rentsch, 1933, p. 15.

p.69. "I still have a faith . . . will save Germany": Putzi's class book entry was quoted in Ernst Hanfstaengl, *Collier's*, op. cit.

p.71. "If only I had" . . . he declared: Helene Niemeyer interview with John Toland, FDRL, Oct. 19, 1970.

p.72. "No, I won't do it . . . I hate about Vienna": Ernst Hanfstaengl, *Hitler: The Missing Years*, p. 129.

p.73. "If only I could . . . The poor fellow": Ernst Hanfstaengl, *Adolf Hitler*, p. 27.

p.75. "But apart from that" . . . he recorded in his diary: Joseph Goebbels, *Tagebücher, Band 1: 1924–1929*, Munich: Piper Verlag, 1992, p. 429.

p.76. Egon, who was allowed to watch . . . their ideological sanctity: Egon Hanfstaengl, *Out of the Strong*, p. 87.

p.78. This new money . . . in a provincial government: Ian Kershaw, *Hitler, 1889-1936: Hubris*, London: Penguin, 1999, p. 319.

Chapter 8

p.80. "Now we're on our way . . . we are trying to accomplish": Ernst Hanfstaengl, "I Was Hitler's Closest Friend," *Cosmopolitan*, March 1943.

p.81. "I always had the feeling . . . she would have liked": Helene Niemeyer interview with John Toland, FDRL, Oct. 19, 1970.

p.82. "The relationship, whatever form it took . . ." he claimed: Ernst Hanfstaengl, *Hitler: The Missing Years*, p. 168.

p.82. "As far as I am concerned . . ." that left Putzi bewildered and outraged: Egon Hanfstaengl, *Out of the Strong*, p. 1.

p.83. On November 1, he rectified the omission . . . number 668 027: Mitteilung des Document Center Berlin von Dec. 9, 1986, quoted in Wilfried Kugel, *Der Unverantwortliche, Das Leben des Hanns Heinz Ewers*, Düsseldorf: Grupello Verlag, 1992, p. 308.

p.83. "Well, now you are about to become a professor after all," he joked: Ernst Hanfstaengl, *Adolf Hitler*, p. 6.

p.84. "Big, dark, blessed . . ." he wrote: Edgar Mowrer, *Triumph and Turmoil: A Personal History of Our Times*, London: George Allen & Unwin Ltd., 1968, p. 207.

p.85. The magazine cabled back . . . She was forced to decline: Herring, *Djuna: The Life and Works*, p. 177.

p.86. "Hanfstaengl, stop being so greedy . . . even the smallest role": Picker, *Hitlers Tischgespräche*, p. 444.

p.86. "A few hours later . . . and political amok-runner": Louis P. Lochner, *What About Germany?*, London: Hodder and Stoughton, 1943, p. 81.

p.86. Hitler was "going very high hat . . . bearing *sons* for the state": Dorothy Thompson, "I Saw Hitler," *Hearst's International-Cosmopolitan*, March 1932.

p.87. "When finally I walked . . .CAN be wrong": Dorothy Thompson, ibid. The article was extended and published as a book by Farrar & Rinehart in 1932.

p.89. "Herr Hitler, what are you . . . keep him from discovering America": Ernst Hanfstaengl, *Hitler: The Missing Years*, p. 178.

p.91. "Baur, you've done your job well . . . from now on": Hans Baur, *Hitler's Pilot*, London: Frederick Muller, 1958, p. 32.

p.91. Also on the tarmac . . . "making himself affable to all": Sefton Delmer, *Trail Sinister: An Autobiography, Volume One,* London: Martin Secker & Warburg, 1961, p. 143.

p.94. "My mother and father are here . . . Hitler is very busy": Putzi's interview with Bavarian television, broadcast in 1972.

p.95. "Herr Hitler, what are you doing . . . this is a deliberate insult": Ernst Hanfstaengl, *Hitler: The Missing Years*, p. 186.

Chapter 9

p.104. "Hitler did not seize power . . . history will fix on him": *Daily Express*, Jan. 31, 1933.

p.104. *The New York Times* got it even more wrong . . . "are hopefully speaking": *NY Times*, Jan. 31, 1933.

p.113. "Now hold your heads . . . by God's gracious aid": Fest, *Hitler*, p. 398.

p.115. "An historic day . . . the Third Reich has come": Quoted in Fest, ibid., p. 410.

Chapter 10

p.118. "Why, Putzi . . . How magnificent": Hamilton Fish Armstrong, *Peace and Counterpeace: From Wilson to Hitler*, New York: Harper and Row, 1971, p. 534.

p.118. In burst what . . . "and brown uniform": Lochner, *What About Germany?*, p. 257.

p.119. A bookish and self-effacing . . . "German people": Notes on Arthur Pope's second interview with Putzi Hanfstaengl, PSF Box 99, FDRL, Dec. 14, 1943, p. 10.

p.120. "It is not a good stage . . . Parsifal and young Siegfried": William C. Bullitt to Roosevelt, Nov. 8, 1936, PSF-30, FDRL.

p.121. "Hitler needs a woman . . . Martha, you are that woman": Martha Dodd, *Through Embassy Eyes*, Garden City, NY: 1940, p. 63.

p.122. According to his son . . . his father had an affair: Egon Hanfstaengl's interview with author, Dec. 2002.

p.122. "His Bohemian life style . . . the whole Nazi hurly-burly like a theatre": *Frankfurter Nachtausgabe*, March 23, 1953.

p.123. The prince . . . "for uniting the different classes": Prince Louis Ferdinand of Prussia, *The Rebel Prince*, Chicago: Henry Regnery Co., 1932, p. 240.

p.123. "Oh, the Jews, the Jews . . . leave Germany to us Germans": Diana Mitford Mosley, *A Life of Contrasts*, London: Hamilton, 1977, p. 107.

p.125. According to Putzi . . . "bathtub with the water overflowing": Interview with Putzi in David Pryce-Jones, *Unity Mitford: A Quest*, London: Weidenfeld and Nicolson, 1976, p. 155.

p.125. "You had to know Putzi to really dislike him," he said: Quentin Reynolds, *Quentin Reynolds*, London: Heinemann, 1964, p. 92.

p.126. "Let me speak . . . he will take care of you": ibid., p. 101.

p.128. "Never come to my house again, you louse": ibid., p. 110.

p.128. "He has neglected . . . like a faithful hound": Bella Fromm, *Blood and Banquets: A Berlin Diary*, New York: Touchstone, 1992, p. 92.

p.129. "He advocates the complete . . ." he said: Will Moore to Miss Marguerite Lehand, Official File 198a, FDRL, Sept. 17, 1933.

p.130. "What are you doing . . . and play for me?": Ernst Hanfstaengl, "My Leader," *Collier's*.

Chapter 11

p.132. Hitler, Egon recalled . . . by his usual standards: Egon Hanfstaengl, *Out of the Strong*, p. 219.

p.133. "Look, boy, that's Austria over there," Hitler said suddenly: ibid., p. 222.

p.133. Their attitude . . . in the seventeenth century: Ernst Hanfstaengl, *Hitler: The Missing Years*, p. 216.

p.134. "Magda calls out *'Engelchen,'*" . . . Putzi would comment: Hans-Otto Meissner, *Magda Goebbels, A Biography*, London: Sidgwick & Jackson, 1980, p. 99.

p.137. "The need for factual evidence . . . the existence of the State": *NY Times*, Aug 30, 1934.

p.138. Göring was livid at first. . . the "horrible rumor" circulating: Philip Metcalfe, *1933*, New York: Harper & Row, 1989, p. 234.

p.139. "Relations between our . . . our two Fascist states": Ernst Hanfstaengl, *Hitler: The Missing Years*, p. 235.

p.139. As he told one American . . . "become more reasonable": Notes on Arthur Pope's second interview with Putzi Hanfstaengl, PSF Box 99, FDRL, Dec 14, 1943.

p.140. "He is constantly" . . . Messersmith wrote: Messersmith papers, Messersmith to Moffat, June 13, 1934, quoted in Marwell, *Unwonted Exile*, p. 124.

p.141. One of the strangest projects . . . out in September 1933: Ernst Hanfstaengl, *Hitler in der Karikatur der Welt*, Berlin: Verlag Braune Bücher, Sept. 19, 1933.

Chapter 12

p.144. "If that is the case . . . to the United States?": Ernst Hanfstaengl, *Hitler: The Missing Years*, p. 242.

p.145. "To object to . . . thing to do": *The Harvard Crimson*, Nov. 8, 1950.

p.146. "To find myself . . . are asking me to come": *NY Times*, Apr. 25, 1934.

p.146. This was intended to . . . "on the sporting fields of Harvard": ibid., June 8, 1934.

p.148. Helene was statuesque in a flowing white evening dress: Metcalfe, *1933*, p. 242.

p.148. "Whether Herr Hanfstaengl's" . . . observed *The New York Times: NY Times*, June 12, 1934.

p.149. *The Harvard Crimson*, . . . "to which he has risen": *The Harvard Crimson*, June 13, 1934.

p.152. "President Roosevelt has sent . . . be no incidents": Ernst Hanfstaengl, *Hitler: The Missing Years*, p. 244.

p.152. "A decided talent . . . and two in retrospect": *Boston Globe*, June 18, 1934.

p.152. According to a German . . . two thousand dollars: *Deutsche Allgemeine Zeitung*, Sept. 15, 1934.

p.152. The essay, entitled "My Leader" . . . their heads held erect: *Collier's*, Aug. 4, 1934.

p.153. "If a car gets stuck in the mud . . . gets drunk on it?": Ernst Hanfstaengl, *Hitler: The Missing Years*, p. 244.

p.154. "What did you mean in your interview" . . . quickly declared over: *NY Times*, June 19, 1934.

p.157. Some protestors then . . . "all imprisoned anti-Fascists": *NY Times*, June 22, 1934.

p.158. "Can any liberal accept . . . burn the books they produced": *NY Times*, June 26, 1934.

Chapter 13

p.160. Although the bride and groom . . . "might enjoy": *NY Times*, July 1, 1934.

p.161. "We are partly responsible . . . rid of him again": Quoted in Kershaw, *Hitler*, 1889–1936, p. 508.

p.163. "I have no comment . . . I stick to my program": *NY Times*, July 1, 1934.

p.167. At Hess's liaison office . . . "if they were chloroformed": Ernst Hanfstaengl, *Hitler: The Missing Years*, p. 248.

p.169. "Okay, now I've told you . . . we fear the worst": Louis P. Lochner, *Always the Unexpected: A Book of Reminiscences*, New York: Macmillan, 1956, p. 244.

Chapter 14

p.172. "Those middle-aged Germans" . . . could not be understood: Philip Gibbs, *European Journey*, London: Heinemann, 1934, p. 386.

p.172. "Everybody is for Hitler . . . regard him as a savior": David Nasaw, *The Chief: The Life of William Randolph Hearst*, New York: Houghton Mifflin, 2000, p. 494.

p.173. "When you are interviewed in Germany . . . for a week or so": Edmund D. Coblentz, editor, *William Randolph Hearst: A Portrait in His Own Words*. New York: Simon and Schuster, 1952, p. 111.

p.173. The media baron . . . "mine and exact": Nasaw, *The Chief*, p. 495.

p.174. "I only had to convince him . . . to impress these Americans": Metcalfe, *1933*, p. 280.

p.175. She was in tears . . . American Beauty roses: Vincent Sheen, *Dorothy and Red*, London: Heinemann, 1964, p. 25.

p.175. Frederick Birchall . . . "mere echoes of Nazi propaganda": *NY Times*, Aug. 26, 1934.

p.176. "I am here to dispense information . . . percentage of deficient children": ibid., Aug. 25, 1934.

p.178. "He used to say often" . . . she was told: Letter dated Aug. 17, 1955, Ana 405, op. cit.

ENDNOTES

p.179. "From that moment on . . ." he declared: *De Telegraaf*, Jan. 19, 1949.

p.180. Hanfstaengl built on his success . . . "False Pretenses and Extortion": *New Yorker Staatszeitung*, May 12, 1933.

p.180. Lüdecke had instead decided . . . "a hot zone of Nazidom": Lothar Machtan, *The Hidden Hitler*, Oxford: Perseus Press, 2002, p. 284.

p.180. "There you are, Herr Hitler . . . What else can you expect?": Ernst Hanfstaengl, Unpublished manuscript of *Hitler: The Missing Years*, Ana 405/47, op. cit.

p.182. "I then waited" . . . he said later: Hanfstaengl's testimony to Advisory Committee to Consider Appeals Against Orders of Internment, Oct. 30, 1939, KV 2/470, Public Records Office, Kew, London.

Chapter 15

p.186. "There was infinite injury . . . call Communists 'swine'": *NY Times*, Nov. 30, 1934.

p.186. "What hurt me most . . . Goethe's or Schiller's house": *Daily Express*, Nov. 30, 1935.

p.187. W. Perkins, one of the solicitors . . . "your great movement": W. Perkins to Hanfstaengl, Dec. 16. 1935.

p.188. The film was almost entirely . . . the German Labor Front: Marwell, *Unwonted Exile*, p. 149.

p.188. "He simply indicated . . . whether he is or is not": William E. Dodd, Jr. and Martha Dodd (eds.), *Ambassador Dodd's Diary 1933–38*, New York: Harcourt, Brace and Co., p. 360–61.

p.189. "I better leave you now" . . . she told him: Putzi's diary, quoted in Marwell, p. 147.

p.189. "My parents got divorced . . . my mother couldn't stand": Egon Hanfstaengl's interview with author, Dec. 2002.

p.190. When she told him about the divorce . . . "few real ladies in Germany": Egon Hanfstaengl to Toland, Mar. 4, 1973.

p.190. "It's nice and quiet here . . . and warn him": Egon Hanfstaengl, *Out of the Strong*, p. 362.

p.191. If Egon received a message . . . steps to leave: Egon Hanfstaengl interview with John Toland, FDRL, March 18, 1971.

Chapter 16

p.195. "You are urgently requested . . . special plane from the Munich airport.": Hanfstaengl in interview with John Toland, FDRL, p. 70.

p.196. "Why don't you comply . . . your influence would be very valuable": ibid., p. 71.

p.196. "How long will I be" . . . came the reply: ibid. p. 72.

p.197. "What are they doing . . . hear of any minerals, you understand": Hanfstaengl's testimony to Advisory Committee to Consider Appeals Against Orders of Internment, Oct. 30, 1939, KV 2/470, PRO.

p.201. 'They hoped that . . . than take after him": Egon Hanfstaengl, *Out of the Strong*, p. 370.

p.203. "Goebbels began casting aspersions . . . intimate knowledge of the Third Reich": Albert Speer, *Inside the Third Reich*, London: Weidenfeld & Nicolson, 1970, pp. 188–189.

p.204. "Hitler knew that . . . told me himself": Pryce-Jones, *Unity Mitford: A Quest*, p. 196.

p.204. "Father, this woman . . . in her eyes": Ernst Hanfstaengl, *Zwischen Weissem und Braunem Haus*, p. 371.

p.205. "He plans a wonderfully . . . " in her diary: Jan Dalley, *Diana Mosley*, New York: Alfred Knopf, p. 243.

p.205. "A joke is supposed . . . dinner with him tonight": Putzi's interview with John Toland, Oct. 14, 1970.

p.205. "God how tired" . . . last diary entry for his birthday: Marwell, *Unwonted Exile*, p. 161.

p.207. "There's nothing mysterious . . . returned from there": Lochner, *Always the Unexpected*, p. 185.

p.210. "We cannot keep . . . unpleasant for your family": Ernst Hanfstaengl, *Hitler: The Missing Years*, p. 288.

p.212. "Did the Führer really . . . That's the law": Egon Hanfstaengl, *Out of the Strong*, p. 381.

p.213. "*Herrgott* . . . now you're here at last": ibid., p. 385.

Chapter 17

p.216. The article, he told von Gersdorff . . . "for all we are intending to do": Putzi to Mary von Gersdorff, April 6, 1937, quoted in Marwell, *Unwonted Exile*, p. 188.

p.216. "It is now apparent . . . standing for this," Putzi wrote: Hanfstaengl to Göring, April 7, 1937, quoted in Marwell, *Unwonted Exile*, p. 189.

p.216. "Hanfstaengl is in London . . . And never let him go": Joseph Goebbels, *Tagebücher, Band 3: 1935–1939*, Munich: Piper Verlag, 1992, pp. 1066–1067.

p.218. On the orders of Martin Bormann. . . "without attracting attention": Friedrichs to Herr Hauptamtsleiter Hederich of the Parteiamtlich Prüfungskommission zum Schutz des NS-Schrifttums, July 26, 1937.

p.220. Larkin, active in the Socialist Party . . . "from 1915 onward": Affidavit of James Larkin, Jan. 22, 1934, quoted in Marwell, *Unwonted Exile*, p. 294.

p.221. If he did so loyally, then he could conduct "an unmolested existence": Weizsäcker to Woermann, March 29, 1938. NARA T-120/F110553-554, quoted in Marwell, *Unwonted Exile*, pp. 289–90.

p.222. "We had a good laugh . . ." Meeker recalled later: Meeker to Putzi, Aug. 28, 1961, ANA 405/45.

p.223. "You will admit that . . . " he demanded: Ana 405/46.

Chapter 18

p.228. "If I felt it was the old Hitler . . ." he recalled later: Hanfstaengl's testimony to Advisory Committee to Consider Appeals Against Orders of Internment, Oct. 30, 1939, KV 2/470, PRO.

p.231. On May 27, he had even sent Göring . . . following week: Putzi–Göring, May 27, 1939, quoted in Marwell, *Unwonted Exile*, pp. 405–6.

ENDNOTES

p.234. "I see myself obliged . . ." he concluded: Putzi to Bormann, August 18, 1939, quoted in Marwell, *Unwonted Exile,* p. 435.

Chapter 19

p.239. As one internee . . . "provided and catered for": Hal Alec Natan, *Barren Interlude, The Story of My Detention (Erlebnisbericht aus der Internierung),* unpublished manuscript, Institut für Zeitgeschichte, Munich, p. 54.

p.245. One of the inmates compared . . . he declared: Marwell, *Unwonted Exile,* p. 450.

p.246. "The inference is irresistible . . . liberty at this time": KV 2/470, PRO.

p.246. "Because I replied" . . . he wrote: Ana 405.

p.247. The Home Office, however, insisted . . . "internees," it said: File H.8040 for Ernst Hanfstaengl, KV 2/470, PRO.

Chapter 20

p.249. "Country Saved from Fifth Column Stab," declared the *Daily Herald: Daily Herald,* May 17, 1940.

p.250. Putzi sent his son . . . "torpedo or air raid bomb," he wrote: Marwell, *Unwonted Exile,* p. 466.

p.255. "Conditions were so bad . . . they finally closed it down": North American Newspaper Alliance, April 22, 1953.

Chapter 21

p.259. Roosevelt had been impressed . . . for a third term in 1940: Ernest B. Furgurson, "Back Channels," *Washingtonian,* June 1996, p. 6.

p.260. As Carter put it . . "event of publicity": The Year of Crisis, John Franklin Carter Papers, April 14, 1945, cit. Joseph E. Persico, *Roosevelt's Secret War,* New York: Random House, 2001, p. 58.

p.261. "What on earth do you think . . . makes them tick": Carter Collection, Oral History, FDRL.

p.261. Sheila Carter was . . . she was carrying: Marwell, *Unwonted Exile,* p. 501.

p.261. "Legally, you are British . . . come to Washington": Putzi's diary, quoted in Marwell, *Unwonted Exile,* p. 501.

p.262. "I doubt in no way . . ." he wrote in his diary: ibid., p. 502.

p.262. "I have been approached . . . ." eccentric and unreliable": KV 2/470 PRO.

p.263. Noting that Putzi . . . publishing them himself: Tamm to Hoover, June 3, 1942, FBI File 100-76954.

p.263. If it were up to the FBI . . . "guarded detention": Tamm to Hoover, March 13, 1942, FBI File 100-76954.

p.264. Maugham's wife . . . "bed with a hyena": Furgurson, *Washingtonian,* p. 17.

p.264. But, as one Foreign Office official . . . "to the experiment": A.W.G Randall at the Foreign Office to FA Newsam at the Home Office, May 22, 1942.

p.265. "I must tell you frankly . . . there are good and bad ex-Nazis," he said: Campbell to Carter, FDRL, June 23, 1942.

p.265. "What do you think . . . his safety while here": PSF Box 98, FDRL.

p.266. As Carter put it . . . "than a military obliteration": Steven Casey, "Franklin D. Roosevelt, Ernst 'Putzi' Hanfstaengl and the 'S-Project,' June 1942–June 1944," *Journal of Contemporary History,* 35, 3 (2000).

Chapter 22

p.268. "We were not well . . . or soldiers allowed": Interview with author, Dec. 2002.

p.269. Although Carter was in . . . for unconventional tasks: Steven Casey, *Journal of Contemporary History,* p. 342.

p.269. Field took an almost . . . "a forceful personality": Henry Field, "Memorandum on Ernst Hanfstaengl," FDRL, Oct. 29, 1965.

p.270. "It was just Hanfstaengl using his brain," he assured the army: Carter Collection, Oral History p. 15, FDRL, quoted in Persico, p. 194.

p.271. "I've never seen anything . . . kill me tonight": Field, "Memorandum on Ernst Hanfstaengl," p. 47.

p.276. Putzi suggested waiting . . . "as after Versailles": Report on Sedgwick's answer to your question, Carter to Welles Dec. 1, PSF Carter 98, FDRL.

p.276. The appointment of a Himmler loyalist . . . "the political desperado": Carter, Observations on the Appointment of General Kurt Zeitzler to the position of Chief of General Staff, Dec. 17, 1942, PSF Box 98, FDRL.

p.277. "He demanded more . . . to roam," Field wrote: Field, "Memorandum," Oct. 29, 1965.

p.278. Putzi was showing . . . "Anglo-Soviet relations": Campbell to Carter, June 23, 1942, quoted in Casey, *J. Cont. History,* p. 352.

p.278. Campbell also wrote . . . a one-month trial basis: Campbell to Welles, Jan. 27, 1943, FO/115/3579/116/1PR.

p.279. Putzi, Carter wrote to Welles . . . "unassailable in Europe": John Carter, "Memorandum to Sumner Welles," Nov. 16, 1942, FDRL.

p.280. Roosevelt summoned Carter . . . "editor of *Cosmopolitan*": Casey, *J. Cont. History,* p. 353.

p.280. On January 4, 1943, Carter . . . accession to power: Jan 4, 1943, PSF (Subject) Carter, FDRL.

p.280. After a brief biography of Putzi . . . "to this Government," he said: Attached to Jan. 4, 1943, PSF (Subject) Carter, FDRL.

p.281. In a detailed eight-page . . . "in this field": Jan. 31, 1943, PSF (Subject) Carter, FDRL.

p.282. In any case . . . "his services at this time": L.B. Nichols to Tolson, April 21, 1943, FDRL.

Chapter 23

p.283. The final version . . . ran to sixty-eight pages: The details are taken from Ernst Hanfstaengl, *Adolf Hitler.*

p.287. On March 8, Putzi wrote . . . he wrote: Carter to FDR, March 8, 1943, PSF, FDRL.

p.288. In May, Carter asked . . . five thousand dollars: Carter to Harold Smith, May 19, 1943, FDRL.

ENDNOTES

p.289. "The sour truth remains . . . an unprecedented scale": Report on Putzi's comments on the German Katyn-Incident Propaganda, May 18, 1943, FDRL.

p.289. On July 14, 1943, he told . . . "German arms again": Report on Hanfstaengl observations on FCC radio-intelligence, FDRL.

p.290. After he had been asked . . . "it won't go unnoticed": Egon Hanfstaengl interview with John Toland, March 18, 1971, FDRL.

p.291. "The death of Hitler would. . . the commander in chief": Henry Field, 1976, op. cit., p. 13.

p.294. "Is there anything sadder . . . how you are!": Katherine Hanfstaengl to Putzi, May 9, 1943.

p.294. In another, she . . . "of their welfare": Katherine Hanfstaengl to Putzi, May 24, 1943.

Chapter 24

p.296. It was a wet and . . . toward Washington: This account is drawn from Alexander Sturm's unpublished 39-page manuscript, *"Bush Hill or Hanfstaengl in Virginia: A memoir dedicated to its hero with highest esteem by his inadequate Boswell,"* contained in Putzi's papers in the Bayerische Staatsbibliothek in Munich.

p.298. Confirmation of this . . . destroyed by Allied bombing: Report on Putzi Hanfstaengl, Jan. 26, 1944.

p.299. For this reason . . . solely on the Nazis: John Carter, Report from Putzi on current developments, Feb. 3, 1944, FDRL.

p.299. In one report . . . postwar Germany: John Carter, Report on Putzi's view on current political developments in Europe, April 28, 1944, FDRL.

p.300. "Guests may come and guests may go, but I stay on forever": Sturm, op. cit., p. 24.

p.300. "Whenever I get into one . . ." in his Lancia: Sturm, op. cit., p. 31.

p.301. "Goethe was twenty years . . . touch of prescience": Sturm, op. cit., p. 34.

p.301. Putzi, he noted . . . resentful of their influence: Report on Arthur Pope's second interview with Putzi Hanfstaengl, Dec. 14, 1943, PSF JF Carter, FDRL.

p.301. If the Nazi regime . . . to play the role of "loyal opposition": Jack Morgan, Report on Conversation, Dec. 24, 1943, PSF Carter, FDRL

p.302. The previous July . . . Putzi was in America: Report on Hanfstaengl suggestion for Propaganda Leaflet for Germany, July 21, 1943, FDRL.

p.303. "Who is going to be there?" . . . "Wait and see": Henry Field, *Dr. Sedgwick (Ernst Hanfstaengl),* Sept. 11, 1976, FDRL, p. 28.

p.304. In one of his own broadcasts, he claimed "a well-known traitor to the Fatherland, now living abroad, was sending lies into Germany by radio and record": ibid., p. 29.

p.304. As he saw it . . . "food and shelter": Carter, JF, Report on Security Arrangements for Putzi Hanfstaengl, Jan. 17, 1944, FDRL.

p.305. He was especially impressed . . . "are beyond praise": Carter to Maj. Gen. Jon T. Lewis, April 13, 1944, FDRL.

p.305. "Confidence in our credibility" . . . he warned: Elmer Davis to Roosevelt, May 24, 1944, FDRL.

p.306. "Even if the scheme . . . and England": Memorandum for the President from the Under Secretary of State, June 7, 1944, PSF 9-7, FDRL.

p.307. "When Hitler and . . . real assurance of peace": Casey, *J. Cont. History,* p. 356.

p.307. The old "Prussian Reichswehr-Junker set . . . seemed to believe," he said: Ernst Hanfstaengl, "Notes on the Present Crisis," Sept. 23, 1943, FDRL.

p.309. Putzi argued that America . . . an Asian war to win: Field, Report no. LIII by Dr. Sedgwick, June 26, 1944, FDRL.

p.309. His gloom extended . . . will be "Stalin-Asia": PSF Carter to Roosevelt, July 11, 1944, FDRL.

p.311. "Having learnt that Bavaria . . . all day long": Ana 405/39, op. cit.

p.312. In an introduction . . . "well worthwhile": Sumner Welles, Introduction to *The Catoctin Conversation,* New York: Charles Scribner's Sons, 1947, p. xii.

Chapter 25

p.318. "From internment camp . . ." in psychological warfare: *De Telegraaf,* Jan. 19, 1949.

p.318. "My aim was to establish . . . their criminal rulers": *Main Echo,* Jan. 29, 1949.

p.318. "Have you ever heard . . . I am punished for that": *Chicago Sunday Tribune,* May 30, 1954.

p.319. "I won't even make . . . firm went bankrupt": Egon Hanfstaengl's interview with the author, Dec. 2002.

p.320. A little later . . . want to meet him: Putzi to Hollis T. Gleason, May 23, 1959, Ana 405/39.

p.322. "It's always painful . . . was twenty-three": Djuna Barnes to Emily Coleman, May 21, 1938, quoted in Herring, *Djuna: The Life and Works,* p. 70.

p.323. Putzi, it complained. . . "anecdotes and gossip": *Die Zeit,* Sept. 15, 1970.

p.324. His father, Egon wrote, was "as excited as a retread bride": Egon Hanfstaengl to John Toland, March 12, 1974.

p.324. It was, her son wrote . . . "organic disintegration": Egon Hanfstaengl to Toland, Aug. 9, 1973.

INDEX

ABOUT THE AUTHOR

PETER CONRADI is the author of *The Red Ripper: Inside the Mind of Russia's Most Brutal Serial Killer* and *Mad Vlad: Vladimir Zhirinovsky and the New Russian Nationalism*. A graduate of Oxford University, he also studied at Munich's Ludwig-Maximilian University and knows Putzi's hometown well. Conradi is the Deputy Foreign Editor of *The Sunday Times* (London). He lives in London with his wife and three children.